Global Climate Change and Natural Resources

2011

Also by Emil Morhardt

Ecological Consequences of Global Climate Change 2011

Global Climate Change and Natural Resources: 2010

Ecological Consequences of Global Climate Change: Summaries of the 2009 Scientific Literature

Global Climate Change and Natural Resources: Summaries of the 2007-2008 Scientific Literature

Biology of Global Change

Global Climate Change: Summaries of the 2006-2007 Scientific Literature

Research in Natural Resources Management

Clean Green and Read All Over

Research in Ecosystem Services

California Desert Flowers

Cannon and Slinkard Fire Recovery Study: A Photographic Flora

Global Climate Change and Natural Resources

2011

A Roberts Environmental Center Annual Snapshot

J. Emil Morhardt, Editor

The Roberts Environmental Center Press

Roberts Environmental Center Press
Claremont McKenna College
925 N. Mills Avenue
Claremont, California 91711
(909) 621-8190

Morhardt, J. Emil
    Global Climate Change and Natural Resources 2011: A Roberts Environmental Center Annual
    Snapshot/ J. Emil Morhardt, Editor.

    ISBN 978-0-9843823-4-7 (paper)

Table of Contents

Forward

J. Emil Morhardt

For the past several years my students and I have been examining the state of global natural resources, particularly in light of global warming and climate change, each year producing a book similar to this one, but based only on scientific technical literature published within the past year. The books are similar in format, but entirely new in content—nothing in the current volume was known (at least in the sense of having been published in the peer-reviewed technical literature) before 2010. The gestation period of these books is very short by commercial publishing standards. The writing for this one was initiated at the end of January, 2011, and the final work was published and available for purchase at Amazon.com, CreateSpace direct, and bookstores and online retailers by the middle of May, 2011. Many of the scientific papers reviewed in it were published, or made available online in prepublication format, during the course of the writing. Most books cover material at least a year old. This one will be superseded by another, more recent one of ours by a year from now. If you are reading this before our next book comes out in May, 2012, you are reading material not likely to be found in most other books.

I was inspired to initiate this series by Bjørn Lomborg's *The Skeptical Environmentalist* (Lomborg 2001), published a decade ago. Although his book was reviled by the environmental community (to which I belong) for a long list of pretty good reasons, it was lauded by *The Economist*, a weekly magazine I also read and respect, and by a good bit of the rest of the non-scientific community, both in academia and in the corporate world, to which I also have ties. I invited Lomborg to visit (which he did) and used his book as a text in my class in Natural Resources Management as a basis for discussing the availability and fate of a wide range of natural resources—supplemented by current scientific papers speaking to the same issues, but usually with the opposite take on the problem. Ultimately the course evolved into the present one that no longer uses textbooks, but is entirely based on current research. At the time, global warming was just beginning to be a public issue, and was, in the eyes of many, demolished by Lomborg's book, along with the fears of shortages in any of our natural resources. Lomborg was, in a sense, living in the 1950s, when there were so few people extant, it really did look like natural resources were inexhaustible.

Now we know better. Global warming and climate change are real and natural resources are becoming limiting. The global peak of oil production may already have passed, and certainly will be in the next two decades—as discussed in Chapter 1—and gasoline at the corner station here in Claremont is well over $4.00/gallon again and going up daily. This week *The New Yorker* has an article about the massive new oil production in North Dakota, facilitated by hydrostatic fracturing of the rock, but even with this advanced "fracking" the fields will only provide enough oil to supply the U.S. for two years, and the new oil isn't likely to lower oil prices any, or change the date of peak oil.

In 2001, Lomborg also disavowed any adverse biological effects of human activities—but as I found out personally when he visited my lab, he isn't a scientist, so he missed much of the subtleties of the research in biological areas. There is, in fact, no question that the World's ecosystems and many of its species are increasingly stressed, and we were already likely to find ourselves on a biologically much simpler planet from human population pressures alone, even without the additional stresses of CO_2-induced ocean acidification and climate change. By mandating biological fuels we are likely making things worse, for even more land is being cleared to produce them.

There are many other issues related to natural resources and climate change as well, and although this book doesn't cover them all, it will give you a broad insight into the current state of many of our natural resources and how they may be affected by global warming and climate change. The first section looks at the state of energy production, along with a chapter on alternate vehicle fuels and how we as a society might deal with the excessive CO_2 in the atmosphere. The second section is about melting ice sheets and glaciers, how water supplies are responding, and how agriculture is doing in the face of the changes. The third is about the ecological effects of climate change—there are many.

There is plenty of interesting information in these pages, and you will come away with a nuanced understanding of the issues, and a better appreciation of the difficulties in finding solutions.

References Cited

Lomborg, B., 2001. The skeptical environmentalist: measuring the real state of the world. Cambridge (UK), 165-172

Section I—Energy Resources

1. The Likelihood and Implications of Peak Oil

Steven Erickson

Few things have proven to be as essential to the development of modern civilization as the recovery and consumption of fossil fuels. Fossil fuels touch every aspect of our lives, and unfortunately they are a finite resource. This finiteness has led many experts to assert that we are approaching—or have already reached—a peak in oil production. This assertion, commonly referred to in the media and literature as Peak Oil, states that oil production will reach a peak in volume after which output will slowly decline. This will be coupled with a steady growth in demand for fossil fuels caused both by population growth and the rapid economic growth of developing nations. This will naturally create massive energy shortages as economically viable alternatives are still relatively far off. If a peak caused by the exhaustion of oil resources does occur, the consequences to global economics, international relations, and even the structure of urban areas would be massive, with some experts predicting a complete change in the makeup society as we know it.

Although on the surface Peak Oil seems to make intuitive sense—there are only so many fossil fuels in the ground—this claim has generated no small controversy, with many economists refuting a production peak caused by the exhaustion of oil reserves. The general argument made against Peak Oil is that technological progress, development of new, unconventional sources of fossil fuels and changes in consumption patterns will allow us to put off peak oil indefinitely. This relies heavily on the theories of supply and demand and substitution; as prices of oil rise new oil fields become economically viable to exploit, new technologies become profitable to develop, and consumers will change their habits to save money. This camp does not deny that a peak in production of oil is possible—after all we are not still using whale oil—but that it will be due to a switch to cheaper new technologies as opposed any sort of geological limitations. Data on the unending upwards revisions on ultimate recoverable reserves (URR) is often used to support this viewpoint as well. Other scientists who support an abiotic origin of oil in an ongoing process within the earth even claim that there may be so much oil deep in the ground that a oil peak is inconceivable and that preparing for it would be a waste of time.

Peak Oil supporters state that this viewpoint is overly optimistic, quoting data on diminishing oil discoveries and growing demand, and returning to the geological viewpoint that there is ultimately only so much oil for us to consume. They claim that once about half of URR is consumed global oil production will peak, which is what happens both in individual fields as well as regions as a whole. This sort of regional peak was predicted and did in fact happen in the US during the 1970s, giving some credence to the Peak Oil camp. Supporters also point to the slow progress in oil replacements like liquefied coal, stating that these options will not be ready in time to offset an oil peak.

A peak in fossil fuel production and the subsequent decline in oil production has important ramifications not only for global economic growth and quality of life, but also for models of climate change. The burning of fossil fuels is the primary source of anthropogenic CO_2, the leading culprit behind climate change. If climate change models wrongly predict the amount of fossil fuels available in the future then they will in turn wrongly predict the total amount of carbon dioxide in the atmosphere as well as the total amount of warming in the coming decades.

Unfortunately, proving or disproving Peak Oil is a fairly difficult task. Public data on oil reserves are generally inadequate in both quantity and quality, and most data are kept private by the companies or governments which generate them. There are also many different methods to try to prove or disprove the theory, with economists tending to view the total quantity of oil as a fluid process depending on many economic, political, and technological factors, while geologists view total supplies as a static volume. As such, there has been no consensus on Peak Oil.

In this summary articles reviewing the data will first be covered, giving a look at the state of the data and the possible conclusions that can be drawn from it. Following will be articles who's authors have looked at these data but have come to opposing conclusions on the likelihood of an oil peak as well as the effects of such a peak on commonly used climate models. Also investigated is the theory of abiotic oil generation and whether or not it might stave off a potential resource peak. Several articles that attempt to predict what a post peak world might look like economically, politically, and socially and how policy makers can model and plan for potential risks involved with fuel shortages are presented. The articles in support of Peak Oil generally agree upon 2030 as a likely date for the peak in oil production. Finally, a single article on a problematic portion of the liquefied coal production process is summarized to illustrate the difficulties encountered in finding a replacement for oil. The research done by these authors not only provides a good treatment of the data but also illustrates the conflicting and at times equally sensible views on Peak Oil while avoiding much of the politics that often colors views on the issue.

Estimates of Peak Oil Muddled by Incomplete Data, Differences in Terminology and Varying Theoretical Views

A peak in oil production due to resource exhaustion is a familiar topic to most. However, as of now no consensus has been reached as to likelihood of whether or not we will encounter this peak in the short run, and if we will, when will it occur. Although there are many reasons why divisions of opinion would occur, among them varying levels of optimism and fields of study, Sorrell *et al.* review current peak oil research done by the UK Energy Research Centre (UKERC) to explain that some of the main drivers of the uncertainty surrounding peak oil estimates are that the data are sparse and often privately owned, scientists use different and changing terminology, and the assumptions underlying models of oil production and consumption are not necessarily the same. Taking this information into account, the authors then go on to predict that oil production will probably reach a bumpy plateau and then decline rather than a form a true peak.

Sorrell *et al.* summarize the UK Energy Research Centre's (UKERC) findings in their independent review of the evidence for a peak in oil production. They go on to analyze the various factors influencing the difficulty in both predicting peaks in oil production and getting these predictions taken seriously in the scientific community. They conclude by explaining what needs to be done to the models to make them more reliable as well as giving their opinions on current estimates of future oil production.

One of the first problems examined is the ambiguity and quality of data. First of all, publicly available data are scant and therefore not very useful. Commercial sources are better, but are also expensive and sometimes impossible to obtain. Further augmenting the problem is the division of reserves into proved (1P) and proved and probable (2P). Neither of these terms has an especially standardized meaning, and because of the lack of data availability scientists must make assumptions in order to get any sort of estimate.

The process of estimating resource size is also fraught with uncertainty. Geological models are often used for relatively unexplored regions and economic models are typically used to plot out production in areas that are well explored. According to the authors, neither of these techniques take their weaknesses fully into account. They surmise that most techniques will be pessimistic in their estimates. In order to improve the situation, Sorrell *et al.* (2010) suggest new models that use both historical and geologic data along with economic and political data, but they may provide very different results from previous models for estimating regional recoverable resources.

Estimating actual oil supply is just as difficult. Both curve fitting and econometric models are used to try to map out supply, but fitted lines lack theoretical basis, and econometrics may not do a better job of predicting future output. The authors state that the ideal model would be one based from the bottom up using project data, but most companies closely guard their data, making that information difficult to attain. The authors assert that although such supply models for a given level of available resources can estimate a peak to within a decade, they can not provide much precision beyond that.

Sorrell *et al.* conclude the paper by discussing the timing of the peak. They say that current estimates of URR made by the US Geological Survey (USGS) are around 3345 GB. This estimate puts a global resource peak at around 2030. The authors conclude that if one wants to justify that an oil peak can be put off beyond this date they must rely on some tenuous conclusions, including low demand growth, a reversal in the 40 year trend of declining oil discoveries, and a cumulative production at the date of any potential peak that exceeds 50% of the global URR.

The Special Report on Emission Scenarios Overestimates the Quantity of Future Recoverable Fossil Fuels

The Special Report on Emission Scenarios (SRES), compiled in 2000 by the Intergovernmental Panel on Climate Change (IPCC), is a collection of forty possible global emission outcomes over the next 100 years that have served as a basis for many projections on global climate change. Unfortunately many of these scenarios have missed the mark and are no longer entirely plausible. Höök *et al.* (2010a) have reviewed the data and have concluded that due to an over-reliance on outdated works as well as a certain unnecessary optimism with regards to mankind's technological progression, the SRES greatly overestimates the amount of recoverable fossil fuels that will be available to humanity through the year 2100. This has ramifications not only for the overall economic outlooks projected by the SRES, but also for the report's estimates of total greenhouse gas output, as the burning of fossil fuels accounts for about 57% of anthropogenic greenhouse gas in the atmosphere. Therefore, the SRES needs to revise downwards its estimates of total CO_2 in the atmosphere for all of its scenarios to compensate for its overstatement of available resources.

Höök *et al.* reviewed not only the projections for fossil fuel production provided by each of the 40 SRES emissions scenarios and the assumptions made and research used in reaching these projections, but also the relevant literature and statistics that have been published since the SRES's 2000 publication. After this review they concluded that the IPCC had been overly optimistic about the amount of fossil fuels that could be viably extracted within the next century, and had therefore overestimated the amount of CO_2 emissions possible during that time period. Many of the scenarios seem to project the recovery of more fossil fuels than are currently thought to exist, place too much weight on the quantity and feasibility of unconventional fossil fuel reserves, and put unreasonably large demands on the growth of fossil fuel production capacity of several hydrocarbon rich countries.

The authors believe that these errors stem from the SRES taking an optimistic view of future oil production. The report essentially takes the viewpoint that we should not look at oil reserves as a fixed quantity, but rather a fluid amount linked directly to our technical knowledge, with the implication that as our technology progresses, our ability not only to use fossil fuels more efficiently, but also to extract unconventional fossil fuels such as coal-bed methane or oil contained in oil shale which were once not viable, will allow us to extend our production of fossil fuels almost indefinitely.

Höök *et al.*, on the other hand, identify various studies that show that the depletion of fossil fuel reserves increases costs enough to offset any gains from new technology, a fact that the SRES seems to ignore.

They also identify studies that show that the worldwide production of unconventional oil would be required to attain a growth rate of 10% per year for the next 20 years in order to meet SRES projections, which according to Höök and others in 2009 is a feat that has never been attained by any energy system in history.

Finally, the authors point out that even the quantity and economic viability of unconventional fossil fuels may be in question. The SRES uses scant detail to assume that coal-to-liquid technology, supposedly a key player in the sustained usage of fossil fuels, is much cheaper than current literature would suggest. Moreover, the estimated quantity of gas hydrates, another key unconventional fossil fuel, have recently decreased by three orders of magnitude, from 10^{18} m^3 to 10^{15} m^{3,} due largely to an increase in geological knowledge. This means that many of the sources used by the SRES have become obsolete and that the conclusions based on those sources are suspect at best.

The authors purport that all of these factors necessitate numerous revisions downwards in regards to the expected output of fossil fuels, and that already several scenarios contained in the SRES can be ruled out. If the IPCC would like to avoid such exaggerated figures on resource availability in the future the authors suggest that the IPCC would do well to hire more resource experts the next time around.

Steven Erickson

Predictions of an Imminent Exhaustion of Oil Resources Based Solely on Fallacy

Following the recent rise in oil prices, the term peak oil has become a popular buzzword. Predictions on the potential timing of such a peak vary, but some sources predict that the earth could reach peak oil within the next decade or so. However, Radetzki (2010) warns that predictions of an imminent peak in oil production should not be taken seriously, as the major arguments made for this coming peak by groups like the Association for the Study of Peak Oil (ASPO) are largely fallacious with little scientific or economic support. Radetzki goes on to state that a peak in oil production is conceivable, but it would be caused by political or market forces, not a decrease in availability.

Radetzki scrutinized several of the main arguments made by the ASPO in regards to a supposed coming peak in oil production. These arguments include the fixed and limited nature of base oil reserves, that a peak in oil production would occur when half of the ultimately recoverable resources (URRs) are exploited, and that oil discoveries are declining and insufficient to meet the unending increase in demand. Radetzki works to discredit each of these arguments, claiming that they are only "chimeras".

Radetzki first addresses the assertion that oil will peak when half of the URR has been consumed. He states that although oil fields do reach peak production when about half of the exploitable oil is used up, there is no convincing reason that this should hold true for global oil production. He goes on to explain that even if this were the case, we lack the ability to ascertain when this halfway point has been reached, as even "resource pessimist" Colin Cambell, a leading player in the Peak Oil Movement, has added 300 billion barrels to his estimates from the URR. Radetzki states that due to the steady advance of technology, the URR is not a simple sum of total resources that can be easily burned through, but rather a result of fluid processes which result in its continual expansion. This holds especially true with oil prices over $60 per barrel, as this makes many novel methods of oil extraction more plausible.

Radetzki goes on to consider problems raised concerning the slowdown in oil discovery in recent decades. Radetzki explains that the ASPO's data on the diminishing size of new discoveries is underestimating the total amount of oil being found. This is largely because they ignore an important concept called appreciation. The amount of oil first estimated in a new field is normally about six times smaller than actual reserves due to continuing development of the field and improvement in recovery technology. In the ASPO's comparisons they use the figures from the fully appreciated oil discoveries in the 60's and the 70's, but use the preliminary estimates for newer discoveries, ignoring any appreciation that might occur. It is in this way that, although the quantity and size of new discoveries appears to have slowed, we still see increases in the base reserves.

Radetzki concludes that although peak oil is a possibility, it will not be due to limited resources. Instead, the economics of energy may change, making newer methods of energy generation preferable to the burning of fossil fuels. If this occurs then demand will naturally fall and production of oil will peter out. Another threat to oil production is resource nationalism—the majority of exploitable oil is controlled by governments—which would effectively cut off certain countries from the natural wealth of resource rich countries. This would indeed cause a production crisis in effected countries, and according to Radetzki is much more likely than an exhaustion of our useable reserves.

Regardless of Its Veracity, The Theory of Abiotic Oil Formation Does Not Negate The Peak Oil Hypothesis

Throughout history mankind has produced many theories to explain the origin of oil; Aristotle, for example, believed that petroleum was "the result of exhalations from the deep earth." By the mid 18th century theories of biotic oil formation—that oil and coal originate from biological remnants subjected to the heat and pressure of the earth—were already entering the mainstream. These biotic theories remain the most prevalent today, and have proved the most successful in predicting locations of large oil reserves. However, in the 1950's, theories of an abiotic origin of oil, first proposed in the early decades of that century, were revived in Russia. Recently, proponents of this theory have stated that deep in the Earth's mantle there lie vast oceans of oil that make preparations for a peak in oil production a waste of effort. However, Höök et al. (2010b) state that regardless of the viability of the abiotic oil formation theory, such reserves would at most only delay the onset of peak oil, as a resource is still considered finite as long as extraction is more rapid than renewal. Therefore, unless abiotic processes create oil on the order of several hundred thousand barrels a day, they will not be able to help us stave off a peak in oil production.

Höök et al. surveyed and summarized the research on the origins of both biotic and abiotic oil formation theories and the empirical evidence present for both. After analyzing these data, they reexamine the argument for peak oil taking into account potential reserves created by abiotic oil formation, concluding that unless the "strong" theory of abiotic oil production is true—that is that abiotic oil processes create large quantities of oil over short periods of time—then peak oil will at the very most delay the onset of this production peak.

Much evidence has been provided to show that hydrocarbons are the result of biotic processes. Chemical analysis has shown a link between chlorophyll in

19

living plants and porphyrin pigments—a type of nitrogen found in fossil fuel reserves—which originate primarily from chlorophylls. Carbon isotopes found in hydrocarbons have also been shown through mass spectroscopy to be the same isotopes favored by living organisms, and oil has also been shown to contain many biomarkers and chemical fossils. Furthermore, biodegradation caused by microorganisms has been shown to result in petroleum being transformed into heavy oil. Höök et al. explain that these theories on degradation could explain all petroleum formation.

The theory of abiotic oil generation, supported primarily by chemists with little geological experience, relies primarily on experimental work that suggests that under high pressures and heat, hydrogen and carbon combine to create hydrocarbon chains. However, drillings in Sweden in the 1980s, which thus far have been the most serious attempt at proving abiotic oil formation, failed to find any recoverable amount of oil.

Some scientists propose that the fact that some oil reservoirs exist in rock formations not traditionally associated with oil is proof that abiotic oil generation does exist, however geological studies show that these reservoirs were created by migration of oil from sedimentary source rock nearby through commonly understood mechanisms. Another argument proposed by abiotic oil supporters is that these abiotic oil reserves are at great and largely unexplored depths, but to this date very little oil has been found at depths greater than 5000 m. Furthermore, studies show that oil generally converts into natural gas at temperatures greater than 200 °C, temperatures that generally exist below 5000 m. Höök et al. conclude from their review that although it is possible to create abiotic oil in the laboratory, there has thus far been no evidence suggesting any sort of commercially viable accumulation of abiotic oil in the earth's mantle.

Höök et al. close their paper by addressing what effect, if any, abiotic oil formation would have on peak oil. Their main point revolves around the idea of what it means for a resource to be finite. The authors state that a resource is renewable if and only if its rate of replenishment is greater than its rate of depletion. They use the production of whale oil in the 19th century to illustrate this point. Although whales are able to reproduce, the resource was still finite as whales were killed much more quickly than they could reproduce, causing a very clear peak in whale oil production. They then go on to divide abiotic oil generation theories into two main groups, a weak theory and a strong theory. The weak theory states that oil forms abiotically at rates similar to those assumed in conventional biogenic theories, while the strong theory states that oil reservoirs are replaced more quickly than we deplete them. This rate of replacement would be about five orders of magnitude greater than what is known in conventional oil formation theory.

If the weak theory holds true, then it makes little difference whether or not oil is generated biotically or a abiotically, as we are still consuming petroleum at a rate faster than it is being replaced, and a peak in oil production is inevitable. If the strong theory were true, then a production peak could potentially be put off indefinitely. Unfortunately, the authors state that even the most optimistic supporter of abiotic oil has no ability to prove such claims. Therefore, even if abiotic oil generation is real and has created large reserves deep in the Earth's mantle, its effect on the arrival of peak oil production would ultimately be minimal.

A Model to Include Risks of Peak Oil in Current Urban Planning

High gasoline prices in 2005 made it clear that spikes in fuel costs will cause people to modify their behaviors. These changes ranged from the increase in consumption of more efficient vehicles, changes in driving behavior such as driving at lower speeds and carpooling, to the reduction of optional trips that an individual may have wanted to take but could not afford. Given these effects, it would make sense for risk models in urban planning to include risks to certain development forms caused by reduced supply of fossil fuels, but thus far no one has attempted to model these effects. Krumdieck *et al.* (2010) attempt to rectify this by aggregating various predictions on peaks in conventional oil, they created probabilistic models showing the probability of a peak at a given time and the amount of oil available in the future. They also create impact models to show how these changes will affect behavior and the ultimate value of certain urban developments. Their model showed that the larger the urban sprawl, the greater the calculated risk factor. They conclude that it is essential that transportation risks created by an oil peak must be considered when planning urban areas and that these risks would be best mitigated by concentrating population centers and creating incentives to ride public transportation or use active modes of transportation like cycling or walking.

Krumdieck *et al.* must first calculate the probable supply of oil in order to know how large of an impact an oil production peak will have on civic life. They create this distribution by fitting a curve to peak projections by various experts rather than trying to pick a single expert to base their claims on. These predictions tend to cluster around 2010, and all of them fall before 2030. The resulting distribution is bell-shaped and results in a probability function that projects the probability of a peak in a given year. They then take the cumulative probability of this function to calculate the probability that a peak will have occurred by a certain year.

Then, in order to calculate future oil supply for a given year, similar probabilistic functions need to be estimated in order to find future growth rates and rates of decline. Before peak, growth rates tend to center around 1.6% and estimates of post-peak declines center around 3% per year. A Gaussian probability function was then created for each of these rates.

Finally, to create the ultimate probabilistic estimation of oil supply, a Monte Carlo simulation was used to integrate the three probabilistic models, generating a set of possible oil supplies spread across a probability function. Among the figures generated by this production, it is predicted that there is only a 5% chance of having more than 28 billion barrels/year in 2035, which is about the yearly production of conventional oil in 2005. The authors suggest that it is likely that by 2035 we will have about 60% of the oil supply as existed in 2005. As urban planning projects typically look forward as much as 40 years it is clear that an oil peak needs to be considered when looking at potential risks to viability.

After creating a function for oil supply, an impact function was also necessary to illustrate the effects of an oil peak on individual behavior and aggregate this to find the ultimate effect on various modes of urban planning. The authors theorize that the primary consequence of rising fuel prices will be a change in travel demand. This will manifest itself by a change in the quantity and nature of trips. They create a metric to measure the essentiality of trips. Trips are divided into three groups: optional, necessary, and essential. Optional trips are trips that can be cut without an overall loss of utility, necessary trips are trips which an individual would not cut if they could avoid it, and result in a loss of either social or economic wellbeing. Finally, essential trips cannot be cut without significant loss to personal health and overall quality of life. The authors define all trips as 20% optional, 30% necessary, and 50% essential.

Given the projections on fuel supply produced by the model, it is likely that there will be a disparity between unconstrained—or business as usual— demand and energy supply. Impact is then characterized by the types of strategies available to deal with this disparity, which would depend on organization of the city and transportation methods available. Low impact strategies are defined as those in which energy consumption is lowered but all economic and social participation is maintained. This would be realized by an increase in the use of fuel efficient vehicles, public transportation and active modes of transportation such as walking or cycling as well as through decreased trip distances and other behavioral changes. Medium impact results imply a cut in optional trips. High impact strategies are those in which necessary trips are cut, and very high impact strategies result in a loss of essential trips. The larger the supply and demand disparity, the more difficult it will be to avoid suffering medium and high impact effects.

These models of fuel supply and supply demand disparity impact are then used to calculate the risk factor of a peak in conventional oil. This model, which incorporates unconstrained energy demand, energy supply, and the various ways in which people can change their behavior to deal with the disparity between the two, comes up with several conclusions. The first is that behavioral changes generate the least impact. These are facilitated by a dense city requiring little driving with good public transportation. The other conclusion is that a reduction to trips significantly increases the risk factor, a possibility faced by more spread out cities with poor public transportation. Although these conclusions seem trivial, the authors point out that this is the first time they have been modeled in a mathematical fashion that can be included in risk analysis models for the planning of future projects.

In order to test this model, the authors applied their formula to the city of Christchurch, New Zealand. Christchurch was predicted to nearly double in population between 2005 and 2041, and the city has four different plans for expansion: an unplanned, business as usual approach, Plan A, in which the city borders expand little and the focus is on population density, Plan B, which would allow growth to push out along developed areas, and Plan C, which would primarily involve growth in the suburbs of Christchurch. The development model used had oil supply about 20% over what the model showed was likely for 2041, and risk was calculated with this assumption. Unsurprisingly, although the risk factor was significant for all plans, Plan A had the lowest risk.

The World After Peak Oil If No Satisfactory Energy Substitute is Found

It is difficult to predict what sort of world we will face if a peak in oil production is caused not by the eventual phasing out of oil but by an exhaustion of supply. This is even more true if technological optimists' prediction of the creation of a substitute for oil as our main industrial energy resource proves false. Friedrichs (2010) offers several possible scenarios for this post oil world based on three different historical cases. Countries may resort to military predation as Japan did before and during World War 2, undergo totalitarian retrenchment similar to what occurred in North Korea during the 1990s, or they may rely on improvisation and community in order to adapt to the lack of key resources in a manner similar to Cubans after the fall of the Soviet Union. He goes on to explain that the response would vary depending on historical and political factors in a given country. Friedrichs also offers the example of the failure of the post Civil War South to adapt in a timely fashion to the loss of a key economic resource—slaves—as justification for his views that the world would likely have a very difficult time replacing oil with a new resource after a production peak.

Friedrichs used three historical case studies of countries facing acute oil shortages to extrapolate what the world could look like if oil production reaches a peak and no reasonable substitute is found. From these studies he derives four hypotheses: "The greater a country's military potential and the perception that force will be more effective than the free market to protect access to vital resources, the more likely there will be a strategy of military predation," the less democratic and pluralist a country, the more likely those in power will institute totalitarian retrenchment, the less individualistic a country, the more likely there will be an "adaptive regression to community based values" and finally that peak oil will create winners and loses, that power will shift from oil importers to the exporters, as well as from private oil companies to public ones. Finally, using the post-war American South as a basis, Friedrichs posits that the transition from oil will not be smooth, and that the adaptation may take more than a century.

The first of Friedrichs' hypothesis is reached following his analysis of Imperial Japan's behavior before and during the War in the Pacific. After concluding that Germany's defeat in World War I was due largely to its inability to secure a large enough resource base the leaders of Japan decided that in order to ensure Japanese success they would have to directly control the resources they would need. In the face of trade embargoes on oil, Japan invaded Manchuria, South East Asia, and many Pacific islands. Using this as his basis, Friedrichs surmises that countries with the ability to project their power, particularly the United States and to a lesser extent China, will resort to military predation in order to secure oil after the markets are no longer deemed a convenient or reliable way to meet energy needs.

Friedrichs' second hypothesis, that countries with a weak democratic tradition and histories rife with dictatorship will experience a retrenchment of totalitarianism, comes from the events in North Korea following the collapse of the Soviet Union. After the Soviet Union dissolved North Korea no longer received oil in return for political corruption. This led to a complete collapse of the country's economy, including its highly industrialized agricultural sector, leading to widespread famine that killed 3–5% of the population. At the same time, the elite ruling class continued to enjoy the privileges that it had grown accustomed to while oil was still prevalent. Friedrichs believes that countries in Eastern Europe, Southeast Asia, and Africa with their totalitarian pasts will be particularly susceptible to this retrenchment.

In contrast, Cuba scraped by reasonably well after oil shipments from the USSR ceased in the early nineties. This experience is the basis of Friedrichs' third hypothesis, that countries with a strong sense of community and are not accustomed to the consumption levels of the industrialized West will be able to subsist through wide-scale socioeconomic adaptation. Due to Cuba's tight knit neighborhoods and knowledge of traditional agriculture Cubans were able to live at a subsistence level through Urban agriculture that ranged from gardens on the roof to chickens in apartments. Though living without cheap oil certainly made daily life unpleasant, Cuba did not experience any of the widespread famine suffered by average North Koreans. Friedrichs writes that countries that still rely largely on subsistence agriculture in Sub-Saharan Africa and Latin American countries with societies still based around the family and community as opposed to the individual will be the ones most able to make these adaptations.

Finally, Friedrichs warns that optimism in regards to oil being superseded by new fuels may be unwarranted. He points out that the American South took nearly a century to achieve a quality of life similar to that of the North after its economy lost its key resource, namely slaves. Even though a guide to what should be done existed in the northern states, the South still failed to make adaptations necessary to life post-slavery because of their attachment to the old ways of doing things. Friedrichs concludes that losing oil in the 21st century will have a similar effect on our economy as the emancipation of the slaves had on the American South, and that we have no convenient models to lead us away from the scenarios presented in Friedrichs' paper.

Demand Management of Oil Will be a Persistent Problem after Peak Production

An eventual peak in oil production is viewed by many to be the unavoidable consequence of the consumption of a resource that is by its very nature nonrenewable. Debate continues as to when this peak will eventually be reached, and it depends largely on our ability to sustain oil production through new methods of exploiting unconventional sources of fossil fuel. Hughes and Rudolph (2010) point out that avoiding a peak depends largely on oil fields that have yet to be discovered, and that unconventional oil sources are costly not only in terms of their energy return on energy invested (EROEI), but also with regards to the amount of carbon dioxide expelled in their extraction. When an eventual peak is reached, jurisdictions will primarily be limited to three different methods of coping: reduction of demand for energy, replacement of oil with other sources of secure liquid fuel, and restriction of new demand for energy to sources not based on fossil fuel. The authors conclude that the third option seems more likely, but that problems such as finding clean sources of electricity generation and the difficulty of obtaining natural gas in gas-poor regions would still present significant hurdles to our transition away from oil.

Hughes and Rudolph (2010) analyzed production and demand growth, sources, alternatives, and production outlooks for oil to reach an opinion on the likelihood of an oil peak. They then proceed to offer possible policy reactions to this peak if it were to occur on a timeline similar to that presented by the International Energy Agency (IEA). They conclude that if a peak due to resource exhaustion were to occur, it would be extremely taxing upon the world's economies, and the resulting problems would not be overcome in a simple and timely manner.

Hughes and Rudolph begin by emphasizing the importance of oil in to-day's world. They state that oil represents 34% of the world's total energy demand, with coal and natural gas making up another 47.4% of aggregate energy demand. This was made possible by the exponential and unprecedented growth of oil production. From the dawn of the 20th century all the way through the 1970's, oil production doubled about once every ten years. Following the oil shocks of 1975 and 1980 growth in oil production has continued, though in a less dramatic linear fashion.

The authors go on to analyze the sources of this oil production. They say that about 85% of oil is produced from conventional sources, for example onshore reserves and those situated in shallow water. However, these sources have largely been in decline, forcing oil companies to resort to more energy intensive unconventional sources, such as the oil sands of Canada or the heavy oil of Venezuela, as well as substitutable liquid fuels such as liquefied coal and natural gas and fuels created from biomass.

The main difference pointed out between these two sources is not their ultimate product, but rather the amount of energy required to obtain the fuel. In the beginning of the 20th century it has been estimated that oil reserves in the US had an EROEI of nearly 100, while the estimated EROEI of newer conventional crude oil wells is closer to 11, with biofuels currently yielding an EROEI somewhere between 1.0 and 3.2. The authors conclude that if increasing demand for oil is to be met, it will be both expensive and environmentally harmful.

Hughes and Rudolph move on to address the theory of peak oil. Although peak oil has been criticized for its missed predictions in the past, the authors remind the reader that methods of predicting oil production have been improving and such predictions should not be taken lightly. They examine the production outlooks provided by the IEA, which show an increase in liquid fuel production through 2030. However, the authors point out that this depends largely on crude oil that has yet to be found as well as a growing reliance on liquid natural gas. If either of these prospects do not pan out, a peak or plateau in oil production would likely be reached between 2020 and 2030.

The authors do state that although the IEA's study is rigorous, there is a shortage of data regarding oil reserves in the Middle East, as much of these data are unavailable to the public. It is unclear whether this would make IEA under or over-estimate the total amount of remaining reserves.

If a peak occurs, meeting future demand for oil would be an unprecedented challenge to world governments and economies. The authors explain that accommodating such a large change would require long-term planning that would likely require a decrease in energy consumption. Strategies to meet the peak would fall under three main labels: reduction, replacement, and restriction. Reduction would involve lowering energy use through conservation and efficiency, replacement would require replacing oil with other liquid fuels, and restriction would limit new energy demand to non-oil sources.

Hughes and Rudolph conclude that restriction will be the most likely strategy, and that for at least the near term energy usage would likely be restricted to natural gas and electricity. This of course presents its own unique problems. Providing natural gas to gas poor regions like Europe would require either new pipelines or the large-scale liquefying of gas. Either of these solutions would subject places like Europe to intense political pressure from suppliers of natural gas. The major problem with electricity on the other hand is the steady supply of environmentally sustainable energy. Countries like the United States and China have already shown a willingness to rely on their massive coal reserves, which is not environmentally desirable. The authors state that perhaps the best options are renewables such as solar and wind, despite the fact that they would require a change in energy consumption attitudes, from one where usage determines output to output determining usage.

Activated Sludge Process with a Fixed Biological Media a Viable Way to Treat Coal Gasification Wastewater

Coal gasification is often seen as a key to future energy production. It takes advantage of plentiful coal supplies, particularly in the United States and China, in order to create liquid fuels, as well as to produce the hydrogen gas used in the hydrogen fuel cells that many predict will eventually come to power most of our transportation infrastructure. Unfortunately, the process of coal gasification creates wastewater containing many pollutants harmful to the environment, including ammonia (NH_4-n), cyclooctadiene (COD), and phenol. Because of this, the continuing and future viability of coal gasification requires effective processes to purify the wastewater that its creation and refinement produces. Traditionally an activated sludge process (ASP) is used to treat this wastewater. Han *et al.* (2010) found that if a soft fixed biological medium is added into the treatment tanks, about 80% of pollutants can be removed in a manner more stable than traditional ASP treatment.

Han *et al.* studied the effects of submerged biofilm on the ASP. Traditionally ASP does a good job in removing phenol and COD, but has a relatively small effect on NH_4-n in the system. The biofilm added contained nitrifying bacteria to breakdown the NH_4-n in the wastewater.

The ASP uses a two stage process, with each stage composed of one large tank and one sedimentation tank, with a total volume per stage of 7000 m^3. The effluent from the coal gasification is mixed with residential wastewater and then flows through the first tank and moves on to the tanks of the second stage in a process that takes about 42 hours. Each stage works through the same method, with the sludge adsorbing and biodegrading the phenol and COD's, and the bacteria on the biofilm nitrifying the NH_4-n. The research team measured the levels of COD, NH_4-n, and phenol in the wastewater before it entered the system, after the first stage, and upon its exit of the system. These measurements continued over the course of an entire year.

The results of the experiment were very promising, generating only a few problematic points in the data. COD removal rates after the two stages averaged out to be around 80%. The concentration of COD ranged from 550 to 1760 mg/L in the untreated wastewater, with concentration rates dropping to about 200 mg/L after completing the second stage.

Similarly, phenol rates were greatly reduced following the ASP. The influent total phenol concentrations ranged from 95 to 345 mg/L, and the effluent total concentrations were around 25 mg/L. The average total rate of phenol removal was 90%.

The study points out one main drop in filtration capacity by the first stage of the ADP in the 5 weeks between weeks 35 and 40. Normally the first stage of the process filters out 70% of COD and 80% of phenol, but during this period that rate dropped to 60% for both pollutants. Han *et al.* suggest that the problem might lie in the process by which the sludge removes these compounds. They state that it is possible that the sludge became saturated with pollutants through adsorption and that the process of biodegradation did not work quickly enough to break down the compounds, allowing unadsorbed contaminants to continue on to the second stage. This did not affect the concentration levels after the second stage, which was able to make up for the deficiency in the first stage tanks.

The rate of removal of NH_4-n from the wastewater began fairly low, but ultimately reached 80% after 15 weeks. The influent NH_4-n concentrations ranged from 60 to 110 mg/L, and after 15 weeks the concentration in the effluent was down to around 15 mg/L. Thanks to the biofilm inserted into the tanks, nitrifying bacteria were able to adhere onto them and grow successfully. This was not possible during the traditional ASP process, but the bacteria took time to multiply, leading to the low rates of nitrogen filtration and the beginning of the experiment.

The first stage of the ADP had problems removing NH_4-n even after the 15 week period in which removal rates finally rose to 80%. The authors hypothesize that this was due to a competitive mechanism in which heterotrophic bacteria were preying upon the nitrifying bacteria. This was particularly a problem in the first stage, in which the wastewater still had a high concentration of organic matter due to mixing of the coal gasification wastewater with sewage from the surrounding residential area. Predation was not a problem in the second stage, as concentration of organic matter was much lower.

Given these results, Han *et al.* conclude that ADP with a soft biological medium inserted could remove most NH₄-n and organic pollutants from coal gasification wastewater. Additionally, they concluded that this process was more stable than traditional ADP.

Conclusions

Given the evidence it is clear that ongoing research is necessary to establish the likelihood of peak in oil production. This will require a large amount of cooperation across academic fields as well as obtaining better data, which may or may not be possible. This work will be vital to determine whether the world should be preparing for a massive change or not? Are we actually only harming ourselves by spending on new technologies that would mitigate the effects of an oil peak that will never come? Given the importance of oil production to our current way of life and the effects its consumption will have on the lives of generations to come through global warming, it is crucial that these questions are answered. Unfortunately the community is still undecided on Peak Oil, and it may only be through experiencing a global peak in oil production that a consensus can be reached.

References Cited

Friedrichs, J., 2010. Global energy crunch: how different parts of the world would react to a peak oil scenario. Energy Policy 38, 4562–4569.

Han, H., Li, H., Du, M., Wang, W., 2010. Treatment of coal gasification wastewater by full scale activated sludge process with fixed media. Bioinformatics and Biomedical Engineering (iCBBE), 2010 4th International Conference on, 1–4

Höök, M., Sivertsson, A., Aleklett, K., 2010a. Validity of the fossil fuel production outlooks in the IPCC emission scenarios. Natural Resources Research, 63–81

Höök, M., Bardi, U., Feng, L., Pang, X., 2010b. Development of oil formation theories and their importance for peak oil. Marine and Petroleum Geology 27, 1995–2004.

Hughes, L., Rudolph, J., 2010. Future world oil production: Growth, plateau, or peak? Current Opinions in Environmental Sustainability special issue Energy Systems.

Krumdieck, S., Page, S., Dantas, A., 2010. Urban form and long-term fuel supply decline: A method to investigate the peak oil risks to essential activities. Transportation Research Part A 44, 306–322.

Sorrell, S., Speirs, J., Bentley, R., Brandt, A., Miller, R., 2010. Global oil depletion: A review of the evidence. Energy Policy 38, 5290–5295

Radetzki, M., 2010. Peak oil and other threatening peaks—chimeras without substance. Energy Policy 38, 6566–6569.

2. Environmental Impacts of Electricity Production

Lucinda Block

According to Weber *et al.* (2010), 40% of US CO_2 emissions originate from electricity generation and distribution. Due to the increasingly serious global warming impact of fossil fuels like coal and natural gas used for electricity production, many researchers have focused efforts on analyzing more environmentally benign sources of electricity. Not only do many wish to substitute fossil fuels used for electricity generation with renewable sources of energy like solar, wind, hydropower, geothermal, hydrokinetic, or biomass, but given the potential of renewable electricity generation, electrification of other sectors (like transportation) is being viewed as a viable climate change mitigation strategy (Jacobson and Delucchi 2011).

In this chapter, I review several lifecycle analyses (LCA) of different renewable energy sources used for electricity generation. Laleman *et al.* (2011) analyzed the environmental impact and potential of rooftop photovoltaic technology in regions of low solar irradiation and offered a detailed explanation of the LCA indicators used along with their advantages and disadvantages. This explanation gives context to studies done by Butner *et al.* (2010), Miller *et al.* (2011), and Ozbilen *et al.* (2011) that assessed the impact of electricity generation from biomass and hydrokinetic energy and hydrogen production for energy storage.

The study by Howarth *et al.* (2011) calls into question the assumption that natural gas has a much lower global warming potential than coal; for example, Laleman *et al.*'s data from the Ecoinvent v2.0 database show natural gas to have about half the global warming potential of hard coal. Howarth *et al.* considered natural gas production from unconventional sources such as shale, and calculated that fugitive methane emissions of just 2–3%, well within the possible range for both conventional and shale gas production, make natural gas more impactful than coal and oil.

Weber *et al.* emphasize the sources of uncertainty in calculating emissions factors, or estimated average quantity of CO_2 emitted per unit of energy consumed. Though crucial to conducting LCAs, the accuracy of emissions factors is greatly complicated by regional variability. The authors examine this variability and offer recommendations for dealing with uncertainty.

Davis *et al.* (2010) offer a larger picture of global greenhouse gas emissions by calculating the cumulative future emissions of existing energy infrastructure, or our "committed" CO_2 emissions. The authors assume that it is much harder to decommission functioning energy infrastructure, and by assuming future emissions from existing infrastructure to be inevitable, one gets an idea of how much leeway remains in which to improve energy efficiency and reduce greenhouse gas emissions. Whereas Davis *et al.* calculate committed emissions, Jacobson and Delucchi optimistically propose a global scale solution for a low to no-carbon world. By analyzing the feasibility of necessary infrastructure, Jacobson and Delucchi describe a world entirely powered by wind, water and sunlight and conclude that barriers are more social and political than economic or technological.

Photovoltaic Technology in Regions of Low Solar Irradiation: A Broad Assessment of Environmental Impact

Whereas most lifecycle assessments (LCAs) use one-dimensional indicators and only apply to areas of high solar irradiation, Laleman *et al.* (2011) used both one-dimensional indicators and the multi-dimensional Eco-Indicator 99 (EI 99) to conduct a broad assessment the environmental impact of various photovoltaic (PV) technologies employed in areas of low solar irradiation such as Canada and Northern Europe. Furthermore, they used these same indicators to compare PV systems to other sources of electricity production. The authors found the energy payback time of PV systems to be less than 5 years, and the global warming potential to be approximately 10 times lower than a coal plant and 4 times higher than a nuclear power plant or wind farm. The authors obtained significantly different results using EI 99 compared to one-dimensional indicators, and thus stressed the importance of carefully evaluating a combination of different environmental impact assessment approaches. Ruben Laleman, Johan Alrecht, and Jo Dewulf of Ghent University in Belgium used lifecycle data from the Ecoinvent database (v2.0) to assess the environmental impact of six different PV technologies under conditions of low solar irradiation (900-1000 kWh/m²/year). As opposed to only using a one-dimensional indicator such as Cumulative Energy Demand (CED), Energy Payback Time (EPT), or Global Warming Potential (GWP), as many other authors conducting LCAs do, Laleman *et al.* compared environmental impact findings of these one-dimensional indicators to the multi-dimensional EI 99. The authors also compared their findings of PV environmental impacts to the impact of other electricity sources such as hard coal, natural gas, and the Belgian electricity mix.

The authors' findings of PV technology's environmental impact for the one-dimensional indicators—CED, EPT, and GWP—were comparable to previous literature conducted on the subject, but their findings for the EI 99 had very little correlation with the one-dimensional indicators (at most 22%). Therefore, they stress the importance of employing a multi-dimensional indicator, especially along-side one-dimensional indicators, in order to give the most nuanced picture possible of environmental impacts.

Besides assessing environmental impact for various environmental indicators—mineral extraction, fossil fuels, respiratory effects, ozone layer depletion, ionizing radiation, climate change, carcinogenics, land occupation, ecotoxicity, and acidification and eutrophication—EI 99 categorizes those indicators into three main dimensions: human health, ecosystem quality, and the depletion of non-renewable resources, and creates three different "perspectives"—i.e., three different ways to deal with the subjective process of weighting and normalizing results based on different rankings of preferences, values, and attitudes. The three perspectives are Hierarchist, Egalitarian, and Individualist. The Hierarchist represents the view of the "average scientist" who is presumed to follow the IPCC's (International Panel on Climate Change) assessment reports on the effects of climate change, balance short- and long-term concerns, and bases her views on consensus. The Egalitarian greatly values ecosystem quality, considers the very long term—another way of saying she is concerned with sustainability—and is highly risk-averse, potentially resulting in overestimation of risks. The Egalitarian is prone to consider all possible negative environmental effects of a phenomenon like climate change as definite. This view contrasts with that of the Individualist, who only considers "proven" effects (as opposed to effects based on consensus but around which there remains some doubt). The Individualist does not place any importance in fossil fuel depletion; rather, she only considers the depletion of minerals relevant. Furthermore, the Individualist's perspective lies within a short-term time frame, whereas the Egalitarian thinks in terms of a very long time frame. Laleman *et al.* emphasize the need to clarify and outline these different perspectives in LCAs employing EI 99 so as not to cause serious misinterpretations, and for clarity's sake they also include unweighted results.

First, the authors evaluated environmental impact using one-dimensional indicators for the following six PV technologies: Cadmium Telluride (CdTe), $CuInSe_2$ (CIS), ribbon Si, multi crystalline Si (multi c-Si), mono crystalline Si (mono c-Si) and amorphous (a-Si). The newer technologies are the CdTe, CIS and ribbon Si. Using the same figure for yearly energy output and the same conversion coefficient for electricity generation efficiency, the authors' calculations for CED and EPT indicators are proportional to one another. Whereas CED measures total energy required to construct the PV system over its lifetime, EPT measures the amount of time until the PV system produces more energy than was required for its construction. In these analyses, the newer technologies were found to be more efficient than older ones, requiring less than 30,000 megajoules equivalent per kilowatt-peak (kilowatt-peak [kWp] is a measure of solar energy output under laboratory conditions; a standard home installation is considered to be 3 kWp in this study) for their construction. All PV types had an EPT of less than 5 years in low irradiation conditions. CdTe, CIS and ribbon Si EPTs were about one year less than those of the other PV systems, though this difference decreased as irradiation conditions increased. In high solar irradiation regions like Spain, EPTs were only 2–3 years.

The GWP measures quantity of greenhouse gases emitted over the life-cycle of a PV system. As with CED and EPT indicators, the GWP indicator showed the three newer PV technologies, along with multi c-Si, to have less impact than the three older ones (approximately 5000 kg of CO_2 equivalent compared to approximately 6000 kg of CO_2 equivalent).

The EI 99 results differed significantly from the one-dimensional indicators. Using the Hierarchist perspective, CdTe was found to have the highest impact score, and greatly exceeded the scores of the other newer technologies (450 compared to 317 and 353). A breakdown of impact scores according to individual environmental indicators shows that most impact originates from fossil fuels and respiratory effects. The authors note that reducing the energy input of PV production will decrease the impact related to fossil fuel extraction, respiratory effects, climate change, acidification and carcinogenics as they all relate to one another.

In order to compare the environmental impact of PV technology to other sources of electricity, the authors selected the multi c-Si system, as it has the largest market share. They employed both a pessimistic (20 year) and optimistic (30 year) lifespan estimate for the PV system, and using both GWP and EI 99 indicators they compared the impact for 1 kWh (kilowatt-hour) produced by the various electricity sources.

The GWP analysis showed PV electricity to have a markedly lower impact than fossil fuel based sources (even with an expected lifespan of 20 years, the PV's GWP was 0.12 kg of CO_2 equivalent per kWh (kgCO$_2$-eq/kWh) compared to 0.53 for natural gas). The Belgian mix is surprisingly low, at 0.33 kgCO$_2$-eq/kWh, due to the high (55%) proportion of nuclear energy contribution. The GWP of PV electricity was found to be approximately four times higher than nuclear and wind and ten times lower than coal (the authors claim their impact assessment for nuclear takes into account the impact of radiation on human health).

The EI 99 results for compared environmental impact across electricity sources varied greatly depending on the perspective used. Because the Individualist perspective does not "value" fossil fuel extraction as having an environmental impact, the mineral extraction associated with PV construction is weighted very highly and thus the total impact of PV is very high for the Individualist compared to the Egalitarian and Hierarchist perspectives. Since PV technology requires a significant level of aluminum, iron, and copper, the Individualist finds PV to be much more impactful than natural gas, whereas the Egalitarian and Hierarchist find natural gas to be significantly more impactful. In the unweighted category of ecosystem quality, PV is about twice as impactful as natural gas (and both are small compared to coal). In the category of human health and resource depletion, PV impacts are negligible, natural gas impacts are small, and coal impacts are high. Though a comparison of mineral ore extraction across electricity sources show that PV requires a relatively large amount of mineral ore, an EI 99 assessment of overall resource depletion shows mineral extraction associated with PV to be negligible compared to the fossil fuel extraction required for other electricity sources. With regards to the issue of mineral ore required for PV construction, the authors indicate that the removal of the aluminum frame used for PV panel installations would greatly reduce overall environmental impact, and they recommend an efficient recycling program for the ores.

The authors conclude that PV systems have a relatively low environmental impact even in areas of low solar irradiation, especially compared to fossil fuel based sources of electricity, though mineral extraction requirements should be taken into consideration. Lifetime energy production ranged from 4 to 6 times lifetime energy consumption, and could reach 12 times lifetime energy consumption in sunny regions. Lifetime greenhouse gas emissions were significantly lower than fossil fuel based sources of electricity production. The EI 99 analysis showed that when fossil fuels were considered to have a negative impact on the wellbeing of future generations, PV systems were found to be less impactful than natural gas, coal, and the Belgian electricity mix. The weighting step of EI 99 analysis greatly affected results, making the Individualist perspective consider PV more impactful than natural gas—as the authors point out, many would consider the large weight the Individualist assigns to mineral extraction to be illogical or irrational in this case. The authors suggest this implies a need for great care and consideration of complexities in conducting a LCA. Furthermore, due to low correlation of EI 99 results with one-dimensional indicators, Laleman *et al.* recommend the use of various indicators for a thorough and comprehensive LCA.

Lucinda Block

The Environmental Impact of Electricity Production from Biomass: A Comparison of Poplar and Ethiopian Mustard

Spain has set the goal of producing 12% of its primary energy demand through renewable sources in its Renewable Energies Plan 2000–2010, and power generation from biomass represents an important contribution to meet this goal. Butner et al. (2010) evaluated the environmental performance of two biocrops used for electricity production, poplar and Ethiopian mustard. Using a Life-Cycle Assessment (LCA) approach, the authors calculated environmental impacts for electricity generation from the two crops and compared values to natural gas generation and the Spanish electricity mix in order to assess whether or not these crops are environmentally competitive with conventional sources of power. They found poplar to be less environmentally impactful than Ethiopian mustard, mostly due to higher production yields. Electricity from biomass had more impact in three of six environmental categories than natural gas power and less impact in all categories compared to the mix of electricity supplied to the Spanish grid.

Isabela Butnar from the Universitat Rouvira I Virgili along with Julio Rodrigo, Carles M. Gasol, and Francesc Castells selected poplar and Ethiopian mustard for the study due to their high yields in Spain. They chose poplar in particular because of its strong environmental performance and high yields in Mediterranean areas compared with annual herbaceous crops, though its cultivation also consumes large amounts of water. The two crops also differ significantly from one another: poplar is a perennial crop with a sixteen-year cultivation period, and Ethiopian mustard an annual herbaceous species.

The authors considered cradle-to-grave impacts of the different processes required to produce electricity from poplar and Ethiopian mustard, including field work, the use of farm machines, and the transport of materials associated with production such as fertilizer, herbicides, and packaging, as well as the transport of produced biomass to the power plant. To calculate this last impact, Butnar et al. considered two different distances, 25 km and 50 km. The authors based these distances on the percentage of available land for biocrop production at different plant capacities: when the required cultivated area of biomass for a given plant capacity exceeded 15% of the regional irrigated arable land, they calculated a distance of 50 km from the field; otherwise, they calculated a distance of 25 km.

Along with distance values, Butnar et al. varied the power plant capacities and productivity yield values to calculate the environmental impacts of twelve different scenarios. The three power plant capacities considered were 10, 25, and 50 MW. The authors used two different productivity values for each crop, the lower limit of their productivity yield range and the average value. For poplar these values were 9 and 13.5 t/ha, respectively, and for Ethiopian mustard they were 4.72 and 8.07 t/ha.

Using SiAGROSOST, a software tool created by their research group, the authors found optimum values for minimizing environmental impact in the variety of scenarios mentioned above for ten different environmental indicators, though only six indicators were included in the report: acidification, global warming, human toxicity, ozone layer depletion, abiotic depletion, and photochemical oxidation.

As expected, for all indicators, environmental impact decreased when biomass productivity increased. Because of its higher productivity per hectare, poplar outperformed Ethiopian mustard, having less environmental impact across all indicators. In general, a greater distance between fields and power plants (50 km as opposed to 25 km) implied greater environmental impact. In turn, this had implications for the optimal power plant size—the larger capacity of 50 MW plants required more biomass cultivated area than 15% of the regional irrigated arable land, and thus the quantity of biomass required to run the plant at full capacity was not available at a 25 km distance. This increased the environmental impact of 50 MW plants, despite their generally higher efficiency in energy production.

The two crops performed differently in their relationship with productivity, transport, and environmental impacts. Poplar's impacts were more closely associated with transport, and Ethiopian mustard's with productivity. When transport distances increased, poplar's environmental impact increased more than Ethiopian mustard's environmental impact did. When productivity decreased, Ethiopian mustard's environmental impact increased more than poplar's did. This information has implications for planning the use of different types of crops for biomass electricity generation: while both productivity and transport distance are important, either factor may be more important for different crops.

By calculating the contribution of individual fieldwork activities—between fertilizers, harvesting, pesticides, and others—to the impact of crop cultivation, the authors found that fertilization is by far the most impactful step of cultivation (accounting for up to 78% of acidification and up to 82% of global warming impact). However, replacing mineral fertilizers with natural fertilizers such as livestock manure could significantly reduce the environmental impact of fertilization, which, along with soil characteristics and weather, greatly contributes to crop productivity.

Butnar *et al.* compared their calculated impact values for biomass with electricity production from natural gas and the electricity put into the Spanish grid, which is largely dependent on fossil fuels. They found that biomass electricity had a worse environmental profile than natural gas in the areas of acidification, human toxicity, and photochemical oxidation, and a better environmental profile in the areas of global warming, abiotic depletion, and ozone depletion. Biomass electricity had a better environmental profile than the Spanish electricity mix in all areas. However, it is important to note that Butnar *et al.* did not calculate the impact of transport and distribution of electricity in their biomass LCA, while values for natural gas and the Spanish mix include transport and distribution. Additionally, Butnar *et al.* failed to account for the disposal of ashes from the combustion of biomass in their LCA.

Butnar *et al.* found that electricity generation from poplar is more environmentally competitive than from Ethiopian mustard, and that power plants of 10 and 25 MW are more environmentally competitive for biomass electricity generation than 50 MW plants in the region of Tarragonès. The authors recommend thoughtful biomass management plans that include recycled residues, e.g. from the cleaning of public parks. They also state that in order to keep environmental impact of electricity generation from biomass low, biomass productivity must be optimized, and distances between field and power plant must be minimized.

A Baseline Life-Cycle Assessment for Hydrokinetic Energy Extraction

Miller *et al.* (2011) used life-cycle assessment methods to evaluate environmental impacts of hydrokinetic energy extraction (HEE), which have not previously been quantified. The authors established a baseline methodology for doing so, and compared their LCA findings for HEE with other energy systems across a variety of environmental indicators. HEE is considered an environmentally benign form of renewable energy, and by harnessing kinetic as opposed to potential energy, avoids the sediment movement and impact to ecosystem of conventional hydroelectric power generation. HEE collects energy from the kinetic movement of water without constructing a dam, and therefore avoids large ecosystem disruptions and changes to water flow and volume associated with hydropower electricity generation. In this study, the authors focus on HEE from rivers, as opposed to tidal flow or waves. They focus on the Gorlov system, which uses a helical crossflow turbine. Miller *et al.* found the Gorlov system compared closely to small hydropower and to have the lowest life-cycle impact of all energy systems considered.

Veronica B. Miller, Amy E. Landis, and Laura A. Schaefer of the University of Pittsburgh employed the Tool for the Reduction and Assessment of Chemical and other environmental Impacts (TRACI) to conduct their Life-Cycle Impact Assessment (LCIA). They considered upstream and downstream impacts of HEE, small hydropower, coal, natural gas, and nuclear power. The small hydropower considerations included the dam structure, tunnel, turbine, generator, plant operation, and dismantling. The calculation of coal plant impact included the coal production and preparation, coal processing, storage and transportation, and the calculation of natural gas impact included gas field exploration, natural gas production, gas purification, long distance transportation, and regional distribution.[1] The HEE LCIA included raw materials used to construct the Gorlov system, transportation, assembly, operation, and decommissioning.

Miller *et al.* compared different energy systems to each other across many environmental indicators to calculate which energy source implies the most environmental impact, and more specifically, how Gorlov HEE and hydropower compare to one another, but they do not mention how they controlled for the variable of energy output between different types of electricity plants. The authors found that among all energy systems considered, coal and gas power plants had the highest environmental impacts related to global warming, acidification, eutrophication, ecosystem disruption, and smog formation. Nuclear power was most the most impactful energy system in terms of ozone depletion. Gorlov HEE and small hydropower had negligible global warming impacts compared to the other energy systems. A comparison of Gorlov HEE and small hydropower showed that small hydropower was more impactful than Gorlov HEE across all indicators but respiratory effects and acidification. The authors attribute these impacts to the production of copper, which is used for the Gorlov HEE generator, though they mention that methods of SO_2-free copper production are currently being investigated. The ecotoxicity of Gorlov HEE was shown to be less than 2% of that of small hydropower.

The study shows that Gorlov HEE is less impactful across almost all environmental indicators than small hydropower. Nonetheless, the study should be viewed as a rough basis for estimating the life-cycle environmental impact of HEE. The data used for this study came primarily from estimates, as opposed to from a case study. Additionally, many considerations were not taken into account: fish and local river ecology health was not taken into account, though Miller *et al.* suggest that a new LCIA category could be created and this impact could be calculated using estimated fish passage from HEE computational fluid dynamics and fish swimming data. The authors did not consider in their assessment the variety of fiberglass types used for turbine blade construction. Furthermore, the study did not account for negative environmental effects of dam construction, such as changes to overall water flow and temperature differences, or the benefits of hydropower, such as its reliability as a renewable source of energy and the benefit of creating a reservoir.

---

[1] The authors neglect to mention whether their data for the impacts of natural gas production have been updated to reflect recent developments in natural gas extraction from unconventional shale. See Howarth *et al.* (2011).

Lucinda Block

Re-evaluating Lifecycle Greenhouse Gas Emissions of Natural Gas Production

Natural gas is widely regarded as a transitional or bridge fuel: though still a fossil fuel, it is believed to have less global warming potential (GWP) than oil or coal. In this paper Howarth *et al.* (2011) re-examine that assumption by calculating fugitive methane emissions from both conventional and unconventional gas resources, namely shale gas from high-volume hydraulic fracturing. Shale gas production has boomed in recent years, exceeding conventional production in 2009, and is expected to constitute a large part of the gas used to transition from fossil fuels to renewable energy. However, few scientists have evaluated the greenhouse gas footprint of unconventional gas, and in light of recent findings that methane has an even greater GWP than previously believed, it is imperative to reassess the GWP of natural gas production from conventional and unconventional sources. Howarth *et al.* calculated that 3.6–7.9% of methane from shale gas production escapes through fugitive emissions and venting, a percentage 1.3–2.1 times higher than from conventional gas production. They found shale gas to have a larger GWP than oil and coal on a 20-year timescale, and to have a larger GWP than oil and comparable GWP to coal on a 100-year timescale.

Howarth *et al.* used two recently available reports for their data, a 2010 Environmental Protection Agency (EPA) document on greenhouse gas emissions from the oil and gas industry and a 2010 Government Accountability Office report on natural gas losses on federal lands. The former document is the first update on oil and gas emissions factors since 1996, when the agency produced a report that served as the basis for the national greenhouse gas inventory for the past decade. Howarth *et al.* remark that the 1996 study was neither based on random sampling nor comprehensive; instead, data were collected from model facilities through voluntary reporting. The EPA acknowledge in their new report that emissions factors are much higher from some sources than originally thought, and that the first report was published at a time when methane emissions were not a significant concern.

Because recent studies suggest that methane has a greater GWP than previously thought—having 33 times the GWP of CO_2 when examined on a 100 year timescale, whereas previously thought to be 25 (IPCC 2007)—and because of the presumably low methane emissions factors used in recent years to calculate greenhouse gas inventories, Howarth *et al.* focus in this paper on calculating the fugitive methane emissions and emissions from venting throughout conventional and unconventional natural gas production.

The main differences the authors find in methane emissions between conventional and unconventional gas production occurs during well completion. The

40

extraction of shale gas requires high-volume hydraulic fracturing, a process in which large volumes of water are pumped into wells in order to fracture and re-fracture the otherwise impermeable shale and stimulate gas flow. Much of this water returns to the surface as "flow-back," carrying with it large quantities of methane. Howarth *et al.* used fairly uncertain data to calculate the flow-back emissions of five different unconventional formations, with some of it coming from PowerPoint slides of EPA-sponsored workshops. They took the mean of methane losses from flow-back as a percentage of total lifetime production of the well, resulting in a figure of 1.6%.

To calculate the total percentage of gas loss from well completion the authors had to add to this number the methane lost from "drill-out," the stage of high-volume hydraulic fracturing in which producers drill out the plugs used to separate fracturing stages. Because drill-out emissions were not available for individual formations, Howarth *et al.* used the mean of EPA drill-out emissions estimates (142,000 to 425,000 m^3 of methane; mean=280,000 m^3) multiplied by the average lifetime production of four of the rock formations used to determine flow-back emissions. Because of the higher lifetime production of these formations compared to others examined in a study of twelve formations, the calculation resulted in a conservative estimate for drill-out methane emissions as a percentage of gross well production of 0.33%. Combined with flow-back emissions, Howarth *et al.* calculate that 1.9% of gross shale gas production is emitted during well completion as an uncertain but highly conservative estimate. This figure contrasts with an emissions estimate of 0.01% of gross gas production for conventional wells using EPA data.

Howarth *et al.* calculate a series of ranges for other potential sources of fugitive methane emissions in conventional and shale gas production. The authors attribute the same methane loss ranges to both conventional and unconventional gas production for equipment leaks and routine venting, since the same technologies are used for both types of gas once they are connected to a pipeline. The low end of 0.3% represents the use of best available technology, and the upper estimate of 1.9% does not include accidents or emergency venting.

Fugitive emissions from transport, storage, and distribution of natural gas can also be assumed to be the same for both types of gas production, as conventional and shale gas are an identical commodity at this point of production. The authors employed the figure of 1.4%, calculated in a 2005 study by Lelieveld *et al.* as the lower estimate of average gas loss combining transport, storage, and distribution losses. They found the estimate's upper limit using a bottom-down approach, calculating the disparity between measured gas produced at the wellhead and measured volume of gas purchased and consumed as an end product. The authors calculated an upper limit of 3.6% by taking the mean of the State of Texas's data for missing and unaccounted gas in the years 2000 and 2007. Howarth *et al.* believe 3.6% to still be a conservative estimate, given that industry fought a proposed hard cap on missing and unaccounted gas of 5% in the state.

The authors also provided a range of methane losses for "liquid unloading" and gas processing. Liquid unloading is a process often needed for conventional well production and sometimes for unconventional well production, in which liquid is unloaded to mitigate water intrusion as reservoir pressure drops when a well matures. Though methane losses from liquid unloading were estimated at 0.02–0.26% of gross production, because some wells do not require liquid unloading, the authors used the range of 0–0.26%. Surprisingly, they used the same range for both conventional and shale gas, despite acknowledging that liquid unloading is primarily required for conventional wells. Logically, conventional gas should have been given a higher estimate for liquid unloading than shale gas, but the authors do not address this.

Similarly, the authors provided the same range for both conventional and shale gas for emissions from gas processing. Howarth *et al.* explain that both conventional and shale gas vary in quality when extracted, and thus sometimes require processing that creates more methane emissions. However, they do not address the question of whether one type of gas or the other has a higher average quality when extracted. Instead, the authors provided a methane loss range of 0%, representing no processing, to 0.19% of production for both types of gas. This area of uncertainty goes unaddressed in the study.

Howarth *et al.* calculated the total fugitive methane loss as a percentage of gross production at 1.7–6.0% for conventional gas, and 3.6–7.9% for shale gas. Compared to coal (both surface- and deep-mined) and diesel oil on a 20- and 100-year timescale, the authors found the GWP of shale gas to be 1.2–2.1 times greater than coal and 1.5–2.5 times greater than oil on a 20-year timescale. On a 100-year timescale, they found the GWP of shale gas to be comparable to coal and up to 1.4 times greater than oil. The high estimate GWP of conventional gas was also significantly higher than oil and coal on a 20-year timescale and comparable on a 100-year timescale.

Comparing their estimates for conventional gas fugitive methane emissions to other peer-reviewed literature, the authors note that although two of three studies found lower estimates for fugitive emissions, these studies used GWP factors for methane that are now known to be too low and still concluded that in many cases a switch to natural gas from coal could aggravate rather than mitigate the effects of climate change. Lelieveld *et al.* concluded that natural gas would be worse than oil if fugitive methane emissions exceeded 3.1% of total production, and worse than coal if they exceeded 5.6%. Adjusting that study's GWP factor for methane to account for recent findings, Howarth *et al.* claim that fugitive methane emissions of only 2–3% make natural gas more impactful than oil and coal, well within both their emissions ranges for conventional and shale gas.

In conclusion, the authors emphasize that rather than promoting continued use of oil and coal, they warn against policymaking that relies on natural gas as a bridge fuel and assumes that gas implies lower carbon emissions per unit of energy produced compared to other fuels. However, they acknowledge that there is a large amount of uncertainty in fugitive methane estimates and recommend further study, given the importance of the topic.

Evaluating the Uncertainty in Calculating Greenhouse Gas Emissions for Electricity Generation

Because 40% of U.S. CO_2 emissions come from electricity generation and distribution, the ability to calculate CO_2 emissions per unit of electricity consumed is crucial in order to perform a life-cycle analysis (LCA), be it of a product or process. However, the greenhouse gas emissions associated with an individual entity's electricity consumption is nearly impossible to calculate given the nature of electricity grids. For this reason, LCA practitioners often employ emissions factors, or estimated average quantity of CO_2 emitted per unit of energy consumed. Unfortunately, emissions factors vary greatly both spatially and temporally due to different energy sources used for generation, as well as differing plant efficiencies. The authors point out that in addition to electricity coming from varying sources (for example, hydroelectric power provides much of the Pacific Northwests's electricity due to the natural availability of that resource), electricity systems are quite complex because deregulation in the 1990s connected more remote customers with more remote generators, making it even more difficult to trace the source and associated greenhouse gas emissions of one's electricity. In this study Weber *et al.* (2010) calculated the variability in emissions factor estimates and demonstrated the uncertainty in using these estimates for LCA and policymaking. The authors also make suggestions for how to deal with this uncertainty.

Christopher Weber, Paulina Jaramillo, Joe Marriott, and Constantine Samaras examined the uncertainty of emissions factors at various geographic levels of the U.S. and in different locales by collecting different emissions factors for CO_2, SO_2 and NO_x (though CO_2 contributes primarily to global warming and is thus the main focus of the paper). The authors acknowledge that they did not take into account the emissions of upstream supply chains for electricity generation, noting that accounting for upstream emissions would only slightly increase uncertainty. The authors calculated emissions factors along several potential regional delineations of the electric grid. The emissions factor with the largest geographical area was the U.S. continental average (0.69 kg CO_2/kWh), followed by three regions based on electrical grid connectivity—the Eastern, Western, and Texas Interconnects. At a smaller level, Weber *et al.* used the 24 subregional grid delineations as defined by the EPA's eGrid and used in the Greenhouse Gas Protocol, a tool for conducting LCAs. Finally, the authors used data collected by the U.S. Energy Information Administration through voluntary greenhouse gas reporting since 1992. The different datasets considered form seven independent estimates of electricity emission factors for every combination of U.S. state, eGrid subregion, and grid operator (whether independent system operators or regional transmission operators).

For their dataset, the authors calculated a coefficient of variation (COV), or the normalized standard deviation. A higher COV meant more variation between different estimates for electricity emissions factor, and therefore a higher uncertainty of amount of CO_2 emitted per unit of electricity generation in the region. The average CO_2, COV for all delineations, or districts, considered out of 101 total was 0.19 (an average uncertainty of ±40% at two standard deviations) and ranged from a maximum of 0.70 to a minimum of 0.08. The districts with highest associated uncertainty were those that had smaller or larger than average local or regional emissions factors. Since electricity grids do not correlate closely with state borders, emissions factors estimated along state lines had higher variation than those estimated according to eGrid delineations.

The authors conclude that LCA practitioners and policymakers generally do not have access to the data required in order to calculate a specific consumer's electricity-related greenhouse gas emissions. Therefore, for practical purposes, Weber *et al.* recommend that standards organizations provide clear guidelines for conducting LCA calculations, and by standardizing these calculations reduce overall comparative uncertainty between different LCAs. The authors suggest that standards organizations should discourage the use of political borders in calculating emissions intensity for a particular area, as this unnecessarily increases uncertainty. Furthermore, researchers should report kWhs consumed alongside the assumed grid emissions factor within an appropriate electricity system delineation, in order to increase transparency and allow for normalized comparisons of a specific product. If estimating indirect CO_2 emissions is required, Weber *et al.* suggest that researchers provide a range for the emissions factor. In that case, if an entity wants to guarantee an emissions reduction or carbon neutrality, it can use the highest range of emissions factors.

In public policy decisions, choosing a set of emissions factors will raise issues of equity. If too general a set of emissions were to be used and an emissions trading market were to be set up, local distribution companies buying lower-carbon electricity would obtain an advantage, and local distribution companies buying higher-carbon electricity would be at a disadvantage. Additionally, using more locally specific emissions factors could potentially penalize energy users in areas that have higher-carbon electricity simply due to natural resources. For example, electricity in the Pacific Northwest will be lower-carbon because of the regional hydroelectric resources. An industry located in the Pacific Northwest stands to lose less from policies to reduce carbon emissions than industries in other regions.

The authors note that while it may be possible, depending on required level of accuracy for the investigation, to choose an appropriate emissions factor (e.g., if an industry operates in many locales throughout the country and the investigation does not require a particularly high level of accuracy in emissions calculations, one could use the national average emissions factor), consistency in calculating the indirect emissions of electricity consumption is of highest importance, along with transparency and reproducibility of methods.

Estimating our Commitment to Global Warming

Transitioning from a fossil fuel-based economy to one based on renewable energy is impeded by widespread existing energy infrastructure: not only primary energy infrastructure such as coal-fired power plants, but also transportation infrastructure such as motor vehicles or airplanes and residential infrastructure such as natural gas-burning furnaces or stoves. Unless this infrastructure is prematurely decommissioned or widely retrofitted with expensive carbon capture and storage technology, this "infrastructural inertia" represents committed CO_2 emissions as we move into the future. Davis *et al.* (2010) calculated the cumulative future emissions of existing energy infrastructure and found that if we completely discontinued the production of net CO_2-emitting infrastructure, existing infrastructure alone would contribute 496 gigatonnes of CO_2 to the atmosphere between 2010 and 2060, increasing mean global temperatures by 1.3 °C. Noting the difference between this quantity and estimated future warming, the authors conclude that the sources of most emissions are yet to be built. However, they believe that extraordinary efforts are required to prevent the continued expansion of CO_2-emitting infrastructure.

Steven J. Davis and Ken Caldeira of the Carnegie Institution of Washington along with Damon Matthews of Concordia University in Montreal used datasets of worldwide CO_2 emissions from directly emitting infrastructure such as power plants and motor vehicles as well as estimates of emissions produced by industry, households, businesses, and other forms of transport to predict cumulative global CO_2 emissions through 2060. Historical data provided them with lifetimes and annual emissions of infrastructure. The authors estimated emissions from non-energy sources such as land use change or agriculture using the International Panel on Climate Change's (IPCC) Special Report on Emissions Scenarios A2 scenario. They used an intermediate-complexity coupled climate-carbon model, the University of Victoria Earth System Climate Model, in order to calculate changes in atmospheric CO_2 and temperature based on emissions.

Davis et al. calculated a cumulative 496 gigatonnes (1 Gt=10^{12} kg) of global CO_2 emissions between 2010 and 2060, with 282 and 701 Gt CO_2 being the lower and upper bound estimates. Accounting for non-energy CO_2 emissions, the total atmospheric CO_2 in this scenario stabilizes below 430 parts per million (ppm), with an increase of global temperatures of 1.3 °C (1.1–1.4 °C above pre-industrial levels or 0.3–0.7 °C above current temperatures). The authors calculate emissions through 2060 (as opposed to through 2100, as with many other climate predictions) because by 2060 all energy-related sources of CO_2 emissions are predicted to be no longer functional. Whereas they calculate a mean cumulative emissions of 496 Gt CO_2 from existing energy infrastructure, scenarios considering the continued expansion of fossil fuel-based infrastructure through 2100 predict cumulative global emissions of 2986 to 7402 Gt CO_2. In those scenarios, global temperatures increase by 2.4–4.6 °C above pre-industrial levels and atmospheric CO_2 stabilizes above 600 ppm. Internationally, a rise in temperature of 2 °C and an atmospheric CO_2 level of 450 ppm are considered to be the benchmark past which geophysical, biological and socioeconomic systems are especially vulnerable. Thus, the authors note, as existing energy infrastructure does not surpass the benchmark, the infrastructure that represents the most threatening CO_2 emissions has yet to be built.

Existing energy infrastructure is concentrated in highly developed countries such as Western Europe, the United States, and Japan and populous countries experiencing rapid development, particularly China. China accounts for the greatest energy inertia, where almost one quarter of worldwide electrical generating capacity has been commissioned as coal plants since 2000. The young age of its existing infrastructure compared to that of the U.S., Japan, or Western Europe also contributes to China's large emissions commitment, approximately 37% of the global total. However, emissions commitment per capita in China is comparable to Japan and Western Europe and far less than that of the U.S. (136 tons CO_2 per person versus 241). Davis et al. emphasize the importance of historic emissions in already developed countries and consumption in those countries as a driving force of Chinese emissions. They also note that committed emissions per unit of GDP is much higher in developing countries than already developed ones, showing that infrastructural inertia of emissions is greatest where industrialization is occurring but incomplete.

Davis et al. conclude that although their estimates of cumulative committed global emissions of CO_2 do not push us past the threshold of 450 ppm CO_2 and 2 °C of warming, avoiding great quantities of CO_2 emissions from not yet built infrastructure will require a tremendous political effort and shift, partially because of the supporting infrastructure for CO_2 emitting devices such as highways or factories that produce internal combustion engines. Though their findings do not have groundbreaking implications for climate change studies, the study provides a useful benchmark of what future emissions are inevitable without high-cost retrofitting or halting of industry and what future emissions can more easily be reduced.

The Feasibility of Powering the World with Wind, Water, and Solar Power

Jacobson and Delucchi (2011) address the pressing problem of climate change by proposing to produce all new power worldwide from wind, water and sunlight (WWS) by 2030 and to replace pre-existing energy sources with WWS by 2050. In this Part I of their two-part study, they assess the feasibility of doing so by calculating global end-use energy demand in a WWS world and comparing it to that of a world powered by fossil fuels as projected by the Energy Information Administration. They also examined worldwide capacity for WWS energy production and the limitations of materials used for the construction of WWS infrastructure. They estimated that about 3,800,000 5 MW wind turbines, 49,000 300 MW concentrated solar plants, 40,000 300 MW solar PV power plants, 1.7 billion 3kW rooftop PV systems, 5350 100 MW geothermal power plants, 270 new 1300 MW hydroelectric power plants, 720000 0.75 MW wave devices, and 490,000 1 MW tidal turbines can meet global energy demand in 2030 with a 1.0% increase in land use, and found that barriers are primarily social and political rather than technical or economic.

Mark Z. Jacobson and Mark A. Delucchi found a decrease in global end-use energy demand in 2030 compared to the Energy Information Administration's projections, which predicted demand will increase from 12.5 trillion watts (TW) to 17 TW in the year 2030 given an energy supply similar to today's, constituted by 35% oil, 27% coal, 23% natural gas, 6% nuclear, and the rest from biomass, sunlight, wind, and geothermal. In the WWS scenario proposed by the authors, all end uses that can be electrified would use WWS power directly, and end uses that require combustion (like industrial processes) would use electrolytic hydrogen produced with WWS. Heating and cooling processes would employ electric heat pumps, and batteries, fuel cells, or a hybrid of the two would replace liquid fuels in non-aviation transportation. Aviation would use liquefied hydrogen to then be combusted. Jacobson and Delucchi calculated that an all WWS world would require approximately 30% less end-use power than the EIA projections for our current heavily fossil fuel-powered world. This is due to some increases in efficiency, for example, in the case of using electricity directly for heating or electric motors, as well as modest conservation measures (increases in efficiency through better insulation, more efficient lighting and heating, passive heating and cooling in buildings, and large-scale planning to reduce energy demand) and subtracting the energy requirements of petroleum refining.

The authors investigated the availability of renewable resources that could potentially be exploited for power production in order to evaluate whether these could meet global energy demands in 2030. They found that wind and solar power in likely-developable locations could each provide enough power by themselves to meet global demands, with wind power potentially providing 3–5 times global demand and solar power potentially providing 15–20 times global demand. Concentrated solar power (CSP) could also meet global demand and has the ability to store energy for night usage, but it requires more land than PV and can use about 8 gal/kWh of water in a water-cooled plant, compared to almost no water for PV or wind. At the same time, air-cooled plants could be a viable alternative to water-cooled plants in areas of scarce water resources. Although other WWS technologies like wave power, geothermal and hydropower have much less energy potential (between 0.02 TW for tidal power and 1.6 TW for hydroelectric), Jacobson and Delucchi say they will be more abundant and economical than wind or solar in many locations and that since wind and solar power are variable, these other technologies could help stabilize electric power supply.

In the WWS power generation scenario created by the authors, 50% of power will come from wind, 20% from CSP plants, 14% from solar PV plants, 6% from rooftop PV, 4% each from hydrothermal and geothermal plants, and 1% each from wave and tidal energy. Calculating combined footprint and spacing areas required for these technologies led Jacobson and Delucchi to the conclusion that their WWS scheme will require an additional 1.0% of global land area.

The authors found that resource availability of bulk materials like steel and concrete is unlikely to constrain the development of WWS power systems. Some of the rarer materials used for WWS technologies include neodymium for electric motors and generators, platinum for fuel cells, and lithium in batteries, however, could present problems. Wind power is currently limited by neodymium requirements for permanent magnets in generators. Solar power is limited by silver reserves, although research suggests that opportunities exist to produce PV power with low cost and commonly available materials. Current neodymium requirements for electric motors similarly imply a need to develop alternative motors that do not use rare-earth elements. Global reserves of lithium are limited and in order to satisfy requirements for electric vehicles and other uses, a global recycling program is needed. Similarly, a platinum recycling program would be required in a scenario of producing 20 million hydrogen fuel cell vehicles per year, which could easily deplete platinum reserves in less than 100 years. Although Jacobson and Deluccchi expect the cost of recycling or replacing neodymium or platinum to be negligible, this is dependent on a drastic improvement in worldwide recycling infrastructure and in many cases finding viable alternatives to existing technologies.

Jacobson and Delucchi find a world powered entirely by wind, water and solar power to be feasible, with a marked decrease in global end-use energy demand, a 1.0% increase in land use, and some need for technological substitutions and/or recycling programs for materials used in renewable energy construction. The authors recommend replacing all new energy with WWS by 2030 and all existing energy with WWS by 2050. The study does not provide a life-cycle analysis of implementation of the proposed WWS technologies. This would potentially be useful, as it would require a measured analysis of all environmental impacts, including impacts of natural resource extraction for new infrastructure. Interestingly, Jacobson and Delucchi neglect to consider factors like the CO_2 emissions from the chemical process of making cement, which would be required on a large scale for the production of wind turbines in their scenario.

The authors have published Part II to this study, in which they consider reliability, system and transmission costs, and policies needed to implement worldwide WWS infrastructure.

Conclusions

In order to avoid the most serious consequences of climate change, we will have to make large strides towards rapidly reducing greenhouse gas emissions. By replacing fossil fuels with renewable sources of energy for electricity generation, this may be possible. Jacobson and Delucchi outline the feasibility of powering the world entirely with practically zero-carbon sources and suggest that barriers are political and social in nature rather than economic or technological. However, those barriers are not negligible, and would require significant mobilization. Our infrastructural inertia, as estimated by Davis *et al.*, commits us to an increase of between 282 and 701 Gt CO_2, or an increase of 1.1–1.4 °C over pre-industrial levels. While LCA is a useful tool for estimating total environmental impacts of electricity generation, it has some disadvantages (Laleman *et al.*) and frequently does not include economic feasibility of a technology. Studies that consider disadvantages of different methodologies and carefully express uncertainty are most useful when evaluating the environmental impact of fuel sources used for electricity generation.

References Cited

Butnar, I., Rodrigo, J., Gasol, C. M., and Castells, F., 2010. Life-cycle assessment of electricity from biomass: Case studies of two biocrops in Spain. Biomass and Bioenergy 34, 1780–1788.

Davis, S. J., Caldeira, K., Matthews, D., 2010. Future CO_2 emissions and climate change from existing energy infrastructure. Science 329, 1330–1333.

Howarth, R. W., Santoro, R., Ingraffea, A., 2011. Methane and the greenhouse-gas footprint of natural gas from shale formations. Climate Change Letters, forthcoming.

Jacobson, M. Z., Delucchi, M. A., 2011. Providing all global energy with wind, water and solar power, Part I: Technologies, energy resources, quantities and areas of infrastructure, and materials. Energy Policy 39, 1154–1169.

Intergovernmental Panel on Climate Change, 2007. IPCC Fourth Assessment Report (AR4), Working Group 1, The Physical Science Basis. http://www.ipcc.ch/publications_and_data/ar4/wg1/en/ch2s2-10-2.html.

Laleman, R., Albrecht, J., and Dewulf, J., 2011. Life Cycle Analysis to estimate impact of residential photovoltaic systems in regions with a lower solar irradiation. Renewable and Sustainable Energy Reviews 15, 267–281.

Lelieveld J., Lechtenbohmer S., Assonov S. S., Brenninkmeijer C. A. M., Dinest C., Fischedick M., Hanke T., 2005. Low methane leakage from gas pipelines. Nature 434, 841–842.

Miller, V., Landis, A., and Schaefer., 2011. A benchmark for life cycle air emissions and life cycle impact assessment of hydrokinetic energy extraction using life cycle assessment. Renewable Energy 36, 1040–1046.

Weber, C., Jaramillo, P., Marriott, J., and Samaras, C., 2010. Life Cycle Assessment and Grid Electricity: What Do We Know and What Can We Know? Environmental Science & Technology 44, 1895–1901.

3. Our Oceans: Renewable Energy Sources of the Future?

Juliet Archer

The ocean–based renewable energy industry is still in its infancy, despite some early innovations. For example, the Rance tidal power plant of Saint-Malo, Ille-et-Vilaine, France, began producing energy more than forty years ago, in 1967. Currently, the plant produces 540 million kilowatt hours (kWh) of energy annually (EDF 2011). Yet, ocean–based renewable energy in general, including tidal energy, remains underdeveloped. This is partially due to a lack of knowledge in designing full scale systems; such is the case with salinity gradient power plants (Veerman *et al.* 2010). In addition, knowledge of the magnitude and type of environmental effects resulting from ocean renewable energies is insufficient. In some cases progress is also hampered by viewshed concerns from residents in coastal communities, such is often the case for offshore wind energy because of its high vertical profile (Save Our Sound 2011). In other cases, there is a lack of public and/or private investment in marine renewable research and development. Despite these current challenges, there is much potential for the development of technologies that harness this vast renewable energy source. In light of climate change and increased pollution, now, more than ever, we need ocean–based renewable power in order to decrease our dependency on fossil fuels.

An Overview of Ocean Renewable Energy Technologies

The untapped potential of ocean renewable energy is vast like the oceans' uncharted depths. And like the deep ocean, it is also mysterious, since most technologies that capitalize on the sea as an energy source are still in the early stages of development and testing. Therefore, Bedard *et al.* (2010) state that it is unclear which technologies will be the most cost efficient and reliable while producing the fewest environmental effects. The technologies currently being developed include ocean wave, thermal, tidal/open-ocean current, tidal barrage, salinity gradient and shallow and deepwater offshore wind energy. Among these, only shallow water off-shore wind energy has reached the status of a fully-deployed commercial technology. Part of the reason the other technologies are not yet commercial is because of the time it takes for development and testing. This process, from initial concept to deployment of a full-scale model in natural waters is estimated by Bedard *et al.* to take at least 5 to 10 years. Consequently, the future for ocean energy technology is bright since only a glimmer of its potential impact has been seen.

In their review, Bedard *et al.* explain the history, current status and different concepts or designs of each of the above mentioned ocean energy technologies. As of their writing, only 4 mega-watts (MW) of wave energy have been installed worldwide. Most of the deployments of concepts such as point absorbers, overtopping terminators, linear absorbers, and oscillating water column terminators (OWC) have been small-scale prototypes. In the United States, further installation of wave energy technology has been hindered by a lack of standardized facilities in which to test wave energy devices in the open ocean. However, these and other challenges are recognized and are being met by private and public groups, such as the Northwest National Marine Renewable Energy Center (NNMREC) funded by the United States Department of Energy (DOE), and Pacific Gas and Electric (PG&E). In Portugal these problems have already been confronted, resulting in the first commercial wave energy plant being deployed in 2008. Furthermore, demonstration projects are continuing and planned at other sites around the world, including Australia and Ireland. If these early projects are successful, Bedard *et al.* predict that wave energy technologies with a total of 100 MW of capacity will be deployed in five to ten years.

Tidal current or hydrokinetic ocean energy technologies have only been installed in rivers or less than one kilometer from coasts. The three types of water turbines that exploit the kinetic energy of moving water are axial, cross-flow and combination axial and cross-flow turbines. In addition there are also non-turbine designs such as oscillatory hydrofoils, hydro venturi and vortex induced motion devices. In the United States, hydrokinetic technology has been tested in New York's East River but like wave energy, hydrokinetic technologies lack proper infrastructure to deploy and test devices in tidal passages. However, in-stream demonstrations in rivers continue around the world. If results are successful, the authors expect that tidal energy capacity will increase by 1–10 MW within five to ten years. Despite studies in the 1970s determining minimal adverse environmental effects, technology has not yet been developed to harness the power of open-ocean currents, like the Gulf Stream.

Offshore wind energy is a promising resource because high-wind areas are located near some of the world's largest coastal cities. In comparison to onshore wind energy technology, offshore technology does not suffer from the same transportation and installation restrictions. However, the cost of infrastructure and logistical support for offshore units is significant and capital costs are typically double those of onshore turbines. Therefore, offshore units tend to be larger in order to maximize the value of the infrastructure. In 2008, the worldwide capacity of offshore wind energy was 1,471 MW. This is insignificant in comparison to the almost 121,000 MW of total installed wind power in the same year (Global Wind Report 2008). Overall, the industry is challenged by high costs, especially of operation and maintenance, in comparison to mature land-based wind technology. However, Germany, China and the United States, among other countries, are all in processes of adding new capacity. Furthermore, the first full-scale floating turbine was deployed in 2009, exemplifying the infancy and potential growth of the offshore wind industry.

Ocean thermal energy conversion (OTEC) technologies extract energy from the difference in temperature between cold deep ocean water (less than 40 °F) and warm surface water (more than 80°F). The challenge of developing commercially viable OTEC energy technologies is currently being undertaken by a number of small companies, some of which are funded by the DOE. The major difficulties in the commercialization of OTEC are that the capital costs are high and the resource has a low-energy density. At the time of writing, no major commercial OTEC technologies have been installed.

Salinity gradient energy conversion technology, like OTEC, extracts energy from a physical gradient. Salinity gradient power or osmotic power exploits the differing salt concentrations in fresh and sea water. The methods for this process are reverse electrodialysis (RED) and pressure-retarded osmosis (PRO). Currently, the Netherlands and Norway are the only countries developing salinity gradient technologies for commercial use. In the Netherlands, plans have been proposed to exploit the salinity differential between the Afsluitdijk dike and the ocean with RED technology. In 2009, Norway installed the world's first salinity gradient power plant using PRO technology, designed for 10 kW of capacity. If this plant is successful, then the construction of commercial osmotic power plants is probable in the next few years. Based on the current state of ocean renewable energy technologies, rapid growth in the use of ocean–based renewable energy can be expected.

Designing Prototype Tidal Current Turbines in Taiwan

Since the island has limited energy resources, developing renewable energy projects is an imperative for the government of Taiwan. Although it has a few onshore wind turbines, ocean-based renewable energies are an obvious alternative since the country is surrounded by the Pacific Ocean. This line of thinking has secured National Science Council funding for Tsai *et al.* (2010) to begin the design and testing of prototype tidal current turbines. The team plans to conduct field tests between Keelung Harbor and Keelung Island because of the high speeds that currents achieve while traveling over Keelung Sill. Tsai *et al.* are primarily focused on designing blades, with an ideal camber and pitch, and turbines, which will move automatically to take advantage of the changing direction of currents. Once a prototype is designed, they will test for the design's dynamic response to irregular waves and winds, non-uniform currents, and typhoon conditions. If they are successful, Taiwan will be closer to its goal of increasing renewable energy to 10% of total capacity by 2025.

Cheng-Han Tsai and colleagues at the National Taiwan Ocean University and Minghsin University of Science and Technology have undertaken five related projects in order to install a 3 kW current generator on Keelung Sill and to better understand the dynamic responses of tidal energy converters. The first three projects aim to simulate and assess the tidal current power surrounding Taiwan and especially that of the Keelung Sill area. To accomplish this challenging task, Tsai *et al.* use a numerical model, in situ measurements and satellite images. In order to simulate tides numerically, the model used a finite difference method[2] to solve control equations. In addition, a vertically integrated continuity equation and equations of motion in x and y directions were used along with a hydrostatic equation[3] that determined pressure at depth z. To measure water velocity, the model averaged volume transport over depth. The numerical model shows that strong currents are present at Keelung Sill. However, the model is likely an underestimation of current velocity because it shows a maximum velocity of only 1.0 m/s in a 24-hour cycle.

In order to verify their model, Tsai *et al.* are conducting in-situ measurements of the currents at Keelung sill three times, for at least one month each. The velocity is measured by deploying Aquadopp Profilers (at depths of 5m, 10m, 15m, and 20m) in addition to a RCM-7 current meter (at 20m). These instruments are deployed at five different sites on Keelung Sill during each testing period. Preliminary measured results show that the current speed in this area can be as high as 2.2–2.4 m/s depending on the depth, 15–20 m, respectively. These early results confirm the team's suspicion that the numerical model underestimated current speed. From these measurements the power (in Watts) of the current can be calculated, using velocity, an efficiency coefficient, the water density and the blade sweep area.

The third project of Tsai *et al.* is to determine water depth, tidal elevation, and tidal energy around Keelung Sill using high frequency satellite images. The

---

[2] "Finite-difference methods approximate the solutions to differential equations using finite difference equations to approximate derivatives" (Wikipedia)

[3] "The form assumed by the vertical component of the vector equation of motion when all Coriolis, earth curvature, frictional, and vertical acceleration terms are considered negligible compared with those involving the vertical pressure force and the force of gravity" (American Meteorological Society)

scientists will use a Formosa-2 satellite that has a sun-synchronous orbit. The images will be used to calculate temporal-variable water depth, which can then be compared to the in-situ data. This information will also be used to estimate tidal elevation and energy. Developing a tidal current turbine is the fourth project presented in this paper. The team's objective is to find the ideal configuration of blade camber and pitch so that the turbine will produce the maximum power output, based on the current speed. The team also plans on designing a turbine that moves, on its own, in response to a current's change in direction. If Tsai *et al.* succeed, the turbine will always face into the current and therefore maximize its power production. Before testing on-site, the power generation capacity of the design will be tested at the National Taiwan Ocean University's cavitation tunnel.

The last project planned is the assessment of the dynamic response behavior of the new turbine. This project will begin with the installation of the team's 3 kW turbine design at Keelung Sill. The scientists are interested in this topic because there are few data available on the response of turbines to the forces of winds, waves, and currents. Their hypothesis is that the blade will experience the most load variations. The team is especially interested in the effect of extreme forces, present during typhoon conditions, on the blades and structure of turbines. This information is pertinent because of their government's goal of increasing renewable energy production and its emphasis on ocean-based renewable energies. If ocean current energy production is to be a viable option for Taiwan, then turbine designs must withstand typhoon conditions[4]. Although these on-going projects are not complete, significant results are expected based on the ambitious goals and detailed plans that have been laid out in this paper.

Reverse Electrodialysis: Optimizing Performance in Up-Scaled Systems

Reverse Electrodialysis (RED) is a salinity gradient power (SGP) process whereby electrical power is produced from the reversible mixing of waters that have different salinity concentrations, such as river and sea water. This technology has promise as a future source of clean and sustainable energy, with an estimated global potential of 2.6 TW for all forms of SGP. However, previous research has been done on a relatively small scale. In order to create commercially viable RED power plants, researchers must first determine how to maximize the performance of large cell stacks. When trying to solve this problem, Veerman *et al.* 2010 found that there exists a tradeoff between the hydrodynamic and electrical requirements of spacers. In a RED system, spacers are open structures which separate alternately

---

[4] An average of three to four typhoons hit Taiwan each year. (Central Weather Bureau of Taiwan)

stacked cation (CEM) and anion exchange membranes (AEM), provide stack stability, and increase turbulence within the compartments. In attempting to maximize performance, Veerman et al. also considered other parameters such as, flow direction, residence time, flow velocity, and electrode segmentation. Their research is significant because it provides a "[f]irst [s]tep" towards the goal of producing commercial electricity from a RED power plant.

J. Veerman and colleagues, from Wetsus (Centre of Excellence for Sustainable Water Technology) and the University of Groningen, compared the performance of small and large laboratory RED stacks. In these stacks, power is generated by the potential difference between sea and fresh water over a membrane and the movement of ions through that membrane. The "large" stacks contained either 25 or 50 cells each, while the "small" stacks consisted of 50 cells each. Cell dimensions of the small stacks, which have been the focus of previous research, measure less than 10 by 10 cm^2. These small stacks have a total active membrane area of 1 m^2. In this study, Veerman et al. also utilized larger stacks with cell dimensions of 25 by 75 cm^2 and total active membrane areas of either 9.4 or 18.75 m^2. With these large RED stacks, the researchers also determined the impact of others parameters, when attempting to maximize performance at the lowest possible investment and operational costs. The researchers employed NaCl and hexacyanoferrate electrode rinse solutions, depending on which parameter they were testing. In using these applied electrode solutions, the study drifts from its focus on maximizing the performance of commercial SGP technology because these solutions are only used in laboratories. More advanced systems must be employed in RED power plants. For "sea water" they used a 30 g NaCl/L solution and for "river water" they used a 1 g NaCl/L solution.

The authors found that hydrodynamic power losses are greatest at high flow rates. On the contrary, they also found that losses from co-ion transport and osmosis were significant at very low flow rates. Therefore, net power density (W/m^2) and energy efficiency are maximized at optimal rather than maximal or minimal flow rates. In studying the effect of residence time on power density, Veerman et al. used Fumasep and Qianqiu membranes, cross-, co-, and counter-current flow directions, and 25 and 50 cell large stacks. The authors found that the generated electricity of stacks was mostly independent from the aforementioned parameters. Similarly, the number of cells had no effect on power density. This signifies that losses from shortcut currents, which increase as the number of cells increase, are minimal. Co-current and counter-current operations were also tested, to determine which mode is more efficient in RED stacks. In counter-current mode, river water flows downward and sea water flows upward. However, in co-current mode both river and sea water flow upward. Contrary to evidence from other processes, the authors found that co-current mode resulted in a higher power density within the RED stacks. The researchers explained this surprising discovery based on the competing effects of a high potential difference near the inlet side and a high conductivity near the outlet side. Furthermore, the authors speculated that co-current operations minimize the pressure within the compartments and thus minimize leakage. Lastly, thin, delicate membranes and open spacers, both of which maximize power density, can be used with co-current operations.

Veerman *et al.* also considered the effect of electrode segmentation on generated power (W). The power of a segmented stack was found to be 11% more than that of an unsegmented stack. However, segmentation may not be practical in actual RED power plants because it is probable that segmentation's small advantage disappears at high flow rates. Furthermore, segmentation requires the use of complicated and costly electronics, which may reduce its theoretical benefits. The authors also measured the pressure from fluid resistance in the manifolds, bore holes, and compartments—around the supply and drain holes and where uniform flow exists—in order to calculate hydrodynamic losses. Fluid resistance in the manifolds and bore holes resulted in negligible and very low losses, respectively. Around the outlet and inlet holes, on the other hand, resistance was very high and these areas accounted for the majority of fluid resistance within the system. When graphed against flow velocity (cm/s), uniform spacer resistance for horizontal and vertical operation in co-current mode had approximately equal slopes. To decrease fluid resistance, the authors recommend that more inlet and outlet places be created and that very open spacers be used around supply and drain holes. The researchers conclude by recommending that future RED designs utilize very open spacers, co-current operation, and very thin membranes.

Maximizing the Efficiency of Offshore Wave Energy Converters: A Vital but Challenging Task

Although approximately 4 MW of wave energy have been installed worldwide, questions of how to maximize converter efficiency still exist (Bedard *et al.* 2010). Igic *et al.* (2011) explored this question by investigating how the overall performance of the Wave Dragon (WD) wave energy converter changed based on different control strategies and electrical system configurations. The authors modeled these dependencies using a computer simulation of one turbine-generator connected to an AC/DC/AC converter and an infinite grid. Results for torque, DC link voltage, power, speed, output voltage, and current were presented in relation to the height of the turbine head. Using a permanent magnet generator (PMG), Igic *et al.* found that the line to line voltage of their simulation was 690 V and the maximum current value was 50 A. In addition, their simulation was deemed appropriate for use in prospective studies of wave energy power take-off systems. Even though further research is still needed, the authors' case study and simulation results should be considered in the design of future offshore wave energy converters.

Igic and colleagues examined various electrical system configurations and control strategies of the WD offshore wave energy converter in regards to overall system performance. First, Igic *et al.* presented a case study which thoroughly described the potential electrical systems, grid connections, and generators that could be used with the WD. Next, they described models and presented equations representing PMG and frequency converter control. In these models and equations, both generator and grid side control mechanisms were considered. Lastly, the team built a MATLAB simulation model by utilizing the "power system tool box" in order to investigate how the overall system performance was impacted by generator characteristics and control strategies. The authors made some minor assumptions while constructing their model. For example, the influence of converter harmonics and torque fluctuation was ignored. In addition, the AC/DC and DC/AC converters were both portrayed as voltage-controlled voltage sources (VCVS). Furthermore, the authors chose various parameters, such as stator resistance, inductance, and flux induced by magnet, for the PMG simulation. Finally, to focus solely on performance of the system control, Igic *et al.* assumed that the turbine was connected to an infinite utility grid.

The simulation results of this paper pertain specifically to the WD wave energy converter. The WD is a floating barrage that creates electrical energy from wave power. It is composed of three parts which are analogous to a human's mouth, arms and stomach, which work together in the process of deriving energy from food. The main part of the WD is a large floating reservoir that faces incoming waves. This part is analogous to the mouth because it is where the waves enter the system via a curved ramp. As the waves overtop the ramp and enter the reservoir, potential energy is created by the difference in relative elevation. The arm-like reflectors assist in directing waves towards the reservoir and typically increase the rate of energy capture by 70%. Finally, the 16–20 low-head water turbines are like the stomach because they are used to convert the hydraulic head[5] within the reservoir into the end product, electricity. The multiple small turbines provide the many advantages, such as efficient flow rate regulation, shorter draft tubes, higher speeds and allowing the performance of maintenance activities while production continues. In order to maximize efficiency and thereby performance, a control scheme of three phases is applied to the production process. The first phase is the careful regulation of the platform's floating level in order to maximize the amount of power flowing over the ramp, given ocean conditions. The second phase is controlling the

---

[5] "The force exerted by a column of liquid expressed by the height of the liquid above the point at which the pressure is measured. Although head refers to a distance or height, it is used to express pressure, since the force of the liquid column is directly proportional to its height." (Engineering Dictionary)

water level inside the reservoir in order to minimize energy loss from losses of pressure head and due to overflowed water. The last phase controls turbine and generator speed in order to maximize turbine efficiency based on the instantaneous turbine head[6].

Results from the single turbine-generator-frequency converter unit are shown in relation to turbine head height. When water head (m) is relatively high, torque (Nm), turbine speed (rpm), and the amount of power (W) delivered to the grid are also relatively high. The DC link voltage (V) does not have a similar positive correlation with the turbine head. Output phase voltage (V) is constant throughout the simulation and shows no relationship to turbine head. The output phase current (A) shows a pattern similar but not analogous to the height of the turbine head. The authors also found that torque quickly decreases to zero as the cylinder gate closes. This ensures that the WD will use the greatest amount of water potential energy within the system. Igic *et al.* conclude by recommending that the relationship between power fluctuation and voltage near the grid connection point be examined by incorporating a grid model into their simulation.

Offshore Wind Energy: A Viable Option for California?

In the future, offshore wind energy could provide 174–224% of California's (CA) current electricity needs (Dvorak *et al.* 2010). This estimate is based on the development of floating and other turbine tower support technologies that will enable the placement of turbines in deep water (50–200 m). The advancement of these technologies is critical to the viability of offshore wind energy in CA since approximately 90% of wind resources are located in deep water. Utilizing only existing technologies, for depths up to 50 m, the estimate decreases to wind energy providing 17–31% of the state's electricity needs. Compared to Southern (SCA) and Central CA (CCA), the Northern coast (NCA) has the greatest potential for immediate development. NCA's potential annual delivered energy by turbines at depths of 0–50 m, utilizing winds speeds ≥ 7.0 ms^{-1} is 63.1 terawatt hours (TWh). This potential delivered energy would offset approximately 36% of CA's current carbon electricity sources. Although NCA has the most shallow water wind resources, it has limited transmission capacity compared to the other regions. At the time of writing, the potential for offshore wind energy has not yet been developed in CA or elsewhere in the United States.

M. J. Dvorak and his colleagues quantified CA's potential for offshore wind energy by locating potential turbine sites using bathymetry data, modeling multiple years of mesoscale weather data and then calculating the potential energy

---

[6] "the level of difference between the reservoir level and the mean sea level"

and power provided by offshore turbines. To give context, the CA coast was divided into three areas, NCA, CCA, and SCA. Within these regions, potential sites were classified by depth using high-resolution bathymetry data. To determine average offshore wind speed, a mesoscale model version 5 (MM5) weather model was run for all of 2007 and for the months of January, April, July, and October of 2005 and 2006. This modeling allowed the calculation of annual and seasonal average wind speeds at turbine hub height (80 m) as well as the average power density of the wind resource. The modeling data were validated using offshore weather buoy data from the National Oceanic and Atmospheric Administration (NOAA) National Data Buoy Center (NDBC) for years 1998–2008. The MM5 data very closely matched the NDBC buoy data.

To estimate the energy production potential, the number of turbines that could be built and the potential production capacity of each site was calculated. The REpower 5M, 5 MW wind turbine, requiring 0.44^2 km of area, was used for all calculations. In calculating turbine density, the authors accounted for surface area that could not be utilized due to shipping lanes, wildlife areas, viewshed considerations, etc., by including a conservative 33% exclusionary factor. The turbine capacity factor (CF) is defined as the ratio of actual output over a period of time and maximum output at nameplate capacity over that time. It was calculated for each site using the relationship between average wind speed, rated power and rotor diameter of the REpower 5M turbine. This calculation allowed annual energy and average power output to be calculated for each site. In all calculations, winds were assumed to follow a Rayleigh probability distribution over time.

The results show that the potential for wind energy in CA is significant, but not currently feasible, in all regions. The relatively shallow waters of NCA have the most potential using current turbine foundation technology. The development of sites in CCA is limited because most resources exist far from San Francisco and in deep waters. The Farallon Islands is one such site whose development is dependent on lengthy undersea transmission cables and a study of the environmental effects of wind turbines on nearby bird, marine mammal, and fish populations. SCA has similar problems since the CA Bight shields the Los Angeles coast and sends most winds to sites 50 km or farther from shore. These distant sites include Point Conception, San Miguel Island and Santa Rosa Island. If technologies for deepwater resources are developed, then the combination of SCA's high demand and many grid interconnection points will make it an ideal region for offshore wind energy development.

A hypothetical, but currently feasible, wind farm near Cape Mendocino in NCA is proposed by the authors. The farm would be located in water that is less than 50 m deep and therefore could utilize current monopole or multi-leg turbine foundations. It would occupy about 138 km² in area and contain 300 REpower 5M turbines. The farm could be connected to the local electrical grid via an existing power plant in Humboldt Bay. The authors predicted that it would be most productive in summer months and that its hourly activity would be consistent throughout daytime hours. This represents a significant advantage over onshore wind farms which peak at night and thus do not match the high daytime summer demand. Using the aforementioned exclusionary factor, the proposed farm could replace 4% of CA's current carbon electricity generation. This great potential to offset carbon energy sources suggests that offshore wind energy sites should be seriously considered in CA.

Offshore Wind Farms: Environmental Impacts Are Not Benign

As is with other relatively new industries, the environmental effects of offshore wind energy have not been fully examined. In their comprehensive review, Wilson *et al.* (2010) find that although many gaps in knowledge exist, overall, offshore wind generation does result in adverse ecosystem effects. These effects were generally minor, but their magnitudes are dependent on the sensitivity, migration patterns, mating and feeding habits of the specific fish, benthic invertebrates, birds, marine mammals, and other creatures which inhabit potential wind energy sites. Negative environmental effects during the exploration, installation, operation and decommissioning of wind farms result from increased noise, the presence of electromagnetic fields, habitat loss and degradation, and the potential for collision with turbines. There is also evidence that environmental benefits may result from offshore wind energy generation. For instance, the towers and foundations of offshore wind turbines have been found to act as artificial reefs which may increase fish and benthic populations. Furthermore, wind farms may deter commercial fishing, especially the use of beam-trawling, creating, in effect, wildlife protection areas. The authors caution that the magnitude and direction of environmental consequences, especially long term, are not well examined and thus additional research is needed.

Wilson and colleagues at the Institute of Estuarine and Costal Studies at University of Hull (Hull, United Kingdom) determined the potential environmental effects of an offshore wind farm using a conceptual model or "horrendogram" and then analyzed these effects relative to an undeveloped offshore site. The authors separately analyzed environmental effects during the different phases of a project, such as exploration, construction, operation and decommissioning. They further classified their findings based on whether the impact was likely to have a major, moderate, minor, negligible, nonexistent or beneficial interaction. Wilson *et al.* also considered the persistence (days, weeks, months, etc.) and spatial extent (nearfield, far-field) of an impact. The classification of impacts was based on historic data, recent studies, reports, and expert judgment.

In regards to the seabed, Wilson *et al.* determined that when utilizing current monopile foundations, disturbance and possible alteration of the sediment structure is unavoidable. The alteration of sediment structures occurs when fine particles are released from the drilling of monopiles into hard chalk or other bedrock. Drill cuttings may also smother benthic[7] and other creatures. The installation can also cause scour or erosion of the seabed around the base of the new turbine as the flow of currents in the immediate area changes. To minimize current, wake, and habitat changes, turbines can be spaced further apart so that the affected area is small compared to the size of the entire wind farm. To minimize erosion of the seabed, scour protection can be installed. Depending on the type of material and design used, such as rocky substratum adjoining to sandy substrata, scour protection can also increase the surface area available for colonization.

The authors noted that habitat increases can be especially beneficial for juvenile benthic creatures, such as crabs. This impact would therefore be beneficial to both the benthic ecosystem and commercial fisheries as populations are protected within a certain area yet increase overall. Fish populations have also been shown to increase when wind farms are located in nursery areas, as juvenile mortality decreases and spawning biomass increases. Furthermore, scour protection design considerations that increase complexity, like holes and artificial seagrass beds, can increase the number of fish in an area. Again, increased fish populations would benefit commercial fisheries as larger populations spill out into fishing grounds. However, it is unclear whether habitat creation would offset habitat loss for native organisms and so the overall direction of the impact is unknown. Also, the magnitude of the impact may be dependent on the location of the wind farm and the specific aquatic populations with which it interacts.

Wind farms also have negative impacts on fish communities. For instance, electromagnetic (EM) fields, created by export cable routes and connecting cables, may cause a significant moderate impact, especially on sensitive species like elasmobranchs[8], and teleosts[9], and on other demersal[10], and benthic organisms. Potential EM field impacts include decreased hunting performance and incomplete migrations. The significance of these EM field effects is dependent on the type and magnitude of current, insulation type, conductor core geometry, particulars of the seabed, and the depth of the cable (if buried). In addition, noise and increased turbidity during the construction phases may have moderate to minor impacts on

---

[7] benthic –adj.: of, relating to, or occurring in the depths of the ocean

[8] elasmobranch –noun: any of a subclass (Elasmobranchii) of cartilaginous fishes that have five to seven lateral to ventral gill openings on each side and that comprise the sharks, rays, skates and extinct related fishes

[9] teleost –noun: bony fish

[10] demersal –adj.: living near, deposited on, or sinking to the bottom of the sea

hearing specialists and visual predators, respectively. Noise pollution can also occur during operation and may lead to sublethal effects like disturbances in fishes' gathering of information about other fish (prey, predators, competitors, and mates) and locations (migration routes and feeding grounds). Overall the many potential feedback loops make it difficult to predict precisely how wind farms will impact fish and benthic organisms.

The effect on mammals and coastal and sea birds is, on the other hand, overwhelmingly negative. For instance, the probability of collision with turbine blades is especially high if species pass through often. This impact can be mitigated by proper placement of wind farms in regards to wind currents and birds' foraging and breeding areas. However, the probability of collision for large birds, which cannot easily maneuver may be unavoidable. Times of low visibility and/or high winds are likely to exacerbate the problem. Bats are also especially susceptible to collisions because of their curiosity and attraction to the turbines' artificial lighting and high insect populations. In the long run, habituation to wind farms has been shown to decrease avian mortalities as birds learn to recognize the wind turbines as dangerous. Improving turbine technology, by using larger blades that rotate more slowly, for instance, may also decrease the collision rates of birds and bats.

Another potential impact on avian creatures is habitat loss and resulting displacement as birds avoid the turbine structures. If the required diversions, and thus extra energy expenditures, are large enough, then the wind farm can become a barrier and may reduce the breeding and survival rates of the population. As with fish populations, the impact of habitat loss on bird populations is dependent on location. For example, if the farm is located near an estuary or on a coast, then it may decrease the area available for feeding or roosting. Furthermore, if a wind farm is poorly located in regards to adjacent developments then cumulative effects may be detrimental to bird populations. Cumulative effects may occur if a chain of wind farms is located in a flyway corridor for a rare species. More information via improved predictive and observational models is needed in order to determine the significance of the above impacts on birds and mammals.

Marine mammals like cetaceans (dolphins, whales, and porpoises) and pinnipeds (seals and sealions) may be significantly impacted by the noise produced by wind farms. These marine mammals are extremely vocal and some also use echolocation to communicate, navigate, avoid predators, forage, and locate other individuals. The noise interference with these activities would be greatest during exploration and construction. Noise interference would also occur, at minimal levels, during operation. The results of this interference may include displacement (temporary or permanent), changes to feeding and social behaviors, and reductions in breeding success, stress, and death. The magnitude of these effects is dependent on the mammals' habituation to noise, low-frequency hearing abilities of specific species, sound-propagation conditions, and ambient noise levels. To decrease the cumulative effects of a proposed wind farm, location decisions should give consideration to the breeding and migration patterns of marine mammals in relation to existing offshore activities.

Wilson *et al.* recommend a number of improvements to the technologies and processes of determining and measuring the environmental effects of proposed offshore wind farm sites. The technologies recommended are very specific to each affected organism, while some of the processes are in the form of general guidelines. For example, the authors recommend that future research distinguish between real and perceived impacts of offshore wind farms. Additionally, they advise that monitoring be in proportion to the actual effects and not to the publics' perceived effects. They also advise monitoring programs for endangered, protected, and ecosystem key organisms. Lastly, the authors emphasize the many gaps in knowledge and the need for studies focusing on long term effects. Wilson and colleagues conclude by acknowledging that offshore wind farms are not entirely environmentally benign. Yet the authors remind readers to weigh the costs with the environmental benefits, including the creation of renewable energy.

Before Scotland Increases Marine Renewable Energy Capacity, It Must First Assess the Potential Impacts on Local Cetacean Species

The government of Scotland aims to increase renewable energy power to 50% of total electricity demand by 2020. To meet this goal, Scotland will likely to turn to marine renewable energy sources since it has commissioned or proposed United Kingdom Strategic Environmental Assessments (SEA) on wave, tidal, and marine wind energy, respectively. Additionally, the Crown Estate has announced that ten sites, within Scottish waters, will be available for marine wind energy development. However, the best methods for mitigating negative impacts on local cetaceans, including protected species, have not been determined. Thus, Scotland is conflicted. Should it increase its marine renewable energy capacity to the detriment of cetacean species? Or should it proceed with caution, in order to protect the cetaceans, and disregard its renewable energy goal? Dolman and Simmonds (2010) suggest that long term baseline research and real-time monitoring and mitigation methods be developed. Furthermore, they advise that the Scottish government employ adaptive management in all planning processes so that early learning can be incorporated into future plans. If Scotland is able to adopt some of Dolman and Simmonds' recommendations, then perhaps it can have both –reliable marine renewable energy and healthy cetacean populations.

Sarah Dolman and Mark Simmonds examined the negative effects of marine renewable energy technologies on cetacean species with regard to political drivers and cetacean conservation. They described the current legislative, political and legal situations in light of the urgent problems presented by climate change. The authors also presented the current research and understanding of how wind, wave and tidal renewable energies impact local cetacean species including harbor porpoises, bottlenose dolphins, baleen whales, and white beaked dolphins. Finally, after synthesizing the above information, Dolman and Simmonds presented their analysis of current best practices in marine renewable energy. Lastly, the authors presented key factors in Scotland's attempt to implement best practices in marine renewable energy development.

Dolman and Simmonds found that both the UK and the Scottish government have ambitious plans to increase their renewable energy capacity. However, one challenge for developing Scottish marine renewable energy is that the UK parliament, not the Scottish government, has the authority to develop "within 200 nautical miles of the UK coastline." Yet, the Scottish government is responsible for administering any developments. As the authority, the UK government has completed a SEA to consider the environmental implications of its plan to produce a total of 33 GW of offshore wind energy. Nonetheless, the UK government has not evaluated the environmental effects of wave or tidal power.

Another consideration in marine energy development is the legal protections of certain species. The authors reported that Scotland has 24 cetacean species that are "strictly protected" under the EU Habitats Directive. This law also requires that Special Areas of Conservation (SAC) be set aside for protected species. Currently, Scotland does not have adequate SACs for its protected species, such as small bottlenose dolphins and harbor porpoises. Scotland also has national laws aimed at protected vulnerable species. Scotland's laws operate at the individual level, so that it is an offence to "deliberately or recklessly disturb or harass any cetacean… in a manner that is…likely to significantly affect its local distribution or local abundance." Since this law includes "recklessly disturb[ing]" a cetacean as an offense, the authors predict that lawful activities, such as building wind turbines, may result in offenses. Lastly, Dolman and Simmonds explain that even though marine renewable energies may mitigate the threat of climate change, environmental laws must still be followed.

The numerous potential negative impacts from wind, tidal and wave energy are presented in the paper not as eventualities but as "conquerable" problems. With the construction of each energy system, pile driving has a significant impact because it results in noise and damage to the sea bed. In addition, increased vessel activities, habitat degradation, operational noise, and the method used to decommission plants are potential impacts for all three technologies. Some of these impacts have already been observed. For example, at a Danish wind farm, porpoise detections decreased over long ranges during pile driving. Most of the effects, including pile driving, are still being considered to determine the significant of their impact on cetacean species.

The authors conclude by presenting specific recommendations for the Scottish government. They advise that selecting an optimal location is a chief concern. To accomplish this, they recommend collecting data, on an appropriate scale, in order to determine habitats, species densities, distributions and population trends, among other things. Once a location has been selected, the Scottish government should then conduct a "full and transparent" Marine Spatial Planning. This Spatial Planning should be integrated with UK and Scottish SEAs to decrease important knowledge gaps and improve coordination. Monitoring should also be done in a coordinated way. The authors recommend that industry, the Crown Estate and the UK and Scottish governments work together to conduct baseline and continual monitoring of the chosen site. Lastly, the authors note that independent scientists and marine conservation groups are also needed to answer imperative questions and support industry best practices, respectively. The many considerations and connected factors show that developing marine renewable energy best practices in Scotland will not be easy.

What Are the Environmental and Ecological Effects of Ocean Renewable Energy Development?

Boehlert and Gill (2010) aimed to answer that question in their synthesis, which blends and summarizes previous research on the environmental effects of specific ocean renewable energy technologies. In their synthesis, the researchers focused on offshore wind, thermal gradient, wave, tidal, and ocean current technologies, through all stages of development—construction, operation, and decommissioning. To classify the results in an intuitive way, Boehlert and Gill grouped environmental effects as either stressors or receptors and by level, from effect to impact to cumulative impact. Although the authors created a very organized system for evaluating the environmental effects of ocean renewable energy development (ORED) projects, their synthesizing did not give rise to definitive conclusions. Rather, the authors acknowledged that there is little research on the environmental effects of ORED, and that existing research is clouded in uncertainty. Therefore, the authors ultimately advise that additional baseline data be collected and that longer, more continuous research studies be undertaken.

G. Boehlert and A. Gill from Oregon State University and Cranfield University, respectively, compiled, summarized, and synthesized current scholarly research on the environmental effects of different ocean renewable energy technologies. The authors chose to limit their synthesis to five technologies: wave, wind, thermal gradient, tidal, and current energy conversion. The authors created a framework with six levels for the classification of their results. The first level is the type of marine renewable energy technology. The second level contains environmental stressors. Stressors are aspects of the environment which may be altered during the installation, operation or decommissioning of marine renewable energy technologies. In their definition of stressors, the authors include device presence, chemical, acoustic, electromagnetic field, energy removal, and dynamic effects. Environmental receptors, defined as "ecosystem elements with [the] potential for some form of response to the stressor," are the third level of their framework. Boehlert and Gill include animals, such as fish and marine mammals and birds, the food chain, ecosystem, and physical environment, including benthic and pelagic habitats. The fourth level of their framework contains four potential environmental effects. These are given as combinations of length, long or short term, and magnitude, single or multiple effects. Environmental impacts, such as population change, community change, biotic process alteration, and physical structure or process alteration, comprise the fifth level. The authors distinguish between an "impact" and an "effect." Specifically, an impact indicates the severity, direction, and duration of an effect. Effects are relegated to level four while impacts included in levels five and six. Lastly, cumulative impacts are presented on the sixth level. These impacts are analyzed separately from level five impacts because level six impacts consider the collective impact of all stressors caused by human impacts. Cumulative impacts are considered on spatial and temporal scales. This framework is used throughout the paper to classify and evaluate the environmental effects of marine renewable energy development.

After outlining their entire framework, Boehlert and Gill go on to give detailed explanations of the environmental stressors found in level two. The first, and arguably most obvious, stressor is the physical presence of renewable energy structures in the marine environment. The presence of these devices can result in a range of changes above and/or below the water surface. For instance, ocean wind energy devices have the highest vertical presence above the water. In contrast, ocean thermal energy conversion (OTEC), with its extensive pipe system along the ocean bottom, will have a greater presence below the water. The authors also note that some wave energy devices, like the Pelamis or Sea Dragon, have a significant presence on the ocean surface.

The authors also consider the dynamic effects of a device, as a stressor independent of its physical presence. The moving parts of devices, located above and below the water may have effects on the marine environment. One of the most common effects is "blade strike," which typically describes either a migratory bird or fish colliding with a wind or current energy device, respectively. A less apparent effect of moving parts is the removal of energy from the air, water or waves. In the water, this may result in changes to turbulence, stratification, sediment transport and even changes in currents and tidal range. These changes may result in further changes such as disturbing the foraging activities of shorebirds or changing the distribution of intertidal organisms. Moving large amounts of water, such as the movement of deep cold and shallow warm water in OTEC processes, may entrap mobile species and redistribute nutrients to colder waters. The above environmental effects of moving parts show the importance of studying both short and long term and near and far field effects.

The chemical effects of marine energy devices are not of paramount concern. As Boehlert and Gill explain, the effects of chemicals utilized in marine renewable energy development and operations will be similar to the effects of any other ocean construction projects. The small risk of chemical effects during installation, ordinary servicing, and decommissioning are expected to result from ocean vessel operations. However during ordinary operations, a risk of chemical spills exists, especially for devices which use hydraulic fluids. The effect of a spill from an OTEC could be very damaging because the working fluid would most likely be ammonia, which is extremely toxic to fish. Leaching of chemicals may also occur if anti-fouling paints are used to deter organisms which would foul the device. The authors advocate for more research on the toxic compounds used in marine renewable energy development. In addition, the natural chemistry of ocean systems must be examined to determine whether the potential for negative ecological effects, including the outgassing of carbon dioxide and acidification of upwelled waters, are high.

Acoustic effects of ORED may interfere with the natural acoustic environment, causing a disturbance to animal communication, orientation, reproduction and/or predator and prey sensing. For instance, it is widely known that acoustic changes impact fish and marine mammals. However, new research has shown that lobster and crab larvae may also be impacted. Therefore, acoustic effects must be examined during all phases of development, and on various temporal and spatial scales. For instance, the construction phase is usually considered noisiest and "most acoustically diverse." These different noises may result from increased shipping surrounding the area, seismic surveys, pile driving and/or other construction activities. Currently, data to quantify the noise of ORED are deficient and therefore, hypotheses, such as that devices with underwater moving parts will be the nosiest, cannot be tested. Boehlert and Gill recommend that future research focus on determining the intensity, propagation, and acoustic profile of sounds emitted from various forms of ORED.

Since ORED are required to transmit electricity, all except shore-based OTEC or pressurized water pumps create electromagnetic effects in the marine environment. Industry standards currently require shielding on all cables that transmit electricity, to confine "directly emitted electric fields." However, shielding does not restrict the magnetic part of an electromagnetic field (EMF). This can pose a problem for magneto-sensitive organisms, especially those which migrate long distances or orient using natural geomagnetic fields. Similarly, organisms which are electroreceptive, and use bioelectrical impulses to orient, feed, or mate may be severely impacted by the electromagnetic effects of ORED. However, scientists are uncertain as to the response of marine creatures to EMFs because the data needed to assess an impact does not exist. The authors suggest that "before-and-after baseline assessments" be completed and that the biological significance of effects as wells as possible thermal effects be examined.

The authors also list the possible impacts on the environmental receptors. The first receptors considered are the physical environment, and pelagic and benthic habitat. The physical environment may be changed by the removal of kinetic energy from the water, resulting in local acceleration, scouring, or altered sediment transport, deposition, or thermal regimes. Pelagic habitats will be most impacted by the creation of structures in previously vacant areas. This may increase fish populations which will probably attract more predators to the area. Pelagic organisms may also be impacted through impingement, collisions, or entanglement with ORED. Benthic habits will probably be the most impacted by ORED because of structural modifications and changes to water circulation and currents. Greater biodiversity may result as devices create an "artificial reef," but some species may benefit while others are negatively impacted. Other impacts have similar mixed effects. For instance, "shell mounds" may accrue on the ocean bottom as growth on lines, buoys, and anchors are sloughed off. This will alter the habitat but it may also create a productive habitat for fish. Therefore, research shows, albeit with much uncertainty, that ORED may have both positive and negative effects on the physical environment and various habitats.

Another important group of receptors includes organisms within the broad categories of fish, seabirds, and marine mammals. One surprisingly positive effect on fish is the creation of de facto reserves in areas where ORED are located, if fishing is banned. However, these reserves may result in increased mortality of resident fishes as new species and additional predators are attracted to the area. Migrating fishes, such as salmon, elasmobranchs, and sturgeons, may also be affected by individual EMF, chemical, and acoustic stressors, or a combination of these stressors. Seabirds, on the other hand, will be primarily impacted by the above surface effects of ORED. For example, birds that are attracted to lights may collide with the above-water structures such as wind turbines. Furthermore, even if most seabirds are able to steer clear of turbines, the extra energy required to do so may have a negative impact, especially on local, diurnal migratory species. Since studies show that the impact of additional energy required intensifies as the time period of avoidance lengthens, cumulative impacts should be considered in future research. Seabirds may also be impacted by below surface structures to the extent that such devices increase fish populations, or present collision, entanglement, or blade strike risks for diving birds. Boehlert and Gill recommend that the effects on crucial areas of bird activity, migration patterns, and seabird prey be studied in the future.

Marine mammals receive a disproportionate amount of attention among marine receptors in studies of the environmental effects of ORED. This is not surprising since the group is usually protected, captures more public interest and is more visible than other receptors. Concerns for cetaceans are similar to those for diving seabirds, and include risks of entanglement, collision, and blade strike, especially if fish populations increase near ORED. In addition, marine mammals may be attracted to or repelled by the acoustic emissions of ORED. Also, like fish, there is a potential that EMFs may disturb marine mammals' natural orientation systems. The authors recommend more monitoring of cetaceans and pinnipeds, beginning at that same time as pilot and demonstration projects are launched. In addition, baseline data are needed for marine mammals and their prey species. Lastly, the authors urge that "special attention" be given to the migratory routes and important feeding grounds of marine mammals.

Although the number of studies on ORED has increased, the number that focuses on the environmental effects of these devices is relatively small. Currently, the development of devices and deployment of pilot projects and demonstrations outpaces the understanding of their effects. Thus, the need for more research is urgent and great. Boehlert and Gill advocate for simultaneous environmental research as these new technologies are deployed, in order to identify impacts for receptor and stressor groups and decrease uncertainty. Environmental standards for ORED are also needed, but stringent standards may inhibit new development. In contrast, lenient standards may lead to tremendous environmental damage. In light of these undesirable consequences, the authors recommend that balanced environmental standards be developed. At the end of their synthesis, Boehlert and Gill remind readers that the ultimate goal of ORED is to decrease our dependence on fossil fuels.

Suggestions for Future Research: Resolving Uncertainty and Answering Questions

It is clear from the articles summarized above that a great deal of research must be done, before the deployment of ocean–based energy devices increases significantly. Future research should focus on increasing the efficiency of devices and decreasing the costs of development, operations, and servicing. Lastly, future research should concentrate on making devices as environmentally harmless as possible. Some research and development areas of particular need include designing subsurface cables that are easily installed and do not have a negative impact on electroreceptive organisms, testing large scale salinity gradient technologies, designing structures that can support wind turbines in deep waters, and building standardized wave energy testing facilities. Research on the environmental effects and impacts of marine renewable energy must also be conducted. Specifically, base level data should be collected and then continuous studies, which track effects over several years, should be conducted. Furthermore, specific research on the unique environmental effects of areas where development is proposed should be performed in an expedient, yet rigorous manner. In addition, broader research, the results of which can be generalized to number of different locations, should also be done over longer time horizons. At this point in the development of most marine renewable energy systems, a number of research questions still need to be addressed. Therefore, slow growth in the industry is optimal, since there are still so many questions and the entire impacts of these technologies on the ocean environment are not known with certainty. Even though there is a great need for the development of renewable energy sources, proceeding with caution will lead to the best results in terms of efficiency, cost, and limiting environmental impacts.

References Cited

American Meteorological Society. "Glossary of Meteorology: Generalized Hydrostatic Equation." Accessed February 13, 2011.
http://amsglossary.allenpress.com/glossary/search?p=1&query=hydrostatic+equation&submit=Search

Bedard, R., Jacobson, P., Previsic, M., Musial W., Varley, R., 2010. An overview of ocean renewable energy technologies. Oceanography 23, 22–31.

Boehlert, G., Gill, A., 2010. Environmental and ecological effects of ocean renewable energy development: A current synthesis. Oceanography 23, 68–81.

Central Weather Bureau of Taiwan. "Typhoon's Impact on Taiwan." Accessed February 13, 2011.
http://www.cwb.gov.tw/V6e/education/encyclopedia/ty014.html#main001

Dolman, S., Simmonds, M., 2010. Towards best environmental practice for cetacean conservation in developing Scotland's marine renewable energy. Marine Policy 34, 1021–1027.

Dvorak, M., Archer, C., Jacobson, M., 2010. California offshore wind energy potential. Renewable Energy 35, 1244–1254.

The EDF Group. "Marine Energies." Accessed April 3, 2011.
http://businesses.edf.com/generation/hydropower-and-renewable-energy/marine-energies/key-figures-43778.html

Engineering Dictionary. "Hydraulic Head." Last modified 2008. Accessed February 27, 2011. http://www.engineering-dictionary.org/HYDRAULIC_HEAD

Global Wind Energy Council. "Global Wind 2008 Report." Last modified 2009. Accessed January 23, 2011.
http://www.gwec.net/index.php?id=153&L=0.

Igic, P., Zhou, Z., Knapp, W., MacEnri, J., Sørensen, H., Friis-Madsen, E., 2011. Multi-megawatt offshore wave energy converters – electrical system configuration and generator control strategy. Renewable Power Generation, IET 5, 10–17.

4. Nuclear Energy

Carolyn Campbell

Nuclear energy is increasingly being considered as a viable alternative to fossil fuels, as countries around the world struggle to find energy solutions that will both reduce greenhouse gas emissions (GHG) and keep up with the world's continued need for reliable power. This chapter addresses the current state of nuclear power generation, new and developing technologies related to nuclear energy, and options for dealing with radioactive waste.

The first nuclear power plants were opened in the 1950s and since then many countries have come to rely on nuclear generation to meet their energy needs. France gets the majority of its electricity from nuclear power, as does Japan. Both political and cultural factors have driven the nuclear industry in these countries. France's independent executive branch had the ability to institute a nuclear program without objections from outside interest groups. The economic growth associated with the nuclear energy industry is also a major selling point. Studies have found a long-run equilibrium relationship between real GDP, nuclear energy consumption, real gross fixed capital formation, and the labor force in many countries. Additionally, a lack of natural resources in both France and Japan has contributed to the growth of the nuclear industry in these countries.

While nuclear energy has been cited as a potential solution in achieving carbon-free electricity, there are many problems facing its development. Fear of nuclear accidents and nuclear waste has lead to intense public and political opposition. Additionally, nuclear energy projects require a very high initial investment. However, nuclear fission energy is a virtually CO_2-free source of energy, with the majority of environmental impacts coming from the construction of the plant.

Radioactive waste is one of the main stumbling blocks for nuclear energy generation. The United States currently lacks a suitable permanent storage site for nuclear waste, and with more than 103 open-cycle reactors, the problem is growing.

One way to combat the issue of nuclear waste is to decrease the amount of waste that needs to be stored. PUREX reprocessing, technologies that burn nuclear fuel waste, and laser transmutation of nuclear waste could all achieve this. Additionally, emerging reactor technologies, such as TRISO-fueled reactors, can produce more stable and easily stored waste.

With the uncertainties surrounding climate change and our reliance on fossil fuels, nuclear power seems like a practical alternative for meeting the world's energy need. However, the safety and security issues surrounding nuclear energy generation and waste may continue to hider its development. The disaster at Japan's Fukushima Daiichi nuclear plant has reawakened our fear of all things nuclear, setting back progress towards an acceptance of nuclear energy. As the problems associated with fossil fuels and anthropogenic emissions become more pronounced in the following years, will the world be able to overcome its reservations with nuclear power and recognize its environmental and energy benefits?

French Politics, Culture, and Nuclear Power

With over 80% of its electricity coming from nuclear power, it has been suggested that France is a model for adopting a nuclear energy industry. However, Coombs (2010) suggests that France's successful nuclear industry has been driven by the unique political and cultural climate of the country. France's independent executive branch, characterized by a lack of division of power, a weak judiciary, and a reliance on bureaucratic capability, had the ability to efficiently institute a nuclear program without objections from outside interest groups. Additionally, the French people have been won over by the economic growth created by the nuclear industry. Finally, the lack of natural resources in the country has contributed to the growth of the nuclear power program. Coombs suggests that the French government's firm support of the nuclear industry has overshadowed the negative aspects of nuclear power, especially the problem of nuclear waste disposal.

Coombs studied the costs and benefits of nuclear energy by analyzing France's nuclear industry. France began looking into nuclear power during the 1960s in order to decrease its dependence on foreign energy sources and was particularly affected by the quadrupling of oil prices from OPEC countries in 1973. The government began to seriously consider adopting nuclear power and was able to efficiently implement a nuclear program without much objection from outside interest groups. Coombs notes that the French executive-empowering government structure prevents activists from being involved in a transparent debate or influencing policy. Additionally, there is a cultural tendency within France to yield decision-making to the large group of trusted scientists and engineers in the country. Furthermore, French nuclear power has a number of benefits including increased job creation, state revenue, and energy independence. While nuclear power is championed in France, it is often looked upon warily in the United States. Coombs argues that this is not because the French people do not have fears about nuclear waste and accidents, but because their cultural views and political situation influence their support for nuclear energy. Additionally, the French have a lack of choice in the matter, with few alternative natural resources and a government structure that does not support political debate on such matters.

Despite the success of nuclear power, the disposal of nuclear waste continues to be an issue in France. The idea of burying the waste has brought up ideas of the profanation of soil and desecration of the Earth. Additionally, a rural/urban divide has been intensified with rural populations protesting against the Parisian's energy waste ending up in their backyards. In order to combat these issues the state has proposed "stockpiling" the waste. This implies reversibility; that the waste will not be buried and forgotten and that future scientists may learn how to reduce or eliminate the toxicity. However, nuclear waste is a long-term problem that France has yet to develop a permanent disposal facility for. While France has come up with a way to "reprocess" fuel from spent nuclear rods, much of the revenue from this process comes from outside the country. This means that other countries, including Japan, Germany, Switzerland, the Netherlands, Belgium, and Italy, are shipping their waste to and from France. This transit of nuclear waste only increases the likelihood of an accident. However, Coombs argues that the French public places the economic benefits derived from nuclear power above the possible health risks.

Coombs concludes that since France's nuclear program has led to enormous economic benefits, the negative byproducts of nuclear energy have been overlooked. The French government was able to institute a nuclear program due to an executive-empowering institutional structure and a trusting public. However, other countries must weigh both the costs and benefits of nuclear power when searching for renewable energy alternatives.

Nuclear Energy Consumption and Economic Growth

Nuclear energy is an important energy source for both long-term energy and environmental strategies and can address energy needs in areas with scarce resources. Additionally, nuclear energy has been found to have an impact on economic growth. Apergis *et al.* (2010) studied the relationship between nuclear energy consumption and economic growth within a multivariate panel framework for the period 1980–2005. Using a heterogeneous panel cointegration test, the authors found a long-run equilibrium relationship between real GDP, nuclear energy consumption, real gross fixed capital formation, and the labor force. Additionally, the panel vector error correction model revealed bidirectional causality between nuclear energy consumption and economic growth in the short-run and unidirectional causality from nuclear energy consumption to economic growth in the long run. These results support the feedback hypothesis that energy consumption and economic growth are interrelated and thus may serve as complements to each other.

Nuclear energy is an important power source of a growing interest as the world develops long-term energy and environmental policy. The *Energy Information Administration* anticipates that electricity generation from nuclear power will increase from approximately 2.7 trillion kilowatt hours in 2006 to 3.8 trillion kilowatt hours in 2030. This increase can be attributed to concerns regarding greenhouse gas emissions from fossil fuel energy sources, volatility of world oil and gas prices, as well as political issues faced by countries dependent on foreign oil. In discussing nuclear energy as an option for sustainable development, it is important to address its impact on economic growth. Four main hypotheses have been linked with the causal relationship between energy consumption and economic growth. First, the growth hypothesis predicts that energy consumption will both directly and indirectly impact economic growth as a complement to labor and capital in the production process. This hypothesis is supported by unidirectional causality from energy consumption to economic growth. Second, the conservation hypothesis presumes that energy conservation policies that reduce energy consumption and waste do not negatively impact economic growth, supported by unidirectional causality from economic growth to energy consumption. Third, the feedback hypothesis suggests that energy consumption and economic growth are interrelated and serve as complements to each other. This hypothesis is supported when there is bidirectional causality between energy consumption and economic growth. Finally, the neutrality hypothesis assumes that energy consumption is a relatively small component of overall output and therefore has little or no impact on economic growth, supported by the absence of any causal relationship.

In order to determine the relationship between nuclear energy consumption and economic growth the authors analyzed annual data from 1980 to 2005 for Argentina, Belgium, Bulgaria, Canada, Finland, France, India, Japan, Netherlands, Pakistan, South Korea, Spain, Sweden, Switzerland, U.K., and U.S. Included in the multivariate framework were real GDP, real gross fixed capital formation, total labor force, and nuclear energy consumption. First, a heterogeneous panel cointegration test was conducted for both panel data sets, one including France and one excluding France due to its heavy dependence on nuclear energy. The test revealed a long-run equilibrium relationship between real GDP, nuclear energy consumption, real gross fixed capital formation, and the labor force. Second, to infer the causal relationship between the variables, a panel of error correction models was estimated. The authors found short-run bidirectional causality between nuclear energy consumption and economic growth and long-run unidirectional causality from nuclear energy consumption to economic growth. The short-run bidirectional causality supports the feedback hypothesis and suggests that energy policies designed to increase the production and consumption of nuclear energy will have a positive affect on economic growth.

Sustainability of Nuclear Fission Energy

Nuclear generation is met with public and political opposition due to concerns regarding nuclear accidents and nuclear waste. Additionally, very high initial investment costs make it difficult to find funding for nuclear energy projects. Piera (2010) examines the sustainability issues related to nuclear fission energy by reviewing ongoing lines of research and development in the field and potential alternative reactor technologies. While the analysis points out the major drawbacks of nuclear energy, those related to safety, security, and the environment, Piera highlights that nuclear fission is a sound CO_2-free source of energy. The study argues that nuclear fission has a high maturity in its current state of commercial development and has enormous potential in new phases of industrial development.

Emphasized as an important option for keeping atmospheric CO_2 below 550 ppm, nuclear power plants currently provide 16% of the global electricity generation. While generation is increasing 1% each year, this rate is incredibly modest when compared to the global yearly increase in primary energy consumption. Nuclear fission energy is well suited to meet the needs of future energy policies due to the guaranty of supply, environmental quality, and moderate energy costs. However, nuclear energy development is hindered by public and political opposition as well as financing difficulties.

Throughout the paper, Piera assessed the concept of sustainable development as applicable to nuclear energy. First coined in the Brundtland Report, sustainable development stressed the importance of considering social, economic, and environmental issues to ensure the same development and living conditions for future generations. In this context, energy is a very critical issue. While nuclear energy is considered an important energy alternative with very low CO_2 emissions, current LWR reactors are inefficient. Only 0.55% of the potential energy in mined uranium is converted into heat in the reactors, a fact that hampers the future development of nuclear energy. Therefore, Pierra argues, future research should focus on options for new reactors and fuel cycles that could exploit natural resources up to 70% or more. Additionally, nuclear natural resources could be more completely exploited through nuclear breeding. Even-numbered heavy nuclei, ^{238}U and ^{232}Th, cannot be considered true fuels because they do not undergo fission with thermal neutrons. Through nuclear breeding these even-numbered nuclei can be converted into odd-numbered nuclei, specifically [239]Pu and [233]U.

While nuclear breeding may be a solution for more efficient use of nuclear natural resources, it causes concerns related to nuclear proliferation. [239]Pu seems to be a suitable material for nuclear weapons, a social concern that must be addressed in sustainability assessments. Additionally, the waste burden of nuclear energy hinders the sustainability of nuclear fission energy. While deep geological repositories have been suggested as a solution for waste storage, the radiotoxicity of nuclear waste can last for 1000 centuries. Therefore, to make nuclear energy more sustainable the waste must be reduced as much as possible before its final disposal. The "open cycle" in use today cannot achieve such a reduction. By switching to a closed cycle with nuclear fuel recycling, much less fuel would need to be disposed of.

Another concern with nuclear energy generation is nuclear accidents. The meltdown of Chernobyl-4 had catastrophic affects on humans and the environment. However, the reactor was running an experiment when the accidents took place and the six-safety systems had been shut off. Generation 3 reactors have learned from the Chernobyl accident and in turn have incorporated more advanced safety systems.

In conclusion, Peira proposes four main sustainability technical criteria for nuclear energy. First, nuclear reactors and nuclear fuel facilities must have enhanced safety features. Second, natural nuclear materials must be more highly exploited. Third, radioactive inventory of waste must be minimized before disposal. And finally, proliferation-resistant technologies must be developed. By achieving these criteria, nuclear fission energy will become a more sustainable and viable option for the future.

Hydrogen Production using Nuclear Energy

It is often argued that hydrogen is the transportation fuel of the future due to its high efficiency and versatility of use. One way to obtain hydrogen is nuclear-based production using thermochemical water splitting. Lubis *et al.* (2010) conducted a life cycle assessment (LCA) of this process in order to determine its environmental impacts. The authors studied the impacts of both nuclear and copper-chlorine thermochemical plants using LCA methodology framework from the International Organization for Standardization (ISO) and CML-2001 impact categories. The four main stages of the LCA include: i) goal definition and scope; ii) inventory analysis; iii) impact assessment; and iv) improvement assessment. From this study it was found that the most significant environmental impacts come from the construction of the two plants and the operation of the nuclear plant. In contrast, the operations of the thermochemical plant do not significantly contribute to the overall environmental impact. In order to decrease the environmental impact of nuclear-based hydrogen production, the authors suggest developing more sustainable processes, particularly in the nuclear plant and construction.

The authors undertook a LCA of hydrogen production using nuclear energy. In order to minimize emissions, hydrogen is produced via a thermochemical cycle that involves a sequence of chemical reactions yielding a net reaction of splitting water. This study analyzed the copper-chlorine (Cu-Cl) thermochemical cycle in which nuclear energy from a supercritical water-cooled reactor (SCWR) provides the thermal energy for driving the chemical reactions. Therefore the emissions from the overall system are the sum of the advanced nuclear power plant and the thermochemical hydrogen production plant. The nuclear plant is taken to be rated at 2060 MW_{th} and the entire thermal output of the plant goes to producing hydrogen. The thermochemical plant is assumed to have a hydrogen production capacity of 5200 kg/h of H_2 and a 30-year operational life. All calculations are based on 1 h of operation of the entire plant.

Lubis *et al.* utilized reported literature in order to estimate the emissions of the nuclear and thermochemical plants. It was estimated that 4.29 kg/h of uranium is needed to produce a thermal output of 2060 MW_{th}. For the thermochemical plant the environmental impact was estimated based on the use of chemicals in the process and use of raw materials. In order to produce 5200 kg of H_2, 514,800 kg of CuCl and 189,600 kg of HCl are required. To assess the impact of hydrogen production, the environmental impacts of emitted substances were classified into environmental impact categories. These categories include abiotic resource depletion potential (ADP), global warming potential (GWP), ozone depletion potential (ODP), eutrophication potential (EP), acidification potential (AP), photochemical ozone creation potential (POCP), and radioactive radiation (RAD). The quantitative environmental impacts were then calculated by multiplying the quantity of emitted substances by the relevant classification factor and the GaBi database was utilized to determine the environmental impact of emissions based on inventory analysis.

The LCA produced several findings regarding the environmental impact of nuclear-based hydrogen production using thermochemical water splitting. For GWP, the system emits 0.0025 g CO_2-eq over the life of the plant, with 95% of these emissions attributable to the construction of the nuclear plant and the hydrogen plant. Additionally, regarding the AP, the emissions of the system are 0.00015 g SO_2-eq, with the 99% of emissions coming from construction and the nuclear fuel cycle. Construction contributes significantly to other impact categories including EP, ODP, and POCP, while the nuclear fuel cycle contributes significantly to ADP and RAD. In order to decrease the environmental effects of this system the authors suggest developing more sustainable processes in the nuclear plant and the construction of hydrogen production.

Coupling Thermochemical Water Splitting with a Desalination Plant for Hydrogen Production from Nuclear Energy

Nuclear energy has the ability to provide a significant share of energy supply in the future without the negative environmental impacts associated with current energy resources. While nuclear energy has mainly been used for electric power generation, it can also be used in thermochemical water decomposition to produce hydrogen. Orhan *et al.* (2010) explored configurations for coupling the Cu-Cl cycle with a desalination plant using nuclear or renewable energy and assessed the viability of these systems. It was found that capital cost of the Cu-Cl cycle per unit of hydrogen output is less for a larger capacity plant while production cost remains constant. Additionally, the total cost of hydrogen production is inversely proportional to the relationship with plant capacity. The overall unit capital cost of the coupled system was found to vary with production capacity, but not with the type of desalination method. In regards to energy use, the effect of the Cu-Cl cycle is dominant on the overall efficiency of the system because the desalination plant uses much less energy. The highest efficiency coupled system is the configuration that utilizes nuclear energy to power the desalination plant.

Orhan *et al.* analyzed the different configurations for coupling a Cu-Cl cycle with a desalination plant using nuclear energy to produce hydrogen. The Cu-Cl cycle consists of a set of reactions to achieve the splitting of water into hydrogen and oxygen. The production of hydrogen through this cycle provides a pathway for the utilization of nuclear thermal energy. Orhan *et al.* studied the options for coupling the Cu-Cl cycle with a desalination plant. Case I couples the Cu-Cl cycle with a desalination plant powered by nuclear energy. The desalination process is carried out using the waste energy from the nuclear reactor and the resulting fresh water is decomposed into hydrogen and oxygen through the Cu-Cl cycle driven by nuclear energy. Case II uses recovered energy from the Cu-Cl cycle to drive the desalination process, with the desalination plant as a sub-system of the Cu-Cl cycle. Additionally, process/waste energy from the nuclear reactor is used to power the Cu-Cl cycle. One drawback of this system is the efficiency decrease in the Cu-Cl cycle due to the fact that the recovered energy is used for desalination rather than within the cycle itself. Case III uses nuclear energy directly in the desalination process. The Cu-Cl cycle is powered by process energy from the nuclear reactor and energy recovered from the cycle. Case IV uses solar energy to drive desalination while process and waste energy from the nuclear plant is used for the Cu-Cl cycle. One drawback of this configuration is that solar energy is intermittent and therefore much attention must be paid to site selection. Finally, Case V uses off-peak electricity to power both desalination and the Cu-Cl cycle.

The authors performed a comparison of the cost and energy use of the different configurations. The capital cost of the Cu-Cl cycle was found to vary from 1.8 to 0.3 $/kg H_2 depending on the capacity of the cycle. The capital cost of the cycle per unit of hydrogen output is inversely proportional to the size of the system because the reaction energy of any chemical or physical reaction in the Cu-Cl cycle does not change based on plant capacity. The overall unit capital costs of the coupled system were found to be the same for all configurations since the cost contribution of the desalination plant is small compared to that of the Cu-Cl cycle. Case III had the highest capital and production cost of the desalination plant, using a MSF system, while Case I, using a humidification-dehumidification system, had the lowest cost. The unit energy consumed was also greatest for Case III, but lowest for Case V. Finally, the energy efficiencies of the entire configuration were assessed. The effect of the Cu-Cl cycle on the overall system is dominant, thus the overall efficiency of the systems are very similar for each case. However, it was found that Case I had the highest efficiency since waste energy from the nuclear reactor was used. In contrast, Case II operated at lower efficiencies using recovered energy from the Cu-Cl cycle.

Nuclear Waste Disposal

While there is a growing consensus that increased investment in nuclear energy is necessary to satisfy future energy needs, the United States currently lacks a suitable permanent storage site for radioactive waste. With more than 103 open-cycle nuclear reactors throughout the country, the issue of nuclear waste storage is a growing concern. Schaffer (2010) assesses the current state of nuclear waste in the U.S. and proposes solutions to developing a viable nuclear waste disposal program. First, the U.S. should reopen the licensing process for the Yucca Mountain waste disposal facility. Additionally, to decrease the amount of waste sent to disposal facilities the U.S. should restart PUREX reprocessing plants. Upon taking these initial steps, the government must continue to search for additionally permanent storage sites and appropriate funds to educate local communities about nuclear waste storage. The Department of Energy (DOE) and the Nuclear Regulatory Commission (NRC) should also issue guidelines and promotions to encourage the industry to build new TRISO-fueled reactors. Finally, further research should focus on innovative technologies that burn nuclear fuel waste.

Of the 103 operating commercial nuclear power plants in the U.S., all of them are of the open-cycle, batch type. These plants produce long-lived radioactive waste in the form of ceramic-encased low-enriched uranium oxide pellets packed into zirconium-clad rods. With the 1982 Nuclear Policy Act, the U.S. recognized the need for a consolidated storage site, and in 1987 named Yucca Mountain, Nevada as the site for deep underground repositories. However, in response to pressures from Nevada politicians, the DOE has filed a motion to withdraw the license application for Yucca Mountain operations. Due to this decision, the country's nuclear waste remains stored in on-site tanks and casks, which Schaffer argues is risky, inefficient, and unsustainable. Additionally, as more open-cycle nuclear plants come on line, the problem only gets worse.

Schaffer suggests that there are two main components to solving the open-cycle nuclear waste disposal program. First is the issue of community confidence; in order for a permanent storage site to be developed, community endorsement is required. Therefore, a confidence-enhancing plan should identifying three or four sites instead of just one, specify storage for a nominal period, provide adequate monetary incentives, and disclose the risks and rewards of a nuclear storage site. The second component of a long-term solution for nuclear waste involves reducing the amount of high-level nuclear waste sent to a storage facility. One way to achieve this is through the PUREX (Plutonium and Uranium by Extraction) process in which depleted fuel rods are cut into pieces and dissolved in nitric acid. Uranium, plutonium, and actinides can then be extracted from the resulting liquid. The extracted uranium-235 can be burned in heavy-water moderated reactors or fast-neutron reactors for additional energy, the plutonium-239 can be used to make MOX (mixed oxide uranium and plutonium) fuel, and the actinides can be vitrified in a design that is resistant to water leaching.

Additional technological solutions for decreasing waste are described in the paper. Closed-cycle fast reactor technology, such as an Advanced Liquid Metal Reactor (ALMR), has been studied for many years. ALMR uses energetic neutrons to interact with uranium-238 to eventually produce plutonium-239. Through pyrometallurgical processing, a mix of transnuranic elements from the used fuel can be extracted and the uranium can be reused. This process has advantages over PUREX reprocessing, in a counter-proliferation sense, because it does not produce pure plutonium. An alternative to reprocessing or refining is to produce nuclear waste that is self-contained, depleted to the point where it is not a proliferation problem, and can be stored in underground sites without concerns of water leaching or seismic damage. TRISO (tri-structureal isometric) fuel reactors use fuel pebbles that, after spent, are safe to store without cooling, are resistant to water leaching, and contain highly depleted nuclear materials. By employing such overlooked strategies for waste reduction and reopening the search for a permanent storage site the U.S. will be able to develop a more viable nuclear waste disposal program.

Laser Transmutation of Nuclear Waste

The issue of radioactive waste is a major challenge in the widespread acceptance of a nuclear energy industry. The issues of where to store the nuclear waste and the possibility of radioactive materials leaching into the under-ground water supply seriously undermine the potential of nuclear energy. However, with the ongoing development of ultra-intense laser techniques, researchers are exploring the possibility of laser transmutation of radioactive materials into stable isotopes. Sadighi-Bonabi *et al.* (2009) analyzed the opportunity for transmutation of ^{93}Zr, a highly radioactive nuclear waste with a half-life of 1.53 million years. The authors suggest that through ultra-intense laser transmutation, ^{93}Zr can be converted to ^{92}Zr, its stable isotope. High-energy electron generation, Bremsstrahlung, and photonuclear reactions were observed and the number of reactions that produced ^{92}Zr calculated. It was found that the laser intensity, irradiation time, and repetition rate of laser have strong and direct effects on the yield of ^{92}Zr and the number of reactions.

The disposal of long-lived radioactive waste is a significant challenge for the nuclear industry. Through the development of ultra-intense laser technologies, the possibility of photonuclear transmutation of nuclear waste to more stable isotopes has offered new solutions to solving this problem. When an ultra-intense laser pulse interacts with the radioactive waste, gamma radiations induce nuclear reactions for transmutation of the waste into a stable isotope. Sadighi-Bonabi *et al.* focused their study on Zirconium, particularly ^{93}Zr, a fission product in nuclear reactors with a half-life of 1.53 million years.

In order to assess the number of reactions and laser-induced photonuclear activation of ^{93}Zr, the authors analyzed available experimental data from focusing intensities onto a solid target. For this study, the laser intensity was assumed to be 10^{20} W/cm^2 with a repetition rate of 10 Hz. Calculations were also extended to higher intensities of 5 x 10^{20} W/cm^2, 10^{21} W/cm^2, 5 x 10^{21} W/cm^2, and 10^{22} W/cm^2. The number of reactions was calculated by evaluating the energy spectrum of the laser and a cross section of the photonuclear reaction between threshold and cut-off energy. It was found that the Bremsstrahlug spectrum, relating to the deceleration of electrons, depended on the intensity of the laser, with higher intensities increasing the number of reactions. Additionally, irradiation time and repetition rate were found to have substantial effects on the yield of ^{93}Zr (γ, n) ^{92}Zr and the number of reactions. If the target is irradiated for an hour by a laser light of 10^{20} W/cm^2 at a repetition rate of 10 Hz, approximately 2.7 x 10^7 reactions will occur. By increasing the repetition rate, yield would also increase. However, achieving higher rates also means using more power, and more advanced lasers. Additionally, although increased intensity of the laser would lead to a higher number of reactions and activity, there is an optimum intensity at which a maximum number of reactions is reached and, beyond that point, the overlap between reaction cross-section and the number of photons disappears. For ^{93}Zr (γ, n) ^{92}Zr, this optimum intensity was calculated at 3×10^{21} W/cm^2.

Through this study, it was found that laser intensity, irradiation time, and repetition rate of the laser have a significant, direct effect on the yield of ^{92}Zr and the number of reactions. Maximizing the efficiency of laser technology for the transmutation of radioactive isotopes will prove valuable in future efforts to solve the problem of long-lived nuclear waste.

Japan's Nuclear Crisis

The 8.9 earthquake, and subsequent tsunami, that rocked Japan on March 11, 2011 have lead to severe damage at Tokyo Electric Power Co.'s Fukushima Daiichi nuclear power plant. The problems at Fukushima Daiichi arose due to the failure of the cooling system and the significant loss of water from the cooling pools. As authorities continue to work to reestablish the cooling system, Japanese citizens wait anxiously. Twenty-five years after the meltdown of Chernobyl-4, it seemed that the world was beginning to accept the importance of nuclear power for providing a clean and reliable source of energy in the future. However, the situation in Japan has awakened our fear of all things nuclear. Critics argue that the same thing that is happening at Fukushima Daiichi could happen in the U.S. and that the country would be wise to halt all nuclear energy production. Other, conversely, argue that the Fukushima accident could create a chance for the nuclear industry to "reboot" and look for innovative technologies that may decrease the risk associated with traditional solid-fuel uranium reactors.

The core of a traditional nuclear reactor, such as the Fukushima Daiichi reactor, contains both water and fuel rods made of zirconium and pellets of nuclear fuel, usually uranium, which set off a controlled nuclear reaction. This reaction heats the water, creating high temperature steam, which powers a turbine and generates electricity. A meltdown occurs when the core gets too hot, causing the fuel rods to crack and release radioactive gases. In the worse case scenario, the fuel pellets melt and fall onto the reactor floor, where they can eat through the protective barriers and eventually reach the surrounding environment. In Japan, the reactors are designed to turn off automatically in case of a disaster, with the aim of preventing a meltdown. However, even with the plant shut off, nuclear fuel rods continue to generate a huge amount of heat. In order to cool the fuel, backup generators are meant to pump water into the plant. These generators failed at Fukushima Daiichi, leading the fuel rods to boil off remaining water and become partially exposed. If left exposed for long enough, the fuel rods could melt and leak radiation. In order to avoid this, authorities are pumping seawater into the reactor to cool the fuel rods. However, salt buildup on the fuel rods can allow them to heat up more by blocking water circulation between the fuel rods, and, in the worst case, can eventually lead to a meltdown. Additionally, workers have released built-up gases containing some radioactive material into the atmosphere in order to ease pressure inside the plant.

The problems at Fukushima Daiichi have aroused concerns of similar disaster occurring in the United States. While some critics argue that the US should halt all nuclear power generation others suggest that the accident in Japan lends a chance to recreate the nuclear industry. It has been suggested in recent years that the solid-fuel nuclear reactors, like the ones in Japan, are an outdated technology and should be replaced by a safer and cheaper kind of nuclear energy. According to Matt Ridley of the Wall Street Journal, thorium has many advantages as a nuclear fuel. There is four times as much thorium in the world as there is uranium; it is easier to handle and to process; it "breeds" its own fuel by continuously creating uranium 233; it can produce 90 times as much energy from the same quantity of fuel; no plutonium is produced by its reactions; and it generates much less waste, with a much shorter half life. Neutrons are needed for a thorium reactor to run and can be supplied with a particle accelerator or uranium 235. Both options are highly controlled and are relatively safe. Additionally, the fuel in a thorium reactor cannot melt down because it is already molten, and reactions slow as it cools. Whether it leads to new innovations or a general shift away from nuclear power, the disaster at the Fukushima Daiichi plant will undoubtedly alter the future of nuclear energy generation.

Conclusions

As concerns over greenhouse gas emissions and rising energy prices continue to become more prominent, the utilization of nuclear fuel appears increasingly advantageous. Not only can nuclear power be used for electrical generation, but it also has the ability to be used in thermochemical water decomposition to produce hydrogen, seen by many as the transportation fuel of the future. Additionally, further technological developments in reactors and waste processing may alleviate some of the safety and security concerns surrounding nuclear power. Nuclear energy has the potential to be a significant source of clean energy for the world. Whether or not it will be accepted as such remains open to debate.

Carolyn Campbell

References Cited

Apergis, N., Payne, J.E., 2010. A panel study of nuclear energy consumption and economic growth. Energy Economics 32, 545–549.

Bradsher, K. New problems at Japanese plant subdue optimism. New York Times. March 23, 2011.

Casselman, B., Smith, R. How nuclear reactors work...and the dangers when they don't. Wall Street Journal. March 15, 2011.

Coombs, C., 2010. French Nuclear Power: A model for the world?. Hinckley Journal of Politics. 11, 7–13.

Hayashi, Y., Iwata, M. Japan struggles to control reactors. Wall Street Journal. March 13, 2011.

Lubis, L.L., Dincer, I., Rosen, M.A., 2010. Life cycle assessment of hydrogen production using nuclear energy: an application based on thermochemical water splitting. Journal of Energy Resources Technology 132, 1–6.

Orhan, M.F., Dincer, I., Naterer, G.F., Rosen, M.A., 2010. Coupling of copper-chloride hybrid thermochemical water splitting cycle with a desalination plant for hydrogen production from nuclear energy. International Journal of Hydrogen Energy 35, 1560–1574.

Piera, M., 2010. Sustainability issues in the development of nuclear fission energy. Energy Conservation and Management 51, 938–946.

Ridley, M. Does a different nuclear power lie ahead. Wall Street Journal. March 19, 2011.

Sadighi-Bonabi, R., Irani, E., Safaie, B., Imani, Kh., Silatani, M., Zare, S., 2010. Possibility of ultra-intense laser transmutation of ^{93}Zr (γ, n) ^{92}Zr a long-lived nuclear waste into a stable isotope. Energy Conservation and Management 51, 636–639.

Schaffer, M.B., 2011. Toward a viable nuclear waste disposal program. Energy Policy 39, 1382–1388.

5. Microalgae Biodiesel

Karen de Wolski

As scientific evidence of climate change continues to accumulate, and the potentially devastating effects of this trend begin to manifest, the necessity of finding methods of reducing our greenhouse gas emissions has become salient. The transportation and energy sectors, with their high burning of fossil fuels, are the primary contributors to overall human greenhouse gas emissions. One of the more appealing alternatives to fossil fuels is biofuels, as they are not limited by declining natural stores, nor do they emit nearly as much carbon in their usage. However, current feedstock-based biofuels, such as corn ethanol, are limited because they directly subtract from global food supply while increasing the cost of food worldwide. Therefore, scientists are searching for a different biomass source that could be similarly converted into biofuel and grown on a mass-scale.

Microalgae have arisen as the most promising new source of biomass for biofuel production. They have a relatively high biomass yield compared to other terrestrial plants, and they simultaneously utilize large amounts of CO_2 in their growth cycle. Additionally, microalgae do not require arable land for cultivation and therefore would not affect agriculture if grown on a bulk scale. While there are clear advantages of developing microalgae as a biofuel source, there remain many obstacles and limitations that must be overcome. The cost of microalgae cultivation and conversion must be reduced if they are to be produced on a large scale. Most current research is seeking ways of lowering the cost by increasing efficiency and yield. This research includes finding methods of reducing water usage and nutrient usage, both inputs which remain relatively high for the overall production process.

Studies of microalgae-based biodiesel production have had optimistic results overall. Cost-benefit and life cycle analyses have demonstrated microalgae to be a viable biofuel source, both technically and economically. Many methods of cultivation and conversion are under exploration. These include the traditional method of harvesting biomass, extracting the lipids, and transesterifying them into biodiesel, and the alternative method of extracting ethanol as a direct byproduct of algal photosynthesis. Within these methods, ways of optimizing yield, whether it be by bioengineering microalgal species or utilizing wastewater as a growth environment, have shown marked progress. While much research and development must be accomplished before microalgae can be grown on a large scale and be a globally used biofuel source, in the often pessimistic world of climate change science, microalgae stand out as a reason for optimism.

Microalgae for Biodiesel Production and Other Applications: a Review

As fossil fuel reserves decline and atmospheric CO_2 concentration increases, the need to find renewable sustainable energy sources has become pressing. The current generation of biofuels, derived from food crops and oil seeds, has relatively low negative environmental effects from its consumption, but it is limited in its economic feasibility because it relies on drawing from food supplies. Microalgae are becoming increasingly viewed as an alternative source of biomass for biodiesel creation, as they have many biological and economic advantages. In their 2010 review article, Mata *et al.* outline the viability of microalgae as a biofuel source, discussing areas that need to be considered and further substantiated before microalgae can be used for wide scale fuel production. Additionally, they highlight other ways that microalgae may be used to ameliorate various climate and health problems, including flue gas CO_2 emission mitigation, wastewater purification, and medicinal applications. They conclude that, while having significant potential as an economically and environmentally feasible source of biodiesel, there remains a substantial amount of scientific research and technological advancement that must be completed before microalgae can be cultivated and processed on a large-scale.

Mata *et al.* emphasize the dire need to find renewable and sustainable energy alternatives, listing the negative effects of global warming and high atmospheric CO_2 concentration and implicating the burning of fossil fuels as the main source of greenhouse gas (GHG) emissions. Biofuels are illustrated as a more environmentally friendly alternative, as they have lower combustion emissions per unit than diesel and gasoline. However, current biofuels are limited because they draw from foodstuffs, and they are therefore not only expensive but also lead to an increase in food prices while lowering food availability worldwide. Biodiesel, currently comprising 82% of total biofuels production and derived from vegetable oils and animal fats, cannot meet the current market demands, as both land availability and feed stocks are insufficient. In order to meet demand and ameliorate global warming, it is therefore necessary to utilize an alternative biomass source that is less costly to cultivate and has lower land requirements. Microalgae are currently under investigation as such a source, as they can provide feedstock for multiple biofuels, including biodiesel, ethanol, and methane, while having relatively low cultivation requirements. Mata *et al.* focus primarily on microalgae for biodiesel production, outlining what is already known about microalgae for this use, and what still needs to be elucidated in order to utilize microalgae on a large-scale.

It is estimated that 50,000 species of microalgae exist, and these prokaryotic and eukaryotic organisms are able to thrive in a variety of harsh conditions with high growth and reproduction rates. Extensive collections of algal species have been gathered at many research institutions, the largest being 4000 strains of 1000 species at the University of Coimbra. Microalgae are relatively easy to grow, requiring little attention, able to utilize non-potable water, and needing 49–132 times less land than rapeseed or soy. They reproduce rapidly, completing a growth cycle every few days, and different species are adapted to live in different conditions, making them versatile organisms for cultivation. Microalgae as a source of biodiesel are additionally advantageous in that they can be simultaneously used to remove CO_2 from industrial flue gases by bio-fixation, remove contaminants from wastewater, and provide other useful compounds for various industrial and pharmaceutical purposes. The large-scale production of biodiesel from microalgae could therefore serve multiple positive functions while meeting energy demands.

While the large-scale culture of microalgae began in the 1960s in Japan, study of them as a renewable energy source has been limited by insufficient funding. An R&D program in the United States, carried out between 1978 and 1996, concluded that microalgae as a low-cost biodiesel source were technically feasible, but would require long term investigation and development to achieve. This project began to identify algal strains with particularly high lipid content for oil extraction and to screen for genetic variability between algal isolates, but the research was curtailed in 1995 by a funding cut. Microalgae research has been brought back to the forefront recently by high crude oil prices and the prevalent need to find less environmentally devastating sources of energy. Most contemporary studies focus on the genetic engineering of microalgae to optimize cultivation success and oil production, with an especial concentration on maximizing lipid content.

Current microalgae to biodiesel production processes consist of cell growth in a production unit, cell separation from the growth media, and lipid extraction. From these lipids, biodiesels can be created by methods similar to those used for other biofuel feedstocks. A key step in cultivation is site selection, which must take into account carbon and light availability, and the metabolic requirements of the algal species of interest. Some species have proven difficult to cultivate at high volume, and light and temperature are the most limiting factors for successful growth. Additionally, salinity, turbulence, and contaminants must be controlled as required by each individual species. The authors list a series of studies by different researchers investigating the effects of various growth conditions, including pH, and the concentrations of CO_2, iron, and nitrogen. It is emphasized that different species have relatively individualized requirements, and these must be understood if microalgae cultivation is to be maximized.

Biomass recovery, or "harvesting," can make up to 30% of biomass production cost, but no single method has proven to be optimal. The development of such a method does, however, remain an important area of interest. Harvesting can include sedimentation, centrifugation, filtration, flocculation, and flotation. The two main criteria for harvest method selection are identified as desired product quality and acceptable moisture level. Sedimentation can be used for lower quality products, while the more costly centrifugation produces higher value products. Processing is also an expensive production cost, and it consists of dehydration and cell disruption for metabolite release. Several extraction methods, including solvents, ultrasound, and microwave are currently used or under investigation. Biodiesels are produced from the lipids by a transesterifaction reaction, in which tricglycerides are converted to esters (biodiesel) and glycerol (by-product) through a multiple step chemical reaction. Current industrial transesterification processes are carried out in a stirred reactor in batch mode, although improvements have been proposed that would enable continuous mode production, allowing for decreased reaction time.

Other considerations for microalgae cultivation include culture system type and operation mode. Open-culture systems, such as lakes, are easier and cheaper to build and operate. They are, however, more difficult to regulate and therefore could be limited in large-scale microalgae cultivation abilities. Closed-culture systems, or photo-bioreactors (PBR), while much more expensive, are more flexible, allowing for optimization of pH, temperature, evaporation levels, and CO_2 loss. It has been shown that PBRs have higher volumetric productivity and cell concentrations than open-culture systems, but congruent areal productivity, and the competition between the two technologies is therefore not necessarily as important as the genetic engineering of microalgae to appropriately fit each system type. The second aforementioned cultivation consideration, operation mode, centers on batch versus continuous PBR operation. Continuous mode offer a higher degree of control over conditions, and hence can produce more reliable and higher quality results. However, different bio-reaction types are better suited than others to this mode of operation, and this therefore needs to be understood when designing a cultivation process for any given microalgae species.

The review ends with a brief discussion of other potential microalgae applications. Flue gases from power plants account for over 7% of world CO_2 emissions, and microalgae could be used to diminish these emissions through natural bio-fixation processes. Microalgae could also be used for waste water treatment, as they require common aquatic contaminants (primarily nitrogen and phosphorous) as nutrient sources. Additionally, many species contain chemical compounds that can be used for both industrial and health applications. These include pigments, antioxidants, vitamins, and food additives. These compounds could be extracted from the microalgae processed for biodiesel production, and could therefore potentially offer multiple simultaneous benefits. Several nutritional supplements have also been found in microalgae, including sterols and carotenoids, which could prove highly beneficial for human health. There is also promising evidence to show that microalgae culture could be a significant source of food for aquatic animal rearing. Microalgae can be utilized to culture zooplankton for feeding farmed crustaceans and finfish. Further understanding of the nutritional value of microalgae could hence be widely applied to aquaculture.

The authors conclude that microalgae as a biodiesel source has great promise as a sustainable and environmentally friendly alternative to the current food crop and seed oil derived biodiesels. While much is already understood about the processes required for mass cultivation, much remains unknown. A significant amount of investment and research will therefore be necessary to develop this technology. Given the importance of reducing GHG emissions and supplementing fossil fuels, this capital investment into microalgae development could prove vital for human energy sustainability.

Cost-effectiveness Analysis of Algae Energy Production in the EU

The transition towards renewable energy is being largely driven by the increase in global energy demand, challenges to energy security, and climate change. In the EU, fossil fuels constitute about 98% of energy consumption within the transportation sector. While biofuels are seen as a possible substitute for fossil fuels, having environmental, economic, and political benefits, first generation biofuels have come under fire because of their negative effects, including deforestation, water and soil degradation, and threats to food security. The European Environment Agency, doubting their ability to satisfy the EU's energy needs, has proposed to suspend biofuels until a study has been conducted that weighs the costs and benefits of their production and utilization. These criticisms of first generation biofuels do not, however, apply to other potential biofuel alternatives and their external environmental benefits. In this study, Kovacevic and Wesseler (2010) completed a cost-effectiveness analysis of the possible utilization of algal biomass as a biofuel source. They took into account externalities, including emissions, impact on food prices, and pesticide use. They concluded that the development of biotechnology and the elevation of crude oil prices would lead to algal biodiesel outcompeting other fuels, but a substantial capital investment will be necessary to make this a reality.

Kovacevic and Wesseler sought to quantify both the direct financial and the external cost-effectiveness of producing algae as a biofuel source in the EU. While microalgae are seen as having great potential in this arena, one of the largest obstacles is capital investment required to develop the necessary biotechnologies.

The two characteristics of microalgae most appealing for utilization as an energy source are their high biomass yield relative to other terrestrial plants, and their high utilization of CO_2. Microalgae's efficient conversion of solar energy and utilization of water, carbon, and nutrients leads to a yield 7–31 times higher than palm oil, the best oil-yielding terrestrial feedstock. Recent interest in microalgae has led to an array of research, with studies indicating a vast spectrum of possible yields dependent on various factors and conditions. While biotechnology advancement is seen as a major pathway for improving yield, Kovacevic and Wesseler indicate that this development is not sufficient. Rather, systems must be optimized for all growing conditions if lipid yields are to be high enough on a large scale. Currently, the only successful mass culture productions of microalgae have been achieved with species tolerant to extreme conditions, a limitation that will need to be overcome if microalgae are to be a major fuel source.

In this study, the researchers compared algal biodiesel with rapeseed biodiesel and fossil fuels in the EU-25 transportation sector. Annuities (expressed per GJ of fuel energy delivered to the gas station) were used to aggregate the private and external costs and benefits of each fuel option for the cost-effectiveness analysis, and represented average annual cost to society accounting for production costs, environmental benefits and costs, energy security, and food price impacts. The European Commission's established biofuel target of 10% vehicle biofuel use by 2020 was used as the time frame and production scale for the comparison. This proposal projects 1.48 EJ of biofuel utilization by the target year. Because discount rates for biofuels vary between 3% and 8%, 5% was chosen as the social discount in this study, although 2% and 8% were also applied. Discount rate is important because high discount rates would probably favor fossil fuels over biofuels because biofuels require higher investment.

The researchers calculated the private production costs of the various fuels in question by choosing certain growing conditions and production processes. They assume favorable conditions (high solar radiation, optimal climate, low altitude, proximal seawater source) as would be found in southwestern and eastern Spain and southeastern Italy. They define three cases: a base case, a low-yield case, and a high-yield case. Kovacevic and Wesseler calculated land requirement through previous microalgal studies, and accounted for the relatively low opportunity cost of land use for algal production. They assumed a basic production unit of 400 ha with paddle wheel mixing, pure CO_2 mixing, and anaerobic digestion for nutrient recycling, with carbon supplied from nearby coal plants. Water supply is assumed to be from seawater sources, with replenishment from freshwater. The cost of the pipe network for water transport and pumping is based on other known engineering projects. The transesterification process of biodiesel production is assumed to be equal to the rapeseed biodiesel process. The researchers also calculated the cost of fuel distribution, considering the differences in energy content between diesel and biodiesel.

Rapeseed biodiesel production costs were generated based on current rapeseed growth and processing. Germany, France, Poland, and the UK are the largest EU rapeseed producers, constituting 72% of total EU rapeseed production. The projected 30% yield improvement by 2020 was accounted for, and maximum land utilization by rapeseed oil was calculated to be 29.1 Mha, as compared to 1.35 Mha for microalgae. Fossil fuel production costs were also calculated based on gas station prices and taxes. Three cases were estimated due to the volatility of crude oil prices, and elasticity between crude oil and fuels price were applied for diesel and gasoline.

The researchers next calculated the social cost of fuel utilization by considering external costs, especially environmental effects. These included costs of CO_2, methane, nitrous oxide, volatile organic compounds, particulate matter, sulfur dioxide, and nitrogen oxide emissions. In order to calculate greenhouse gas (GHG) emissions, three drivers were considered: land use change (only applicable for biofuels), fuel distribution and dispensing, and fuel combustion (only fossil fuels). The effect of land use change on GHG emissions accounted for changes in nitrogen emissions from fertilizers, changes in methane emissions from livestock, and cropland conversion. Conversion of grassland for rapeseed cultivation increases GHG emissions because of fertilizer use, while conversion of cropland to algal ponds decreases GHG emissions. Additionally, energy input for processing algal and rapeseed biodiesel production were considered in the calculation. Distribution and dispensing costs were based on previous estimates, and applied for all fuel types. GHGs from combustion were calculated only for fossil fuels because they release carbon.

Next, the impact on food prices of the different fuel types was considered. It was assumed that microalgae biodiesel would have no impact on food prices because of their small land requirement and ability to use marginal land. Rapeseed requires a significant amount of land, and it was estimated that it would necessitate reallocating 70%, 55%, and 54 % of total wheat, barley, and maize acreage respectively across Germany, France, Poland, and the UK. The researchers also account for the costs of fertilizer and pesticide leaching, comparing cost of purchase to theoretical environmental cost. Because energy security has become a major issue surrounding oil dependency, security of supply for biofuels was derived from the EC Biofuels progress report (2007).

The entire analysis is presented as a comparison of annuities. The social cost for the base case of algal biodiesel is 52.3 €/GJ, with significant cost differences for the alternative cases. Rapeseed oil and fossil fuel had total social costs of 36.0 and 15.8 €/GJ respectively. However, the private costs dominated the cost structure of algal biodiesel production, while the externalities constitute a larger percentage of total cost for rapeseed and fossil fuels. The social cost of fossil fuels increases significantly when crude oil prices rise ($100–$200 /barrel). The private costs of both biofuel types are largely due to biomass production costs, with carbon supply and water supply being the primary factors. Food prices impact and GHG emissions are the greatest external costs of rapeseed biodiesel and fossil fuels, while only algal biodiesel has external benefit in GHG emissions mitigation.

Kovacevic and Wesseler conclude that fossil fuels have the lowest private utilization costs while algal biodiesel has the highest cost. This makes sense given the current infrastructure supporting fossil fuel energy production. Rapeseed oil is also relatively supported within the current fuel system. However, there are scenarios in which algal biodiesel can outcompete rapeseed biodiesel and fossil fuels, even with high production costs. This change would come as a result of biotechnology development, increasing crude oil prices, and high carbon pricing. Algal biodiesel has significantly lower external costs than the other analyzed fuel types. It is therefore concluded that environmental costs can be game changers when examining social costs. If environmental impacts are highly prioritized and enable support for biotechnology development through policy change and investment, microalgae could become the lowest cost fuel to society.

Life-Cycle Analysis on Biodiesel Production from Microalgae: Water Footprint and Nutrients Balance

The combination of both federal government-mandated and individual state renewable energy standards, and the increasing body of evidence that feedstock-based biofuels are unsustainable, have led to the critical evaluation of the feasibility of microalgae as an alternative biofuel source. While microalgae show great promise in their relatively low land requirements, high growth rate, and CO_2 absorption abilities, there remain outstanding questions regarding water consumption rates, especially in comparison to current feedstocks. In their 2011 study, Yang *et al.* use known measurements of algal growth parameters, such as evaporation rate, growth rate, and nutrient usage, to quantify the water footprint and nutrient balance of *Chlorella vulgaris,* a species of microalgae. They found that microalgae are competitive with traditional feedstocks in terms of total water footprint, and that freshwater and nutrient consumption could be significantly reduced by using sea-water and waste water as the base water source. The researchers additionally ana-lyzed spatial variation of microalgae growth in terms of solar radiation and tempera-ture, and found that the water footprint would be lowest in the states of Florida, Hawaii, and Arizona.

Yang *et al.* outline the feasibility of microalgae as a biofuel source in terms of water footprint and nutrient usage by drawing from previously gathered metrics to estimate the water and nutrient consumption of *Chlorella vulgaris*. The 2007 Energy Independence and Security Act requires that renewable fuel production increase to 36 billion gallons per year by 2022. The first generation biofuels derived from corn and sugarcane (Brazil) are limited in that they require significant arable land, increase food prices internationally, and do not necessarily significantly reduce carbon emissions. Microalgae are promising as an alternative fuel source because of their high growth rate, smaller land usage (15–300 times more oil per land unit), high lipid content, and CO_2 absorption abilities. However, microalgae are not yet grown on a mass scale, and several outstanding questions remain regarding the life-cycle impacts of large-scale cultivation and biodiesel production. This study seeks to elucidate the water footprint of biodiesel production from microalgae through quantitative measurements and comparisons with current biodiesel production from feedstocks. The researchers calculate the differences between using seawater, wastewater, and freshwater as a culture base, and they additionally account for nu-trient usage and the effects of solar radiation and temperature variation in microal-gae cultivation.

Microalgae biodiesel production necessarily entails culture, harvest, dry-ing, extraction, and esterification. Microalgae are initially grown in culture water (sea, waste, or fresh) in an open pond which must be constantly replenished with freshwater to accommodate evaporation and maintain optimal salinity levels. When sufficiently grown, the microalgae are harvested, dried, and the lipids are extracted to be esterified for biodiesel. Culture water can be partially recycled directly back into a culture pond, and/or discharged into a wastewater treatment system.

Evaporation is the main source of water loss during the culture process, and the authors used lake evaporation rate to approximate open pond evaporation. Microalgal growth is affected by temperature and solar radiation, and data from the national solar radiation database were used to make the appropriate calculations. Additionally, culture ponds need to be supplied with nutrients, and necessary nu-trient concentrations were based on measurements from previous studies. Both harvesting and drying, the second and third steps of the process respectively, are quantified by solid content (ratio of microalgae to water) and recovery rate (ratio of harvested mass to mass after culture). These values were derived from several al-ready established parameters. Because the extraction and esterification of microalgae is similar to that of soybeans, this study substituted water usage rates for biodiesel production from soybean oil (2–10 liters water used per liter of biodiesel produced) for the analogous water usage of biodiesel production from microalgae-derived oil.

The researchers found that, in the absence of recycling harvested water, the water footprint of microalgae biodiesel production is 3726 kg-water/kg-biodiesel. This value can be decreased to 591 kg-water/kg-biodiesel if all harvest water is recycled. The amount of harvest water recycled does not affect the water footprint of the other production processes. Additionally, they found that using seawater or wastewater can reduce the life-cycle freshwater usage by up to 90%. Harvest water recycling can also decrease nutrient (nitrogen, phosphorous, potassium, magnesium, and sulfur) usage by approximately 55%. The use of a mix of seawater and wastewater for algal culture can additionally reduce nitrogen usage by 94% and abolish the necessity of adding potassium, magnesium, and sulfur.

When these results are compared to the water footprint of feedstock-based biofuel, microalgae are demonstrated to be extremely competitive. Increases in both lipid content and growth rate, the two most important parameters, result in the reduction of the water footprint. These two parameters are, however, usually negatively related to each other, and vary depending on species. This study calculated the water footprint for eleven other species using the same methodology and found that the water footprint could be 1–6 times higher than that of *C. vulgaris*.

Geographic variations in solar radiation, temperature, and evaporation must be accounted for when estimating microalgae growth. While microalgae tend to prosper in high temperature/high solar radiation environments, both of these factors are proportionally related to evaporation rate, and therefore cause an increase in water footprint. Taking these factors into account, the researchers calculated that Florida, Hawaii, and Arizona would have the lowest water footprints for microalgae biodiesel production in the United States.

They conclude that, in terms of water footprint and nutrient usage, microalgae could be a feasible alternative to current feedstocks for biodiesel production. The advancement of technology, especially of photobioreactors for cultured growth, could enhance water conservation and increase cultivation efficiency. The use of sea/waste water for culture water would decrease water usage by 90% and greatly reduce the need for nutrient supplementation. Phosphate could prove to be a limiting factor, as it is not found in either of the aforementioned water types, and global phosphate sources are decreasing. However, experimentation with different microalgae species types and phosphate-rich water could overcome this barrier. While much remains to be done before microalgae can be used as a global renewable energy source, freshwater and nutrient usage does not appear to be a limiting obstacle.

Microalgae Cultivation in a Wastewater Dominated by Carpet Mill Effluents for Biofuel Applications

The current global target for biofuel feedstock crop production by 2030 would demand approximately 180 km³ of water, a demand that could be severely limiting given the overall worldwide depletion of freshwater sources. Because microalgae are a promising option for future biofuel production, finding ways to cultivate and harvest them with relatively little freshwater is both valuable and necessary. Chinnasamy *et al.* (2010) studied the feasibility of growing microalgae in wastewater consisting primarily of carpet mill effluents. This is especially appealing because it would not only greatly reduce the freshwater demand of microalgae cultivation, it would also serve to remove contaminants from the wastewater itself. The researchers found that a consortium of 15 native algal isolates could grow in treated wastewater with >96% nutrient removal, and 63.9% of their oil could be converted into biodiesel. Chinnasamy *et al.* conclude that, while these results are promising, more research is needed to elucidate the mechanisms of anaerobic digestion and thermochemical liquefaction in order for this process to be economically viable

Chinnasamy *et al.* sought to determine the feasibility of microalgae cultivation in wastewater primarily consisting of carpet mill effluents. Annual worldwide domestic and industrial water consumption between 1987 and 2003 was estimated at 325 billion m³ and 665 billion m³ respectively. Approximately 247 million tons of algal biomass and 37 million tons of oil could be created if 50% of the wastewater from this consumed water was used for algae production. Due to the variation in wastewater composition, strains of microalgae able to grow in varying environments must be found if the technology is to advance. The wastewater from carpet mills is rich in phosphorous and nitrogen, and the researchers therefore wanted to examine how microalgae could grow in the water and remove the contaminants. They additionally wanted to determine how consortium (multi-species) based technology functions for nutrient removal and biodiesel production.

Wastewater consisting primarily of carpet mill effluent was collected from a utility company in Dalton, Georgia. In order to minimize temporal variation effects, wastewater was collected in large batches for all four seasons. Water was also collected from the treatment facility to enable the characterization of treated versus untreated wastewater. The algal taxa present and biovolume present in the samples were identified via standard protocol. The water samples were incubated in growth conditions to induce algal growth. The algae were then isolated by serial dilution and incubated on BG11 agar plates, from which individual colonies were selected and maintained. Thirteen microalgal strains and a consortium of wastewater isolates were identified and screened, and two freshwater and two marine forms and the consortium were selected for the timescale batch study.

Several different experiments were carried out within the study. First, biomass production and nutrient removal of the consortium was examined by growing the consortium in flasks of filtered and sterilized wastewater as a nutrient medium under two different levels of CO_2 (ambient and 6%) and temperature (15 and 25 °C) conditions. Because the researchers also wanted to know the potential of cultivating the consortium in open ponds, the consortium was also cultivated in treated wastewater in four raceway ponds. The algae were harvested, dried, and the lipids were extracted for biomass analysis. Biodiesel was produced from crude microalgae oil via acid transesterification and base transesterification. The biodiesel was then analyzed with gas chromatography. Biomass of the harvested cells was quantified through filtration, and lipid content was measured gravimetrically with an automated extraction system. Additionally, total nitrogen and phosphorous were determined via a persulfate method.

Because Chinnasamy *et al.* sought to examine temporal variation in nutrient concentration in wastewater, biochemical oxygen demand, chemical oxygen demand, total suspended solids, and several other parameters were measured in both treated and untreated water throughout the seasons. It was found that there are sufficient nutrients in both treated and untreated wastewater to support algae growth. About 27 species of green algae, 20 species of cyanobacteria, and eight species of diatoms were found in the treated and untreated wastewater, with green algae and cyanobacteria dominating both water types in all seasons. The observed variations in responses of different species to different environmental conditions led the researchers to believe that parameters aside from nutrient availability are the most important in determining species composition.

Several different species, including the consortium, were grown in treated and untreated wastewater and standard growth medium. Several strains showed significant growth in both wastewater types. Marine forms were able to grow in treated and untreated water without any supplements, indicating themselves as having possibly the highest potential for growth in wastewater for biofuel in the future. The species with the highest growth in the preliminary screening were subjected to a time-scale study in treated and untreated carpet industry wastewater. Overall, the best performer was the consortium grown in treated wastewater, with the potential to generate 4060 L of oil $ha^{-1} year^{-1}$. The researchers also calculated that it could produce ample biofuel (3860 L of oil $ha^{-1} year^{-1}$) when cultivated in untreated wastewater. For the experiment examining consortium growth in different CO_2 and temperature conditions, it was found that microalgae cultivated in 6% CO_2 at 25 °C had the highest biomass productivity. The consortium's performance was enhanced in treated wastewater. After 72 hours of incubation, nitrate and phosphate were almost completely removed from the growth medium, indicating high nutrient removal abilities. Biomass of the consortium algae grown in the raceway ponds was quantified and analyzed. Interestingly, the consortium had a high protein content (54.6%) and low lipid and carbohydrate content. When algal lipid content is lower than 40%, energetic cost of harvest can outweigh energetic added value of lipid recovery. Therefore, direct energy recovery may be necessary in algae with low levels of lipids.

To examine the viability of consortium algae-based biodiesel production, crude algal oil was extracted from the biomass, chemically analyzed, and converted into biodiesel. The crude algal oil had a free fatty acid content of about 50%, a trait not conducive to biodiesel conversion. However, the total acid esterification showed a product yield of about 70.9%, with losses mainly resulting from oil impurities. While the biodiesel produced had a higher linolenic acid content (27.9%) than is normally acceptable (12%), the researchers speculate that the quality of the fuel could be improved by deriving some biomass from other non-food feedstocks.

The results of this study show that algal oil from mixed cultures of native algae is a feasible source of biostock for biodiesel production. It will be necessary to find economical methods of crude oil refinement to minimize product impurities, and this remains a large obstacle. Despite the low lipid content of the consortium in this study, biomass recovery via thermochemical liquefaction could enhance recovery rates and reduce energy expenditure for algae cultures with low lipid content. Therefore, thermochemcial liquefaction should be studied and developed to make wastewater-cultivated consortium microalgae a commercially feasible process of biodiesel production.

Life Cycle Energy and Greenhouse Gas Emissions for an Ethanol Production Process Based on Blue-Green Algae

Microalgae-based biofuel production has become a major focus of renewable energy development. Much of this research has centered on biodiesel created from harvested algae. In this paper, Luo *et al.* (2010) investigated the life cycle energy use and greenhouse emissions for a different method of microalgae-based biofuel production in which ethanol synthesized via intracellular photosynthetic pathways is collected directly from un-harvested cyanobacteria (blue-green algae). This method is advantageous in that it has lower energy costs and water usage than that of harvest-based microalgae biodiesel production. Luo *et al.* used already available information for this process to complete the necessary engineering calculations and determine life cycle impacts. They found that this extraction method has significantly lower (67–87% less) greenhouse gas (GHG) emissions than gasoline, and that the net life cycle energy consumption can be as low as 0.20 MJ/MJ_{EtOH}, indicating that this process has great promise as a biofuel production method that can meet regulatory requirements and decrease environmental impact.

Luo *et al.* completed a life cycle analysis of blue-green algae-based ethanol production by calculating projected energy usage and GHG emissions using approximate parameters. The ethanol-producing blue-green algae are genetically enhanced photoautotrophic cyanobacteria that are cultivated in CO_2 and fertilizer supplemented seawater in closed photobioreactors (PBR). Because the microalgae require CO_2, the PBRs could be located near a fossil-fuel power plant or industrial facility that outputs CO_2. The calculations in this paper are done under this assumption. When mature, the algae produce ethanol that diffuses into the growth culture. Dilute ethanol-freshwater solution is extracted from the growth medium and purified to fuel grade (99.7% pure) through a series of separation processes. One of the primary determinants of energy usage for this process is initial concentration of ethanol, as higher starting concentrations require less energy for purification. The researchers used concentrations between 0.5% and 5% (weight percent) as parameters for their calculations because 0.5% is too dilute to be cost effective and 5% would likely allow for economical recovery. The life cycle analysis additionally accounts for production and disposal of the PBRs, mixing in the bioreactors, biomass disposal, fertilizer production and transportation, ethanol separation (vapor compression steam stripping, vapor compression distillation, and molecular sieve), ethanol transportation, and combustion.

    Because Luo *et al.* did their calculations based on a range of initial ethanol concentrations, they had to apply ethanol separation processes that would be efficient for the entire range. Standard column distillation would be applicable to the upper end of the range, but is inefficient below 5%. Therefore, they used vapor compression steam stripping (VCSS) as the first separation method, which would concentrate the ethanol between 5% and 30%. For the second separation step, they used vapor compression distillation (VCD), which would result in a 94% ethanol concentration. For the final step (99.7% purification), the researchers chose molecular sieve dehydration. They used an equation accounting for mass flow rate and heat of evaporation to calculate energy required for vaporization in a steam-stripping column. Assuming an 80% efficiency rate for heat exchange and a 1% initial concentration, they found that the net heat input would be 0.18 MJ/MJ_{EtOH}. The stripper column requires electrically-powered steam compression, and the researchers estimated the work required for this process through an equation accounting for the gas constant, temperature, pressure, and adiabatic coefficient. For the 1% concentration reference case and 38% efficient electricity production, this value was estimated to be 0.11 MJ/MJ_{EtOH}. For the molecular sieves stage of purification, heat requirement was found to be between 1 and 2 MJ/kg_{EtOH}. The purification process accounts for the highest amount of energy consumption of this entire ethanol production method.

The energy usage of several other processes was additionally estimated. PBRs must be mixed to ensure uniformity of algae and nutrients, and the energy requirement was estimated to be about $0.056MJ/MJ_{EtOH}$ for a 1% initial ethanol concentration. Compressor-mediated oxygen removal was calculated to require $0.0001 MJ/MJ_{EtOH}$. Water must be pumped into the system and sterilized, and 3 mol of water are needed per 1 mol of ethanol. The energy requirements of water pumping and sterilization were therefore estimated. Energy consumed during delivery of CO_2 into the PBRs, fertilizer transportation and production, bioreactor production, and waste biomass disposal were additionally calculated.

Luo *et al.* also performed a GHG emissions life cycle analysis of this ethanol production process. Cellulosic renewable fuels must have less than 40% GHG emissions than petroleum-derived fuels according to the U.S. Energy Independence and Security Act. However, the act allows for funding for those fuels that have less than 20% of the greenhouse emissions of petroleum-derived fuel, making this figure the goal for biofuel development. The researchers considered grid electricity and on-site combined heat and power (CHP) from gas turbines as two possible electricity sources. It was estimated that grid electricity would produce 700 g CO_2e/kWh, which would mean 13.5 CO_2e/MJ_{EtOH} for on-site electricity alone. If on-site heat process heat was provided via natural gas, it would mean an additional 11 g CO_2e/MJ_{EtOH}. The researchers found that CHP could greatly reduce GHG emissions in comparison to grid electricity due to increased energy efficiency. Emissions could be further reduced significantly if solar power were to be used for process heat supply.

The researchers conclude that the 20% goal can be reached through this process if initial ethanol concentrations are sufficiently high. For a grid electricity and natural gas powered system, this value would have to be 4–4.5%. For a natural gas CHP system, the value could be 1.0–1.2%. The figure decreases to 0.8% if solar heating is used at 80% heat exchange efficiency. This manner of ethanol production has many advantages, including the ability to locate facilities on nonagricultural land, and the relatively low energy, fertilizer, and water requirements in comparison to harvest-based microalgae biofuel production. If initial ethanol concentrations can be made reliably high, the life cycle net energy input and GHG emissions are low enough to meet new regulatory standards.

Variables Affecting the In Situ Transesterification of Microalgae Lipids

While microalgae show great potential as a future source of biomass for biofuel production, there still exist several obstacles for commercial production associated largely with the high costs of biomass production and fuel conversion routes. The majority of current research into fuel conversion involves the extraction of lipids from biomass and their subsequent conversion to fatty acid alkyl esters (FAAE) and glycerol. This research has traditionally used alkaline catalysts for the transesterification process, but these are limited because they result in partial saponification when used with oil reactants that have free fatty acid (FFA) content above 0.5% w/w. The use of hydrochloric and sulfuric acid as catalysts has been explored as a low-cost alternative that is not affected by FFA content. Ehimen *et al.* (2010) sought to determine how to maximize the reaction rate by varying conditions, including temperature, reacting alcohol volume, reaction time, and moisture content. They found that fatty acid methyl ester (FAME) conversions rates were positively correlated with volume and temperature, and that equilibrium FAME conversions approached asymptotic reaction time limits of 8 hours for almost all temperatures investigated.

Ehimen *et al.* (2010) researched how certain reaction variables affect biodiesel production from microalgae lipids in an acid-catalyzed in situ transesterification process. While most research into microalgae-based biodiesel production has focused on alkaline catalyzed transesterification, this type of catalyst is not viable for large-scale commercial biodiesel production because it results in saponification when used with oils that have an FFA content above 0.5% w/w. The use of inorganic acids as catalysts for this reaction has been explored, as biodiesel producing transesterification and esterifiction reactions can be catalyzed in this manner. Previous studies have shown that acidic catalysts result in higher fatty acid methyl esters (FAME) yields than alkaline catalysts, and these yields can be optimized under certain reaction conditions.

In order to reduce biodiesel production costs, several alternatives to conventional transesterification reactions have been explored. This study focused on "in situ" transesterification, a process which reduces cost by eliminating the need for the solvent extraction step, as the biomass oil is converted directly to FAAE. This method could be particularly efficient for microalgae-based biodiesel production because the alcoholysis of the oil in the biomass directly increases biodiesel yields when derived from microalgae biomass oil. Because microalgae lipids tend to have a high FFA content, acid catalysts were used in this study, which sought to find optimal reaction conditions for microalgae-based in situ transesterification. The researchers varied reacting alcohol volume, temperature, reaction time, and process mixing, seeking how to create a reaction which would have the lowest process costs and the best biodiesel yield.

Microalgae oil was extracted from dried *Chlorella* biomass via previously established methods. Several analyses were conducted on the oil sample, including specific gravity (SG), gas chromatography, and titration to determine acid value and FFA content. The researchers carried out the in situ transesterification process with a sulphuric acid catalyst at the different alcohol volumes in question. The SGs of the extracted FAME products were measured to determine the extent of conversion during reaction, as a decreasing SG signifies that the reaction has reached equilibrium conversion between microalgae lipids and methyl esters. The extent of conversion was further verified by a GC, and a calibration curve of the relationship between SG and FAME conversion was created.

After setting up the in situ transesterification reaction, several conditions were varied to maximize output. Five different methanol volumes and four different temperatures were tried, and the FAME product yields and SGs were measured as described previously. Additionally, the researchers tested for the effect of reaction time at each temperature, running a total of eight different reaction times at each experimental temperature. The researchers were also interested in how moisture content and stirring affects the in situ transesterification process. They therefore studied the effects of moisture by air drying and oven drying *Chlorella* samples to nine different moisture contents and subjecting these samples to the process at a constant temperature and alcohol volume. They then subjected the in situ transesterification process to four stirring variations at a constant temperature and alcohol volume and analyzed the product yields as previously described.

The *Chlorella* grown under the culture conditions of this study was found to have a total transesterifiable lipid fraction of 0.276 g oil/g biomass. The SG of the extracted oil was measured at 0.914 at 25 °C. Using the GC analysis of the extracted oil and the chemical equation of the reaction ($MM_{oil}=[3MM_{FA} + MM_{glycerol}] -3MM_{water}$), average molecular mass of the oil was calculated to be 880 g/mol. A calibration curve was obtained by correlating concentration of FAME species and SG of purified product. This curve covers a range of 0% conversion (pure extracted oil) to 92.22% conversion (lowest measured SG), and could therefore be used to predict corresponding percentage FAME conversions for the other reactions run in this study. A strong negative correlation between SG and percent FAME conversion was demonstrated by this curve. The acid value of the oil was found to be 10.21 mg KOH/g, and the FFA content was calculated at 5.11%. Because this is a relatively high FFA content, the use of an acidic catalyst for in situ transesterification reactions was justified for this microalgae oil.

The results of the experiments varying temperature and alcohol volume show that increasing both variables generally increases microalgae oil conversion to FAME. However, no significant trends were observed for temperature levels of 60 and 90 °C. For the experiments investigating the interaction of reaction time and temperature, asymptotic FAME conversion values were not reached in the 12 hour time boundary of this study at room temperature. Highest equilibrium conversion levels were reached in the shortest time (70% at 15 min, 90% at 1 hour) for the 90 °C reaction temperature. Similar asymptotic values at reaction times of 2 and 4 hours were found for the 60 and 90°C conditions, and the researchers state that 60 °C may therefore be ideal because process heating and pressure requirements could be inhibited at the higher temperature. The authors were interested in the effect of moisture content on FAME conversion because the drying process represents a significant cost in biodiesel production. However, the results indicate that drying cannot be avoided, as there was a strong negative correlation between moisture content and FAME conversion. The researchers also sought whether stirring could be avoided as a cost-cutting measure. While stirring the reaction for only one hour did produce high equilibrium conversion levels, the yield was still only 91.3% of a continuously stirred system. Intermittent one hour stirring produced results closer to the continuously stirred reaction, but nevertheless fell short, and the investigators therefore concluded that stirring (at least intermittently) is likely a necessary cost of biodiesel production for the in situ transesterification process.

The authors conclude that increasing temperature, reaction time, and alcohol volume may favor biodiesel production for this particular process. However, energetic cost of the recovery of excess alcohol reactants and increases in FAME purification requirements could potentially limit any cost reductions achievable by these variables. Therefore, further optimization of this process, including studying filtration, evaporation, and extraction, should be studied to make in situ transesterification a viable biodiesel production method.

Optimization of Direct Conversion of Wet Algae to Biodiesel under Supercritical Methanol Conditions

Because conventional processes of biodiesel production from microalgae are both energy and cost intensive, researchers are seeking alternative methods that would minimize these costs, enabling large-scale microalgae-based biodiesel production. The method studied by Patil *et al.* (2011) in this paper was the direct conversion of wet algae to biodiesel in supercritical methanol conditions (SCM). Traditional processes require the drying of wet algal biomass, the extraction of the oil with solvents, and the catalyzed conversion of the algal oil to biodiesel. SCM conditions allow for a single-step process that could circumvent these expensive steps, thus greatly lessening biodiesel production costs. The researchers sought in this study to characterize the optimal conditions under which biodiesel could be created in this manner, varying reaction time, temperature, and wet algae to methanol (wt./vol.) ratio. They used response surface methodology (RSM) to analyze the results and found that reactions run at a temperature of 255 °C for 25 minutes with a 1:9 wt./vol. ratio produced the best results, representing a potential economical and efficient method of biodiesel production.

Patil *et al.* (2011) set out to elucidate the optimal conditions for the one-step reaction of biodiesel formation from wet algae with SCM conditions. This process avoids the drying, extraction, and catalyzed conversion processes which represent great costs in traditional biodiesel production. Under SCM conditions, water is used as a co-solvent that accelerates conversion of fats and oils to fatty acid methyl esters (FAMEs) and increases solubility and acidity. The process set forth in this study produces FAMEs from polar phospholipids, free fatty acids (FFAs), and triglycerides by reducing polarity of high energy algal molecules while increasing fluidity and volatility. This allows for a single-step process in which extraction and transesterification of wet algal biomass are carried out simultaneously, requiring modest temperatures and relatively low energy input. This process has been conducted successfully for vegetable oils at about half the cost of conventional transesterification methods, and the researchers in this study sought to both demonstrate that it could be carried out for algal oil and to elucidate optimal reaction conditions.

Patil *et al.* first characterized the algal samples through various chemical analyses. Lipid extraction of the *Nannochloropsis* species resulted in triglyceride content at 37.72%, other non-polar hydrocarbons/isoprenoids at 8.72%, and polars, glycolipids, and phospholipids at 3.54%. The researchers also used thin layer chromatography, densitometry, and scanning electron microscopy to further characterize the algal sample. Additionally, an FTIR spectra showed this particular algal species to be highly aliphatic and to have hydroxyl, carboxyl, and carbonyl groups, all identified by specific absorption bands. The triglyceride biosynthetic pathway in microalgae is thought to consist of the formation of acetyl coenzyme A in the cytoplasm, the elongation and desaturation of fatty acid carbon chain, and the subsequent biosynthesis of triglycerides. Methanol's intermolecular hydrogen bonding is significantly decreased in the supercritical state, reducing its polarity and dielectric constant, and allowing the alcohol to solvate non-polar triglycerides. This results in a single phase lipid/methanol mixture and produces FAMEs and diglycerides that can be transesterified into methyl ester and monoglyceride and eventually glycerol.

The researchers identified the wet algae to methanol (wt./vol.) ratio, reaction temperature, and reaction time as being the most critical variables affecting product FAME content. They utilized RSM to analyze these variables, a statistical analysis involving a three factorial subset that allows for accurate approximation of true error and significance. Wet algae to methanol ratios between 1:4 and 1:12, reaction times between 10 and 30 minutes, and temperatures between 240 and 260 °C were used in a total of 28 experimental runs. Additionally, Patil *et al.* implemented a general second order linear model with a deconstructionist approach to facilitate parametric evaluation for the predicted response surface and a least square method to predict the values of the involved parameters.

For the actual experiment, 4 g samples of wet algae paste were run through non-catalytic SCM in a micro-reactor under a matrix of the previously described reaction conditions at a constant pressure of 1200 psi. The organic contents containing the non-polar lipids were isolated and analyzed by gas chromatography-mass spectroscopy (GC-MS) with methyl heptadecanoate as an internal standard. The FAME content of the final product could then be calculated by comparing the integrals of the FAME peaks with integrals of the standard peak. A general linear model, least squares, and ANOVA were conducted to analyze the effects of the varied reaction parameters.

The regression analysis showed all three parameters to significantly influence FAME content, confirmed by both P-values and the correlation coefficient ($R^2=0.921$). The researchers created graphs showing response contours of FAME yield against temperature and wet algae to methanol ratio at the three time intervals. The regression coefficients show that reaction time positively affects response up to 255 °C, while higher temperatures are not conducive to transesterification reactions, possibly due to decomposition of oil/lipids and alkyl esters. The ratio of wet algae to methanol had a positive effect on yield up to 1:9, but negatively influenced yield at higher ratios. This may be explained by the reversible reaction being shifted forward as a result of increased contact area between methanol and lipids. This parameter can also interact with reaction temperature to reduce FAME yield due to either FAME decomposition or the reduction of the critical temperature of the reactant/product. High reaction times allowed for completion of the transesterification reaction and thus higher FAME yields. This effect was especially notable at the wet algae to methanol ratio of 1:9 at 255 °C. The experimental analysis and RSM study showed maximum yields under the aforementioned conditions with a reaction time of 25 minutes.

The researchers were also interested in the elemental composition of the algal samples. They therefore subjected raw and residual samples to scanning electron microscopy to produce the elemental spectra. These results showed that the algal cell wall structure was disturbed and fragmented under the SCM condition and that the algal biomass was thermally degraded due to high unsaturated fatty acid content.

The algal biodiesel samples were analyzed by GC-MS to quantify the product. The FAME content was calculated by comparing the FAME peak integrals to the internal standard peak integrals. The algal biodiesel was found to have a large proportion of mono and poly unsaturated FAMEs. The ATR-FTIR spectra of the algal biodiesel were compared to the ATR-FTIR spectra of camelina biodiesel and petro-diesel. The main components of diesel are aliphatic hydrocarbons, which were observed by various peaks on all three spectra.

The authors conclude that this single-step biodiesel production process shows great promise in its shorter reaction time, simple product purification, and maximum FAME conversion. It requires lower energy input than conventional methods, and the process can be successfully optimized by RSM, representing the potential for efficient, relatively low-cost biodiesel production.

Enhancement Effect of Ethyl-2-methyl Acetoacetate on Triacyl-glycerols Production by a Freshwater Microalga, *Scenedesmus* sp. LX1

Declining fossil fuel reserves have led to the necessity of developing alternative sustainable fuel sources. One of the most promising possibilities is microalgae, as they are a renewable resource and have relatively high lipid productivity compared to conventional biofuel feedstock sources. A foreseeable obstacle to the advancement of this technology is the high cost of microalgae-based biodiesel production. Xin *et al.* (2010) sought to elucidate whether the antialgal allelochemical ethyl-2-methyl acetoacetate (EMA) could induce high lipid accumulation in microalgal cells, thus making the biodiesel production process more efficient and cost-effective. They conducted the experiment on a microalgae species known to have high lipid content, *Scenedesmus* sp. LX1, and measured the biomass and lipid productivity post-EMA exposure. They found that EMA could increase triacylglycerol (TAG) lipid and TAG productivity content by 79% and 40% respectively in this species, indicating EMA as a possible method of reducing the costs of microalgae biodiesel production.

Xin *et al.* sought to experimentally determine whether the addition of the antialgal allelochemical EMA could induce higher TAG content per lipid and TAG productivity in the microalgae species *Scenesdesmus* sp. LX1. EMA, a compound isolated from the reed *Phragmites communis*, has been found to inhibit the growth of *Chlorella pyrenoidosa* and *Microcystis aeruginosa,* and the researchers therefore believed that, as an environmental stressor, EMA may result in higher lipid content in microalgae. They chose *Scenesdesmus* sp. LX1 as the experimental subject because it had been previously isolated and is known to have high lipid content. The microalgae were grown in different concentrations of EMA culture and the TAG content per lipid and TAG productivity were measured and calculated.

All microalgae cultures were grown in the same light intensity, light/dark periods, humidity, and temperature. The researchers added EMA to the growth medium in four different concentrations (0, 0.25, 0.5, 1.0, and 2.0 mg/L). Densities of the microalgae cultures were determined by measuring optical density (OD_{650}) every 24 hours. These data were then extrapolated to a logistic model to find algal growth. Biomass and total lipid content were also measured. The experimenters then dissolved the dried lipids in isopropyl alcohol, and they estimated TAGs content by an enzymatic colorimetric method. Significant difference analyses were carried out by Independent-Samples t-tests.

Xin *et al.* found that none of the experimental EMA concentrations had a significant effect on microalgae growth. Through linear regression analysis, they also calculated that carrying capacity of culture was not significantly affected by different EMA concentrations. Lipid content per biomass and TAGs content per lipid were measured after 19 days of cultivation. Different EMA concentration did not induce significantly different biomasses (all about 30%). However, it was found that TAG accumulation was significantly higher ($p<0.01$) in microalgae grown in EMA concentrations of 0.5, 1.0, and 2.0 mg/L (34.8%, 78.3%, and 79.1% respectively). Additionally, TAG productivity was significantly greater in the microalgae samples grown in 1.0 and 2.0 mg/L EMA concentrations.

These results are promising because they indicate that microalgae productivity can be enhanced by EMA without hindering growth rate. This could potentially greatly reduce costs of microalgae biodiesel production. The researchers conclude that, while the exact chemical mechanisms need to be further studied, this experiment partially elucidates a possible method of overcoming the cost-barrier of wide-scale microalgae cultivation.

Conclusions

The studies reviewed in this chapter make it clear that microalgae-based biodiesel production is not merely a far-off dream, but a realizable option for reducing greenhouse gas emissions while finding a source of renewable energy. Most recent experiments and investigations have yielded promising results, although almost all researchers emphasize that there are many areas that must still be significantly explored and developed before large scale microalgae cultivation and biofuel production is a reality. Fortunately, what needs to be accomplished in these underdeveloped areas is relatively elucidated, and the current research is both directed and diverse. Given how many options are being explored and showing positive outcomes, it seems clear that much of the promise demonstrated thus far will be fulfilled. While costs must be reduced and yields must be increased, these requirements seem relatively achievable compared to the many challenges associated with ameliorating climate change.

References Cited

Chinnasamy S., Bhatnagar A., Hunt R., Das KC., 2010. Microalgae cultivation in a wastewater dominated by carpet mill effluents for biofuel applications. Bioresource Technology 101, 3097–3105.

Ehimen E., Sun Z., Carrington C., 2010. Variables affecting the in situ transesterification of microalgae lipids. Fuel 89, 677–684.

Kovacevic V., Wesseler J., 2010. Cost-effectiveness analysis of algae energy production in the EU. Energy Policy 38, 5749–5757.

Luo D., Hu Z., Choi D., Thomas V., Realff M., Chance R., 2010. Life cycle energy and greenhouse gas emissions for an ethanol production process based on blue-green algae. Environmental Science Technology 44, 8670–8677.

Mata T., Martins A., Caetano N. 2010. Microalgae for biodiesel production and other applications: a review. Renewable and Sustainable Energy Reviews 14, 217–232.

Patil P., Gude V., Mannarswamy A., Deng S., Cook P., Munson-McGee S., Rhodes I., Lammers P., Nirmalakhandan N., 2011. Optimization of direct conversion of wet algae to biodiesel under supercritical methanol conditions. Bioresource Technology 102, 118–122.

Xin, L., Hong-ying H., Jia Y., Yin-hu W., 2010. Enhancement effect of ethyl-2-methyl acetoacetate on triacylglycerols production by a freshwater microalga, *Scenedesmus* sp. LX1. Bioresource Technology 101, 9819-9821.

Yang J., Xu M., Hu Q., Sommerfeld M., Chen Y., 2011. Life-cycle analysis on biodiesel production from microalgae: water footprint and nutrients balance. Bioresource Technology 102, 159–165.

6. Impacts of Coal Mining

Rosemary Kulp

Coal provides energy for domestic heating and cooking, transportation services, products, raw materials, energy for industrial applications and electricity generation. In the United States, coal has been a stable primary source for power production since colonial times, increasing in use post industrial revolution and expanding into the consuming sectors of America post 1950. In 1950, U.S. coal production was 560 million short tons (MMst). In 2003, U.S. coal production was 1.07 billion short tons, an average annual increase in coal production of 1.2 percent per year. In the United States today, coal demand is driven by the electric power sector, which accounts for 90 percent of consumption, compared to the 19 percent it represented in 1950. In this chapter the most recent health detriments due to coal mining is covered as well as environmental concerns, and potential technology implementations (Bonskowski *et al.* 2006*).*

Human Health Impacts of Mining

Anesetti-Rothermel *et al.* (2010) used geographic information systems to test the hypotheses that age-adjusted county cancer mortality rates were positively associated with distance-weighted population exposure to coal extraction and processing activities, and distance-weighted exposure measures are more strongly correlated to cancer mortality than exposure based on tons of coal mined in the county. Their results supported their hypothesis in that they found a relationship between population proximity to coal mine features and cancers. All three global spatial autocorrelation tests ran resulted in positive spatial autocorrelation. Other variables, like the tonnage exposure measure, race/ethnicity percentages, education, poverty, primary health care access, etc. contributed significant additional variance and for total cancer and three cancer subgroups, the exposure measure was correlated to higher mortality after controlling for smoking rates. The previous exposure measure, based on tonnage, was not related as strongly to cancer mortality.

Approximately 50% of West Virginia's population resides within just 11counties. West Virginia's counties have an average population density of 94.9 persons, and a median of 51.1 persons, per square land mile. Persons who live in coal mining counties of Appalachia, like the counties of West Virginia have elevated all-cause cancer as well as lung cancer mortality, compared to non-mining counties or the nation, even after controlling for socio-economic, health services and behavioral variables.

The higher cancer mortality in the region has been attributed to behavioral risks such as smoking, poor socio-economic conditions and problematic access to medical care. This experiment conducted an exploratory spatial data analysis to determine if there was a spatial relationship between the existing data. In this study a distance-based index describing, per county, the proximity of that county's population to coal mine features was developed and then used in a regression analysis.

The experiment was conducted with the expectation that distance-weighted population exposure is more highly correlated to cancer mortality rates than the previous measure of tons of county-level coal mining. If cancer mortality is not related to exposure to mining activity, and is only a reflection of socio-economic status or behavior, there would be no improvement in the capacity of the exposure measure to account for mortality rates.

Cancer mortality rates were taken from the Centers for Disease Control and Prevention. The rates were age-adjusted using the 2000 US standard population, and were found for West Virginia counties as the rate per 100,000 person-years for 1979–2004. The person-year approach allowed for aggregation across years to estimate cancer mortality in rural, less populated counties that typify most coal mining locations.

The time period, represented by covariates, was sometimes based on the 2000 Census, and sometimes on more recent estimates when available. These covariates include average poverty rate for 2000–2002, high school and college education rates in 2000, supply of primary care physicians per 1,000 population in 2001, and smoking rate in 2003. Geographic data on activities of the coal mining industry included mining permit boundaries for mining sites, the point locations of surface slurry impoundment dams, the point locations of permitted underground injection sites, and the point locations of coal processing facilities. Most of the data compilation and manipulation was performed using ArcView GIS software,versions 9.2 and 9.3

Within each of the study area's census block groups the mean distance was calculated in km from the nearest mine boundary, the impoundment dam, the injection site, and the preparation plant. The inverse distance for each mine infrastructure type for each block group was then calculated. The mean inverse distances were multiplied by the population of the block group. This resulted in a value per block group/infrastructure type where closer distances and bigger populations have larger values, and farther distances and smaller populations have smaller values.

The tonnage measured, rather than the distance weighted measure, was used for the spatial analysis because tonnage measures from border counties outside West Virginia could be included. However, the mapping of mining activities was available only within the state.

Anesetti-Rothermel *et al.* identified two sources of spatial information for coal processing facilities the US environmental Protection Agency and the West Virginia Department of Environmental Protection (WVDEP) data sets. With the data a basic photo alignment of the point was relocated to a more accurate location. Of 76 entities, 46 were realigned.

The last coal mining data set used in the study was slurry injection sites. These are areas where waste water from mining, drilling or processing has been injected into underground areas for the purpose of storage. Injection sites are permitted by the EPA as National Pollution Discharge Elimination System (NPDES) points. The content of the slurry is monitored at the discharge points as part of the NPDES regulatory process. Mining operations often involve the capture of used water in artificial impoundments, held in place by earthen dams, for the purpose of removing contaminants and non-combustibles. Acid mine drainage (AMD) is also held in surface impoundments. These coal impoundment dams are regulated by WVDEP. Further information involving potential health effects of coal slurry and toxic water will be addressed later in the chapter.

Global measure of spatial autocorrelation was used to measure the level and direction (positive or negative) of association for the entire sample used. The resulting test is similar to a correlation coefficient as it varies between -1.0 and $+1.0$. This test of global spatial autocorrelation was computed using GeoDa 0.9.5-i software. The variables of interest, county-level age-adjusted combined cancer mortality rates (1979–2004) and tonnage of coal production per county (1986-2005), were joined to a georeferenced spatial county layer file of West Virginia and its neighboring counties from surrounding states.

All three global spatial autocorrelation tests yielded a value of $P < 0.001$, showing that the data was not spatially random. The correlations between cancer mortality and the total distance-weighted exposure were higher than the corresponding correlations between cancer mortality and the tonnage exposure measure for all cancer sites. Respiratory cancer was found to be correlated to the distance-weighted measure but not to the tonnage measured.

The superior performance of the distance-weighted exposure measure is consistent with the possibility of environmental contamination from the mining industry as a causal factor in the etiology of cancer for populations residing in West Virginia. The strong association between respiratory cancer and mining boundaries, controlling for smoking, may reflect air quality problems around the mines, especially at mountaintops and other surface mining operations.

This experiment was done under the assumption that current mining reflects past mining and based off of the long history of coal mining in the region but there is the possibility of error if there has been significant change in coal mining technology in the area. Another interesting fact is that the population in West Virginia decreased from 1.94 million to 1.79 million before becoming stable from 1990 to 2000 (1.79 to 1.81 million). The population loss to emigration affected coal-mining counties significantly more than non-mining counties: between 1980 and 1990, the average coal mining county lost 5,233 people to migration compared to a loss of 1,175 people for non-mining counties This could make observed mining effects more conservative than they are, because people exposed in mining areas would develop cancer later in another area later on.

Another experiment conducted on the effects of humans to coal residues used DNA assessment to look for potential detrimental health effects of mining. Da Silvia *et al.* (2010) evaluated genotoxic effects in a population exposed to coal residues from the open-cast mine in "El Cerrejón" Columbia using a cytokinesis-blocked micronucleus test and a comet assay. The 200 individuals tested had no known exposure to previous toxins like coal, radiation, chemicals or cigarettes. One hundred of the individuals were workers exposed to and working in four different mining activities and one hundred individuals were non-exposed control individuals were which acted as controls. Blood samples were taken to investigate biomarkers of genotoxicity; specifically, primary DNA damage, tail length, and percent of tail. Both biomarkers showed statistically significantly higher values in the exposed group compared to the non-exposed control group. No difference was observed between the exposed groups executing different mining activities. These results indicate that exposure to coal mining residues may result in an increased genotoxic exposure in coal mining workers. The study did not find a correlation between age, alcohol consumption and service time with the biomarkers of genotoxicity.

Coal is one of the most abundant minerals in nature and is one of the largest fossil fuel sources of energy. Colombia, a country in South America, has large natural coal reserves and "El Cerrejón" located in northern Guajira, is the world's largest open-cast mine. Coal residues consist of a mixture of substances, containing carbon, hydrogen, nitrogen, oxygen and sulfur. Some basic parameters of coal from "El Cerrejón" are: total moisture (~10%), volatiles (~30%), ash (~8%), sulfur (~1%), carbon (~70%), hydrogen (~6%), oxygen (~5%), and nitrogen (~1%). The main operations carried out in " El Cerrejón " are extraction of coal, and mincing coal for transportation. During coal extraction large quantities of particles of coal dust are emitted and when it is exposed to oxygen and sunlight a spontaneous combustion can occur sending large clouds of polycyclic aromatic hydrocarbons (PAHs) into the environment.

Chronic inhalation of complex mixtures, containing substances such as heavy metals, ash, iron, PAHs and sulfur, can result in lung disorders including pneumoconiosis, progressive massive fibrosis, bronchitis, loss of lung function, emphysema. In addition to direct cellular damage, compounds like PAHs have mutagenic properties that have been associated with an increased risk for cancer development. However, coal dust still remains classified as a non carcinogen for humans according to the International Agency for Research on Cancer.

The primary target cells of inhaled coal dust particles are macrophages and epithelial cells. Activated macrophages (phagocytosis toxicity) produce excessive amounts of reactive oxygen species (ROS) and cytokines. Epithelial cells and fibroblasts which are the main producers of components of the extracellular matrix including collagens, proteoglycans and elastic fibres, are also known to produce cytokines and ROS upon stimulation. Additional phagocytotic cell may be recruited by chemokines produced by the alveolar macrophages as well as epithelial cells, and may amplify local production of ROS and cytokines. Both ROS and cytokines may cause damage or proliferation of local epithelial and mesenchymal tissue and may as such have consequences to lung tissue morphology, and cell turnover. When there is excessive production of ROS, or when there are insufficient defense mechanisms, oxidative stress may result in DNA damage, lipid peroxidation, protein modification, membrane disruption, and mitochondrial damage, all of which capable of affecting cytogenetic damage levels.

These types of DNA damages are usually induced by most of the genotoxic agents which induce DNA breaks at the phosphodiester skeleton or between bases and sugars resulting in abasic sites identifiable under microscopic inspection.

Coal dust has been evaluated in real world field tests in wild rodents in coal mining areas in Brazil and in Colombia however this is the first field test on human exposure to coal ash in Columbia thus far. The exposed group was divided into four groups: Extracted coal transport (n=50) in which the workers are involved in coal transport up to the arrival in the storing centers; equipment field maintenance (n=18) the drivers that spread water on the roads where large quantities of coal dust are generated, coal stripping (n=17) where workers accumulate the coal material after it's been stripped for transportation (and put out the fires caused by coal spontaneous combustion), and coal embarking (n=15) where the workers ship coal in containers to be exported to other countries.

All the individuals included in the study were non-smokers. The exposed group was composed of volunteers between the ages of 24 and 60, medically evaluated and deemed healthy for at least five years at the time of the assessment, with no previous recorded of prescriptions that are known or suspected to have mutagenetic properties. Peripheral blood samples from all 200 individuals were collected by venipuncture with 20 mL of blood being drawn. Thirty micro-liters of isolated lymphocytes were mixed with 270 μL 0.5% of LMA-Invitrogen at 37 °C. This mixture was placed into a slide previously coated with 1.5% of agarose(NMA-Cambrex Bioscience Rockland) and processed at 60 °C. The slides were immersed overnight in lysis solution (2.5 M NaCl, 100 mM EDTA and 10 mM Tris, pH 10.0–10.5, 1% with freshly added 1% Triton X-100 and 10% DMSO) at 4 °C in the dark. Afterwards, the slides were placed for 30 minutes in an alkaline buffer at 4 °C (300 mM NaOH and 1 mM EDTA, pHN13) in order to unwind the DNA. The alkaline electrophoresis was carried out for 30 min at 25 V and 300 mA. This standard alkaline procedure allows single-strand DNA breaks to be detected and lesions are converted to strand breaks under these conditions as well. The gels were neutralized with 0.4 M Tris (pH 7.5) with 3 washes of 5 min each. Finally, the slides were stained with 50 μL ethidium bromide (2 μL/mL) and examined at 40× magnification under a fluorescence microscope.

For each individual 50 cells from each of two replicate slides were analyzed. The cells were classified according to tail size into five classes ranging from undamaged (0) to maximally damaged (4). The damage index (DI) calculation was carried out according to a pre-existing visual classification system. The values for the damage index could range from 0 (100 cells all at class 0) up to 400 (100 cells all at class 4).

The second test, the MN test using the cytokinesis-block technique was chosen because it allows reliable data scoring because only the MN of those cells that have completed one nuclear division are analyzed. Cultures were prepared with whole blood in duplicate. Cultures were incubated at 37 °C in the dark for 46 hours, under 5% CO_2 in a humidified atmosphere. Two parallel cultures were then set in tubes for each sample. The cells were harvested after 72 hours before being treated with a hypotonic solution (0.075 M KCl) and were immediately centrifuged and fixed three times with methanol/acetic acid. The fixed cells were then dropped onto humidified slides and MN registration was performed on coded slides in a double blind test.

The mean values of both biomarkers parameters in the exposed group demonstrated significant differences when compared to the values of the non-exposed control group ($p > 0.001$) using the non-parametric Mann Whitney U-test. The Spearman correlation coefficients for MN frequency with age, and DNA damage (tail length, % of tail DNA, DI) for non-exposed control and exposed groups were not significant ($p>0.05$). The correlations between MN frequency with time of service, and DNA damage with respect to tail length, % of tail DNA and DI, for the subdivided exposed groups, were not significant ($p>0.05$). The effect of alcohol consumption on MN frequencies and DNA damage in all groups using

Mann Whitney U-test and was not found to be statistically significant in any of the groups (p>0.05). There was also no statistically significant difference between the DNA damage between the four different coal mining activities (pN0.05) using a t-test.

The results obtained in Micronucleus frequency show that the values in the exposed to coal mining residuals group (8.6±4.8) are higher compared with the non-exposed control group (2.9±4.0). This clearly demonstrates higher levels of DNA damage in the exposed group (mean tail length=23.4±6.5; mean% of tail DNA=13.1±7.9; mean DI=60.0±39.5) compared to the nonexposed control group (mean tail length=14.3±2.5; mean% of tail DNA=2.9±1.5; mean DI=9.0±6.4). These differences were all statistically significant in the evaluation using a Mann Whitney U-test (p<0.001). This showl that I nthis test the exposure to heavy metal alloids ash and PAH's are detrimental on a DNA level to human health. The effects of poly aromatic hydrocarbons on human health is an interesting topic, especially as it effects in-utero development of children and childbirth.

Chen *et al.* (2010) examined the potential impact of PAH exposure on in-utero fetal death during early pregnancy, specifically missed abortions. Missed abortion refers to an intrauterine pregnancy in which the fetus does not develop normally over a prolonged period of time (typically 6 weeks) or the fetus is already known to have died but the products of conception remain in-utero. Missed abortion is a complication of early pregnancy that occurs in up to 15% of all clinically recognized pregnancies. The scientists conducted a case–control study examining the influence of maternal exposure to polycyclic aromatic hydrocarbons (PAHs), specifically BaP, a five-ring PAH whose metabolites are mutagenic and highly carcinogenic, on missed vs. induced abortions in Tianjin, an industrial city in northern China. Maternal blood, but not aborted tissues, tested showed BaP-DNA adduct levels were strongly associated with the risk of missed abortions. The BaP-DNA adduct levels in maternal blood were found to be significantly and positively associated with environmental exposure, including proximity of the residence to the nearest roadway, commuting by walking, traffic congestion near the residence, and daily average time outdoors. BaP-DNA adduct levels were found to be negatively associated with the consumption of grilled, smoked, or barbecued foods.

Human exposure to PAHs occurs largely through inhalation and diet. PAHs adversely impact birth outcomes and cognitive development in early childhood; including decreased head circumferences, birth length, and birth weight. In animal studies transplacental exposure to benzo[a]pyrene (BaP), a specific type of PAH, has been associated with an increase in xenobiotic (a chemical found in an organism but not normally produced or expected to be present in it, or a substances present in much higher concentrations than usual) metabolism in the placental tissues, fetal loss and a decrease in plasma hormone levels of progesterone; a steroid hormone involved in the female menstrual cycle, which supports gestation and embryogenesis of humans and other species. BaP has also been found to negatively affect estrogen levels and prolactin peptides; which control lactation during breast-feeding. It is hypothesized that fetuses may be particularly sensitive to the impact of toxic PAHs during early pregnancy (e.g. the 1st trimester) because of the rapid development of fetal organs and the higher exposure per body weight of the fetus.

The biologic mechanisms through which parental exposures to PAHs might affect early pregnancy loss are not well understood but may involve the induction of apoptosis (the process of programmed cell death that can occur in multicellular organisms) after DNA damage from PAHs, antiestrogenic effects of PAHs, and binding to the human aryl hydrocarbon hydroxylase to induce P450 enzymes or to receptors for placental growth factors, altering trophoblast (cells forming the outer layer of a blastocyst, which provide nutrients to the embryo and develop into a large part of the placenta. They are formed during the first stage of pregnancy and are the first cells to differentiate from the fertilized egg proliferation as well as its endocrine function and decreasing exchange of oxygen and nutrients between the fetus and the mother. The endocrine system is a system of glands, each of which secretes a type of hormone into the bloodstream to regulate the body's homeostasis.

This study was conducted in Tianjin, the second largest city in northern coastal China. It is an important industrial center and contains a developed sea-land-air transportation network. As one of the fastest growing areas in coastal China, the PAH's levels are considered much higher than in rural areas. This study was conducted during a relatively warm period (April– November), reducing the potential for high PAH exposures from coal combustion during home heating. Data from the Tianjin Environmental Protection Agency showed BaP concentrations to be as high as 14.5 ng/m3 in January compared to only 1.3 ng/m3 in July of 2006.

All study participants were screened to exclude smokers, women with chronic diseases (e.g. hypertension, heart disease, and diabetes), pregnancy complications, women with potentially high occupational exposures to PAH's like bus or taxi drivers, traffic police officers, coal plant workers, coke oven workers, cooks, etc, and those who had resided in the city for less than a year. After scrrening, aproximatly 80 control subjects and 90 test cases were used. Cases with missed abortions and controls seeking induced abortion services were gathered and recorded from four hospitals, including the Main Hospital of Tianjin Medical University, the 2nd Hospital of Tianjin Medical University, the Hospital of Chinese People's Armed Police Forces, and Dongli Hospital. All four hospitals allowed the collection of aborted tissues, but only two of the hospitals gave permission for maternal blood drawings. Thus, maternal blood samples were collected for only a subset of the matched case–control pairs. However the other two hospitals were within a close distance (6 km) of the other two hospitals, and so were not adjusted for in the calculations.

Test cases were pregnant women carrying an in-utero fetus that was confirmed dead by ultrasound measurements before 14 weeks of gestation. Control cases were women with normal pregnancies who requested an induction of an abortion due to an unplanned and unwanted pregnancy. BaP levels were measured via biomarker in maternal blood and aborted tissues.

One hour after the abortion procedure the aborted tissues and maternal blood were collected and a standardized twenty minute interview was administered by trained personnel to the recipient of the procedure. During the interview the demographics and socioeconomic information was collected, as well as the reproductive history (e.g. previous abortion history, and number of previous birth to a fetus with a gestational age of 24 weeks or more); and any factors that may have lead to increased exposure to PAHs during pregnancy, such as time spent outdoors and intransit (commuting), proximity to nearby industrial facilities, traffic activities near residence, cooking activities and fuels used, dietary PAH exposure via grilled, smoked, or barbecued foods, exposure to environmental tobacco smoke, etc.

Two ml of maternal blood were drawn from consenting women by syringe. The aborted tissue was analyzed in total because it is difficult to separate the villous (gastrointestinal polyps) from the embryo early in pregnancy, so all samples contained both embryo and villous materials together. Two different purification kits were used for the aborted tissue and the maternal blood in order to determine the levels of BaP in the aborted tissue and maternal blood. BaP-DNA adducts (the places where BaP is taken up into the neurons) in extracted DNA were analyzed using the high-performance liquid chromatography-fluorescence method, a technique that can separate a mixture of compounds out so that certain compounds can be analyzed for concentration. This specific test detects benzo[a] pyrene diol-epoxide (BPDE) tetrols (a type of PAH) in the DNA adducts and from these concentrations BaP-DNA adduct levels were calculated by dividing the BPDE concentrations by the total DNA concentrations.

A set of multivariate conditional logistic regression models was used to examine the influence of the PAH adduct levels in maternal blood and aborted tissue on the risk of missed abortions. BaP-DNA adduct levels were modeled as a continuous exposure, and compared to subjects with higher adduct levels and those with lower adduct levels using the median adduct level in the control group as the cut point.

Approximately ninety percent (90.1%) of the study participants were between 20 and 35 years of age. Missed abortion subjects were less educated, reported lower monthly household income, and were somewhat younger than the control subjects seeking induced abortions. After controlling for maternal education and household income, maternal blood BaP-DNA level (per adduct/108 nucleotides) increased the risk of having experienced a missed abortion, and when the number of BaP-DNA adducts was categorized according to the median in the control group, the risk of a missed abortion was more than four times higher for those exposed above the fifty percent marker.

BaP-DNA adducts in maternal blood correlated poorly and slightly negatively with the levels measured in aborted tissues (overall r=–0.12, n=102; cases r=–0.02, n=51; controls r=–0.21, n=51). BaP-DNA adduct levels in maternal blood were significantly higher in the case group. The mean number of BaP-DNA adducts in the aborted tissues was somewhat lower in the case (4.8 adducts/108 nucleotides) than in the control group (6.0 adducts/108 nucleotides), however, this difference was not statistically significant (p=0.29). Missed abortions were not associated with the BaP-DNA adducts in aborted tissues regardless of whetherthe adduct levels were treated as a continuous variable or not.

There was an observed risk of increase for missed abortion in women who reported commuting by walking (adjusted OR=3.52; 95% CI, 1.44–8.57), traffic congestion near their residence (adjusted OR=3.07; 95% CI, 1.31–7.16), living near an industrial site (adjusted OR=3.21; 95% CI, 0.98– 10.48), and frequent cooking activities during pregnancy (adjusted OR=3.78; 95% CI, 1.11–12.87). Living close to a roadway and spending more time outdoors was also positively associated with missed abortion. Surprisingly, reporting the consumption of grilled, smoked, or barbecued foods seemed to decrease the risk of missed abortion even after adjustmant for socioeconomic factors (OR=0.22; 95% CI, 0.06–0.86). However, these foods were mostly consumed by women who reported cooking never, or occasionally, rather than routinely.

The lack of an association between missed abortion and PAH adduct levels in aborted tissue, as well as the absence of any correlation between maternal blood and aborted tissues DNA adduct levels in both cases and controls could be due to the more active and complex metabolism taking place in the rapidly developing placental and fetal cells of early pregnancy compared to the fully differentiated lymphocytes of the mother.

Other scientists have proposed that the placenta might act as a protective barrier against some genotoxic components between the circulation of mother and child. PAH-DNA adduct levels in placental tissues have been found to be influenced by the activity of the enzymes cytochrome P450-1A1 and glutathione Stransferases. The overall average BaP-DNA adduct levels (including cases and controls) were about 26% higher in the aborted tissue than in maternal blood. The higher levels measured in aborted tissues in comparison to the maternal blood in this study might be due to the aborted tissues having been collected early in pregnancy when the fetal/villous tissues exhibit a very high metabolism rate in order to form a fully functional placenta.

This study shows that it cannot be assumed that PAH exposures preferentially effect missed abortions. It is even conceivable that the highest exposures lead to earlier spontaneous abortions that may or may not be clinically recognized by women.

The consumption of grilled, smoked, or barbecued foods seemed to decrease the risk of missed abortions while cooking frequently at home increased risk. However, intake of possibly high PAH food items was found to be associated with a low frequency of cooking at home, i.e. the less a woman reported cooking at home the more she may have eaten outside the home; and while this Chinese population seldom cooks, grills, smokes, or barbecues food at home, such foods are easily available from vendors outside the home. While missed abortions were associated with frequent cooking activities, statistically significant correlation were not found between cooking frequency and maternal blood PAH-DNA adduct levels.

In addition to an increased likelyhood of missed abortions, correlations between open coal mining areas and low birth weight in West Virginia, USA. Ahem *et al.* (2010) conducted a cross-sectional analysis to determine if there was significant presence of low birth weight in mothers living near coal mining areas in West Virginia. After adjusting the findings so that mothers who reported smoking or drinking were accounted for, they found that areas with high levels of coal mining elevated the odds of a low-birth-weight infant by 16- 14% (with the lower percentage adjusted for mothers who drank) in areas with lower mining levels, relative to counties with no coal mining.

Coal mining releases toxic chemicals including arsenic, mercury, lead, cadmium, selenium, nickel, and copper into local environments, and the processing of coal involves the use of other toxic chemicals like acryamilides, complex polymers used to separate the coal from the sludge. These compounds are called "trade secrets" by many coal companies and given nicknames like "Comax 1000". This is in addition to the diesel fueled equipment that moves and processes coal. Materials rejected by a cleaning plant tend to be enriched in iron sulfides which oxidize into sulfates, causing the acidification of water that comes into contact with refuse piles. Contaminated water is held in impoundment ponds, or injected underground so as to not accidently become a potable water source.

In West Virginia, mountaintop removal mining has become an increasingly dominant form of coal mining. This form relies on surface explosives and removal of up to 1,000 feet of rock and soil above the coal. While this is an easier and less cost intensive method of reaching coal beds compared to underground mining methods which tunnel into mountains via the sides, levels of airborne particulates are higher in surface mining vs. underground mining operations and result in community level exposure. This is an important point because recent studies have documented significant transplacental transfer of contaminants, including polycyclic aromatic hydrocarbons (PAHs) and environmental tobacco. In addition, the fetus may be vulnerable to pollution stored inside the mother's body; further research on it will be covered later in this chapter.

Birth data were obtained from the West Virginia Birthscore Dataset, 2005–2007 (n = 42,770) while data on coal mining were taken from the Department of Energy, Energy Information Administration (EIA). Covariates regarding mothers' demographics, behaviors, and insurance coverage were included. Mothers who were older, unmarried, less educated, smoked, did not receive prenatal care, were on Medicaid, and had recorded medical risks had a greater risk of low birth weight were not included in the study, reducing the data set from about 45,000 to 42,770.

Birth weight was converted to a yes/no score based on whether birth weight was less than 2,500 g. The independent variables were counties with zero, moderate, or high levels of coal mining. Counties with coal mining were divided into levels of coal tonnage, and the mother's age was converted into younger than 18, 18–39, and 40 and older. Number of previous pregnancies was recorded, including live births, abortions and stillbirths for mothers residing in mining areas.

The results showed a significant association between receiving late prenatal care and elevated risks for low birth weight outcomes. Mothers in mining areas were also found to be at a significantly higher risk of low birth weight before controlling for covariates. Further, there is evidence of a dose response effect, meaning that there was a higher odds ratio of low birth weight in areas of higher levels of mining compared to areas of moderate mining levels. The risk of low birth weight was found to be related to previously established factors as expected.

Before adjustment, living in a high coal mining area increased the odds of a low birth- weight infant by 19%; after adjustment, the odds were still elevated by 16%. For areas with lower mining levels, the odds of a low-birth-weight infant were increased by 13% before adjustment and 14% after adjustment.

Future research needs to refine categories of medical risks to understand the contribution of each of these risks on low birth weight outcomes. In addition, the level of coal mining served as an environmental proxy for air and water contamination, because no direct environmental data related to levels of air particulates or types of water contamination were available. Recent studies have examined the impact of polycyclic aromatic hydrocarbons (PAH's) and fine particles on pregnancy outcomes, finding support for the idea that adverse pregnancy outcome is the result of maternal exposures to airborne particulates themselves, vs. the impact of co-pollutants carried by the particles.

Environmental Effects and Human Health Impact

In the period since 1973, four distinct trends dominated U.S. coal mining technology. First, the popularity of long wall mining, second the increased technology of mining tools (better tools adapted for specific work environs, and longer durability). Third, overall growth in surface coal mining at the expense of underground coal mining and fourth, the accelerated application of surface mining technology in large-scale area mines in the western region in states such as Wyoming, Montana, North Dakota, Texas, Arizona etc. Surface mining is the removal of the top layer of soil and rock in order to expose the coal seam beneath. An example of this method would be mountain top removal or MTR an adaptation of area mining to mountainous terrain. Often on massive scales, MTR removes all successive upper layers of rock and broad perimeters of lower rock layers. It recovers about 85 percent of all upper coal beds contained within the rock layers and large portions of the lower beds. MTR operations may affect the top 250 to 600 feet of Appalachian peaks and ridges; they have recovered coal from as many as 18 coal beds. MTR mining creates huge quantities of excavated overburden that are disposed of as fill in upper portions of adjacent valleys. This mining method is highly controversial environmentally and the contamination of water supplies has been suspected due to coal mining activities like these. Another potential negative side effect of coal mining is coal fires. (Bonskowski, R *et al. 2006*)

A coal seam fire is the underground smoldering of a coal deposit. They are caused by spontaneous combustion or by lightning strikes, grass fires, or forest fires and continue to smolder underground after surface fires have been extinguished, sometimes for many years, before flaring up and restarting forest and brush fires nearby. They propagate in a creeping fashion along mine shafts and cracks in geologic structures. They are problematic in that they release toxic fumes into the atmosphere, reignite grass, brush, or forest fires, and cause the subsidence of surface infrastructure such as roads, pipelines, electric lines, bridge supports, buildings and homes. Coal seam fires continue to burn for decades or even centuries until either the fuel source is exhausted or an underground water table is encountered. Global coal fire emissions are estimated to release 40 tons of mercury into the atmosphere annually, and three percent of the world's annual CO_2 emissions. Subsidence is the motion of a surface (usually, the Earth's surface) as it shifts downward relative to a datum such as sea-level

Uncontrolled coal fires have been reported in many coal-bearing countries such as the United States, Indonesia, China, India, Australia and South Africa. China is the world's largest producer of coal, mining 2000 million metric tons (Mt) of raw coal per year. In China it is estimated that around 10–200 Mt of coal reserves are consumed annually by coal fires or made inaccessible by fires that hinder mining operations. Few studies have focused on the land subsidence accompanying uncontrolled coal fires. This is due in part to the dangerous or remote environment of the regions containing coal fires, which are difficult to access. This prevents ground based examinations like GPS surveys on large scales.

Recent improvements in SAR interferometry have led to new approaches based on the use of a large dataset of SAR images over the same area to overcome limitations of conventional geodesy. The study was conducted in the Wuda coalfield (also named the Wuda syncline), located in the south-central part of the Inner Mongolia Autonomous Region, North China.

The average annual potential evaporation vs. the annual average precipitation indicates very dry climatic conditions. The Wuda coalfield is composed of platform deposits of Upper Carboniferous and Lower Permian Taiyuan and Shanxi Formation, and consists of five coal layers inter-bedded in a sequence of alternating sandstone, limestone and mudstone layers

As in other coalfields worldwide, Wuda's coal fire ignition is mostly attributable to spontaneous combustion and mining-related activities. Due to regular and intensive coal extractions with mechanized longwall methods over the past decades, underground coal mining is still one of predominant deformation factors in Wuda, especially in abandoned coal mine areas. Additionally, significant changes in the topography are potentially due to the dumping of massive overburden waste materials near the mining areas that is a fairly common practice when coal mining. This could be the cause of the negative radar range changes (positive displacements) due to inaccurate compensation of the topographic phase. Other sources of ground deformations in the area are possibly natural geological phenomena such as active neotectonic movements. Currently, small scale private mining in the Wuda coalfield, which is characterized by low levels of mechanization and poor safety standards, has posed the greatest threat concerning the expansion of existing coal fires and the development of new ones. Before 1989 most coal fires in Wuda were isolated and scattered in different places. Subsequently these isolated fires gradually connected into coal fire zones (herein after referred to as CFZs) and have developed to be the largest coal fire region in China.

In the Wuda coalfield, uncontrolled coal fires, particularly subsurface or underground coal seam burning, have resulted in widespread land subsidence due to both the changing volume of the burning coal and the thermal effects in the adjacent rock mass. The land subsidence can cause significant surface cracks and fissures which promotes further subsurface coal burning by providing ventilation paths through which oxygen and water can circulate to support combustion, and hence in turn aggravate the coal burning process and land subsidence.

In this study, the 3D displacement velocities from the GPS measurements that were collected in 2006 and 2008 were then projected into the Line of Sight

(LOS) direction so as to compare corresponding InSAR measurements. A PSI method referred to as Interferometric Point Target Analysis (IPTA) was then used to show the temporal and spatial characteristics of interferometric signals collected from point-likely targets or so-called Persistent Scatterers. This allows a precise estimation of the different phase contributions in terms of deformation, atmospheric, topographic and orbital phases of the area being studied.

The most basic procedure is to use the sums or averages of multiple interferograms, in order to obtain single interferograms. This operates under the assumption that the signal (displacement) in the interferograms has a systematic pattern. So, whereas the atmospheric noise is random for independent interferograms, it is possible to limit the influence of the noise by stacking, or increasing the samples of SAR observations. Basically, the addition of N interferograms with equal duration has a signal that is N times larger than a single interferograms, but the atmospheric noise is only $N^{1/5}$ times larger. If reasonable coherence levels can be guaranteed in the interferograms that are characterized by short time periods and small perpendicular baselines, several temporally-contiguous interferograms can be stacked (subject to data availability) to generate a pseudo–interferogram interpreted in the case of rapid displacement even over a longer period, where no single coherent interferograms exists. The final results obtained by interferometric point analysis consist of height corrections, linear deformation rates, atmospheric phase, refined baselines, phase quality information (temporal coherence) and nonlinear deformation histories for each PT point.

A two dimensional linear regression analysis of the differential interferometric phase was performed on the selected 49 multi-master interferograms. Then, the initial list of persistent scatters points was determined based on the low temporal variability of the backscatter derived from co-registered SLC intensity stacks, and the the spectral properties of each individual SLC data. The negative sign of the deformation rate stands for an increasing distance with time away from the satellite (e.g. subsidence), whereas the positive sign a decreasing distance with time such as lateral movement or uplift.

Primary focus was given to the land subsidence over the CFZ18 area situated in the central of Wuda syncline, which is mostly covered by exposed sandstones and rocks with long, wide surface fissures. The Persistant Scatters averaged displacement velocity maps showed a relatively stable pattern (–5 to 5 mm/yr) in areas near the urban center of Wuda city; in contrast, land subsidence signals are mainly revealed within the Wuda syncline, with a maximum subsidence rate of approximately 40 mm/yr.

In spite of temporal decorrelation resulting in low PS density, the PSI-derived results can highlight three subsidence regions in the coalfields of Shuhaitu, Huangbeici and Wufushan. Field inspections show that they relate to mining activities and surface coal burning, particularly in the abandoned mining areas. Even though the low density of PS points could not permit the restoring of the full shape of secondary bowls in the coal burning center, the resulting displacement velocity map revealed the shape and spatial extent of the subsidence areas within the CFZ18. This land subsidence is evidenced by the displacement history of the PS points near the center of coal seam burning

A clear correlation is shown between the displacement velocities of PS points and their corresponding GPS measurements that were extracted from the 2-D velocity filed. However, in Fig. 7 there is an underestimate in the PSI measurements especially in case of existing high displacement rates typically less than –30 mm/yr. This is probably due to loss information on the PS points undergoing higher displacements. The absolute differences between them were calculated, varying from 0 to 11.3 mm/yr with the average of 5.4 mm/yr and the standard deviation of 4.1 mm/yr.

The results show evident subsidence signals within the coal fire Zones 5, 7, 12 and 13, with mean deformation rate of –20.1 mm/yr, –16.7 mm/yr, –20.6mm/yr and –18.7 mm/yr, respectively. The subsidence patterns observed in the four coal fire zones are evidenced during the in-situ inspections in 2008. Fig. 9 shows that the DInSAR results derived from the three small-baseline interferometric pairs show an accelerated progress of surface deformation from 2003, 2006 to 2008 within the Wuda coalfields. This is exemplified in Fig 10, over the CFZ18area. A correlation between surface subsidence and coal seam burning was evidenced again, by overlaying the coal fire distributions that were mapped in field works in the same years as SAR acquisitions on the three displacement velocity maps.

The PSI method allowed for the retrieval of displacement time series for each PS points over the period of SAR data acquisition and its measurements are more precise than those of stacking DInSAR. However, it is still limited in the areas where a low density of PS points were detected due to large deformation gradient or low coherence, e.g. southern part of the syncline in the Wufushan mining area. Even though it is less precise compared to the PSI method, stacking DInSAR and 2-pass DInSAR that are based on selected interferometric pairs could provide an effective assessment of the magnitude and the spatial extent of land subsidence related to coal fires in Wuda, even in the coal fire zones with relatively rapid deformation.

The resulting InSAR measurements are more sensitive to vertical motion than other components of deformation vectors that are perpendicular to the LOS direction (e.g. horizontal movement) because of the small incidence angle of ENVAISAT ASAR data used in this study. This potentially limits an understanding of ground displacement behaviors related to coal fires. However, this can be accounted for by using a multiple-pass InSAR to derive 3D deformation maps. These maps merge more InSAR data sets at the same location with different orbit directions (ascending and descending) and/or with different look angles.

New technology has also been developed in the past few years, this has resulted in simulation methods are based on a number of geological and mining parameters, typically such as seam thickness, depth of mining, gradient of seam and direction of seam, and have the potential for modeling the magnitude, extent and dynamics of surface subsidence due to underground mining. These new developments will further the knowledge of coal fire behaviors.

Clean Coal Technology

Because China is the Global leader in Coal production, it is the ideal country to study for potential technological development and utilization. Chen and Xu *(2010)* describe coal's role in China's energy system, evaluate current clean coal technologies being implemented, and describe increases and decreases in SO_2 NO_x and CO_2 emissions from the early 90's to 2007. The technologies include flue gas desulphurization technologies and implementation of large scale total energy systems in coal plants to maximize energy output while minimizing carbon emissions. Clean coal technologies currently being developed in China include high efficiency combustion and advanced power generation technologies, coal transformation technologies, integrated gasification combined cycle, and carbon capture and storage.

In China, there are 1,018 billion tons of proven coal resources available and close to 4,500 billion tons in reserves predicted. From 1991 to 2005, the share of energy consumption in both the agriculture and commercial sectors remained around 5%, the industrial sector increased from 67% to 70%, the transportation sector increased from 5% to 10%, while residential use dropped from 18% to 10%. The district heating rate is expected to increase from 30% in 2005 to 40% by 2010 with 40GW of new cogeneration plants for space heating. Cogeneration plants use electric generators that recycle their waste heat to generate steam that powers auxiliary turbines which provide additional power; these systems are also known as total energy systems. Total energy plants are predicted to incorporate an annual coal savings of 25 Mega tonnage coal equivalence (Mtce). China's per capita carbon emissions increased by 4.03% per year from 1980 to 2005, reaching 1.05 tC per capita in 2005. Driven mainly by population expansion, economic growth, urbanization and a booming transportation sector, China's future carbon emissions will continue to increase.

Total coal usage in China for electricity was 76.6% in 2007 with production of 1804 Mtce in China's coal production in 2005, ranking it number one in the world with 38.4% of the world's total coal usage. China's total installed power capacity increased from 66GW in 1980 to 319GW in 2000. It has then more than doubled from 2000 to 2007 with 56.3GW new capacity added annually on average, resulting in a total of 713GW in 2007. Since 1990, the percentage of thermal power from coal has remained at about 75% of the total while the percentage of electricity generated from coal has remained at 80–83%. Coal-fired power plants accounted for over 97% in the total thermal power capacity.

Forty-seven percent of China's energy comes from domestic oil consumption, with the oil mainly coming from the Middle East. The oil demand is expected to increase considerably due to significant growth of the energy consumption in the transportation sector, with significant growth of highway transport and dramatic growth of car usage. Coal is the source of about 70% of the CO_2 emitted from China annually. With structural adjustments in the economy, industry and industrial products, as well as energy efficiency improvements and changes to low-and non-carbon energy sources. Thermal power generation efficiency has increased significantly in the last two decades with the energy consumption per kWh decreasing from 448 gce/kWh in 1980, to 427 gce/kWh in 1990 and further to 377 gce/kWh in 2005. The main contribution to the decrease is the government's policy to develop supercritical (SC) or ultra supercritical (USC) units with unit capacities over 600MW, and large combined cycle units, to develop cogeneration power plants, to retrofit medium-sized stations with capacities ranging from 100 to 300MW per unit, and to gradually close small stations with capacities less than 100MW. The share of thermal power plants with unit capacities above 300MW will increase from 45.5% in 2005 to over 60% in 2010. The increase in energy demand has led to complications with environmental policy regulations, and has negatively impacted the surrounding environment.

Acid rain effects have extended from the Southwest to south of the Yangtse River to form four major acid rain control areas, accounting for 30–40% of the national area. Coal is responsible for 90% of the SO_2 emissions, 70% of the dust emissions, 67% of the NO_x emissions, and 70% of the CO_2 emissions China's total SO_2 emissions increased from 14 million tons in 1981to 25.49 million tons in 2005, though soot emissions decreased from 14.5 million tons to 11.82 million tons. Soot emissions from the power sector of China have been effectively controlled with a 32% reduction in 2005 compared to 1980 due to increased usage of high-efficiency electric dust removal systems.

Energy efficient systems being incorporated in China include required installation of flue gas desulfurization systems on all new coal power projects and accelerated desulphurization retrofits to all coal based generating units larger than 135MW. By 2010 most of the existing 114GW of small units will be decommissioned.

China Huaneng Group's Yuhuan power plant will generate 22 billion kWh of electricity per year. The generation efficiency of the Yuhuan power plant is 45% and the coal consumption is 285.6gce/kWh which is 80.4 gce/kWh less than the national average in 2006

By 2010 supercritical and ultra-supercritical units will account for over 40% of the total newly built thermal power generating units. From 2010 to 2020, new power plants with unit capacities of 600MW and more will all be required to be supercritical

The ease of scale-up, low emissions capabilities, and fuel flexibility make circulating fluidized beds (CFB) a serious option in China for mid-sized (300–450MW) and larger (400–600MW) utility units. There are several 300MW CFB units in operation, including at the China Huaneng Group's Kaiyuan power plant and China is currently building a 600MW CFB plant that, if successful, would be the largest CFB plant in the world. At present, the capital and operating costs of high-efficiency NOx removal technologies is relatively high. Several selective catalytic reduction (SCR) demonstration projects are in operation with about 6000MW of SCR units under construction.

Gasification is a process that converts carbonaceous materials, such as coal, petroleum, or biomass, into carbon monoxide and hydrogen by reaction of the raw material at high temperatures with a controlled amount of oxygen and/or steam. Gasification is a very efficient method for extracting energy from many different types of organic materials and also has applications as a clean waste disposal technique. The primary gasification technologies being developed in China are ash agglomerating fluidized bed coal gasification, non-slag and slag two-stage entrained flow bed coal gasification, two-stage dry feed entrained flow bed coal gasification, coal-water slurry gasification with opposed multi-burners, and coal-water slurry gasification with multiple materials. Methanol is an important chemical feedstock that can also be used as an alternative liquid fuel to oil. Not only does it offer an alternative vehicle fuel, but it can also be used as a feedstock for dimethylether (DME), methanol-to-olefins (MTO) or methanol-to-propylene (MTP) plants

Integrated gasification combined cycle (IGCC) was selected in 2006 as one of the key technologies for future power generation in China according to the National Program for Medium-to-Long-Term Scientific and Technological Development (2006–2010) issued by the State Council of China. China's overall goal is to form clusters of these advanced coal technologies and support the development of China's energy equipment manufacturing industry to achieve efficient, clean, and affordable use of coal define IGCC

Since 1994, eleven domestic research institutes have implemented IGCC technical feasibility under the leadership group. These institutes are cooperating with foreign companies, such as Texaco/General Electric (GE), Shell, and the Asian

Development Bank to develop this technology. The IGCC unit cost is still much higher than that of other kinds of coal-fired power generation plants. However, IGCC offers a similar efficiency to that of USC plants. The USC plants are cheaper, but IGCC offers better air pollution control, lower water demand, and reduced solid waste in addition to lower cost for carbon capture systems retrofitted to the plants.

China is one of the initial members of the Carbon Sequestration Leadership Forum. There are three major national science and technology programs in China sponsored by the Ministry of Science and Technology (MOST): Four key projects are been implemented under the 973 Program, including research on enhanced oil recovery, basic research on polygeneration systems with syngas co-production from coal gas and coke oven gas, basic research on high efficiency catalytic reforming of natural gas and syngas, and research on thermal-to-power conversion processes in gas turbines

Scaling up technology to be mass produced is one of the key engineering challenges of implementing new technology onto the global market. McCauley *et al.* (2010) describe clean coal technologies that Babcock & Wilcox Power Generation Group (B&W PGG) is developing to enable near-zero coal plant emissions, including carbon dioxide (CO_2) emissions. They found that the most cost-effective reduction of these emissions is through further improvements in steam cycle efficiency by advancing ultra-supercritical boilers from current steam temperatures of 600 °C to as high as 760 °C. They go on to explain that in order to capture CO_2, there are two combustion-based technology paths: oxy-combustion and CO_2 scrubbing. Oxy-combustion is applied to the entire plant process and is ready for large-scale demonstration while CO_2 scrubbing can be applied to all or part of plant emissions, with advancements in solvents and process design underway to enable effective processes with coal-fired flue gas. Oxy-coal combustion allows for near-zero emissions of particulate matter, sulfur dioxide, nitrogen oxides and mercury. In addition oxy-coal does not involve inventing and applying new technologies. Instead it is adapted from pre-existing sulfur dioxide scrubbing techniques. In addition to carbon capturing systems reviewed here, results from the U.S. regional carbon sequestration program led by the Department of Energy have shown sufficient reservoir capacity to last well into the next century or longer, primarily in deep underground saline formations. The article concludes with the possibility of large scale operations involving carbon scrubbing technology by 2020 provided a joint global initiative is implemented

Low electrical production in coal technology is the next logical step in coal manufacturing in Asia since use for coal is steadily growing worldwide as, at the same time, world politics has begun singling out coal-fired power plants as a major contributors to global climate change and CO_2 emissions. For coal to continue to drive power generation and economic expansion across the globe in the most environmentally friendly manner, technology must be developed to reduce coal plant emissions to near zero. There are many of these carbon capture technologies under development, however, none are operating at the integrated large-scale needed to move to commercial operation, though some are close.

Oxy-coal combustion is one such technology being considered. Utilizing ultra-supercritical boilers and advanced oxygen production, steam generator technology has demonstrated its flexibility and cycling capabilities. Oxygen production provides a unique opportunity for capture flexibility through the use of multiple compressors, multiple trains, and liquid storage systems. While a CO_2 scrubbing system is another technology for carbon capture. Pertaining to the issue of scaling-up these systems, oxy-coal and RSAT CO_2 scrubbing are ready to meet these challenges.

During the last several years, a resurgent Research and Development effort on high temperature steam plants has pushed towards 1300 °F (700 °C) steam temperature and beyond, referred to as advanced ultra-supercritical steam cycles. Globally, Asia has had a very active plan to accelerate the higher efficiency supercritical steam cycle process for coal combustion, reducing energy intensity from greater than 325 g/kwh (38% LHV) to less than 280 g/kwh (44% LHV) In future technological generation, the plan is to develop the advanced ultra-supercritical steam cycle (700 °C steam temperature), which will have an energy intensity less than 230 g/kwh (53% LHV), and to incorporate carbon capture and reuse or storage.

As power plant emissions have been continually ratcheted downward since the 1970s, emission control systems have significantly increased performance and reduced cost. Higher efficiency is the lowest cost option to achieve CO_2 reduction (compared to capture/storage), and can also achieve gains in updating existing power plants. Historic drivers to achieve higher temperatures were the economics of increased fuel efficiency and lower power cost. Looking at Fig. 2 in the paper we see that 2nd generation steam cycle technology can maintain current plant efficiency while dropping carbon emissions from 0.69 to 0.07 metric tons of carbon dioxide per MWh.

New, high nickel alloys have been developed and are currently in the process of being approved. Some of the most promising materials are Super 304H, Inconel 740, and Alloy 617, with current technological challenges involving preventing fireside corrosion, limiting steam-side oxidation, developing new welding and manufacturing processes, and designing stainless steel headers with acceptable creep life. Creep life is the deformation of plastic that occurs in steel over when held in high temperatures over long periods of time.

Environmental controls likewise continue to improve while benefitting from increased boiler efficiency and furnace operation. The environmental control equipment operates normally with no additional reagents or chemicals required and no new waste streams are generated. Post-combustion CO_2 scrubbing involves scaling up known technology to the sizes currently used for SO_2 scrubbers, with a similar project execution. Sulfur dioxide controls focus on wet FGD scrubbers with a progression of increasing capture efficiency from 70% in the 1970s to the 98 -99% range available today. This oxy-fuel combustion technology has been through small lab pilot testing, large pilot testing, and a rigorous bottom-up integration and optimization analysis

Fig. 3 in the paper shows how oxy-combustion captures CO_2. Combustion air is replaced with oxygen from an advanced air separation unit. Nitrogen that would normally be conveyed with the air through conventional air-fuel firing is excluded. Instead, a portion of the CO_2-rich flue gas is returned back to a conventional pulverizer/burner system, essentially substituting CO_2 for the nitrogen in the furnace. The CO_2 in oxygen combustion influences furnace operation and heat transfer in ways similar to the nitrogen in the air-fired system. These features allow the technology to be used in retrofit and repowering applications. Oxy-combustion creates a flue gas that is primarily a concentrated stream of CO2, rather than nitrogen, and other products of combustion (although greatly reduced nitrogen oxide NO_x). The fraction of the flue gas that is not re-circulated to the burners is sent to a compression and purification unit (CPU). The flue gas leaving the boiler is cleaned using conventional particulate and sulfur removal systems. Remaining particulate is further filtered in the CPU to protect compressor systems.

A NO_x removal system is not required on the boiler, as the remaining combustion-generated NO_x is almost completely removed as a condensable in the CPU. To prepare high purity, pipeline quality, CO_2 at the exit of the CPU, a small amount of inert constituents are removed in the CPU. CPU advancements and advantages by Air Liquide (a leading company in carbon technology) are specifically designed to process the flue gas emissions to provide a CO_2 product stream at a specification suitable for the transportation and storage underground. As such, it is a first of its kind.

Several different companies have test piloted the complete combustion/environmental process, utilizing a full commercial-scale burner (100 MBtu/hr) direct-fired from a pulverizer. Oxygen was mixed with flue gas recycled from an ESP/wet FGD system, simulating the commercial process and equipment. B&W PGG carried out oxy-coal combustion tests on the CEDF to evaluate operation and emission from several types of coal, including bituminous, sub-bituminous, and lignite. COMO modeling was used to evaluate and improve the design of the burner and operation of the CEDF. The CEDF test campaign, incorporating the above-mentioned process was a success. Another example would be Lacq Pilot, a project, led by TOTAL, which consisted of oxy-combustion of natural gas in a 30 MWth boiler and subsequent CO_2 purification, transport and storage in a depleted oil field, and Callide Pilot, a project led by CS Energy, which consisted of oxy-combustion in a 100 MWth boiler and subsequent CO_2 purification, transport and storage in a geologic formation.

The experimental results were then used to validate COMO models, which were developed based on experimental data measured from air-fired combustion. From the test results, it was observed that coal combustion characteristics under an oxy-coal environment are different from an air environment. Coal gasification with CO_2 and H_2O significantly affects reactivity and burnout rate. However, by applying a new set of kinetic parameters, the existing model was improved to predict the oxy-coal combustion coal burnout rate The similarity of the oxy-combustion process to air-firing supports its use for both new and retrofit (or repowering) applications. For new units, the plant configuration can be designed to optimize capital and operating costs. Other process improvements have lowered the cost of electricity compared to first generation processes as published by the U.S. Department of Energy. Applying oxy-combustion to existing units is technically feasible, but the economic application will be site specific. In the U.S., there are still many old, small coal units (greater than 50 years old; less than 250 MW) operating at relatively high capacity factor, typically with several units at one plant. Rather than retrofit the existing boiler, repowering these old plants may be necessary to significantly extend the life of the existing site and maintain local support. The major carbon capture studies conducted by the U.S. Department of Energy show that the cost competitiveness of the key technologies being developed for advanced clean coal power generation. In these studies, oxy-coal was the most economically viable.

For post-combustion scrubbers, the technology is one of scale and operating performance rather than component design. Regenerable solvent scrubbing has been used in other industries for sixty years. The goal is to bring it to the coal-fired power generation market at the plant size required, as well as using the flue gas with all its components (ash, sulfur dioxide, nitrogen oxide, and oxygen). Carbon dioxide scrubbers will have the benefit of being back-end processes, and they can be sized to handle any portion of the flue gas. This allows flexibility for partial capture to meet initial capital expenditure limits and the availability of sources to take the carbon dioxide, for either storage or beneficial reuse

The basic process takes the flue gas and contacts it with a solvent (such as an amine) in an absorption tower, where the CO_2 is preferentially absorbed, and the remaining flue gas exits through a typical stack. The CO_2-laden solvent is then sent to a separate regenerator (or stripping tower) where it is heated, driving off the

CO_2, which is then sent to the compression system, and eventually offsite for permanent storage. The clean solvent is regenerated and can be sent back to the absorber tower.

Significant differences exist between the petrochemical/natural gas industry use of this technology and what will need to be deployed in the coal-fired power industry. An amine-based solvent is generically sensitive to system impurities and the process is volume controlled. For example, in petrochemical applications, the effluent gas is generally at very high pressure which allows for smaller equipment sizes, and the gas being treated is very clean (derived from natural gas or petroleum distillation), not having excess oxygen, particulates, sulfur dioxide, or nitrogen oxide. All of these are atypical conditions in coal combustion flue gas. This leads to two distinct technology development tracks, the first dealing with the scale and plant integration, and the second involving the development of optimized solvents for use in coal combustion flue gas with the normal range of contaminants. The solvent used for coal-fired power plants has to incorporate the best of CO_2 holding capacity, absorption rates, regeneration energy use and durability. Durability is defined by the solvent degradation rate (make-up) and attrition due to impurities such as oxygen, sulfur dioxide, nitrogen dioxide and particulate matter. While a robust filtering and reclamation system will be incorporated into the design, there will still be solvent attribution due to irreversible reactions. The rate-based models enable researchers and engineers to make better investment decisions and to design more economical CO_2 scrubbing systems that can withstand changes of process conditions that may be encountered from power plants.

The obstacles for carbon capture, regardless of the technology utilized, all have a similar theme: 1) a worldwide commitment is needed (or at least from the major emitters such as the U.S. and Asia), 2) carbon capture is an added cost to a power plant with no immediate economic benefit, and 3) countries with large coal fleets have a large capital investment that is long-term and cannot be easily displaced. For post-combustion capture, the U.S. has announced the retrofit of a coal plant for a 60 MWe CO_2 amine scrubber by Fluor, and reuse of the CO_2 for EOR. At the same time Fluor has been chosen to supply CO_2 scrubbers for an 800 MWe new build coal plant in Texas. These projects will prove that coal can then remain as the key fossil fuel energy source for base-load power generation needs

However, if firms cannot implement these new technological changes then the technology is useless in terms of benefitting people or the environment. Amadi-Echendu *et, al* (2010) performed three case studies to study how mining firms tackle the issues of technology planning and forecasting especially in the context of depleting ore grades and new legislation. Of particular interest is whether mining firms utilize a structured approach, and, if so, what approaches, methods and tools are preferred. After examining the three firms the scientist found that technology planning and forecasting in mining has not developed fully, and that the processes for technology management in the cases studied are driven by operational concerns, i.e. the market-pull view rather than the technology-push view. They then suggest that a technology roadmapping technique is more suited to the technology-push view dominant with manufacturers, vendors or suppliers, instead of the market-pull view prevalent within operators of asset-intensive businesses.

Coal mining provides a basic raw material for energy supply. Global demand of coal is projected to rise by 1.4% a year, with this demand expected to be strongest in the developing world where the requirement for electricity power generation is expected to account for the bulk of this increase in demand. Mines tend to be relatively large operations in numerous underground sections depending on the resource and its geology. Mining methods such as drill and blast, continuous, and longwall, are carried out using engineered assets that involve large earthmoving equipment, like excavators, roof bolters, shovels, shuttle cars, and trucks. The reliability and availability of the production equipment, the workforce, and the support systems have a large impact on mine performance. Maintenance cost in the mining industry can be as high as half of the production cost, so sustainable management of an asset over its entire life cycle is vital to firms searching for ways to improve business performance. Developing new coal technology that makes it sustainable (except for CO_2 emissions) would pave the way for increases in coal usage. For example technology changes like a continuous miner aligns technological innovations with strategic objectives in order to improve business performance both short and long term.

Depleting ore grades along with new legislation have lead to demand for new direction in mining. Traditionally, production tonnage has been a key driver, however, health, safety and energy efficiency issues have taken on more significance, resulting in many new legislative requirements that also impact on cost and competitiveness. Safety is a major issue in mining. Hazardous, confined work spaces with dangerous machines impact on productivity and cost. Environmental protection through 'green technologies' is also at premium cost to miners.

The current challenge lies in reducing exposure to hazards and minimizing recordable accident case rates towards zero. This requires training and new technologies in production equipment and business systems. Examples of new suggested technology include automation, satellite communications, smart sensors, and robotics.

Changes in technology tend to be abrupt and discontinuous, thus presenting significant uncertainties in mining environments conventionally resistant to change. Many managers are at least aware of the strategic importance of technology because of increasing costs, complexity, and rate of change of technology, and these issues are compounded by competition for, and the globalization of, the sources of technology.

Establishing technology management processes in mining is an ongoing challenge that requires effective communication, dialogue and understanding between the commercial and technological functions of a firm. This case study attempted to decide which distinctive technological capabilities are necessary to establish and maintain health, safety and environmental compliance, as well as production targets and which technologies should be implemented and how these technologies should be embodied in business systems and engineered production assets.

The first case study involved 100 people in the coal mining business, including 80 subjects from coal mines, 4 from research and service providers, and 16 from government establishments. The convenience sample was drawn from 60 participants attending a Coaltech 2020 colloquium, and 40 members of the South African Colliery Engineers Association.

The respondents ranked safety, health and environmental regulations as top drivers for technological innovations in coal mining, like the introduction of a remotely controlled continuous miner which would remove the human operator from the coal face. It was found that factors such as process innovation, technology obsolescence and competition ranked relatively low in this regard. Most of the respondents' organizations used 'scenario planning and trend extrapolation' more often for technology planning and forecasting, rather than the roadmapping technique as propounded in literature

The second case study examined how the requirements for technological innovations are specified in a typical coal mining firm. Coal miners focused on technology that resolved operational problems first and then technology that would provide competitive advantage.

To minimize trial and error, technical problem solving requires knowledge of underground coal mining conditions. The complication is that in order to specify what technology to implement, a technological intelligence of the machine is required which lies with the manufacturer, vendor, or supplier rather than the operator of the equipment.

The study found that current technology improvement projects matched the rate of occurrence of failures only in three sub- assemblies (i.e.,gatheringgearbox,cutterdrumcentreandcutter).

In Case study 3 with platinum mining Only 8 out of 41 respondents felt that the firm had a technology planning horizon greater than 5 years, whereas 28 respondents indicated a planning horizon of between 1 and 5 years. The data indicated that the firm's incremental innovation cycle was about 2.5 years, and that the firm introduced radical innovation every 5 years. Seven respondents didn't know how often the firm introduced radical innovations. Legislation, production targets, and economics ranked as the three to drivers for technology improvements. Scenario planning and trend extrapolation were indicated as the techniques more likely to be applied for technology planning

The three case studies showed that scenario planning and trend analysis has been the preferred approach for mining firms. The case studies also found that safety and environment considerations create the highest impetus for technological innovations in coal mining. What this means is that, as users of technology, firms are more likely to adopt a reactive, instead of a proactive stance on the issue of technology roadmapping.

Conclusions

It is important to note that this paper, although useful in highlighting the benefits of installing and implementing green technology in the U.S., does not address clean coal technology which would also create local job environments and create safer work environments with the addition of new and better working steel products that are currently ready to be implemented in coal retrieval and cleaning. However, even though retrofitting low CO_2 emission technologies are currently ready for scale up installation, there still remains the problem of ammonium compounds used in coal cleaning, contributing to toxic runoff, as well as the poly aromatic hydrocarbons released during the coal retrieval and processing, which are still detrimental to human health as shown in the earlier sections of this article. To conclude, the benefits of clean coal technology do not seem at this point to outweigh the costs in human health or environmental damage in comparison to investing in clean coal technology. Especially with the case study illustrated earlier which shows the slow turn around rate of clean coal technology from its development (and scale up readiness) to actual use in coal facilities. It would seem beneficial either way to invest in the implementation of new green technologies in the United States while watching the development of clean coal in China for further advancement (and possible retrofitting of scrubbing technologies that will eliminate dangerous emissions) to be implemented in existing large coal mining facilities, while shutting down smaller older facilities for the incorporation of wind, PV solar, and nuclear energy plants.

References Cited

Ahem, M. Hamilton, C. Mackay, K. Mullett, M. 2010. Residence in coal-mining areas and low-birth-weight outcomes. DOI 10.1007/s10995-009-0555-1

Amadi-Echendu, J. Lephauphau, O. Maswanganyi, M. Mkhize, M. 2010 Case Studies of technology road mapping in mining doi:10.1016/j.jengtecman.2010.12.002

Anesetti-Rothermel, A., Fedorko, E. Hendryx, M. 2010 A geographical information system-based analysis of cancer mortality and population exposure to coal mining activities in West Virginia, United States of America. *Geospatial Health 4(2), 2010, pp. 243-256*

Chen, Y. Hou, H. Ritz, B. Wu, J. 2010. Exposure to polycyclic aromatic hydrocarbons and missed abortion in early pregnancy in a Chinese population. doi:10.1016/j.scitotenv.2010.02.028

Chen, W., Xu, R. 2010 Clean coal technology development in China doi:10.1016/j.enpol.2009.06.003

Da Silva, J. Espitia-Pérez , L. Hartmann, A. Henriques, J. Hoyos-Giraldo, L. León-Mejía, G. Quintana, M. 2010. Assessment of DNA damage in coal open-cast mining workers using the cytokinesis-blocked micronucleus test and the comet assay. doi:10.1016/j.scitotenv.2010.10.049 2010

Jiang, L., Kong, B., Ma, J., Wang, Y 2010. Potential of small-baseline SAR interferometry for monitoring land subsidence related to underground coal fires: Wuda (Northern China) case study. doi:10.1016/j.rse.2010.08.000

McCauley, K., Zhou, H., Zeng., Zhang, R 2010. Scale-up and operational flexibility for clean coal technology carbon capture systems.

Bonskowski, R. Freme, F. Watson, W (2006) Coal production in the US, a historical overview. Encyclopedia of Energy and Engineering, October 2006.

7. The Future of Hybrid, Battery Electric, and Hydrogen Fuel Cell Vehicles

Laura Silverberg

The competitor to be feared is one who never bothers about you at all, but goes on making his own business better all the time.—Henry Ford

Electric vehicles date further back in history than the average American may know. From the mid-nineteenth century until the early twentieth century, electricity was one of the most popular methods for vehicle propulsion. However, during this time, internal combustion engine technology advanced significantly, allowing for the mass-production of reduced prices of gasoline-run vehicles, particularly under the Ford Motor Company. This led to a significant decline in electric vehicles and by the 1930s, gasoline vehicles eventually pushed them off the market. Recently, however, there have been increased concerns about the environmental impact of gasoline on human health and the environment, the threat of peak oil, and the economic recession of the late 2000s. This has renewed interests in electric cars, which are seen as significantly cleaner, and more ecologically friendly vehicles. Carmakers worldwide have begun the development of these vehicles.

One solution that addresses the needs of researchers, consumers, car manufacturers, and government agency standards is the plug-in hybrid vehicle. This vehicle uses electricity from the power grid as its charge by plugging a cord from the vehicle into a standard outlet. Hydrogen fuel cell technology has also proven to be a worthy alternative to address the threat of global warming associated with environmentally damaging technology. However, a major challenge to fuel cell vehicles is the current, though weak design for on-board hydrogen storage, which may compromise standard vehicle requirements, namely safety, cost, and infrastructure adaptations. Recently though, researchers have developed a high-pressure tank as a possible solution to achieving better fuel cell vehicle range.

Currently, the number of electric vehicles in the market is inconsequential. However, as consumer interest increases and vehicle technology improves, petroleum-based vehicle fuels will be eradicated from the vehicle market. It is up to researchers to work on improving battery technologies to decrease the weight, cost, and recharging time for these vehicles. As of 2011, there are four plug-in hybrid electric vehicles available in the United States: the Chevrolet Volt, the Nissan Leaf, the Tesla Roadster, and the Fisker Karma. Although the selection is limited, Ford, Volvo, Rolls Royce, and Toyota all plan to release their electric vehicle models by 2012.

As humans, we can only control so many facets of global warming. By looking into the operation of future vehicle alternatives, we can easily begin to make changes, not only in our consumption behaviors, but also in our local environments.

Comparative Analysis of Battery Electric, Hydrogen Fuel Cell, and Hybrid Vehicles in a Future Sustainable Road Transport System

With the onset of global warming and climate change, road transport has become responsible for a large part of global anthropogenic emissions of CO_2. Today's road transport, for the most part dependent on oil-derived fuels, generates various pollutants that are harmful to human health. Offer *et al.* (2010) utilize previous studies conducted by the International Energy Agency, hereafter IEA, on alternative vehicle platforms. One platform called for a reduction of 80 g CO_2 km^{-1} to 30 g CO_2 km^{-1} by the year 2030. The other platform suggested that a substantial shift to hydrogen-fuelled cars by the year 2050 could result in 50% less CO_2 emissions. These platforms served as the bases for their comparative analysis of battery electric, hydrogen fuel cell and hybrid vehicles in the years 2010 and 2030. Using data based in technology, cost prediction, and sensitivity analyses of the benefits and drawbacks of alternative fuel-based vehicles, Offer *et al.* reason that a "combination of electricity and hydrogen as a transport fuel could bring additional benefit to the end user in terms of both capital and running cost." The authors label this model a hydrogen fuel cell plug-in hybrid electric vehicle (FCHEV). While the FCHEV carries a significantly low lifecycle cost in comparison to other alternative fuel-based vehicles, alternate data show the FCHEV's insensitivity to electricity costs and sensitivity to hydrogen cost. The authors determine that with future technologies, various shortcomings, particularly involving mass-production and infrastructure, could be solved, presenting hydrogen fuel cell and battery electric vehicles as viable options for a future sustainable road transport system by the year

2030. Offer *et al.* conclude the best platform for future integration of fuel cells is the FCHEV, which, for policy-making purposes, "should be pursued and supported."

G.J. Offer *et al.* analyze two of the three "alternative powertrain technologies considered by IEA as viable options of providing a "sustainable road transport system with near-zero emissions" by the year 2030 (IEA, 2008). By taking these into consideration, the authors create their own form of technical, economic and infrastructural comparisons with the analysis of various barriers to the adoption of battery electric vehicles (BEV) and fuel cell electric vehicles (FCEV). For the most part, these barriers are somewhat 'complementary', although electricity proves more accessible at this point in time, as electricity is already a widely used energy vector. That is not to say, however, that hydrogen is not a practical option for the future. The authors discuss that overcoming technical and economic barriers are important for large scale, mass-produced adoption of alternative-fuel vehicles; however, their study focuses more on the potential economic advantages of the IEA vehicle platforms. Since the BEV and the FCEV models both rely on an electric powertrain and are otherwise identical, the authors claim that "the two technologies should be considered together rather than separately, in a hybrid solution."

Various conclusions can be drawn from the authors' analysis of alternative-fuel vehicles. In terms of capital costs in the year 2010, FCEVs, BEVs and FCHEVs are all far more expensive than the conventional internal combustion engine, hereafter ICE, powertrain. The ICE powertrain will still be cheaper in 2030, although when lifetime fuel costs are factored in, the overall model proves less efficient. According to the authors' "optimistic" and "pessimistic" hypotheses for 2030, capital costs could drop significantly, the FCHEV model presenting the lowest capital cost. The authors also discuss that accurate predictions of the future costs of alternative powertrain sources are not possible at this time. Additionally, any mark-up added at the point of sale were not included in the study. This permits the technologies to be evaluated on an equal playing field, representing economic standings during the year 2010. With more development of powertrain technologies and the revising of cost sensitivity trends, these numbers will be reevaluated and relative to the year at hand. Regarding lifecycle costs over 100,000 miles, the authors concluded that FCHEVs appeared to be cheaper than BEVs and exhibited a wider sensitivity to capital and running costs. ICEs and FCEVs lifecycle costs were significantly higher than FCHEVs and BEVs, around 1.75 times greater. The authors conducted a separate study on battery size that considered BEV lifecycle cost sensitivity to battery size. They found that BEV economics are cheapest if a battery size can be reduced to accommodate a range of only 50 miles, predominantly targeting city-based drivers. The authors recommend a battery electric vehicle with fuel cell range extender as the best platform for integration of fuel cells for future road transport. As the most viable option, this model can compete for space in an electrified transport network and allow consumers to choose between recharging or refuelling their vehicle.

Practical Implementation of an Hybrid Electric-Fuel Cell Vehicle

Electric vehicles are becoming more popular in the consumer world, as the demand for high-performance vehicles continues along an upward trajectory. While the costs of fossil fuels and clean energy are on the rise, vehicles whose power sources operate together within an electric or hybrid framework continue to be in high demand. A major advance in hybrid vehicle research has focused on fuel cell technology. This technology has improved significantly over the past few years, with a major decrease in the cost, the volume and the weight of individual cells. In fact, medium power fuel cells are now available in medium-high efficiency. In order to develop a "competitive product…" "[h]igh performance fuel-cell power modules, batteries and the necessary power electronics …are required" and must be developed for greatest efficiency. Dominguez *et al.* introduce a hybrid vehicle, built from the commercial vehicle GEM eL by Global Electric Motorcars, where the battery stack of the commercial car is supported by a 4 kW fuel cell. The "fuel cell charges the batteries when they have low charge but it provides…power directly to the dc motor drive when it is required by the user." Within the proposed hybrid system, Dominguez *et al.* divide the description of their system into the following subsections: the fuel cell device and the hydrogen storage system, the dc/dc power converter and the auxiliary converters, and the control and monitoring system. These three categories serve as the basis for analysis of the authors' proposed hybrid vehicle. The proposed model has been "experimentally tested in the facilities of the National Institute of Aerospace Technology in Huelva, Spain, where two separate vehicle acceleration scenarios were tested." In both of these scenarios, the authors observed that the fuel cell provides power whether or not the vehicle is in motion. The advantage to this system is that the vehicle range can be extended since the fuel cell module charges the batteries using hydrogen as fuel. The authors determine that after an analysis of their proposed hybrid vehicle system, their data demonstrate a "high robustness and reliability."

Dominguez *et al.* analyze a practical model of a proposed hybrid vehicle, powered by an array of batteries and a fuel cell. The authors section their data into three main systems that have been integrated into their vehicle design. The first subsection describes the fuel cell power module, the HyPM-XR, which is used in the hybrid vehicle. Like any other fuel cell, this powertrain emits nearly zero emissions other than byproducts such as water and oxygen-depleted air. The fuel cell module, suitable for a wide range of "transportation, stationary and portable applications," is highly reliable due to its "modular design, fast dynamic response and high efficiency." The second subsection, focusing on dc/dc boost power converters and auxiliary dc/dc converters, describes the make up of the power electronic system incorporated into the vehicle. The authors make a note of the design system's weight and volume reduction and that the reliability of this model is achieved by the boost converter system located under the driver's seat. The converter is also capable of switching frequencies, barely allowing any noise to emit from the vehicle as it comes to a rest, as well as obtaining a dc voltage output higher than its input. If said voltage ratios were higher, a double-boost system could be used. However, the main reason for utilizing the auxiliary dc/dc converter is "to generate the necessary voltage to supply the secondary power systems such as the selenoidal valve and a computer with a tactile screen (PC-car)," as well as provide "300 watts for 20 seconds in the start-up of the fuel cell system." This PC-car monitoring system, using Labview technology, allows the user to control and monitor the system. This includes the vehicle's status, "the hydrogen load, the hydrogen pressure, the dc voltage of the fuel cell...the battery stack...and possible warnings and errors." By providing liberties to the user to manipulate their own hybrid system, the authors' proposed hybrid electrical-fuel cell vehicle proves to be a good basis and testing platform for future technologies.

In the third and final subsection of the paper, Dominguez *et al.* describe the proposed vehicle's control and monitoring system. Hydrogen, an important facet of the vehicle's design, is stored in the back of the vehicle. The fuel cell uses hydrogen to produce the energy to charge the battery stack when it is needed. When a low battery charge is detected, at a level below 78 volts, the fuel cell injects current to increase the charge. Typically "when a battery charge is applied to a battery stack, its dc voltage increases almost immediately." On the other hand, when the vehicle is in motion, the dv voltage of the battery stack fluctuates. If this is not taken into account, a simple acceleration of the vehicle would trigger a low battery warning. The authors clarify that as part of their proposed model, this is not a problem since the "controller provides the necessary current to charge the batteries or to drive the dc motor directly." However, at the same time, there is current flowing from the fuel cell system to charge the batteries. This process can save energy because the battery stack is left unaware that the user "is demanding more power unless the maximum nominal current of the fuel cell system is achieved." Once the maximum is achieved, the "current from the fuel cell system is saturated and the rest of the power is provided back to the battery stack."

Dominguez *et al.* review two experimentally tested scenarios on their proposed hybrid system. In the first experiment, the vehicle "is moving continuously and the driver is accelerating and braking following a hilly path." Since the fuel cell is providing continuous energy to the battery stack, the battery stack can transfer that energy to the dc motor. In the second experiment, the "vehicle is moving and suddenly…stops." In this scenario, the fuel cell not only provides power as the vehicle accelerates, but also when the vehicle stops and a low battery level is detected; the fuel cell is prompted to continue providing power in order to charge the battery stack. The authors also found that the vehicle range can be increased from 40 kilometers to 100 kilometers, as the only limiting factor is the hydrogen capacity in the vehicle. Furthermore, all experiments were developed under "real weather conditions." The authors conclude that in the future, natural park and tourism vehicles should take advantage of their proposed hybrid system.

The Economics of Using Plug-in Hybrid Electric Vehicle Battery Packs For Grid Storage

In order to increase market acceptance for purchasers of plug-in hybrid electric vehicles, hereafter PHEVs, legislation passed in 2008 provided a subsidy as tax credits for said consumers. PHEVs have the potential to provide services to the electricity sector (vehicle-to-grid, hereafter V2G), in the form of "…peak load shifting, smoothing variable generation from wind and other renewables, and providing distributed grid-connected storage as a reserve against unexpected outages." One of the most advantageous properties of electricity markets is the lack of cost-effective storage. In the absence of energy storage, meeting peak demand becomes difficult and investments in generators and transmission lines must be made. Because of this, the difference between daily peak and off-peak costs can vary significantly within a year.

In regard to V2G services, the authors believe that this system will be more profitable for grid support than the capital cost of batteries that must be remunerated for grid use. In addition to quick battery reaction times, V2G energy has the ability to stabilize or slow fluctuations from sporadic sources, particularly wind or solar sources, and eradicate the need for 'raid ramping' of generators to "match variable power sources." Ramping can also lead to an increase in pollution. Peterson *et al.* evaluate the net revenue, "the net of avoided grid energy purchases from using the energy stored in the vehicle battery pack," of V2G energy sales to determine the 'attractive incentive' for future owners in three separate categories: an organized market, as energy sales to the grid, or capturing values by running the meter slower. While the first two options hold transaction and grid costs, the third option does not. Based on the implications of stored grid electricity, energy arbitrage is examined and potential sale prices of electricity, as well as other pertinent data, are collected from Boston, Massachusetts, Rochester, New York and Philadelphia, Pennsylvania. Each city's hourly electricity markets differed considerably. Based on the authors' findings, profits derived from battery purchases are not incentive enough for vehicle owners to use the battery pack for electricity storage and off-vehicle use.

Peterson *et al.* analyze the potential economic implications of utilizing vehicle batteries to "store grid electricity generated at off-peak hours for off-vehicle use during peak hours." Hourly electricity prices in Boston, Rochester and Philadelphia were used to "arrive at daily profit values, while the economic losses associated with battery degradation were calculated based on data collected" from combined driving and off-vehicle electricity utilization. The authors calculated the revenue from energy arbitrage, degradation costs, and analyzed a sell-before-buy model as the basis for their study. In the revenue model, the authors assumed the PHEV owner was fixed under a real time pricing, hereafter RTP, tariff. With the addition of a transmission and distribution cost of 7¢ kWh^{-1} to the "hourly nodal price" to estimate the RTP, the data resulted in the incentive for owners to use their PHEV for energy arbitrage. The degradation cost study was based on laboratory data from cycling lithium iron phosphate battery cells (LiFePO$_4$) produced by A123 Systems. Using the Chevy Volt's battery pack pricing as the framework for this degradation study, the authors concluded that by using a $5,000 replacement cost, a degradation cost of 4.2¢ kWh^{-1} would apply. The sell-before-buy model entails a battery pack beginning on a day when it is fully charged. From 8 a.m. to 4:59 p.m., the authors designate time for driving exclusively and all other times are allocated for charging. The battery pack is charged at the lowest cost hours possible. In order to determine the amount of battery pack capacity a profit-driven consumer would choose to devote to energy arbitrage, the authors utilize two separate methods. The first method entails the consumer knowing the future TRP where they choose the most expensive locational marginal pricing, hereafter LMP, hour to use the battery pack for home energy use and the cheapest hour after to recharge. In this scenario, the vehicle is fully charged by 8 a.m. The second method calls for knowledge of previous RTPs to determine the hours least expensive to recharge the vehicle. While this method may mis-predict the cost of recharging since it is purely based on speculation, the battery pack energy can be used for home energy as well. The profit is calculated as the revenue cost from energy arbitrage, therefore doubling the incentive for consumers.

Peterson *et al.* provide significant data resulting from their various studies. Using the three cities as the framework for examining electricity market costs, the maximum annual profit ($118) occurred in Philadelphia in 2008, whereas in Boston, the least profitable city, a consumer's profit would only result in $12–48 based on a particular year's market. Based on estimated profit analyses, the authors concluded that increased battery size would not increase the profit greatly due to the limitation of local circuit infrastructure in the three cities.

The authors presented sensitivity analyses on the effect of battery pack replacement cost on profit. Only if the battery pack replacement cost is set to zero, so too will be the cost of degradation. This would yield the maximum profit, particularly in Philadelphia. The difference between peak and off peak is higher in the Pennsylvania New Jersey Maryland Interconnection LLC, hereafter, PJM, than the other regional transition organizations, hereafter RTOs. In this scenario, Boston becomes more profitable than Rochester. The authors also discuss the interest of grid operators knowing when vehicle owners will make their energy available for sale on a given day. Philadelphia was found to be most profitable when PHEV consumers participated in energy arbitrage 56% of the days between the years 2003–2008. However, if the battery pack replacement cost is $10,000, this percentage decreases to 38%.

The results indicate that vehicle owners are not likely to receive sufficient incentives from energy arbitrage to increase the use of car batteries for grid energy storage. The maximum annual profit is between $142–249 in all three cities due to the small variation present in LMPs. If degradation cost is included, the maximum annual profit would only range from $12–48 in perfect circumstances, although more realistically, it would range from $6–72. The authors suggest that if a large number of consumers decide to participate in energy arbitrage, the profit would decrease since the LMP spread would be lowered. Grid net social welfare benefits were also considered. The authors found that the increase of construction and use of peaking generators are similar in size to the energy arbitrage profit. Since there may only be ≈$300–400 of annual net social welfare benefits that can be transferred to the owner of a PHEV, it is unlikely that large-scale usage of grid energy storage will be appealing to a large number of said vehicle owners.

A Multi-Level Perspective on the Introduction of Hydrogen and Battery-Electric Vehicles

Battery-electric and hydrogen vehicles have the ability to change a significant number of challenges present in the current automobile sector. These changes pertain to internal combustion engines, hereafter ICEs, by targeting the rise of global climate change, deterioration of air quality, high fuel prices, and the security of energy supplies. Van Bree *et al.* attempt to address all questions regarding the transition to these alternative vehicles, particularly focusing on the relationship between car manufacturers and consumers and the developments that could interfere. As environmental issues become more urgent, the likelihood of adopting new alternatives becomes more likely. While it is made clear that neither alternative automobile technology is considered superior to the other or to conventional vehicles, only with technical progress can an answer be provided on the futures of the technologies. The authors divide their paper into six sections. Beginning in section two with an explanation of their methodology, the authors give an overview of the relationships between technology and society. Sections 3–5 describe the automobile within the current system of personal transportation. Section 6 describes two scenarios that could aid in the transition to alternative fuel vehicles, hereafter AFVs. Section 7 discusses the implications of these scenarios in the context of the current economic situations and the role policy makers place in supporting technology. The authors conclude that the development of technology of the coming years "will lay the foundation for the dynamics of the coming transition" to both fuel cell and battery electric vehicles.

Van Bree *et al.*, in an effort to tackle the problems regarding the transition to AFVs, clarify that the transition itself is based in the joint development of technology and society. In order to fully comprehend the transition, the authors state that a multi-level perspective, hereafter MLP, should be embraced. In the MLP, three levels are examined: the middle level, the socio-technical regime consisting of the socio-technical system, actors, and rules regarding typical behavioral patterns in the carmaker-consumer relationship, which comprises all elements pertaining to production, distribution, and use of technology; the top level, landscape developments, developments meant to put pressure on the regime and can open a "window of opportunity" for breakthrough technologies; the bottom level, technological niches, the location for new technology development that have the means to be protected from market pressures.

Colleagues Geels and Schot provide an extension of the patterns that describe the transitions in the MLP in four pathways, all differing in the types of timing of multi-level interactions: transformation, regarding moderate landscape pressure; de-alignment and re-alignment, addressing sudden and diverse landscape pressure; technological substitution, presenting fully developed niche technology; and reconfiguration, similar to the transformation pathway with moderate landscape pressure, though with the addition of subsequent adoptions of symbiotic elements of niche technologies "lead[ing] to changes in the basic architecture of the system." In the event that "no niche-innovation has sufficiently developed, a competition between niche technologies may result, from which one winner emerges, as in the de-alignment and re-alignment pathway." Regardless, the pathways system is simply meant to provide further guidance to the scenarios that delineate a possible transition to AFVs.

The third section of the paper focuses solely on the socio-technical system for land-based road transportation. The automobile, "its cultural and symbolic meaning, markets and user practices, and the production system and industry structure" are all examined. The most central actors present in this system include car manufacturers, consumers and fuel providers. Other groups, namely non-governmental organizations, attempt to influence the system. The purchasing process is an important place to begin the study, in that it helps to describe how the car market works and how consumer preferences play a role in the carmaker-consumer relationship. Van Bree *et al.* gather that "safety, reliability, and comfort are the most important criteria for the buyers of any vehicle. Together with price, they can be considered the primary [purchasing] decision criteria." Additionally, with rising fuel prices, the most sensible response for consumers is to "switch to more fuel-efficient cars, rather than opting for driving less." The authors also assess the variety of automobile models that have reached the market over the last decades and the competition that arises between car manufacturers, the increasing modularity of car design, and the relevance of vehicle upgrades to users, all enabled by "consumer expectations and car-manufacturers' drive to increase profitability."

The fourth section considers two niche-innovations, battery-electric vehicles, hereafter BEVs, and fuel cell vehicles, hereafter FCVs, and the barriers that they face. These barriers include "the chicken and the egg problem," "mismatch with consumer preferences," and "high cost." The authors disregard hydrogen from these barriers, although they do assess hydrogen as a technological-niche, since it takes place "in a highly protected environment and…[its] stability is low, i.e. a standard technical solution has not been decided on yet." The electricity-niche is also evaluated.

In the fifth section, Van Bree *et al.* describe three relevant landscape developments: fuel prices, supply security of fossil fuels, and environmental stresses. The authors' most important observation is that "supply, relative to demand, will be more constrained in the future." Imbalances between supply and demand will cause oil prices to increase, particularly due to limited reserves. It is up to local governments to combat the effects of fossil fuel combustion by tightening emission standards.

The sixth section focuses on the segments of the transition process in the MLP. Linkages, otherwise known as "transition seeds," present between various levels of the transition trajectory, have the potential to trigger change within market dynamics, particularly between consumer and carmaker behaviors, and can lead to new development. The authors assess two sets of scenarios as a means to accept the transition to AFVs. In the first set, tightening emissions regulations influences carmakers to scale up their vehicles and commercialize their products. The second set of scenarios pertains to rising fuel prices. This encourages carmakers to implement plug-in versions of their vehicles, and later with battery-electric and fuel cell vehicles. These two sets of scenarios provide different implications for the actors and infrastructure involved. The authors determine that while both FCVs and BEVs can coexist in a competitive market, the adoption of the BEVs would require more changes.

Van Bree *et al.* conclude their paper in section seven, reinforcing the potential that the institutionalized relationship between carmakers and consumers has to shape the transition from ICEs to BEVS and FCVs. While the economic collapse has severely affected the United States, the authors, suggesting the first set of scenarios, find it necessary to restructure the car industry. Products should be more fuel-efficient and plug-in hybrid electric vehicles should be implemented on a mass scale, starting with the public push for the Chevrolet Volt as the foundation.

Future Vehicle Society Based on Electric Motor. Capacitor and Wireless Power Supply

Over the past decade, various international conferences on electric vehicles have focused on the discussion of the rise of developing automobile technologies to make the shift from internal combustion engine vehicles (ICVs) to pure electric vehicles, hereafter EVs. In the future, EVs will be connected to the existing electric powertrain infrastructure, and supercapacitors, rather than conventional batteries, will function in charging these vehicles. Supercapacitors have a "long operating life, large current density, and environmentally friendly composition." With this power, EVs powered by supercapacitors can operate for more than twenty minutes, even after a charge of only thirty seconds. In this scenario, the efficiency of these EVs increase, and the recharge time is reduced. Hori discusses a wireless power transfer system based on magnetic resonance and the efficiency in power transfer it enables. Equipped with an electric motor, EVs have three major advantages for traction control systems, antilock braking, motion control, and estimation of road surface conditions: quick and accurate motor torque generation—a motor can be attached to each wheel, and motor torque can be estimated precisely. Hori concludes that EVs that utilize electric motors, supercapcitors, and wireless power transfer, eliminate the need for engines, high performance lithium ion batteries, and large charging stations.

Hori presents a plug-in hybrid electric vehicle, hereafter PHEV, as the transitional state between ICVs and EVs. With PHEVs, users can utilize nighttime generated electricity during the day and can utilize daytime electricity after a half-day's charge in the evening. The excess of daytime electricity will prove to be beneficial for electric power companies. Hori hopes that PHEVs will lead to a progressive reduction in gasoline usage and familiarize users with a pure EV lifestyle. By eliminating the requirement of gasoline engines and complex hybrid control systems, the purchase and maintenance costs of the vehicle will be reduced.

As a replacement for conventional batteries, Hori presents the supercapacitor model, also known as an electric double layer capacitor, hereafter EDLC, as a physical battery needed to run EVs. In comparison to the conventional model, supercapacitors have long operating lives, extremely high power densities, and use environmentally friendly materials in their make-up. The EDLC energy density, on the other hand, is rather low; improvements for increasing energy density will require a significant amount of time. However, that is not to say that the current amount of energy density is insufficient for operating EVs. In fact, when the capacitors utilize anywhere between 50 and 100 Volts, more than 75% of the charged energy can be used. This is not the case for conventional batteries. Additionally, with a short charging time for these capacitors, EDLC-operated EVs can function for longer than twenty minutes on thirty seconds worth of charging. Hori presents the "Capacitor Car," a concept first utilized by buses in Shanghai, as a suitable and potential transport system for the majority of large cities. Hori details the ubiquity of electric consents and suggests the revamping of vehicle range and infrastructure to apply EV technology to larger scale electric pursuits.

Hori highlights the three main advantages of EVs and the ways in which ICVs are incomparable to their highly sophisticated model: quick torque response of motors, distributed motor installation, and tractable motor torque. The torque response of electric motors is 100 times faster than that of engines. The only energy losses result from the friction between the tire and road surface. With the application of adhesion control, the tire would evade the problem of friction losses. Hori explains that "[t]he most important advantage of these EVs is motion control." In regard to motor installation, a single EV motor can be "divided into 4 and installed into the wheels of the EV without any significant cost increase, which is not the case with cars." This is entirely different from conventional 4-wheel drive or 4-wheel steering, which are based on "driving force distribution using differential gear." Motor torque can be determined from motor current. In EVs, force is transferred from the tire to the road by using "the driving force observer." Running sensors in the vehicle can inform the driver of road surface conditions, significantly improving driving safety.

Hori proposes a wireless power transfer system for supplying energy to moving objects. In this system, capacitor batteries will play an important role as a buffer system. This will reduce the dependence on gasoline stations, thereby reducing the costs affiliated with charging gasoline-operated vehicles. Hori mentions the most recent experimental results of wireless power transfer using approximately 10 MHz frequency. The total efficiency of the energy transfer between the two antennas is over 90%. Good robustness of the wireless power transfer system against gap variation and antenna displacement is presented.

Hori mentions that fuel cell vehicles, FCVs, are no longer a viable choice for the future of automobile technology, as they use 100 g Pt per vehicle. Instead, he suggests that FCV vehicle range can be reduced. He concludes that enhancing vehicle technology with the usage of electricity from a power network can revolutionize daily commutation.

A Web-based Light Electric Vehicle for Homecare Use—A Pilot Study

With the rapid increase in biomedical technology, the mortality rate of elderly people in economically developed areas has decreased. However, according to a recent public health survey, problems associated with the aging community in Taiwan have become particularly severe. In this paper, authors Cheng *et al.* (2010) present an economically viable light electric vehicle design for the homecare of elderly. User needs, application feedbacks, and human factors are taken into account and incorporated into their web-based interactive platform. The goal for this project is to develop a light electric vehicle that can be used for easing the mobility of the elderly both indoors and outdoors. Within their one-year integration project, supported by the National Science Council of TAIWAN, the authors propose and analyze various innovative platforms. These platforms include: "industrial design, biomedical engineering [for healthcare monitoring and vehicle safety checking], mechanical design, power electronics [for green energy development of solar cells], communication technology [for both indoor and outdoor wireless positioning], and information management [regarding computer technology of a built-in health monitoring system]." The authors conclude that their proposed vehicle can provide multiple positive functions for homecare use.

Cheng *et al.* assess their project from three perspectives: from a technological viewpoint to "build an integration innovation of multiple technologies"; from the industry viewpoint, to "develop an add-on value of the culture electric vehicle for elderly use"; and from the welfare viewpoint, to "promote the humanity of devices." The project was divided into six research groups focusing on the innovative platforms described above, in order to best develop the proposed light electric vehicle. However, since the research groups are located at varying distant sites, a web-based interactive platform was developed to alleviate discussion and communication problems among the groups. Cheng *et al.* make note of the importance of collaboration between the varying research groups. In order for one research group to incorporate specific design elements into the light electric vehicle, it is up to another research group to develop that design. This partnership is important for the success of the vehicle.

Industrial design, power control and management, health monitoring and safety checking, information integration, and management are analyzed. Industrial design consists of the survey users' needs for utilizing the light electric vehicle, the size and design of the vehicle, and the proposal of its conceptual design. The authors provide various views of the proposed light electric vehicle for outdoor use and its detachable chair for indoor use. The authors design a power control and management system to meet the needs of the vehicle. A figure outlining the power supply system is included in the paper. A health monitoring system measuring the ECG signal for vital signs has also been incorporated into the design of the light electric vehicle. Seat pressure and declined level are measured for safety checking. Additionally, a blockdiagram of the system and an image of the developed circuit board that controls the measurement of the ECG signal are provided. The authors integrate a computer screen shot of the management system of the light electric vehicle into their assessment.

The authors conclude that while the interaction information platform may provide a slight solution for communication problems, it is still difficult to discuss the innovative platforms among the participating research groups. However, that is not to say that the future design and implementation of the light electric vehicle is incapable of providing various beneficial functions for homecare use.

RD&D Cooperation for the Development of Fuel Cell, Hybrid, and Electric Vehicles within the International Energy Agency

The rising level of CO_2 emissions is becoming more concerning for a growing population dependent on roadway mobility. Fuel cell vehicles, hereafter FCVs, can provide a significant alternative and sustainable form of transport that combines "energy efficiency, emissions reductions, and reduced petroleum use." This paper summarizes the report of Annex XIII in 2010 by compiling "an up-to date, neutral, and comprehensive assessment of current trends in fuel cell vehicle technology and related policy." Telias *et al.* (2010) include a review of the most current components of the fuel cell battery stack, batteries, and hydrogen storage with commentary on the successful results of fuel cell vehicle demonstrations projects worldwide.

Telias *et al.* assess two applications of fuel cell technology, a system that can be seen as a power converter unit providing "electricity and heat and therefore provid[ing] an analogous function in combination with an electric machine as the internal combustion engine in a conventional vehicle." The first system functions as an energy converter, used in conjunction with an electric motor to propel the vehicle. The second application of the system analyzes its auxiliary units where power may not be needed at all times, particularly when the vehicle is not in motion. Generally with FCVs, the auxiliaries are significantly lower than that of the demands of the vehicle propulsion. In both applications of the system, the fuel cell can be directly linked with an electric motor, creating a pure fuel cell power train. It is only when the powertrain is combined with an energy storage system that the powertrain becomes a hybrid. Pure FCVs, systems that can manage with the dynamic power demands of the vehicle, require maximum power; the power demand of the car matches the maximum output power of the fuel cell system. The production of power from the fuel cell system has to react instantaneously since there is no energy storage system within the vehicle. This is dynamic power adaptation. In addition, the fuel cell starting time must be in the same range as an internal combustion engine or battery electric vehicle. Finally, the power output of a fuel cell system, while temperature-dependent (the power output of the fuel cell may be reduced at a lower temperatures), must not be overly-reduced at the ambient temperatures at which it is expected to operate.

Telias *et al.* briefly evaluate two configurations of hybrid FCVs. The conventional hybrid contains batteries that store collected braking energy and supply peaking power, or as an alternative, use a supercapacitor for short-term peak power demands. The plug-in hybrid system can be used with or without a connection to the electricity storage grid—it can be charged from the fuel cell system, or charged with electricity. This allows the user to drive moderate distances using grid-supplied electricity.

FCVs require technologically advanced components that are not found in conventional vehicles today. The major components of a typical FCV include: fuel cell system power electronics (consisting of a fuel cell stack offering significant potential for cost-effective production based on economy of scale, and a motor controller, DC/DC converter, and inverter), fuel processor, current inverters and conditioners, and a heat recovery system), electric machines (use alternating current to provide traction to the wheels of the vehicle, therefore enabling propulsion; an energy storage system, and a hydrogen storage system.

Polymer electrolyte fuel cells, hereafter PEFCs, are typically applied for automotive use. Low-temperature fuel cells show good performance regarding nominal power, cold temperature performance, and service life. High-temperature PEFCs have substantial advantages regarding water management and CO-tolerance, but function slightly less well under low-temperature conditions. Generally, PEFCs can be operated at low pressure with more simple auxiliaries, which result in less power demand for the air compression. In this scenario, humidity control is needed. In a high-pressure scenario, power density can be increased, allowing the water volume for humidity control to be reduced with the addition of a compressor unit. The majority of FCVs today take advantage of high power, high energy, and long cycle life energy storage devices to improve system performance. These energy storage devices can provide assistance to the fuel cell system during events in which temperature and fuel delivery to the fuel cell stack result in voltage drops during high-load demands. Currently, energy storage systems available for use in FCVs include "lithium-ion, nickel-metal hydride, and lead-acid batteries, as well as ultra capacitors." Onboard hydrogen storage systems are also required for FCVs. The development of an onboard system to store hydrogen fuel still remains an inhibiting factor for the widespread commercialization of hydrogen. Research and development of additional technologies is still being conducted.

Worldwide, various FCV demonstration projects have been used as a basis for development of future hydrogen infrastructure performance. These demonstrations offer the opportunity to "gather valuable data—including fuel economy, and other factors—that can be used in working towards creative solutions to technical barriers facing hydrogen fuel cell technology in automobiles." Telias *et al.* highlight select results of "notable passenger vehicle demonstrations" from around the world including: North America, the European Union, and Japan. Over the next decade, these project committees will focus on infrastructure development and preparing the market for the introduction of their vehicle models in the transportation sector worldwide. Additionally, the authors assess the international trends in funding for RD&D activities regarding fuel cell and hydrogen technologies for transport applications and the policies that provide the framework of development for these activities. In the United States, the Fuel Cell Technologies Program is responsible for the research and development of: hydrogen production and delivery, hydrogen storage, fuel cell stack components, as well as various aspects of the safety standards, technology, marketing, transportation, and distribution of fuel cells. In the European Union, the Multi-Annual Implementation Plan of the "Fuel Cells and Hydrogen Joint Technology Initiative" is responsible for the research and development of: transport and refueling infrastructure, hydrogen production and distribution, stationary power generation and combined heat and power, early markets, and cross-cutting issues. In Japan, The "Cool Earth – Innovative Energy Technology Program" gives "priority to 21 technologies based on their potential to reduce CO_2 emissions and to deliver substantial performance improvement, cost reduction, and increased diffusion as well as technologies where Japan could have the global lead." In this program, the development for FCVs foresees cost reduction through technology development and improvement of durability and cruising distance over the next decade.

While there has been significant development of battery electric vehicles and plug-in hybrid electric vehicles, manufacturers are continuing research efforts on FCVs. The list of shortcomings of FCVs has been reduced dramatically, although improvements regarding investment costs of the powertrain and installation of the proper fueling infrastructure need further development. Telias *et al.* suggest learning from the compressed natural gas infrastructure network for fueling stations or introducing the fuel cell system as a "range extender" in combination with a driving battery plugged or unplugged. While the authors anticipate competition over the technologies of the pure battery electric vehicle and the FCV, the favored outcome of the two systems will be based in its superior "combination of costs and convenience."

High-Energy Electrode Investigation For Plug-In Hybrid Electric Vehicles

While various high-energy-density electrode materials for lithium-ion (Li-ion) batteries exist, Lu *et al.* (2011) suggest that other engineering approaches, such as electrode optimization, be considered to meet the energy requirements for plug-in hybrid electric vehicles (PHEVs). The authors investigate the impact of the electrode thickness on the energy density of Li-ion batteries, although their findings show that the electrode thickness would affect the battery's "integrity, electrochemical performance, and cycleability." That is why it is important to find both an appropriate and practical thickness of the electrode for high-energy batteries. The authors also found that the hybrid pulse power characterization (HPPC) test indicates that the electrode resistance is "inversely proportional" to the electrode thickness. This allows for the use of thicker electrodes, practical thickness measuring around 100 μm, in Li-ion batteries to meet standard PHEV power requirements. The authors also find that cycle performance shows that cells with a "higher loading density have a similar capacity retention to cells with a lower loading density."

Lu *et al.* assess high-energy electrode density levels for the purpose of meeting the energy requirements for PHEVs. In fiscal year 2009, the Department of Energy (DOE) began its pledge to enable the development of PHEVs with a 40-mile all-electric range. However, along with other challenges regarding Li-ion batteries in the HEV application, the issue of cycle life, as well as providing sufficient energy within the weight and volume requirements of PHEVs became apparent. Currently, there is no commercially available high-energy material to meet the needs of the proposed 40-mile PHEV. However, this issue can be addressed by engineering approaches. Thus far, various possibilities have been investigated for experimental and modeling techniques including electrode porosity and inactive additives. Both of these possibilities can be utilized to improve the energy density.

Lu *et al.* examine a series of cathode and anode electrodes with varying thicknesses and porosities that were prepared using a small laboratory coater. Both lithium half-cells and fuel cells were created in an "inert atmosphere glove box with an oxygen level of less than 5 ppm." Additionally, the results of the electrochemical performance of coin cells, investigated using the HPPC profile, were also used in the study to determine thickness effects.

While no commercially available electrode materials currently exist to meet the weight and volume requirements of a 40-mile PHEV, it is important to consider battery structure optimization to increase battery energy density, for example, by increasing electrode thickness. Using a battery design model based on PHEV energy requirements, the authors experiment with various cathode and anode electrode thicknesses. They found that the cathode electrode should be thicker than 130 μm if only 70% of the total battery energy will be utilized and that the "battery weight reduction rate levels off when the electrode thickness is greater than 100 μm." This is due to less weight and volume from the current collector and separator. The authors also evaluate the relationship between the electrode thickness and coating weight before and after calendering. Electrode integrity gets worse when the electrode thickness reaches above 100 μm. Thicker electrodes, however, do not affect the useable capacity of the NCA cathode material at a low cycling rate, although it is affected by the electrode thickness at a higher discharge rate. Due to this, better binder strength must be developed which will allow for thicker electrodes and volume expansion. The authors determine that within the relationship between the deliverable capacity and discharge rate of NCA half-cells, the usable capacity will drop significantly when the discharge rate increases.

Power performance of the NCA half-cells with varying electrode thicknesses also utilized the HPPC test. Area specific impedance (ASI) of the half-cells decreases as the electrode thickness increases and levels off according to the results from the half-cell and full-cell. Lu *et al.* clarify that "[t]his does not necessarily mean that the cell with the thicker electrode always has a higher power capability," thus confirming that thicker electrode cells must be discharged at a higher current density. This process can offset the lower impedance. However, this combination can cause tension on the transport of lithium ions in the electrolyte, limiting its rate capability. The last test regards the assessment of capacity fading of cells with various electrode-loading densities. No obvious difference was observed for the full-cells under this condition.

The authors conclude that while the HPPC test results indicate that the electrode impedance is "inversely proportional" to the electrode thickness, this is will allow for good power capability of the Li-ion battery with a higher loading density in the future. Higher loading densities have similar capacity retention as lower loading densities.

Conclusions

As threats of global warming increase in intensity, it is important to implement major, life-altering transformations for a prompt reduction of greenhouse gases. While taking all vehicles off the road is a highly impractical option, alternative vehicle models that contribute zero emissions must be considered. Currently, further engineering designs and implementation strategies are being developed, though based on an unreliable market, the future of the mass-implementation of electric vehicles is unknown. Perhaps with legal regulations set for vehicle development and emissions standards, all conventional engine vehicles will be prohibited. While this may prove economically difficult, particularly for those who must purchase new vehicles, individuals' impacts on the planet will become more widely recognized, and our society's collective ecological impacts will decrease dramatically. Once electric vehicles prove successful for individual vehicle owners, the technology can be applied on a larger scale to public transportation.

References Cited

Cheng, K., Liang, T., Lu, C., Shih, D., Cai, D., Hsu, M., Huang, J., 2010. A Web-based Light Electric Vehicle for Homecare Use – A Pilot Study. 2010 International Conference on Computational Aspects of Social Networks, 175–178.

Dominguez, E., Leon, J.I., Montero, C., Marcos, D., Rodriguez, M., Bordons, C., Ridao, M.A., Fernandez, E., 2010. Practical Implementation of an Hybrid Electric-Fuel Cell Vehicle. IEEE Proceedings from the Annual Conference of IEEE, 3828–3833.

Hori, Yoichi, 2010. Future Vehicle Society Based on Electric Motor, Capacitor and Wireless Power Supply. The 2010 International Power Electronics Conference, 2930–2934.

Offer, G.J., Howey, D., Contestabile, M., Clague, R., Brandon, N., 2010. Comparative analysis of battery electric, hydrogen fuel cell and hybrid vehicles in a future sustainable road transport system. Energy Policy 38, 24–29.

Peterson, Scott B., Whitacre, J.F., Apt, Jay, 2010. The Economics of Using Plug-In Hybrid Electric Vehicle Battery Packs for Grid Storage. Journal of Power Sources 195, 2377–2384.

Telias, G., Day, K., Dietrich, P. 2010. RD&D Cooperation for the Development of Fuel Cell, Hybrid, and Electric Vehicles within the International Energy Agency. 2010. World Battery, Hybrid and Fuel Cell Electric Vehicle Symposium & Exhibition, 1–6.

Van Bree, B., Verbong, G.P.J., Kramer, G.J., 2010. A Multi-Level Perspective on the Introduction of Hydrogen and Battery Electric Vehicles. Technological Forecasting & Social Change 77, 529–540.

Wenquan, L., Jansen, A., Dees, D., Nelson, P., Veselka, N.R., Henriksen, G., 2011. High-Energy Electrode Investigation For Plug-In Hybrid Electric Vehicles. Journal of Power Sources 196, 1537–1540.

8. Carbon Sequestration: a Comparison of Various Methods

Anna Fiastro

Climate change is a global issue that affects people and the environment. Over the past two centuries there has been an increase in greenhouse gases in the earth's atmosphere. This is in part due to human activities such as burning fossil fuels and biomass, activities that have been increasing since the 1700s with the industrial revolution. The burning of these compounds has changed the composition of the atmosphere and as a result, the earth's average temperature has increased, which in turn has influenced precipitation, storm patterns, and has led to a rise in sea level. These changes have a direct affect on agriculture and water supply, as well as ecosystem health and biodiversity.

One method to combat these extreme effects is carbon capture and storage. This chapter focuses on two approaches to capturing carbon. First, carbon that has already been released into the atmosphere in the form of carbon dioxide can be collected. Secondly, carbon can be collected before it has even been released into the atmosphere from industrial processes which continually emit new carbon dioxide into the atmosphere in massive quantities. Once the carbon has been captured there are various methods for storing it in a sustainable and long term way. This chapter discusses the most up-to-date scientific information concerning this carbon sequestration and compares the effectiveness of various methods, including geological and ocean sequestration as well as use in industrial processes such as concrete production.

Sequestration of CO_2 in Geological Formations as Carbonate Minerals

Atmospheric carbon dioxide concentrations have been steadily increasing over the past century causing detrimental effects on the earth's climate. In addition to efforts to decreased future carbon emissions, the capture and storage of current CO_2 in the atmosphere is an important component of a long-term solution for reducing CO_2 concentrations. One method proposed for this is geological CO_2 storage. This is a process in which CO_2 emissions are pumped into geological formations instead of into the Earth's atmosphere. Since the CO_2 being inserted into the rock is buoyant when compared to the rock and surrounding water, there are different trapping mechanisms to insure that the CO_2 does not resurface to be released into the air. The focus of a paper by Matter and Kelemen (2009) is "mineral tapping" in which dissolved CO_2 reacts with water and the minerals of the surrounding rock to form solid carbonate that will remain in place. This is a long-term storage solution for large quantities of CO_2. The success of this solution, however, depends on the type of physical and chemical properties of the location chosen for injection.

The emissions are pumped to depths of over 800 meters where the combination of temperature, pressure, and salinity, in addition to the pH of the location, induce a fluid-rock reaction that causes carbonate mineral formation. Early studies examined deep aquifers in sedimentary rock because of the porous nature of this rock. It was thought that space was a necessary characteristic of the host rock because it offered a place to deposit the carbonate mineral product. Sedimentary rock includes sandstone, siltstone, shale, and limestone, however these types of rock have very low mineral trapping potential. This is seen in prediction models run in various labs, and in field observations of natural CO_2 reservoirs leeching into rock.

The field of research then looked toward aquifers containing 'basic' silicate minerals, such as olivine, serpentine, pyroxenes, plagioclase, and basaltic glass. It was found that silicate minerals buffer the pH in these reactions making them essential for enhancing mineral storage. It has been shown in laboratory experiments and in natural analogues that these types of rock react rapidly to form carbonate minerals. These types of rock are also commonly found on every continent. This makes the capacity for CO_2 storage in carbonate enormous.

The original concern with mineral trapping was requirement for space. The reactions are often self-limiting because they fill in empty space and can create boundaries between the unreacted CO_2 and fluid. As was mentioned earlier, this was the advantage of sedimentary rock originally being examined. The porous nature of the rock is important to ensure ample room for product creation. It was thought that optimal rock containing silicate minerals would not be porous enough to have a continued reaction and convert all of the CO_2 to carbonate. As a solution to this, it was hypothesized that the crystallization will fracture the rock to increase permeability. This has been proven to occur in both laboratory simulations as well as in naturally occurring systems. The fracturing that occurs creates more space for the carbonate product to be deposited and allows the reactants to continually come in contact with each other, forming more carbonate.

Another aspect that makes this process a favorable solution to CO_2 capture is the self-heating cycle that occurs. Heat is given off from the initial reaction and remains to speed up the continued reaction of more and more CO_2, increasing the overall reaction rate. With continued reactions taking place, the elevated temperature is maintained and so is the speedy reaction rate. This results in more and more CO_2 being sequestered.

The combination of silicate minerals, fracturing and excess heat allow for large quantities of carbon dioxide to be captured and deposited in underground aquifers as carbonate minerals. This is a solution to increased CO_2 levels that is being examined further.

Sequestration of CO_2 in Basalt Geological Formations along the Eastern Seaboard of the United States

Carbon capture and storage has been proposed as an important component to a well rounded plan to control increasing carbon dioxide levels in the earth's atmosphere. One method for sequestering CO_2 is to pump new emissions into geological formations. Previous research has shown basalt and ultramafic rock reservoirs to be good, secure, long term locations for the sequestration of CO_2. Goldberg *et al.* (2010) examined the potential of various reservoir sites in the Central Atlantic Magmatic Province (CAMP) basalt flows to be sequestration sites for large cities along the eastern seaboard of the United States.

The Central Atlantic Magmatic Province (CAMP) lies on and off shore along the eastern coast of North America. CAMP consists of numerous basins of thick continental sediments with veins of basalt running through them. These basins were created during the Triassic and Jurassic time periods. Since these events, other seismic activity and interactions with water and the atmosphere have caused some of these rock formations to erode, while the remainder have become stratified with varying thickness and composition over a large area. This stratification has lead to ideal conditions for CO_2 injection and sequestration.

What has occurred is that layers of very thick and dense basalt have surrounded areas of less dense and porous basalt. The porous basalt allows space for a chemical reaction to occur between the minerals of the basalt and the injecting CO_2 creating a mineral carbonate that fills in the cracks. The dense basalt layers seal the pumped CO_2 and the carbonate product in the basin so that it is harder for it to be reintroduced into the environment and atmosphere.

These authors speculate that these types of layered formations can be found in the Orange Mountain basalt, the Newark Rift Basin, the Long Island Rift

Basins, and the South Georgia Rift Basin. This is based on sampling data, density and porosity profiles, computer modeling, and scientific speculation. These sites are close to major metropolitan areas on the east coast of the United States, allowing them to work efficiently as storage locations for areas of high industrial CO_2 output. The speculated size of the reservoirs also offers the potential to store massive amounts of CO_2. For example, estimates show that one basin could contain the equivalent emissions from 3 or more coal-fired power plants for up to 40 years.

Further study is necessary to confirm the existence of these basins, and demonstrate their suitability to act as sequestration locations. Studies would include high-resolution survey mapping, followed by drilling in and around locations. Pilot injection projects would then be conducted and monitored to determine the safety and effectiveness of this form of capture and storage. Goldberg *et al.* also suggested that research should first be conducted at on-shore sites as they are more accessible and cost effective, and then offshore sites can be explored with the increased technology and knowledge.

The Effects of Injecting CO_2 into Deep Bethypelagic Layers of the Ocean

In the face of increasing CO_2 levels in the atmosphere, one approach to reducing new CO_2 emissions is carbon capture and storage. Yamada *et al.* (2010) examine the technique of dissolution; injecting CO_2 into deep layers of the ocean. The limited mixing of these deep waters would prevent the CO_2 from entering the atmosphere for a long time, but the CO_2 could affect the prokaryotic populations at these depths and their associated nutrient cycles. The research looked at the effects of increased CO_2 on these populations by capturing samples of them in water samples from deep in the Pacific Ocean and conducting laboratory experiments on them, increasing CO_2 levels and evaluating the effects.

The plan for dissolution is to inject CO_2 into the benthypelagic zone, which ranges from 1000 to 3000 meters from the surface. This is an important area for the regeneration of nutrients and organic material. The layers of the ocean are separated by temperature and salinity gradients that prevent mixing. Due to limited mixing of the layers of the ocean it is thought that the CO_2 would not move up and not be introduced into the atmosphere; the CO_2 would dissolve into the surrounding water and remain at depth, causing a decrease in the pH, also known as acidification, but only locally. It is important to look at the effects of these elevated CO_2 levels on the systems that operate in these layers, specifically the prokaryotes who are responsible for these nutrient cycles.

Yamada *et al.* took water samples from two different locations in western North Pacific at 2000 meters deep, and used these in experiments within 10 days of sampling. Carbon dioxide injection conditions were simulated by bubbling air containing different concentrations of CO_2 though the tanks containing the samples. The pH, total cell count, and heterotrophic prokaryotic production rates were monitored in each sample. Although there was variation between the sites, thought to be due to seasonal differences, clear results were obtained. The bubbling of CO_2 increased the acidity of the water (decreased the pH). The total cell counts remained relatively constant independent of pH, but the heterotrophic prokaryotic production rates decreased with increasing acidity. Simply said, with more CO_2 in the water, productivity of the organisms living in it decreased went down.

It seems counter-intuitive that total cell count would remain the same while productivity went down. In order to further examine this, the researchers looked at the direct viable count, or the number of thriving prokaryotic cells capable of growth. This was shown to decrease with acidification, explaining the decreased productivity rates.

Another trial was run in which acidification was simulated by adding a chemical buffer. This showed similar results to the CO_2 bubbling method. As pH decreased and acidity increased, prokaryotic growth and production were lowered.

In these experiments, acidification suppressed bacterial activity more than Archaea activity. The significance of this is not fully understood, and further research is necessary to look at the life histories of different types of Archaea to better understand their reaction to changing pH levels.

Long-term Effectiveness of Different Types of CO_2 Sequestration

Increasing levels of CO_2 in the earth's atmosphere are causing changes to the climate on a global scale. Methods have been proposed to reduce the amount of carbon in the atmosphere as well as to decrease the amount of new carbon emissions being released. Carbon capture and storage has become a prominent proposal for collecting CO_2 from industrial outputs and sequestering them in various places. Many methods and locations have been proposed for carbon storage. Shaffer (2010) has researched and predicted the long-term effectiveness and consequences of different storage techniques, including deep ocean sequestration, onshore geological storage, and deep-ocean sediment storage. He compared these to a "business-as usual" emissions model, based on projections if no changes are made to current practices, and to a desirable future emissions model, which is the 'best-case' scenario for avoiding strong global warming. All the projections are drawn out to 50,000 A.D. Shaffer found that these methods offer short term solutions, because CO_2 is leaked and reintroduced into the atmosphere causing a delayed global warming effect. He concludes that the best way to free ourselves and future generations of this climate burden is to dramatically reduce emissions now.

Shaffer used the IPCC SRES model for the 'business–as-usual' and 'best-case' scenarios, and the Danish Center for Earth System Science (DCESS) model to make the long-term projections for the onshore and offshore scenarios. He compares the partial pressure of atmospheric CO_2, the geologically stored CO_2, the mean atmosphere and ocean warming, ocean carbon inventory change, and the 'dead zone' volume fraction of each method for the 50,000-year time scale. The change in pH and change in CO_2 was also predicted at the oceans surface and at 3,000 meters depth, for each scenario.

The 'business-as-usual' scenario had the highest CO_2 partial pressure and the most atmospheric and ocean warming for all that scenarios and the peaks in all three of these categories were the earliest on the time scale. This is to be expected because it does not involve any attempt to reduce the CO_2 emissions or their effects. This scenario also resulted in the highest fraction of global ocean volume to be considered a dead zone, meaning that there would be very little oxygen dissolved in the water to support life. "Business-as-usual" had a dramatic effect in the amount of carbon in the surface layers of the ocean, but did not have the greatest overall change in the amount of carbon in the ocean. In this category it was overshadowed by the deep-ocean sequestration. This analysis shows that some action should be taken in the face of increasing atmospheric carbon levels.

In deep-ocean sequestration, CO_2 is pumped into the cold, lower layers of the ocean that do not readily mix with the upper layers. In the long term this method for storing carbon has similar effects as the "business-as-usual" on atmospheric partial pressure of CO_2, atmospheric and oceanic warming, and the fraction of the ocean that is a "dead zone," but not until 2,000 years later. Then the ocean becomes mixed sufficiently to release the sequestered CO_2 to the atmosphere. Since in this method the CO_2 is directly introduced into the water, it does increase the amount of carbon in the ocean more dramatically than any of the other methods.

Another approach analyzed is onshore geological storage, where emissions are injected into geological formations deep underground. With this approach, there is a possibility of CO_2 leaking from the geological container and being introduced to the atmosphere. Therefore, this method was analyzed using three different leakage scenarios; rapidly, moderately, and weakly leaking projections. The rapidly leaking geological formation scenario had effects similar to the deep-ocean and the ocean sediment methods with severe affects on all the measured factors, but the effects where delayed when compared to current practices. The moderately leaking scenario was about half as severe as the rapidly leaking scenario and the peak was delayed by about 5,000 years after the 'business-as-usual.' The slowly leaking scenario had very little effect at all and was similar to the 'best-case' scenario, at least

50,000 years out when it was starting to show the same trends as the other scenarios, with rising effects in ocean carbon inventory and atmospheric and ocean warming. This is to be expected because the slow leakage would cause a more drawn out and subtle effect on the factors being examined, but an effect none the less.

The last method analyzed is to inject CO_2 into deep offshore ocean sediments. This projection was done assuming that the sequestered carbon would 'rapidly' leak from the rock confines. Since this is an offshore injection site, it will leak into the deep ocean layers. Thus, the projections are similar to those of deep ocean sequestration, but delayed 1,000 years by the CO_2 leaking out of the rock.

Shaffer concludes that while all these methods seem to minimize the effects of CO_2 emissions, the long-term effects are still present. He suggest that the best solution is to stop new emissions as soon as possible instead of trying to hide them away, and have them come back to cause trouble for future generations.

Effects of Iron Fertilization on Diatom Populations and Domoic Acid Concentrations.

Iron fertilization has been proposed as a solution to increased levels of CO_2 in the atmosphere and the resulting acidification of the world's oceans. Iron fertilization is a process in which iron is added to areas of open ocean to induce phytoplankton blooms; the species of phytoplankton targeted sequester CO_2 in their cells removing it from the atmosphere and upper levels of the oceans. The idea is that as these cells die they will sink to the bottom of the ocean with the acquired carbon where it will remain. It is important, however, to weigh the benefits of this procedure against the possible consequences. Silver *et al.* (2010) have shown that iron fertilization leads to increased biomass of diatom species from the genus *Pseudo-nitzschia,* which are known to produce the neurotoxin domoic acid (DA). This increase is directly correlated with increased levels of DA in the environment. This neurotoxin has been shown to have negative effects in both coastal and oceanic ecosystems, as well as at depth below fertilization sites; and the extent of this increases still is not fully understood.

Silver and colleagues surveyed 34 stations ranging from the Pacific subarctic to the Southern Ocean, some of which were historic iron fertilization sites. They collected and analyzed near surface water samples and sediment samples. They quantified and identified eleven *Pseudo-nitzschia* species from these samples and measured DA concentrations in the cells and water of each sample.

A correlation was found between increased *Pseudo-nitzschia* cell abundance and increased DA concentrations. Eleven species from the genus were identified in the samples, some containing just one species and some up to 4 different species. Due to the method of data collection toxin levels could not be assigned to specific species. Variability in toxin levels was attributed to different combinations of species as well as between variability among individuals or cells within a species. This variability is due to varying physical and chemical conditions as well as different strains within the species. This, however, does not affect the clear correlation between cell abundance and DA toxin levels.

It was also found that increased levels of DA toxin and *Pseudo-nitzschia* abundance was linked to areas of historic iron enrichment experimentation. While it has not yet been shown that these elevated toxin levels impact higher trophic levels in oceanic ecosystems, as seen in coastal regions, it has been proven that DA has reached levels that pose a threat to the oceanic ecosystems.

The data from this study also suggest that DA neurotoxins are delivered to deeper depths in the intact cells of these *Pseudo-nitzschia* species and at higher rates with iron fertilization. In areas where prior studies using iron fertilization took place, intact diatom cells containing DA were found in sediment samples that correlated with blooms occurring after fertilization.

Sequestration of New CO_2 Emissions by Reacting with Seawater

Human activity has caused the CO_2 levels in the atmosphere to increase to dangerous levels, resulting in changes in the earth's climate. Everyday new CO_2 emissions are being released from various sources and adding to this problem. Carbon intensive industrial plants, such as coal-fired power plants, contribute a large portion of these waste gas emissions. Wang *et al.* (2011) have investigated the use of magnesium and calcium ions to react with the emitted CO_2 to form a carbonate precipitate. The carbonate is a very stable substance that sequesters the carbon and keeps it from separating and mixing into the atmosphere. The authors propose the use of seawater as the source for the magnesium and calcium ions, particularly waste seawater from desalination plants with high ion concentrations. They determined the optimal conditions to push this reaction to form the most carbonate precipitant.

Wang *et al.* focused on the mixing of salt water with the CO_2 emissions from coal power plants. They used various equations to calculate the possible carbonate precipitation under different conditions and carbon emissions. They found that the pressure of the carbon containing gas and the acidity of the salt solution were the two driving factors of the reaction, and determined the optimal partial pressure and pH range.

For this reaction to happen the CO_2 from the gas must be absorbed into the liquid. By increasing the pressure of the gas, more CO_2 passes into the liquid and is available to form carbonate ions. The atmospheric pressure allows the ocean to take up CO_2 from the atmosphere naturally, but this is a slow process. Increasing the pressure to more than 1 atmosphere speeds up the formation of carbonate. Emissions from most industrial plants are in a gas form that has a partial pressure several times higher than that of the atmosphere. Therefore, the mixing of this gas with seawater should accelerate the process.

Wang *et al.* established that an enhanced alkaline solution would also lead to increased carbonate precipitation. Increased pH drives the buffer equilibrium from CO_2 towards the formation of carbonate ions (CO_3^{2-}). These ions then react to form the carbonate, which is precipitated out, sequestering the carbon in a stable condition. The more basic the solution, the more carbonate ions there are to form carbonate. There is however a threshold for this trend, where the pH is too high and unwanted precipitates are formed. Seawater does not have the optimal pH to push this reaction; however increasing its pH is a very difficult. The authors propose several ways to increase pH, including electrolytically, but with the technology available today, they are all expensive processes.

Pressure and pH cause more carbonate ions to be present to react with other positive ions to form the carbonate solids. The author's analysis of the various cations in seawater found that magnesium and calcium are abundant enough and strong enough cations to precipitate carbonate anions. The condensed seawater that comes from desalination plants as well as underground brine offer high concentrations of these ions to react with the carbonate ions.

Finally, Wang *et al.* applied these ideas to an existing coal-fired power plant. When the pressure of the gas and pH of the solution where known, the amount of precipitate could be calculated and the amount of carbon sequestered could be predicted. The addition of alkaline seawater to emissions seems to be a promising method of carbon capture and storage in the form of carbonate precipitate.

Possible Negative Implications of Ocean Urea Fertilization

Since the industrial revolution, there has been an ever-increasing concentration of CO_2 in the atmosphere contributing to global climate change. Ocean fertilization is one proposed method of carbon capture and storage; it is the use of fertilizers to stimulating the growth of phytoplankton species that take up CO_2 in their growth. One fertilizer being proposed is urea, a nitrogen rich organic compound. Unlike nitrogen fertilization, research of the effectiveness of urea as an ocean fertilizer is only being conducted by one laboratory at the University of Sydney, which has connections with Ocean Nourishment Corporation (ONC), a company that has the patent on the procedure. The environmental and social aspects of this procedure must be fully examined to determine if it a safe and effective solution for carbon sequestration before it is implemented on a large scale. Mayo-Ramsay (2010) discusses the process of urea fertilization, and its ability to reduce atmospheric levels of carbon and stimulate fisheries. She also examines its possible effects on the Sulu Sea, the leading site being considered.

Ocean urea fertilization utilizes a nutrient solution produced by mixing urea with other limiting nutrients. This nutrient solution is then put in the ocean where it increases the abundance of phytoplankton, and the resultant uptake of carbon from the atmosphere. This stimulation at the lowest trophic level is thought to trickle up the food chain and increase marine productivity of larger fish. The two benefits that are outlined are the sequestration of carbon and the increase in fish populations, which could help in the face of a global food shortage.

Professor Ian Jones is the head of the Ocean Technology Group at the University of Sydney, the only laboratory conducting research on urea fertilization. He also has interests in the Ocean Nourishment Corporation, an Australian commercial organization that has patented its urea fertilization technology. While the company claims to have conducted research on its technique and possible implications, no peer reviewed scientific articles have been published. The company did not consult the local governments or communities that would be affected by this experimentation.

Other scientific discussions and studies being conducted by independent groups have identified various possible dangers related to ocean fertilization. Added fertilizer can lead to the creation of hypoxic zones (areas void of oxygen) as well as the release of nitrous oxide (N_2O). This increase in nutrients can lead to an imbalance in the different species of phytoplankton and ecosystem composition. There is also a question of whether or not such fertilization actually leads to carbon sequestration. While the phytoplankton blooms do take up CO_2, the carbon must not be released back into the atmosphere in order for it to be an effective solution for climate change. In this case, the dead material constructed from the carbon must sink to the bottom of the ocean, but evidence shows that the phytoplankton stay on or near the surface creating a scum.

The proposed urea fertilization plant would pump urea into the Sulu Sea southeast of Asia. This site was selected because it is a fairly enclosed body of water that lacks nutrients but has sufficient phosphorous. While this might seem like a good location, the limited circulation can intensify the possibility of anoxic conditions with increased nutrients.

The other proposed benefit of the program is increased marine productivity, which would supposedly stimulate the local fisheries. Currently there is a vibrant aquaculture industry in the region and long-term production of fish through this method has not been proven. Even if there were increased productivity, the management of this fishery would become very complicated. The proposed site in the Sulu Sea is bordered by a number of States. The Ocean Nourishment Corporation has proposed a specific fishing license that would be necessary to fish in the waters affected by their plant, but would be nearly impossible to determine which fish were wild and which were grown under the influence of the fertilization conditions. Such a license would also be detrimental to the local fisher-people who rely on the fish for their survival, presenting a serious legal barrier to the viability and completion of this project.

Another legal concern is the distribution of the carbon credits obtained through the carbon sequestration. Currently the International Organization for Standardization is coordinating a system to validate and verify greenhouse gas accounting. The benefits of the program would need to be quantified and distributed among the States and organizations participating in the project, but the number of States involved makes this process difficult to agree upon, implement, and regulate.

CO_2 Sequestration in Various Industrial Cement Products

The concentration of CO_2 in the atmosphere has increased dramatically, which is causing irreversible change to global climate systems. Carbon capture and storage is one course of action proposed to remove some of this excess CO_2 and decrease the amount of new CO_2 being emitted. It is known that calcium will react with CO_2 under certain conditions and create calcium carbonate ($CaCO_2$), a stable compound that sequesters the carbon in a way that it is not reintroduced into the atmosphere. Furthermore, there are several industrial, calcium-carrying materials that can participate in this reaction. Previous research has shown that concrete can take up CO_2 as carbonate while it is curing. The incorporation of $CaCO_2$ into the concrete makes the material stronger. It also makes cement more compatible with wood materials for the production of products like wood-cement particleboard. The carbonation also reduces shrinking by about 50% as cement sets and makes the material less permeable to water. Currently, this practice is not used because the cost of producing CO_2 is so high that it is not economically feasible. However, it has been proposed that if recovered CO_2 were used, then this option would become economically possible with the introduction of a carbon credits or carbon tax systems. Monkman et al. (2010) compared different scenarios for using emitted CO_2 for this process and looked at the environmental and economic viability.

The authors compared recovered CO_2 to untreated industrial flue gas emissions in their ability to carbonate 4 different cement products. The recovered CO_2 was imitated with highly concentrated and pressurized CO_2. For each exposure, a continuous supply was used, causing constant pressure and CO_2 concentrations to mimic flue gas which is emitted at a pressure higher than atmospheric pressure. The cement product was closed in a chamber with the pressurized gas and allowed to take up the CO_2. After the designated period of time the chamber was emptied and refilled with flue gas. This process was repeated about seven times, and each time the carbon uptake gradually slowed down as it reached saturation. The amount of carbon taken up was quantified by the percent gain in mass of the cement.

Concrete masonry units (CMU) are one industrially produced product that was examined. CMU were found to be the ideal candidate for carbon uptake because it is porous and already cured in a closed camber, making the addition of a gas easy. Concrete paving stones were also looked at. They are not subjected to any special curing scheme so they could easily be placed in a large sealed room filled with gas for the carbonation treatment. Fiberglass mesh reinforced cement is a product that is cured with high pressure and moisture. Because if this, a large surface area to volume ratio is necessary, which also lends itself to carbon uptake. The last product examined in the study was cellulose fiberboard, used in place of asbestos cement. The curing steps for this material can also easily be replaced by carbonation curing, giving the benefit of hydration of the material and carbon sequestration. Both the fiberglass mesh cement and cellulose fiberboard benefit from a lowered pH, protecting the material from alkali corrosion.

All four of these materials would benefit in strength and durability from carbonation, and their curing processes could easily be replaced or supplemented by carbonation curing. In all cases the uptake from recovered CO_2 was greater than uptake from flue gas.

It is also important to compare the energy and CO_2 penalties for recovering, compressing, and transporting the CO_2 in order for it to be used. When this is taken into consideration, recovered CO_2 is still the most viable option, because it is already at high concentrations. The compression and transportation of flue gas makes it only feasible if the curing process occurs on site. The transportation associated with recovered CO_2 can also be compared to other capture and storage methods, such as geological storage, which would result in equal or more transportation emissions.

Part of the analysis of processing emissions is the comparison of carbonation curing with steam and autoclave curing, the methods predominantly used in the industry. The emissions from carbonation curing are less than one tenth of those associated with steaming and autoclaving. This method is also attractive if one takes into account the possible trading value of carbon and improved technologies reducing energy use in production phases.

One last analysis was done looking at the carbon uptake of ladle slag fines as a replacement for sand. This was done using a different CO_2 exposure process than the other materials. The particulates were exposed to gas made up of 50% CO_2 at atmospheric pressure. This was meant to replicate flue gas without the compression step that is so energy expensive. The material was found to have a modest carbon uptake of about 10% after almost 60 days. This is not thought to be the best opportunity for carbon sequestration but other calcium-rich slags may serve this goal more affectively.

Conclusions

In theory, carbon sequestration is an integral part of any plan to curb the effects of global warming and climate change. While some of these methods are proving to be very promising, greater action must be taken to face this issue head on. Currently there are no large-scale projects to sequester new emissions or emitted carbon from the atmosphere. Most importantly, hiding carbon away in the corners of the earth is only a Band-Aid solution. A dramatic reduction in new emissions is the most affective and stable long-term solution to climate change.

References Cited

Goldberg, D., Kent, D., Olsen, P., 2010. Potential on-shore and off-shore reservoirs for CO_2 sequestration in Central Atlantic magmatic province basalts. Proceedings of the National Academy of Science 107, 1327.doi:10.1073/pnas.0913721107.

Matter, J., Kelemen, P., 2009. Permanent storage of carbon dioxide in geological reservoirs by mineral carbonation. Nature geoscience. doi:10.1038/NGEO683.

Mayo-Ramsay, J., 2010. Environmental, legal and social implications of ocean urea fertilization: Sulu sea example. Marine Policy. 34, 831–835.

Monkman, S., Shao, Y., 2010. Integration of carbon sequestration into curing process of precast concrete. Civil Engineering. DOI:10.1139/L09-140.

Shaffer, G. 2010. Long-term effectiveness and consequences of carbon dioxide sequestration. Nature Geoscience. DOI:10.1030/NGEO896.

Silver, M., Bargu, S., Coale, S., Benitez-Nelson, C., Garcia, A., Roberts, K., Sekula-Wood, E., Bruland, K., Coale, K.,2010.Toxic diatoms and domoic acid in natural and iron enriched waters of the oceanic Pacific. Proceedings of the National Academy of Science 107, 0762.doi:10.1073/pnas.1006968107.

Wang, W., Hu, M., Ma, C. 2011. Possibility for CO_2 sequestration using seawater. Bioinformatics and Biomedical Engineering 4, 1–4.

Yamada, N., Tsurushima, N., Suzumura, P., 2010. Effects of Seawater Acidification by Ocean CO_2 Sequestration on Bathypelgic Prokaryote Activities. Journal of Oceanography. Vol 66, p 571–580.

Section II—Water Supply and Agriculture

9. Effect of Global Warming on the World's Ice Cover

Sachi Singh

One of the most important consequences of global warming is the loss of mass from the Greenland and Antarctica ice sheets and land-based glaciers around the world (Smith 2011). Today, coastal glaciers in West Antarctica are thinning, land-based glaciers are retreating and large icebergs are being calved from the Greenland ice sheet (GrIS). Increased rates of ice thinning and ice flow is said to be consistent with increases in global surface temperatures.

In order to study the mass loss from ice sheets and glaciers, scientists analyze surface mass balance estimates—which is the difference of snow and ice accumulation and ablation—in the context of increased surface temperatures. While there is a strong positive correlation between increased surface temperatures and rates of melting, reduced albedo and precipitation can also have a major effects on glacier dynamics. Tedesco *et al.* (2011) found that the strong negative surface mass balance of the GrIS in 2005 was caused by high surface temperatures, as well as reduced albedo, longer melting season and an increase in the number of days that bare ice was exposed in the GrIS.

Ocean circulation patterns and ocean/fjord temperatures are other factors that significantly influence ice sheet dynamics. A rise in global sea-surface temperatures enhances basal sliding, which increases glacier speeds and undermines the integrity of calved ice and sea ice. In 2003 and 2005, the southeast outlet glaciers of the Greenland ice sheet retreated significantly, while in 2006, the glacier speeds decreased and the ice sheet re-advanced. The deposition of cold water into the East Greenland Coastal Current (EGCC)—which brings fresh, cold water to the coast—strengthened the cold current, decreased sea-surface temperatures and slowed down glaciers speeds in 2006 (Murray *et al.*, 2011). Submarine melting is said to be another cause for the acceleration of glacier speeds and mass loss of outlet glaciers. In a study of a major outlet glacier in the GrIS, the Straneo *et al.* (2011) concluded that the stratified waters of the Arctic and the Atlantic oceans significantly increased submarine melt in the summer seasons. Thus, regional ocean-ice sheet interactions can control the mass loss of coastal and outlet glaciers.

Supraglacial debris have also been observed to influence glacier dynamics and modify their responses to climate change. Scherler *et al.* (2011) studied the effect of debris cover on surface velocities of 286 Himalayan glaciers; they found that debris cover influences anthropogenic and natural radiative heat transfer. Their results indicated that an increase in debris cover leads to a reduction in melt rates, and slows down the glaciers' response to rising temperatures. Thus, to improve estimate accuracy, topographic variations should also be factored into future mass-balance calculations.

Multi-decadal mass balance observations are required to estimate long term trends in ice sheet dynamics. While the mass balance estimates can accurately predict the mass loss from the ice sheets, Rignot *et al.* (2011) claim that these estimates are not sufficient to predict the non-linear contributions of the ice sheets to the rise in sea-level. Sea-level rise is the most important consequence of the melting ice sheets and glaciers. Rignot *et al.* used two independent methods of analysis to estimate that the mass loss from the Antarctica and Greenland ice sheets was three times that from mountain glaciers and ice caps. They concluded that the mass loss from ice sheets will be the biggest contributor to sea-level rise in the forthcoming decades. These results are in agreement with Radic and Hock's (2011) findings, as both papers conclude that the Intergovernmental Panel for Climate Change's (IPCC) projections for the contribution of ice sheets to sea-level rise may be too conservative. In fact, Radic and Hock predict that there will be a significant reduction in glacier volume by 2100 and that some mountainous regions may even lose upto 75% of their present ice volume.

These accelerated glacier speeds and significant ice loss also increase the frequency of volcanic activity (Tuffen, 2010). An increase in volcanic activity could disrupt the stability of ice sheets and cause massive floods and mudflows down the slopes of the volcano. The thinning of ice also reduces sub-glacial explosions—as a consequence, there will be an increase in explosive eruptions that are associated with large amounts of ashfall and pyroclastic debris.

Thus, recent research has unequivocally shown that the world's ice reserves are shrinking; this not only causes sea-level rise, but also has massive implications for coastal and polar habitats.

Reduced Albedo and Accumulation Contribute to Negative Surface Mass Balance of the Greenland Ice Sheet

The year 2010 saw a large increase in near-surface temperatures along the coast of the GrIS; consequently, these unusually warm surface temperatures led to a huge increase in surface melting over the GrIS. To further explore this phenomenon, Tedesco *et al.* (2011) used data from satellite sensors, surface glaciological observations and regional atmospheric models to study the surface albedo, accumulation and the number of days bare ice was exposed over the GrIS in 2010. Their results indicated that the high near-surface temperatures over the GrIS led to a strongly negative surface mass balance—defined as the difference between accumulation and ablation of ice and snow—which was further intensified by the decrease in albedo and the increase in the number of days bare ice was exposed in the GrIS. Thus, the authors concluded that these anomalous conditions led to a longer melting season and contributed to the strongly negative surface mass balance of the GrIS in 2010.

In large areas of the ablation zone in the south of the GrIS, the melting season had started 50 days earlier than the average melting season (measured from 1979 to 2009) and had ended exceptionally late in 2010. While the increase in surface melting can be positively correlated with the increase in near-surface temperatures, recent studies have shown that the melting of the GrIS also depends on the accumulation, radiation, and refreezing and sublimation conditions. The surface mass balance is also strongly correlated with albedo because when melting increases, the grain size of the snow increases and which consequently, decreases the albedo. In this study, the authors used moderate-resolution imaging spectroradiometer (MODIS) albedo product to study anomalies in albedo; they also used data from automatic weather stations and regional surface and energy models to study the surface mass balance anomalies in 2010. They found the largest negative albedo anomalies occurred in August along the south west coast of the ice sheet; they hypothesized that the reduced amount of snowfall, enhanced melting and increased number of bare ice exposure days could have led to the 2010 albedo anomalies. While the early melt season was triggered by the large increase in near-surface temperatures, the reduced accumulation and albedo were more likely to be responsible for the premature bare ice exposure. Thus, the authors inferred that the anomalously warm conditions reduced the accumulation and albedo, which led to the strongly negative surface mass balance of the GrIS in 2010.

Debris Cover Affects Himalayan Glaciers' Response to Climate Change

The Himalayan glaciers are an important source of drinking water, agriculture and hydropower for central and south Asia, however, the remoteness of these glaciers makes ground-based data collection tricky. Thus, scientists are forced to use glacier retreats and advances to measure the impact of climate change on the glaciers. However, Scherler *et al.* (2011) claim these approaches are not entirely accurate as supraglacial debris can affect the the glacier's response to climate change. In order to asses this further, the authors analyzed 286 glaciers in the greater Himalayan Range between 2000 and 2008. They discovered that glaciers that are heavily covered with debris and have stagnant (not moving), low-gradient terminus regions have stable fronts while the monsoon-driven glaciers are retreating. Their results indicate that Himalayan glaciers dynamics seem to be heavily dependent on the debris cover, and show no uniform response to climate change.

Supraglacial debris are said to influence the terminus dynamics of glaciers and modify their response to climate change. To further study the terminus dynamics of the glaciers in the greater Himalaya region, the authors studied the frontal changes and surface velocities of 286 glaciers between 2000 and 2008. They also mapped debris cover to test whether regional disparities in debris cover accounted for the spatial variations in glacier terminus dynamics. The authors found that the regional distribution of stagnant glaciers with stable fronts varied significantly in the greater Himalayan region: they were most common in the Hindukush, southern, and northern central Himalayas and were completely absent in the Karakoram region. Since accumulation areas in Karakoram are relatively steep, stagnant glaciers are absent and cannot account for the stable or advancing glaciers in the region. The authors claim that the westerly-derived winter precipitation could explain the positive mass balance disturbance in Karakoram.

In all other places, the formation of stagnant ice relies on low-gradient slopes and is confined to the terminus region of debris-covered glaciers with shallow gradients. The authors claim that debris-cover—which is almost always a few centimeters thick—leads to a reduction in melt rates and slows down the glacier's response to climate change. Debris-cover also influences anthropogenic and natural radiative heat transfer. Thus, the authors conclude that topographic factors, which usually vary with terrain, have significant effects on the glacier's response to climate change and should be accounted for in future mas-balance calculations.

Ocean Regulation Controls Ice Sheet Mass Loss in the Southeast Greenland Ice Sheet

During the years 2003 and 2005, the southeast outlet glaciers of the GrIS underwent dramatic thinning and the ice sheet significantly retreated; surprisingly in 2006, the acceleration rates of the two largest outlet glaciers of the ice sheet decreased, causing the ice sheet to cease thinning and re-advance. In this paper, Murray *et al.* (2010) explore this synchronous acceleration and thinning of the ice sheet, and propose that regional factors have the greatest impact on these ice sheet-ocean interactions. They conclude that the ice sheet mass loss in the southeast GrIS is primarily caused by the warming and cooling of the coastal waters around the coastal glaciers.

Atmospheric warming and ocean/fjord temperatures both significantly affect glacier dynamics. Atmospheric warming can lead to increased sea-surface temperatures. which enhance basal sliding and increase glacier speeds. Consequently, the meltwater can enter the crevasses of the glaciers and increase the rate of glacier calving. Similarly, warm surface waters can reduce the extent of fjord ice and undermine the integrity of the ice melange (which are small pieces of calved ice and sea ice), which can eventually lead to higher rates of calving and faster flow conditions. In the paper, the authors analyzed the flow speeds, surface elevation, and calving front positions for tidewater terminating glaciers in southeast Greenland to determine the relationship between oceanic processes and glacier dynamics. From the analysis of the sea-surface temperatures, they found the the glacier speed-up of 2003 was not caused by the increase in surface meltwater and basal sliding; instead, it was caused by the warm surface waters that were brought to the southeast coast of Greenland by the Irminger Current (IC). The IC—which brings warm, high salinity water from the Atlantic—bifurcates to the west of Iceland, causing one of its branches to flow southwards along the southeast coast of Greenland; the East Greenland Coastal Current (EGCC)—which brings fresh, cold water to the coast—flows right by the IC, along the landward side of the continental shelf. The authors found that the 2003 speed-up of glaciers—associated with warm IC and weak EGCC—led to a large deposition of cold water into the EGCC; this increased ice discharge into the EGCC strengthened the cold current, decreased the sea-surface temperatures and subsequently, slowed down the glaciers in 2006. Thus, the authors conclude that the ice sheet's input provided a negative feedback to the EGCC, which controlled the ice sheet mass loss and re-stabilized the coastal glaciers.

Ocean Stratification Causes Submarine Melting in a Major Greenland Outlet Glacier

Submarine melting is said to be a potential cause for the widespread acceleration and mass loss of outlet glaciers. Since 2000, the retreat and acceleration of outlet glaciers accounts for 50% of Greenland's net mass loss. To further explore this phenomenon, Straneo *et al.* (2011) conducted surveys of the Sermilik Fjord, which is a major outlet of the GrIS, in August 2009 and in March 2010. Their data revealed that both the cold, fresh Arctic waters (PW) and the warm, salty subtropical waters from the North Atlantic (STW) cause submarine melt in the summer, while only the STW drives the melt in the winter. Thus, due to the stratification of the waters, the ice edge is organized into multiple overturning cells, which increases the rate of fjord melting with depth.

Ocean-driven melting has important implications for ice sheet variability and sea-level rise. Typically, submarine melt rates are estimated from mass-balance calculations using ice-flow and ice-thickness data, however, these calculations do not provide any information on the water mass and circulation responsible for the melting. In this study, the authors surveyed a major outlet glacier of the Greenland ice sheet and collected measurements for the summer and winter conditions in the fjord. They determined that the thermal forcing of ambient waters (the heat availa-ble to melt the ice) and the circulation at the ice edge are the main factors that drive submarine circulation. They found that in the summer, both PW and STW cause submarine melting in the fjord, leading to large seasonal changes in stratification of the waters. Temperature and salinity data along the fjord show that the PW and STW layering is preserved even at the glacier's terminus. Analysis of the summer data reveals that there are multiple overturning cells along the fjord, which give rise to non-uniform heat transport and increase the rates of melting with depth. These two observations reinforce the hypothesis that the PW and STW strongly influence circulation and melting at the ice edge.

Thus, the authors conclude that the single overturning cell model is not sufficient to understand the submarine melting rates of the Greenland ice sheet. They believe that the Greenland glacier dynamics are the complex consequence of the interface of the Atlantic/Arctic waters, as well as the changes in large-scale ocean circulation.

Efficient Subglacial Drainage Systems Reduce Velocity and Duration of Ice Flow at Warm Temperatures

Recent studies on the mass balance of the GrIS have shown that the thick-ening of the sheet's interior is offset by its mass loss near coastal regions due to basal lubrication (a process by which the surface meltwater penetrates to the base of the ice sheet and enhances basal sliding). To study this mechanism further, Sundal *et al.* (2011) observed the spatial and temporal variations in ice flow of six glaciers in the GrIS over a period of five years. They found that there was a significant increase in the speed of the ice flow in the summer in comparison to that in the winter. Peak rates of ice flow are known to be positively correlated with an increased degree of melting; however, this trend is not universally observed, as ice speeds slow down significantly in warm summers. The authors hypothesize that a more efficient sub-glacial drainage system contributes to the reduction in ice velocities in warm sum-mers.

The combined effect of increased surface melting and ice sheet flow is said to hasten the mass loss of the GrIS; however, recent data models on the mass loss of the GrIS have not been able to incorporate the effects of surface melting induced acceleration into their predictions because little is known about the hydraulic forces associated with the melting. To explore these hydraulic forces, the authors studied the satellite observations of ice flow recorded in the southwest corner of the GrIS to examine the development of the ice flow in years of markedly different melting. They found that the average winter speed of glaciers (122 m/year) was significantly lower than the speed in the summer (138 m/year); they also observed an increased variance of glacier speeds over the summer. Thus, the authors conclude that the seasonal variations in melting drives the seasonal variations in ice flow. The variations in the timing, extent and quantity of surface run-off, and variations in the routing of water at the base of the the ice-sheet could all contribute to the seasonal ice flow cycles. The authors investigated further to find that the ice flow in the late summers was three times shorter and significantly slower than that in the early summer. While some scientists believe that greater melting induces greater ice velocity, the authors believe that even though the peak rate of flow increases with high melting, an efficient subglacial drainage system leads to a reduction in the speed as well as the duration of the flow. Since basal lubrication alone cannot explain this phenomenon, the authors claim that the glacial drainage adjusts to accommodate an increase in ice flow; abundant meltwater could trigger a change from an inefficient cavity system to an efficient channelized system of drainage, which could lead to a reduction in subglacial water pressure and ice speeds. These patterns have been observed in the High Arctic and Alaskan valley glaciers.

Since the rates of surface melting of the GrIS are said to double over the 21st century, it would be useful to gain a deeper understanding of the mechanism that drives these changes in subglacial drainage patterns.

Multi-Model Analyses Reveals the Regional Contribution of Mountain Glaciers and Ice Caps to Future Sea-level Rise

Scientists believe that mountains glaciers and ice caps have been a major contributor to the rise in global sea-levels over the past decades. In this paper, Radić & Hock (2011) investigate the Intergovernmental Panel for Climate Change's (IPCC) projections for the global sea-level rise in the twenty first century, and they conclude that these estimates are not wholly accurate as they do not account for the effects of precipitation and the regional factors influencing the rise in sea-levels. The authors projected the changes in volume of all the ice caps and glaciers on Earth in response to twenty first century temperature and precipitation projections from ten global climate change models (GCMs) reported by the IPCC. They conclude that glaciers in Arctic Canada, Alaska and Antarctica would be largest contributors to the rise in global sea-levels in 2100. Thus, there will be a significant reduction in total glacier volume by 2100, and some mountainous regions may even lose up to 75% of their present ice volume.

The Fourth Assessment Report of the IPCC predicts that the wastage of glaciers and ice caps will lead to a 0.07 to 0.17 m rise in global sea-levels in the twenty first century. Another study found the accelerating rates of mass loss from the glacier mass balance data between 1995 and 2005; the authors of this study used this model to predict a 0.240±0.128 m rise in sea levels, assuming this rate of acceleration is constant. In order to resolve these discrepancies, Radić & Hock studied the volume changes of mountain glaciers and ice caps in 19 spatially resolved glacierized regions. To quantify future volume changes, the authors developed a calibrated mass balance model to applied it to all the glaciers available in the World Glacier Inventory (WGI-XF). According to their multi-model means, glaciers around the world will cause a 0.124±0.037 m rise in sea-level by 2100. Assuming the GCMs are accurate, the authors predict that there will be a global ice volume loss of 0.124±0.037 m SLE (sea level equivalents) by 2100. The volume loss varies considerably from region to region; the smallest loss was predicted to be in Greenland and High Mountain Asia, and the largest in the European Alps and New Zealand. However, these places are not significant contributors to the future rise in sea-level. The glaciers in Arctic Canada, Alaska and Antarctica are estimated to be the largest contributers to the rise in sea-levels. While there are some uncertainties associated with the rise initial setup of the model, this study reveals the main regional contributers to sea-level rise and pinpoint the areas that are most vulnerable to glacier waste. Thus, if warming continues as expected, glaciers will be a large contributer to sea-level rise around the world.

Contribution of the Greenland and Antarctica Ice Sheets to Future Sea-level Rise

In recent years, the rates of thinning and flow of ice sheets have been increasing rapidly all around the world. Typically, researchers use surface mass balance estimates to measure this mass loss and predict future trends in ice sheet mass balance. However, Rignot et al. (2011) claim that surface mass balance calculations do not accurately represent the ice sheet's contribution to sea level rise. In their paper, the authors used the rate of change of mass loss coupled with surface mass balance calculations to study the contribution of the ice sheets of Greenland and Antarctica to sea-level rise. Their results revealed that over the last 8 years, the Greenland and Antarctica ice sheet loss has accelerated by 36.3 ± 2 Gt/yr, 3 times more than the acceleration from mountain glaciers and icecaps. Given the magnitude of this acceleration, the authors conclude that ice sheets will be the major contributor to sea-level rise in the 21st century.

Multi-decadal mass balance observations are required to estimate long term trends in ice sheet mass balance. While the mass balance estimates have improved significantly in the last decade, they are not sufficient to predict the nonlinear contributions of the ice sheet to rise in sea-level. In this paper, the authors used the mass budget method (MBM) and the gravity method to estimate the temporal variations in the mass balance of the Greenland and Antarctica ice sheets. The MBM calculates the ice sheet's rate of mass change by comparing the surface mass balance from regional atmospheric models to the ice discharge—which is calculated using glacier velocities and ice thickness data. The gravity method uses data from the Gravity Recovery and Climate Experiment (GRACE) to estimate the rate of change of mass as a function of time. Using both these models, the authors estimated that in 2006, the Greenland and Antarctic ice sheets had a combined mass loss of 475 ± 158 Gt/year, equivalent to 1.3 ± 0.4 mm/year rise in sea-level. They also estimated in the last 18 years, the acceleration in mass loss was 21.9 ± 1 Gt/year for Greenland and 14.5 ± 2 Gt/year for Antarctica, with a combined total of 36.3 ± 2 Gt/year acceleration in mass loss. Since this acceleration is 3 times larger than for mountain glaciers and ice caps, the authors concluded that the mass loss from ice sheets will be the biggest contributor to sea-level in the forthcoming decade. Thus, the IPPC's projections for the contribution of ice sheets to sea-level rise may be too conservative.

The Current Rates of Ice Thinning Accelerate the Frequency of Volcanic Hazards and Eruptions

There is a strong positive correlation between the melting of ice and the acceleration of volcanic activity. Since glaciers and ice sheets on volcanoes are melting rapidly, Tuffen (2010) concludes that there will be an increase in volcanic eruptions and hazards in the 21st century.

Rapid thinning and recession of ice has been observed on many active and dormant volcanoes. The current ice recession is caused primarily by increased global temperatures, reduced precipitation and regional geothermal and volcanic pressures. Similar ice recessions in the past have been associated with massive increases in volcanic activity. In the past, the thinning of ice has resulted in more explosive eruptions and the collapse of volcano edifices. While it is difficult to quantitatively compare the current ice recession to the past ones, Tuffen is certain that the frequency—and possibly the magnitude—of volcanic eruptions will increase significantly in the 21st century.

There are several hazards associated with thinning ice: any disturbance caused by volcanic eruptions disrupts the stability of the ice sheets and causes large floods and destructive mudflows down the slopes of the volcanoes. The meltwater, which is formed as a consequence of the melting ice, can outwash plains, collapse dams and causes massive devastation of life and property. The thinning of ice can reduce sub-glacial eruptions, which leads to more explosive eruptions with increased ashfall and pyroclastic debris. The thinning of ice causes large scale destruction, but also causes an increase in the frequency of volcanic eruptions. The most dramatic example of the correlation between the thinning of ice and increased volcanic activity was observed in Iceland, where the unloading of ice caused a decompression which lead to a greater degree and depth range of mantle melting; consequently, there was a huge increase in the rate of magma eruption on the individual volcanic systems 1.5 ka after the deglaciation of the area. This indicates that Iceland volcanism responds to the change in ice thickness very quickly. While these trends have been observed in eastern California and western Europe, there is little analysis on whether the magnitude of the eruptions increase during deglaciation events. To further explore this, Tuffen compared the inferred rates of melting during the past glaciation events with the current rates of melting; while he could not conclusively construct the rates of ice thinning during the last glaciation due to different local geographic and geothermal discrepancies, he did observe that the current ice recession is considerably shorter that ones in the past. In order to shine more light on the relationship between climate change and volcanism, Tuffen suggests that future research should be conducted to understand the time scale of the volcano's response to ice thinning and the broader feedbacks between volcanism and climate change.

Conclusions

"Glacial retreat is one of global warming's most visually compelling manifestations." Even though there are regional variations in ice flow and mass loss, scientists predict that the Earth is warming and that the ice is shrinking in most areas (Schmidt, 2011). These accelerated glacier speeds contribute heavily to sea-level rise and the increase in frequency and magnitude of explosive volcanic eruptions, which could have disastrous impacts on coastal and polar habitats, as well as human life and property.

References Cited

Murray, K., Scharrer, K. , James, T. D., Dye, S. R., Hanna, E., Booth, A. D., Selmes, N., Luckman, A., Hughes, A. L. C., Cook, S., Huybrechts, P. 2010. Ocean regulation hypothesis for glacier dynamics in southeast

Greenland and implications for ice sheet mass changes. doi:10.1029/2009JF001522.

Radić, V., Hock, R. 2011. Regionally differentiated contribution of mountain glaciers and ice caps to future sea-level rise. Nature Geoscience. doi:10.1038/ngeo1052.

Rignot, E., I. Velicogna, M. R.van den Broeke, A. Monaghan, and J. Lenaerts. 2011. Acceleration of the contribution of the Greenland and Antarctic ice sheets to sea level rise, Geophys. Res. Lett., 38, L05503, doi:10.1029/2011GL046583.

Scherler, D., Bookhagen, B., Strecker, M. R. 2011. Spatially variable response of Himalayan glaciers
to climate change affected by debris cover. doi: 10.1038/ngeo1068.

Schmidt, C. W. 2011. Out of Equilibrium? The World's Changing Ice Cover. Environment Health Perspectives 119, 20–28.

Smith, J., H. 2011. More and More Melting. Science 331, 1367.

Straneo, F., Curry, R. G., Sutherland, D. A., Hamilton, G. S., Cenedese, C., Våge, K., Stearns, L. A. 2011. Impact of ocean stratification on submarine melting of a major Greenland outlet glacier.
<http://hdl.handle.net/10101/npre.2011.5670.1

Sundal, A. V., Shepherd, A., Nienow, P., Hanna, E., Palmer, S., Huybrechts, P. 2011. Melt-induced speed-up of Greenland ice sheet offset by efficient subglacial drainage. doi:10.1038/nature09740.

Tedesco, M., Fettweis, X., van den Broeke, M. R., van de Wal, R. S. W., Smeets, C. J. P. P., van de Berg, W. J., Serreze, M. C., Box, J. E. 2011. The role of albedo and accumulation in the 2010 melting record in Greenland. Doi:10.1088/1748-9326/6/1/014005.

Tuffen, H. 2010. How will melting of ice affect volcanic hazards in the 21st century? Philosophical Transactions of the Royal Society A 369, 2535–2558.

10. Desalination

Erin Partlan

The issue of fresh water availability is growing more severe as global populations continue to increase. In addition, climate change effects have the potential
to accelerate freshwater losses as precipitation patterns shift and glaciers melt.
Without action in the near future, these water losses will greatly impact the lives of
people around the planet, especially those already living in water-poor environments. Covich (2010) proposes several governmental actions that can be taken to
counteract freshwater shortages, ranging from updating water legislation to investing in climate forecasting technology to upgrading water storage and treatment
infrastructure. However, he includes surprisingly little discussion on improvement
of technology; the scope of his technological improvement is the replacement of
outdated systems with modern ones. While his suggestions are definitely applicable,
and while technological advances will require more lead time than political action,
improvements in water treatment technology will nevertheless be important in future water policy. This chapter will focus on studies of the technology and surrounding issues of desalination for drinking water production.

In its most basic form, desalination is the separation of salt from water of
non-potable salinity. The technologies that accomplish this utilize one of two methods. Membrane desalination utilizes the principle of osmosis through a semi-
permeable membrane. Examples of this include reverse osmosis (RO) in which water is forced through the membrane against its natural gradient, and electro-dialysis
(ED) in which salt ions are pulled out using an electrical current. Thermal desalination utilizes the principle of distillation, and also comes in various forms such as
multistage flash distillation (MSF), multiple-effect distillation (MED), and vapor
compression (VC). In each of these processes, water is heated to form steam and is
subsequently distilled to recoup the purified water. These are the most common
desalination technologies and many others have been and will be developed.
Desalination does not occur without cost, however. The law of mass conservation
requires that the feedwater, or the input flow to the desalination plant, be broken

into a product flow with a lower salt concentration and a byproduct flow with a higher salt concentration. The disposal of this byproduct, or brine as it is most commonly called, can be tricky since some cases produce brine that is twice as concentrated as the feedwater. The most popular method of disposal is return of brine to the ocean. As the ocean is such a large body of water, it is able to absorb the concentrated brine without affecting its overall salt concentration. However, in close proximity to brine outflows, high salt concentrations can still be detrimental to wildlife, especially as mixing is only due to diffusion. Since brine is denser than seawater, after an initial period of turbulence, the brine tends to settle into smooth flowing streams that do not diffuse well into the surrounding water. Thus, while desalination is undoubtedly a noble effort in solving water shortage issues, care must also be taken to ensure that it does not cause damage.

Lastly, desalination must be carefully considered economically, as the construction of large plants is a costly investment. Also, these plants require power in order to separate salts against their gradient, often using fossil fuels to do so. Careful plant design of both technology and implementation can be crucial for the success of a desalination plant. In addition, the use of renewable energy for powering desalination has also been heavily explored. As we shall see in the first study, not all desalination occurs in large plants or with the use of energy-dense coal and oil.

Heat-absorbing Materials Useful for Increased Solar Still Efficiency

The solar still is the simplest form of solar-powered desalination. It uses the mechanisms of evaporation and condensation—the same processes used in other forms of distillation—to purify the water. In a solar still, water is kept in an airtight container. As the water heats up, it evaporates and becomes water vapor. The lid of the still serves as the condenser to transform the purified water vapor back into water and the water slides down the slope of the lid to a collection point. Murugavel *et al.* (2010) built and tested a solar still with a roof-like glass lid, shallow basin, and insulation. They investigated the effects of various insulating and heat-absorbing materials on the efficiency of the still, since operation effectiveness of the still depends on the amount of water evaporated, which depends on the amount of heat added to the water, among other things. The materials tested here included rocks, brick, metal, and cloth. The results of their testing showed that a ¾ inch layer of quartzite rock on the bed of the still performed the best. Murugavel *et al.* also performed theoretical calculations using energy balances and heat transfer equations to determine the theoretical efficiency possible for the chosen parameters. While the quartzite rock performed the best in tests, the actual efficiency was still far from the theoretical efficiency.

Murugavel *et al.* built and tested the solar still in Kovilpatti, India. They crafted a basin from mild steel plate, created a glass cover with a north and south slope, and insulated it with glass wool. In testing, a minimal water depth of 0.5 cm was used. Measurements were taken of the influx and outflux of water and of the temperature of the body of water and the water vapor. Also, atmospheric conditions were monitored to ensure that factors were controlled between test days. From incident solar radiation and ambient temperature data, the authors conclude that this is a valid assumption. The materials used to collect extra heat on the basin were ¼ inch quartzite rock, ¾ inch quartzite rock, ¼ inch washed stones, 1½ inch cement concrete pieces, 1¼ inch brick pieces, mild steel trimmings, and a light black cotton cloth. Multiple trials were run with each material, and while the overall productions hovered around 3.5 L/day of water, the ¾ inch quartzite material performed slightly better than the rest at 3.66 L/day of water.

In the theoretical testing, the authors use thermodynamic equations to model the heat influxes and outfluxes of the system. They note that they are novel in their approach as they use a variable term for the transmittance of solar energy through the glass cover, a term usually assumed to be constant. The resulting equations in their modeling are expressions for the instantaneous and overall water production of the solar still. However, when the parameters from the test of the ¾ inch quartzite rock are used, it was found that four-fold increase in the production rates was theoretically possible. While the authors note several areas of discrepancy—the change in water volume and depth over time, a higher proportion of water vapor inside the still, and differences in the absorptivity of the different testing materials—these results imply that the heat-absorbing material used has a minimal impact on improved efficiency, and that instead, focus should be put on improving the design of the solar still itself to better utilize the incident energy.

Hydrogels as Forward Osmosis Desalination Draw Agents Feasible with Thermal-Pressure Dewatering

In reverse osmosis, water is moved across a membrane using an applied pressure. In contrast, forward osmosis does not typically require this pressure, though it can be used for added efficiency, and instead takes advantage of natural osmosis from a high to low concentration of solutes across a semi-permeable membrane. In the desalination process of forward osmosis, molecules chosen as a draw agent are used to create a higher concentration than the water being desalinated. Thus water naturally flows across the membrane to dilute the draw agent. To finally reclaim the desalinated water, the draw agent is removed. This can be done in several ways, with distillation being the most common. Therefore, draw agents are designed to be removed with a minimal energy cost; effectively, a low distillation temperature. The work done by Li *et al.* (2011) is on the use of hydrogels—complex polymer chains with a high concentration of hydrophilic regions—as draw agents. Upon taking in water, the polymers also expand to create an additional drawing force to pull water across the membrane. Lastly, hydrogels can be externally stimulated to change hydrophilic regions to hydrophobic ones, thus expelling purified water from the hydrogel. In this study, Li *et al.* look into two possible external stimuli—hydraulic pressure and a combination of hydraulic pressure with low temperature thermal processing. It was found that the polymer poly(sodium acrylate)-co-poly(N-isopropylacrylamide)—PSA-NIPAM for short—was the most effective when both water intake and dewatering were taken in account.

Li *et al.* tested four different hydrogels to see the effect of ionic charge on water intake and thermal sensitivity in water expulsion. The flux of water across a membrane was measured over time, and it was found that the charged polymers affected a greater drawing force on the water. In all four cases, the flux of water decreased over time as expected as the hydrogels filled with water. This decrease in flux will occur in all batch-operated forward osmosis processes since it is dependent on the difference in solute concentration. For dewatering, Li *et al.* used hydrostatic pressure at varying temperatures and on hydrogels with varying water contents. It was found that dewatering at room temperature for short times (two minutes) was not effective as all hydrogels released less than 5% of their water, even when comparing hydrogels with 50% water content vs. 80% water content. However, when dewatering was performed for the same amount of time and pressure at an elevated temperature of 50 °C, it was highly effective; the non-charged, thermally-sensitive polymer only released 5% of the 80% water content hydrogel at room temperature, but it released 75% at the elevated temperature. Other hydrogels did not experience as marked a change with warming, but there was some improvement; the charged, thermally-sensitive polymer released 3% of a 66.7% water content hydrogel at room temperature, compared to 17% at the elevated temperature. Overall, considering both the processes of forward osmosis and dewatering at an elevated temperature, PSA-NIPAM was found to be the most effective.

Li *et al.* suggest that this hydrogel can be effectively used with optimization of conditions. While the authors showed that thermal-pressure dewatering is feasible, they suggest that further research be conducted to determine the effects of other stimuli on the hydrogels—for example, using solar energy to stimulate the hydrogel using both heat and light.

Variable Salinity Desalination Plant Feasible for Treating Inconsistent Rainfall

Desalination plants are usually geared to be very efficient at processing water of uniform salinity. In Singapore, heavy rains occur often, but usually in short, interrupted bouts. As a result, a plant geared to the low salinity of rainwater would be very inefficient during dry periods. A solution to this problem is variable salinity desalination (VSD) that is able to switch between low salinity rainwater and high salinity seawater. Seah *et al.* (2010) evaluated a pilot VSD plant on the Tampines River in Singapore and found that it was successful at treating both water feeds. This VSD plant utilized reverse osmosis treatment with microfiltration of the feed water. They found that due to the low salinity of rainwater, the energy consumption of the plant is greatly reduced since the energy needed to process low salinity water is about one-fourth the energy needed for high salinity water, and the overall energy usage of the VSD plant is about half that of conventional desalination plants. In addition, the authors found that fouling of the reverse osmosis membrane could be avoided by switching between high and low salinity feedwater every three days.

This plant is located in an estuarine section of the Tampines River. Low salinity water is obtained from the river, largely supplied by rainwater, and high salinity water is obtained from the ocean. In particular, this plant uses reverse osmosis desalination technology prefaced by screening and microfiltration and followed by disinfection. The product of the plant is added to existing high-grade reclaimed water. Technologically, in order to process both high and low salinity, the plant reroutes water through similar infrastructure when the feedwater is switched. Though the plant was designed for 50:50 division between low and high salinity processing, in 2008, this plant operated at low salinity 60% of the time and at high salinity 40% of the time. Since low salinity desalination requires significantly less energy than high salinity (seawater) desalination, the energy requirements of the VSD plant were greatly reduced. Annual energy usage was 1.11 kWh/m^3 for low salinity desalination and 4.86 kWh m^{-3} for high salinity desalination, averaging 1.86 kWh m^{-3}.

Seah *et al.* discuss current and future improvements of the VSD plant over conventional desalination plants. First, they discuss a rubber weir that is used for flood control of the Tampines River. They postulate that by refining control of the weir, the flow rate of water to the desalination plant can be optimized. Secondly, they note that this VSD plant successfully uses microfiltration in place of multimedia filters and dissolved air flotation. They also found that the conventional RO filter cartridge was not needed as the microfiltration outflow was sufficiently filtered, and will continue to monitor the effect of removing the cartridge. Thirdly, this VSD plant is designed to avoid scaling of precipitating solutes on the RO membrane, thus avoiding the need for pH adjustment or anti-scalants. Fourthly, this VSD plant utilizes testing for membrane and microfiltration performance. Total organic content of the permeate, or the filtered side of the membrane, is used as a continuous measure of the membrane performance, thus notifying operators of either ageing membranes or other damage. A pressure decay test is used in addition to conventional sampling tests for microfiltration performance. Fifthly, the authors found that by switching between low and high salinity feedwater, the chance of membrane fouling, a large problem in conventional plants, was greatly reduced. They found that the optimal time to spend in each mode is three days.

Wind-powered Membrane Desalination Feasible with Minimal Energy Storage

Reverse osmosis (RO) is a desalination process that uses pressure to force high salinity water through a semi-permeable membrane. Since the production rate depends on the pressure difference, which in turn depends on the power supplied, the fuel of choice is energy-dense coal and oil. However, not only are fossil fuels unsustainable, but polluting as well. Park *et al.* (2011) studied the possibility of powering an RO plant with renewable wind power. The advantage to using wind power is that there is a steady supply of wind along coastal areas where desalination plants are most commonly placed. However, without energy storage as a buffer between the wind turbine and the plant, changes in wind speed and direction translate directly into changes in RO pressure and flow rate. While changes in power supply are expected with any power source, this is particularly troublesome for wind energy as wind flux typically changes by 12% per second, compared to the 1% change on average of solar flux. Park *et al.* tested their RO model with brackish feedwater using both a programmable power supply and an actual wind turbine. Issues arose such as a maximum power output of 300 W from the turbine, system shutdown under low wind speeds, salt diffusion across the membrane during shutdown, and a wind speed threshold for feedwater with a high osmotic pressure. However, the authors found that desalination performance under wind conditions of more than 7.0 m/s and turbulence of less than 0.4 was similar to that of steady state conditions, thereby concluding that directly connected wind-powered desalination is feasible with energy buffering to prevent system shutdown.

Park *et al.* used a test bench model of a reverse osmosis desalination system. They examined variables of average wind speed, oscillations in wind speed, and turbulence. Most situations were created with a programmable power supply and then verified using a wind turbine in a wind tunnel. Two brackish water concentrations were used–2750 and 5500 mg/L NaCl–and testing occurred under wind speeds ranging from 3.7–8.7 m/s. Using the power supply, they tested steady state wind speeds (no turbulence or oscillation) and programmed oscillating wind speeds with a turbulence intensity of 0.4 (0.6 being extreme fluctuations and 0.0 being no fluctuation).

They found that under steady state conditions, the optimal power outputs were 120 W for low concentration feedwater and 180 W for high concentration feedwater. The maximum power output for their experimental turbine was 300 W as safety mechanisms were activated under high wind speeds. They also found that while all wind speeds produced permeate flows with acceptable salt concentrations using low concentration feedwater, high concentration feedwater required a minimum of 120 W (corresponding to a steady state wind speed of approximately 5.3 m/s). Under oscillating conditions, they found that low wind speeds with low frequency oscillations produced the lowest permeate flows. This was caused by system shutdown due to low membrane pressure as a direct result of low power supply. They found that shutdown occurred at power outputs of less than 40 W for three seconds. Also, due to the low wind speeds, the system had difficulty restarting, thus further reducing productivity under these conditions. Another issue with system shutdown was the diffusion of salt across the membrane, resulting in a raised permeate salt concentration. Due to this diffusion, the maximum shutdown period for high concentration feedwater is three minutes as the permeate will reach unacceptable salt concentrations at this point. To re-achieve permeate salt concentration within two minutes after a shutdown period, 240 W was needed for high concentration feedwater compared with 120 W for low concentration feedwater. In contrast, high frequency oscillations did not permit shutdown even during low wind speeds as the pressure always returned quickly and thus did not differ greatly from steady state conditions.

The third variable tested was turbulence, measured by the amplitude of the oscillating wind speeds. The authors found that wind conditions of more than 7.0 m/s and turbulence of less than 0.4 adequately resembled steady state conditions. At less than 7.0 m/s, the system was able to reach low enough pressures to reach shut-off. In the extreme case, the osmotic pressure of the high concentration feedwater combined with the low power supply of low wind speeds resulted in zero permeate production.

Lastly, the authors used a wind turbine inside a wind tunnel to perform verification tests. They found that the wind speed did not always correspond with the power output due to complexities in the system, though the membrane pressure still depended directly on the power output. However, the system performance still compared well with the steady state test results using the power supply. The authors were also able to demonstrate an exponential decay in the membrane pressure after system shutdown, thus providing an explanation for the buffer time during low wind speeds. In addition, the wind tunnel tests displayed a 50% production loss with large wind speed fluctuations. However, the authors note that this type of turbulence is not typical and only observed in extreme conditions. They also note that large power fluctuations should not be significantly detrimental as their test membrane has been used for over 250 hours under extreme turbulence. Overall, the authors conclude that wind-powered membrane desalination is feasible despite any drawbacks.

We saw that both wind and solar power are feasible options for powering desalination, though in different applications. We also saw that technology is constantly changing, both in the manipulation of existing processes to the invention of new ones. However, desalination is not a standalone process. Issues such as the ethical disposal of concentrated brine or the effect of environmental conditions are just some of the concerns that arise in operating a desalination plant.

Dilution of Desalination Discharge is Predictable

Discharges from desalination plants are emptied into natural bodies of water, and the differences in pH, temperature, and chemical composition can have detrimental effects on the organisms living there. While it is not an optimal disposal method, sufficient dilution can minimize any detrimental effects. In this study, Marti *et al.* (2011) performed tests on a desalination plant with dense discharge to verify the results of Roberts *et al.* (1997) in which an empirical scaling was produced to correlate Froude number with dilution. The dimensionless Froude number is used to characterize flows in relation to a carrying velocity. In the near field directly from the discharge nozzle, flows are governed by the jet pump and thus will have F>1, while in the far field, the discharge flow matches the speed of the surrounding water and should have F<1. To achieve better mixing and therefore dilution, it is necessary to have turbulent flow, which corresponds to higher Froude numbers. Any mixing that occurs in the far field is a result of background turbulence as the discharge will have settled into layered flow by that time, so therefore, it is necessary to ensure that proper mixing is accomplished in the near field. Data for the dilution at various points corroborated results from the scaling study of Roberts *et al.*, however as the scaling was not created for F<20, the authors recommend further testing as they found the dilution to be higher than expected if the results from Roberts *et al.* are extrapolated. While the authors do not make a statement on the sufficiency of the dilution, if there is more dilution than expected as the velocity of the flow slows, this could mean better conditions for the surrounding aquatic environment.

Marti *et al.* performed tests on the desalination plant during its regular maintenance period in order to test discharges of variable flows. Using its shut down and ramp up periods, data were taken for flows at full velocity, two-thirds velocity and one-third velocity. To determine dilution, measurements of salinity were taken at various heights in the water column; a total of 207 measurements were taken for the three flow rates. Measurements were also made of the background water currents and general meteorological data such as temperature. Over the three testing periods, the temperature shifted only slightly, but the water currents varied in magnitude and direction as the second day of testing coincided with an incoming storm. The study found that layered flow still occurred, and that the salinity column off the ocean floor varied for the three flow rates—four to eight meters for one-third flow, five meters for two-thirds flow, and nine meters for full flow.

The study of Roberts *et al.* resulted in empirical correlations for the thickness of the bottom layer and the minimum dilution achieved at the mixing zone edge with Froude number. For the bottom layer thickness, data collected showed the height of the discharge flow to be less than two meters for reduced flow and between two and three meters at full flow. These data correspond roughly to the predicted values. The dilution achieved by the time the water reached the edge of the mixing zone was 50—55 times the initial discharge for reduced flows and 50—65 times for full flow. Again, these correlate with the predicted values. Marti *et al.* also found that dilution was higher than expected as flows dropped in velocity. This may be explained using the water flow data, which show that the discharge is entering a current going in the same direction and thus dilution should be increased. Further research is recommended to determine the applicability of Roberts *et al.* at these low flow rates.

Desalination of San Joaquin Valley Agricultural Drainage Water Possible with Effective Plant Control

The San Joaquin Valley has the highest agricultural output in America, but its future is in jeopardy. The salinity of its already shallow water table is increasing to the point that areas of land must be retired from use. By using desalination, irrigable water is produced and the volume of brine is decreased. However, the high salt content of the feed water can result in mineral surface scaling on the desalination membranes if it reaches saturated concentrations, which decreases plant productivity. By adding antiscalant compounds, this threshold can be artificially lifted—twice as much for gypsum, and as much as sixty times more for barite. McCool *et. al* performed tests on water samples at each location to determine the concentration of these salts, and the effect that these concentrations would have on a full-scale desalination plant. The authors conclude that while desalination plants are theoretically feasible in the San Joaquin Valley, they must be carefully tailored to each location and regularly monitored.

McCool *et al.* used two approaches to estimate the feasibility of desalination plants at five locations in the San Joaquin Valley. First, water samples were taken and tested to determine the theoretical feasibility based on known saturation values of various salts. The saturation limit is dependent on the fraction of water that is attempted to be removed through desalination as well as the pH of the feed water. The authors also used software to compute the theoretical recovery limits at each location based on the water samples. Secondly, other recent work has preliminarily identified that certain combinations of salts can lead to lowered saturation points. For this reason, bench-scale plate-and-frame reverse osmosis (PFRO) was performed for each location.

From the water samples, the various sites showed great spatial and temporal variability as salinity could differ by up to an order of magnitude between sites and over time. It was found that calcite was above saturation and that gypsum was near saturation at each site, though again, each varied greatly throughout the year. Since the feed water salt concentrations determine specific design aspects for a desalination plant, it is necessary to tailor each plant for a particular location as there is too much variability in the San Joaquin Valley for one design to work throughout. In addition, traditional reverse osmosis plants are not typically able to handle large variations in salinity and the temporal changes experienced in the San Joaquin Valley may be problematic.

In using software to compute the theoretical recovery limits, highs and lows from the water samples were used. Also, the saturation limits used in modeling were slightly different from actual data, in particular for calcite as it was assumed that the concentration of this salt could be negated with changes to the pH of the feed water. Without this adjustment, calcite would be the limiting factor to the productivity of a desalination plant. By shifting the pH down to 6.0, gypsum becomes the limiting scalant. However, the recovery rates are still very limited. The authors suggest that feed-back process control will be required for any plant in the San Joaquin Valley.

In bench-scale testing, the reverse osmosis process was utilized for each location and under various conditions—at natural pH, at a lowered pH, and with or without the addition of antiscalants. In some tests (reduced pH with the addition of antiscalants), no scaling was observed and the decrease in outflow over time is consistent with known changes due to compacting of the membrane. Without the antiscalants, however, the decrease in outflow was much greater with visual scaling on the membrane at both natural and reduced pH. In fact, scaling occurred at a greater magnitude at the reduced pH, speculated to be a result of decreased bicarbonate, which is a large factor in preventing gypsum scaling. Again, the authors conclude that while desalination plants are theoretically feasible in the San Joaquin Valley, they must be carefully tailored to each location and regularly monitored.

Chlorine Byproducts from Reverse Osmosis Desalination not likely to Pose Health Risks to Humans or Aquatic Environments

Reverse osmosis (RO) is a common method of water filtration, and in particular, desalination. Of commercial desalination using filter membranes, RO makes up 80%. It operates by applying pressure to brackish water on one side of a membrane that is only permeable to water, thus creating purified water on the other side of the membrane. In practice, however, the intake water is chlorinated in order to remove organic matter such as algae that can cause problems with the system. This in turn results in chlorine by-products, some of which can cause chronic health problems or even be lethal at sufficient concentrations. In addition, desalinated water is often blended with available freshwater, which may also contain the same organic compounds, thereby making total concentration levels unacceptable. The concern addressed in this study is whether these by-products are released in harmful concentrations either for human consumption or the aquatic environment (Agus and Sedlak 2010). The study focused on a pilot plant in Carlsbad, CA and though the study found that some of the organic compounds produced were prevalent enough to be tasted, none were harmful.

Eva Agus and David Sedlak looked at the Carlsbad desalination plant and also obtained water samples from the coastal regions of California, Florida, and Singapore. These samples were used as a comparison to the Carlsbad data and were chosen as they are likely locations for the placement of water-processing plants. In the Carlsbad tests, samples were taken at two different times (summer and winter) and with two different chlorination dosages. To model blending of desalinated water with freshwater, samples were taken from the Colorado River, NV and the San Pablo Reservoir, CA, which are rich and poor in bromide respectively, a compound that can pass through RO filters relatively well. For the samples from the various coastal regions, after controlling for pH, one chlorination dosage was used to match the Carlsbad tests. For all samples, measurements were taken at various times over a period of three days.

The Carlsbad plant samples had less organic compounds than expected; this is attributed to the fact that it was designed for higher water purity and also, as a pilot-scale plant, gives less opportunity for the formation of by-products due to a shorter holding time. The organic compounds that were detected were found to vary both seasonally and with chlorine concentration. As a result, the authors recommend that tests be run during different times of the year in order to ensure that none of the water produced is harmful. The study also found that even after blending the desalinated water with the chosen freshwater samples, while the bromide concentrations increased greatly, they remained safe for consumption. It is also noted that the results of this test were conservative since no pre-treatment of the freshwater was performed, a process that would normally be done in a commercial plant.

For the samples from the coastal locations, none were found to exceed standards for organic compounds after chlorination. However, it was found that the types and proportions of compounds varied by locations, even though the method and dosage of chlorine were held constant. It is likely that the initial variation in organic compounds dictates the type of reactions that occur after chlorination. Therefore, the authors recommended that tests be performed at the site of a desalination plant to ensure that the compounds present in its outflows are not harmful. In particular, they note that some compounds would be tasted at the levels produced and may be a factor in the consumer desirability of the desalinated water.

The technical aspects–plant design, process development, brine disposal–are all very important considerations for desalination. However, non-technical elements also play a role. Desalination plants require heavy initial investment in the form of both money and time as large plants are costly to build and require extensive surveying to find a proper location for the plant. In the above studies, we saw how desalination can adversely affect the natural environment. Clever design in plant location can minimize environmental impact, and at times, make desalination more economical.

Economics of Desalination

Cost estimation for industrial plants is usually performed with the assistance of aggregated data and estimates by knowledgeable bodies. Younos (2010) discusses the many factors that affect desalination plant cost and evaluates their impact on total cost. In addition, he describes several cost estimation models that are used for desalination plants. Costs are broken into one time construction costs, including both direct and indirect costs, and recurring operation and maintenance costs. The primary factors that determine the magnitude of these costs are feedwater salinity, plant capacity and the location of the plant. One of the more costly aspects of plant location is brine removal as coastal plants can use cost effective surface water disposal while inland plants must use more expensive alternatives. Younos concludes based on aggregated desalination plant cost estimates that fixed costs play a large role compared to maintenance costs, and that brackish water treatment only differs from seawater treatment in energy costs.

Younos defined the following costs pertinent to the construction and operation of a desalination plant. The direct construction costs of implementing a desalination plant include costs for land, production wells, surface water intake structure, equipment (i.e. for water treatment), buildings and brine disposal. Indirect costs include construction overhead such as labor costs and tools, owner's costs such as administrative fees, freight and insurance costs, and resources reserved for contingency. The recurring operations and maintenance costs are separated into fixed insurance and amortization costs and all other costs, including energy, equipment replacement and cost of chemicals. For each site, these costs will be based on the quality of the feedwater, the plant capacity, the location of the plant, and any regulation requirements that may exist. For example, low salinity feedwater will cost less in terms of energy usage, large capacity plants cost more initially but are more efficient in the long run, and costs associated with water intake, pretreatment and brine disposal will depend on the plant surroundings. Younos points out that brine disposal plays a large role in desalination plant design due to its dependence on site location and regulations. In addition, there are multiple options for brine disposal including surface disposal, disposal with wastewater plant effluent, deep well injection, on-land dispersal such as evaporation ponds, spray irrigation, percolation, and zero liquid discharge. For coastal plants, surface disposal to large bodies of water is common and cost effective. However, this is generally not an option for inland plants. Options for inland plants depend on the characteristics of the plant location and techniques such as deep well injection and zero liquid discharge can be costly.

Younos also describes three cost estimation models that are particularly useful for evaluating desalination projects. WTCost, a model from the Bureau of Reclamation, includes thorough and detailed plant cost estimates for the following desalination technologies: reverse osmosis (RO), mechanical vapor compression (MVC), multiple effect distillation (MED), multi-stage distillation (MSF), nanofiltration (NF), and electrodialysis reversal (EDR). The the Desalination Economic Evaluation Program (DEEP) developed by the International Atomic Energy Agency (IAEA) is a model for evaluating the effects of various energy sources on a desalination plant, particularly looking at nuclear sources versus other alternative energies. However, this model was not intended for industrial use and is not as detailed in non-technical costs. The third model is the Reverse Osmosis Desalination Cost Planning Model, a product of Water Resources Associates (WRA), which includes 33 different parameters for desalination plants and is similar to WTCost. While Younos did not perform the cost estimation himself, Sandia National Laboraties aggregated the work of others who have used such methods to estimate the costs of desalination plants. Based on this report, which differentiated estimates by both technology and feedwater quality (brackish vs. seawater), Younos concludes overall that fixed costs are actually a large component, equipment replacement is actually relatively small, and that the only major difference between brackish water and seawater desalination is the cost of energy.

Erin Partlan

Multi-criteria Decision Analysis is Useful for Determining Optimal Desalination Design

While desalination processes can generally be applied interchangeably to different situations, the different methods vary in cost effectiveness depending on external conditions. Two categories of desalination methods are included in this study—thermal and membrane. Thermal desalination technologies include multistage flash (MSF) distillation, multiple-effect distillation (MED), and vapor compression (VC). Membrane technologies include reverse osmosis (RO) and electrodialysis (ED). For any of these technologies, optimization of plant design is based primarily on the salinity of the water (usually categorized into low salinity brackish water and high salinity seawater), quality of water product, and volume of production. For this study, however, other factors such as environmental impact and political preference were also taken into consideration. Afify (2010) looked at five different location types including three aquifers (brackish water) and two coastal settings (seawater). Each location differed in the type of water usage, ranging from small scale use along the desert fringes of Egypt to coastal tourism and resorts. Afify used Multi-criteria Decision Analysis (MCDA) to determine the best technology for each location. He found that, independent of water usage, ED is preferred for brackish water treatment, though RO would be better for larger desalination volumes, while MED is slightly preferred for seawater followed closely by MSF and RO. For any of the technologies, a higher water usage is preferred as it is more cost effective over small scale plants.

Afify used the method of MDCA to evaluate the selected desalination alternatives for a range of location scenarios in Egypt. MDCA uses weighted numerical values for each evaluation criterion so that criteria of varying importance can be used altogether. Furthermore, numerical valuations of qualitative aspects allow them to be included in this method. However, there is no set method for determining the weighting values, and as a result, the interpretation of importance or quality as numerical values can be fairly arbitrary.

Afify looked at five different water sources—low-usage desert fringe aquifers, the moderate-usage Nile aquifer, low-usage coastal aquifer, seawater for tourism, and seawater for coastal city development. The last water source is based on plans to construct new villages and cities along the Red Sea in order to accommodate a growing population (10.7 million by 2025). This scenario incorporates medium to large scale desalination plants into these establishments during initial construction. In comparison, seawater for tourism would utilize small scale desalination systems. For the three aquifers, though they are all brackish water, they vary in salinity. The Nile-fed aquifers have the lowest salinity, whereas the coastal aquifers have high salinity bordering on seawater. The desert aquifers are medium salinity oases. However, Afify notes that as aquifer water is a relatively non-renewable resource, and are generally in areas of low development in Egypt, use of aquifer water for desalination should be limited.

Afify assigned values for each alternative (permutations of water source, desalination technology, and plant size) across five categories—investment costs, operation costs, quality of produced water, environmental impacts of brine outflows, and political preference. Costs were measured in Euros, water quality in ppm, and political and environmental factors were rated out of ten. To rank the categories, Afify used percentages of these values to create two weighting scenarios. In both scenarios, the best technology for each situation was the same: large-scale MED for coastal cities, small-scale MED for coastal resorts, small-scale ED for oasis aquifers, medium-scale ED for Nile-fed aquifers, and medium-scale ED for coastal aquifers. Afify uses these results to recommend a plan of action for coastal development—one large MSF desalination plant for the city of Suize and five MED plants for all other cities along the Red Sea.

Conclusions

With the combination of technical and non-technical improvement in the field of desalination, there is hope that desalination will someday be a safe and effective process that can be used worldwide. In particular, the development of desalination for rural areas is needed greatly as access to water can sometimes involve walking many miles to less than sanitary water sources. Climate change forecasts do not predict a decrease in precipitation; instead they predict a shift away from already dry climates towards already wet ones. While the total amount of water does not change, this can be devastating for people living in these already dry climates that do not have the resources to relocate. All in all, desalination efforts will not be the only solution to this impending crisis. The policy suggestions of Covich are certainly well worth considering. Hopefully, by conserving water in as many places as possible and producing water using as many methods as possible, the effects of water shortage can be successfully mitigated.

References Cited

Afify, A., 2010. Prioritizing desalination strategies using multi-criteria decision analysis. Desalination.250, 928–935.

Agus, E., Sedlak, D., 2010. Formation and fate of chlorination by-products in reverse osmosis desalination systems. Water Research 44, 1616–1626.

Li, D., Zhang, X., Yao, J., Simon, G., Wang, H., 2011. Stimuli-responsive polymer hydrogels as a new class of draw agent for forward osmosis desalination. Chem. Commun. 47, 1710–1712.

Marti, C., Antenucci, J., Luketina, D., Okely, P., Imberger, J., 2011. Near-Field Dilution Characteristics of a Negatively Buoyant Hypersaline Jet Generated by a Desalination Plant. Journal of Hydraulic Engineering, 137, 57–65.

McCool, B., Rahardianto, A., Faria, J., Kovac, K., Lara, D., Cohen, Y., 2010. Feasibility of reverse osmosis desalination of brackish agricultural drainage water in the San Joaquin Valley, Desalination 261, 240–250.

Murugavel, K., Sivakumar, S., Ahamed, J., Chockalingam, K., Srithar, K., 2010. Single basin double slope solar still with minimum basin depth and energy storing materials. Applied Energy 87, 2, 514–523.

Park, G., Schäfer, A., Richards, B., 2010. Renewable energy powered membrane technology: The effect of wind speed fluctuations on the performance of a wind-powered membrane system for brackish water desalination. Journal of Membrane Science 30, 34–44.

Resources for the Future, (2010). Adaptations to sustain high quality freshwater supplies in response to climate change. (Issue Brief 10-05). Washington DC: Covich, A.

Seah, H., Khoo, K. L., Chua, J. Y., Toh, D., Chua, S. C., 2010. Cost effective way to harvest estuarine water: variable salinity desalination concept. Journal of Water Supply: Research and Technology 59, 452–458.

Younos, T., (2010). The Economics of Desalination. Journal of Contemporary Water Research and Education 132, 39–45.

11. Tropical Cyclones and Global Warming

Brian Nadler

Tropical cyclones are storm systems that are often characterized by a "large, low-pressure center", as well as "numerous thunderstorms that produce strong winds and heavy rain"(NCOAA, 2011). These tropical weather events develop over warm bodies of water and are known for their significant force and destruction they cause. However, there is not a great deal of collected data on tropical cyclones, and this is currently being cited as a potential future threat. For many climatologists, the ability to predict tropical storm events in the long term is severely limited by the lack of data in many ocean basins. Cyclones are classified into three main groups: tropical depressions, tropical storms, and hurricanes/typhoons. These events typically occur when a disturbance in the atmosphere instigates the climatological conditions necessary for a cyclone to form—and can also be influenced by other environmental conditions such as Madden-Julian oscillation, El Niño-Southern Oscillation, or the Atlantic multi-decadal oscillation.

It is desirable to compile further data on how global warming correlates with tropical cyclones. Global warming is demonstrated to cause an increase in sea surface temperature (SST), which has a direct corollary relationship with the strength of tropical storms in an ocean basin. However, sea surface temperature is not the only variable when examining weather phenomena such as cyclones; variables such as vorticity, currents, and thermodynamic factors are also important. By expanding studies and predictor models, it will be possible to develop a further understanding of how tropical storms are affected by changes in climate indices due to global warming.

Tropical storms have a devastating effect on human life and local economy, and as global warming continues, there is noted increase in frequency and intensity of tropical storms in some oceanic basins. If there is an increase in tropical storms, it is likely that an increase in tropical storm damage will occur as well. A great deal of tropical storm damage occurs on the coast and in some inland areas, as a result of the high winds and massive flooding that can take place. In addition, there is much debate over where the increases in tropical storms will take place; in some ocean basins there is a decrease in cyclone activity, while in others there is a great deal of increase. It is still uncertain how great an effect global warming has on tropical cyclone genesis, but a large portion of scientific studies done in the past year are attempts to quantify the effects of climate change on each of the variables involved in tropical storm creation. It is desirable to examine the effect of climate change on tropical storm events through present and current data in order to have a more precise method of determining the physical changes that might be brought about by global warming.

Climate Change Having a Significant Impact on Processes that Cause El Niño, Affecting Weather Events

Climate Change is thought by many scientists to be at the forefront of issues facing the global community. With the increase in greenhouse gases, there is expected to be a significant shift in natural variability, with climate being a primary concern (Collins *et al.* 2010). One of the most important climate patterns is the El Niño-Southern Oscillation (ENSO), a large shift of Pacific trade winds from westerly to easterly directions. It is possible to examine these changes through the use of complex coupled global circulation models (CGCM), which suggest that there will be a significant change in the mean climate of the Pacific, played out partly in El Niño variability. However, it is still too early to determine whether there will be an increase or decrease in ENSO activity, or if its intensity will be heightened, since one or more of its causative characteristics will be modified by global warming's effect on climate.

There are many outside variables that factor into the variability of the ENSO, and how much each factor plays a role has been the subject of a great deal of debate. Changes in mean climate, sensitivity to climate change, mean upwelling and advection, thermocline feedback, sea surface temperature/wind stress feedback, atmospheric damping or variability, or surface sonal advective feedback all affect on ENSO formation. However, Collins *et al.* decided to determine what had the most significant effects on ENSO characteristics to more accurately determine future changes due to global warming.

The study utilized information on all of the previously stated characteristics. It was observed that all of the ENSO characteristics were increased to the point where they would have a significant amplification on ENSO activity, save for atmospheric damping, which seemed to reduce variability. The projected changes were modeled using an inter-annual standard deviation of a mean sea-level-pressure index, in which a positive or negative change indicated a strength or weakness of the ENSO, respectively. The sensitivity of ENSO to climate change was also observed using climate reconstructions over the past millennium. In order to compensate for variation in externally forced changes in ENSO characteristics, multiple runs using the same model were performed. It is noted that this is not possible in a real-world scenario, and that natural variability may be obscuring changes that are caused due to global warming.

The authors found a significant relationship between climate change on the process and feedbacks that determine the characteristics of ENSO. The only negative linear relationship is between atmospheric damping feedback and ENSO strength. The overall tendency for larger ENSO events is expected to increase greatly, and the decrease in atmospheric damping will lead to a likely decrease in ENSO variability. For any other feedbacks, there is expected to be little change; there is very little evidence to suggest there is any significant effect otherwise.

The increase in El Niño strength due to global warming will have an important effect on tropical storm activity. More tropical cyclones tend to form during El Niño years in the Eastern Pacific, whereas conversely, more cyclone activity is present in the Atlantic during La Niña years. Being able to determine how the correlation between the strength of ENSO events and frequency and intensity of tropical storms is essential for preparing against future storm activity.

Increase in Frequency of Intense Hurricanes due to Climate Variability in Latter 21st Century

Many recent models of climate change and weather events suggest that the frequency of tropical cyclones will decrease, but the intensity will increase alongside the upward trend in rising climate. The models, however, are flawed and unable to project hurricanes with an intensity rating of category 3 or higher. Bender *et al.* (2010) examined the future of global warming on Atlantic hurricanes, using a method of downscaling that allowed for a more realistic distributional projection of hurricane intensity. The model depicts a significant increase in frequency of category 4 and 5 storms in the latter half of the 21st century, with the number of storms doubling, although the overall frequency of tropical cyclones globally is expected to decrease. The results were similar in two different operational models, indicating a high degree of certainty in the findings. Such data are also dependent on the global climate models used for determining environmental conditions, so future studies should reexamine the findings using updated climate models as well as improved hurricane simulation models, if they exist.

Due to rising sea surface temperatures and a possible increase in hurricane activity in the Atlantic, concerns have been raised that a positive correlation between the two events might exist. There is a great deal of variation among studies, however, a large portion suggest an increase to some degree of hurricane intensity. These models were unable to simulate major hurricanes of category 3 or higher, translating to winds exceeding 50 m/s. Bender *et al.* improved the simulations of the hurricane intensities by downscaling the models from a previous study, and applying a similar method to two hurricane models that yielded similar results.

M.A. Bender and colleagues conducted the studies while at the National Oceanic and Atmospheric Administration and Geophysical Fluid Dynamics Laboratory (GFDL). Comparisons were made between observed and control storm counts from the GFDL, downscaled, and categorized from 1980 to 2007. The results were used in the storm averages for the two hurricane models used in the study. The results do not take into effect the mix of aerosol effects. The rescale of the hurricane model shows a growing trend in hurricane activity that, although not devastating at the present time, could pose a significant threat in the latter half of the 21st century. The largest increase of intense hurricane activity is projected to occur in the western Atlantic, which was demonstrated in three of the four models run.

The authors found a significant relationship between climate change and hurricane strength. In the downscaled models, in 80 years the number of category 4 and 5 hurricanes increased by a cumulative 81%. The hurricane season is predicted to shorten, as well as there being a decrease in the number of hurricanes in other areas around the globe, such as in the Caribbean. The authors suspected the data might be slightly skewed to increase in the latter half of the data due to more capable hurricane monitoring tools being more readily available.

An increase in hurricane intensity due to climate change will have potentially enormous economic and global consequences. Being able to determine intensity and locations of increase in hurricane frequency, we can further determine how climate change affects tropical storms, as well as provide incentive to limit climate change and to plan ahead in areas that are often in the path of hurricanes and major tropical storms.

Observing Climate Effect on Hurricanes Through Hurricane Clustering Methods

When measuring hurricane variability, there are several important variables. Storm intensity, duration, frequency, genesis location, and track all contribute in part to the observed data. In addition to these direct effects that change the thermodynamic state of the storm, there are also indirect effects, most notably climate variations that affect circulation patterns such as the El Niño Southern Oscillation Event (ENSO) (*Kossin et al.* 2010). The changes in atmospheric currents and vertical wind sheer affect North Atlantic hurricane activity by altering the storm duration. There is an increasingly important need to examine hurricane track in order to determine if there is a correlative relationship between climate change and storm intensity. The results suggest that it is not beneficial to utilize Atlantic tracks when observing hurricane models when attempting to quantify the global effects of climate change and track. It is important to include different variables for each track in order to determine how tropical storms and hurricanes have responded to changes in climate variability. According to projections, systematic increases in landfall and statistics and distributions of storm intensity are likely to occur, which makes it difficult to predict climate activity.

The possibility is raised that climate change might significantly affect storm frequency in areas such as the North Atlantic. In order to further explore such a possibility, Kossin *et al.* separated tracks from the North Atlantic hurricane database from 1950 to 2007 and clustered them into four groups based on techniques used in other ocean basins. The composites of each group vary from each other, demonstrating that the different oscillation events have influential holds on North Atlantic tropical storms and hurricanes.

J.P. Kossin and colleagues conducted this research at the University of Wisconsin. Data were obtained through the hurricane database (HURDAT) that is maintained by the National Oceanic and Atmospheric Administration (NOAA). A range of 58 years was covered, from 1950 to 2007, and composite analysis of the sea surface temperatures at those times were recorded using a reconstructed database. Other regional composites were performed at the National Centers for Environmental Prediction—National Center for Atmospheric Research (NCEP—NCAR). The results showed that when considered by individual clusters, the largely documented increase in North Atlantic hurricanes is confined to deep tropical systems, correlated to regions that display positive SST trends.

Throughout the study there were various differences in tropical storm longevity and intensity, and the proportion and destructiveness of landfalling storms were indentified. The results of the study suggest that it is not useful to consider Atlantic tracks in their entirety when quantifying the climatic control of tropical cyclogenesis and track, which storm activity is dependent on. This adds to the challenge of predicting future hurricane or tropical storm activity because it requires that climate models do two things: capture systematic changes in circulation patterns throughout the atmospheric region, and observe mean thermodynamic state changes. More in-depth research will be necessary to improve these attempts at clustering data, for at best, the analyses in this study are only useful as a rough tool for separating tropical storm and hurricane tracks, and it is stated that caution must be used when relating differences within a tropical storm cluster to actual physical mechanisms.

Brian Nadler

Projections of Changing Cyclone Frequency in Relation to Climate Change Demonstrating Uncertainty

While a steadily increasing global temperature is not much in dispute, the effect of such a warming on climate is subject to much debate. Knutson *et al.* (2010) compared older modeling studies, which tended to project a decrease in overall cyclone frequency with newer, higher resolution studies, which are more likely to predict an increase in the most intense cyclones. The newest methods of projection, satellite analysis, and downscaling techniques are examined, as well as the newer, high-resolution projection models of tropical storm activity. The results suggest that while climate models are progressively more reliable, we cannot identify anthropogenic signals in past cyclone data, and therefore are severely limited in our ability to make projections with current data. Further research is highly recommended by Knutson *et al.* in order to enhance the reliability of climate-relevant observations in the future, since there is a high level of societal impact of tropical storms.

The primary challenge for tropical cyclone detection and attribution research is determining whether or not an observed change in tropical cyclone activity exceeds the natural variability of the event, and if so, attributing the change to a specific climate forcing. For projections in the future, the ultimate goal is to develop a reliable projection of these changes in factors that influence cyclone activity, as the resulting effect on storm frequency, track, and distribution.

T.R. Knutson and colleagues conducted their research with the World Meteorological Organization, along with support by the West Australian Government Indian Ocean Climate Initiative. In all models, there was a strong tendency to project an increase in stronger tropical cyclones over the 21st century. Detection and attribution was observed for characteristics such as tropical cyclone rainfall, genesis, tracks, duration and surge flooding, as well as activity versus sea surface temperature. It was also observed that tropical cyclone frequency would likely remain the same overall, but that there would be a shift to more radical tropical storm activity, of a range of category 4 or higher.

Throughout the study there were numerous variables that were identified as having a potential effect on tropical storm activity. Knutson and colleagues were able to improve several aspects of cyclone activity projections, resulting in their predictions that tropical cyclone frequency will remain essentially the same, along with a global increase in the average frequency of strongest tropical cyclones. It was recommended that newer models be created that have an increasingly more detailed spatial resolution and new approaches for observing past tropical cyclone records that would reduce uncertainty of causes of past changes, and be able to better predict future tropical cyclone activity. Future projections of variables such as sea-level rise, regional storm structure, and storm characteristics, need to be taken into account, as well as examining the assumption that there will be no future changes that have a markedly different effect on tropical cyclone behavior than is seen today.

Predicting Tropical Storm Frequency and Intensity By Expanding Studies and Predictor Models

Being able to explain, predict, and understand changes in tropical storm activity is of great societal importance in terms of economic and social impact, and has been studied intensely by scientists around the globe. There is a great variation in tropical storms on different time scales, varying from intra-seasonal to multi-decadal, and a great deal of argument about whether tropical storm frequency and intensity are sensitive to climate change. Villarini *et al.* (2010) examined the empirical understanding between tropical storm frequency and large-scale climate conditions by examining the climate indices that tropical storms are often associated with. The group of scientists modeled not only the North Atlantic climate basin, which is the typical target of studies, but also expanded their analysis to include all tropical storm activity that lasted longer than two days and was recorded as U.S. landfall events. Only tropical storms that last longer than two days were recorded since shorter storms are likely to produce negative results. The authors found that it would be best to use a family of models with Atlantic and tropical storms as covariates.

Villarini and colleagues used a statistical approach to examine the relationship between tropical storm count and climate indices, expanding on further studies by also including tropical storms recorded as U.S. landfall events, rather than only covering the North Atlantic basin. A Poisson distribution model was also utilized to examine the dependence of counts on climate indices, accounting for over-dispersion or under-dispersion of tropical storm counts. The model is able to predict inter-annual variability, however, another model will be necessary to examine decadal variability as well. For all the models, Atlantic and tropical sea surface temperatures (SST) are retained as significant covariates, supporting an idea proposed by Vecchi that the increases or decreases in Atlantic SST are preferable to the values of tropical SST in predicting tropical storm count in the U.S. land areas and the North Atlantic basin. The Poisson model of distribution was determined to be the best method for evaluating the data. The scientists suggest running a further experiment modeling U.S. landfall count with the overall storm count for the North Atlantic in order to get a wider swath of data that would be much more accurate in predicting tropical storm changes and reduce anomalies in data.

Expanding such studies will allow for a better understanding of the ways that we can further predict tropical storm variability, along with patterns and variation.

Using Analysis of Climate Change Effects on Cyclone Frequency and Intensity to Mitigate Damage Risk

In terms of damages, hurricanes and tropical storms are a significant source of social disruption and economic hardship. According to many scientific studies, as well as the Intergovernmental Panel on Climate Change, the enhanced greenhouse conditions will lead to stronger tropical storms, and therefore higher levels of damage cost. A study conducted by Li and Stewart (2011) developed an analysis to assess growing cyclone damage risk and the economic viability of hazard mitigation strategies in order to reduce the potential impact of these events. The analysis utilized an approximation for cyclone wind intensity and frequency in combination with reconstruction patterns in Queensland, Australia. The mean annual wind changes over 50 years were examined in order to rule out annual variability in wind speed change. It was determined that average wind speeds are increasing rapidly, and that building new houses to withstand higher wind velocities and retrofitting older houses to withstand the wind velocities would be economically beneficial in the long run. Further studies will need to be conducted to further examine increases in flooding and storm surge activities due to climate change and their impact on an economic and social level.

According to evidence in recent scientific reports, enhanced greenhouse conditions will lead to an increase of intensity in tropical storms and cyclones. While there is regional variability, the overarching idea is that frequency and intensity will increase. Li and Stewart examined the impact of tropical storms and cyclones on Queensland Australia in various predictor models that cover a wide range of wind speed increases. Other parameters that are not yet fully understood, such as sea surface temperature (SST), storm trajectory, rainfall rates, etc, are not taken into account and are left for future study. Three different mitigation strategies were created in order to examine their cost-effectiveness over time at reducing tropical storm damages, all of which assumed that wind speeds would gradually increase to 110% of current levels.

The first mitigation strategy involved retrofitting foreshore construction, or housing construction closer to the ocean, which is projected to reduce damages by 15.8 million dollars if a severe cyclone hits, 15% less damage than if nothing were done. The second strategy involves retrofitting all houses built pre-1980s, but there is only minimal benefit from the upgrades. The third strategy is an attempt to improve enhancements in new construction farther away from the shoreline, which has a varying effect due to economy viability of the times. It was discovered that the retrofitting of foreshore construction would be the most useful method of protection due to the high likelihood of stronger tropical storms along the coastal areas.

For future studies, it is recommended that other variables be considered rather than merely examining risk in comparison with damage costs, since some of the strategies developed are not the most economically viable when correlated with the increasing damages by gradually higher tropical storm winds. Also, being able to look at effects of SST and other causes of heightened tropical storm activity in correlation with damage increases would also be beneficial in examining how much potential damage might be caused in the future due to the combination of all the effects warming has on tropical storm activity, and running an predictor analysis on the data.

Changes in Tropical Cyclone Frequency not Strongly Correlated with Sea Surface Temperature

Despite the devastating weather and climate events that have occurred globally throughout the past half-century, tropical cyclone activity has decreased. This is true even while sea surface temperatures (SST), which are positively correlated with potential energy in tropical storms, have increased. A scientific dilemma is why, with the increase in SSTs and global warming that are necessary for typhoon genesis, would there be a decrease in numbers of tropical storms. Zhou *et al.* (2010) imply that the explanation for this phenomenon is based in the second law of thermodynamics. They arrived at this by examining the tropical storm genesis in concordance with the inter-tropical convergence zone (ITCZ). Their results suggest that sea surface temperatures are only one of the necessary conditions for tropical cyclone genesis, and that the low-level vorticity, or tendency for elements of the fluid to "spin", associated with ICTZ variations should be a fundamental factor for tropical cyclone genesis. They conclude that the causality between SSTs and tropical storm frequency is suggested is not yet fully understood and should be examined further.

Zhou *et al.* examined the Western North Pacific (WNP) as a model that might explain the relationship between unusual SSTs and tropical storm number. They used NCEP/NCAR 2.5°x2.5° resolution reanalysis data from the National Centers for Environmental Prediction/National Center for Atmospheric research to examine the correlation between SST and surface wind divergence/convection. Zhou and company then used the second law of thermodynamics to try and explain the implications of SST variation and why sea surface warming around the western Pacific is not as dramatic as it is over the central and eastern Pacific. Then, they developed equations, showing a predictable pattern in the changes in SST in various regions, which also helped to explain further temperature variation.

They discovered that there is a gradual increase in the 20-year mean of SSTs over the North Pacific, related to surface wind convection over the ITCZ, but that originally warmer areas will experience a much weaker warming, because of heat lost through diffusion. This leads to the weakening of the ICTZ trough as seen in recent studies, thereby leading to the decreased number of tropical storms. Additionally, a wind component was discovered to have a much more important role over thermodynamic factors than previously considered.

The authors found that warmer SSTs in the western North Pacific can cause fewer tropical cyclones, indicating that sea surface temperatures are only one of the necessary conditions and do not definitively lead to an increase in tropical storm numbers. Examining the effects of other variables on tropical cyclone frequency will help better understand the results proposed by this study.

Dynamic Conditions of the Atmosphere Accounting for the Opposite Trends in Tropical Cyclone Count in the Pacific

Tropical cyclones are considered to be one of the more devastating weather phenomena in terms of their effect on human life and global economy. How global warming will affect these events is widely debated amongst scientists. It is understood that tropical cyclone genesis is dependent on sea surface temperature (SST), since a higher SST provides a cyclone with higher ocean thermal energy. Tropical cyclones typically develop from a tropical disturbance, and only a small percentage of cyclones result from such disturbances. It is implied that with higher SST levels and a temperature increase there will be a similar increase in tropical storms, however, there are opposite trends of cyclone frequency in the western and central Pacific. Li *et al.* (2010) created and examined a model that would explain the variations in the tropical cyclone genesis in different areas of the Pacific. Their results suggest that the major factor that accounts for the distinctly opposite tropical cyclone trends is the constantly changing condition of the atmosphere. They conclude that the projected shift in tropical cyclone activity might pose a great threat to Hawaii and the central Pacific islands.

Li *et al.* examined data demonstrating opposite effects of global warming in different areas of the Pacific. They created a high-resolution global model that can more accurately predict the results shown in previous studies. The model was then tested to ensure that it is applicable to a wider range of results than just Pacific tropical cyclone increases and decreases. The authors used data from the International Pacific Research Center in Hawaii, Korea Ocean Research and Development Institute, First Institute of Oceanography in China, and the GFDL, NOAA in

Princeton New Jersey to compile a suitable model to predict tropical cyclone genesis. The results suggested an increase in variations in atmospheric conditions in the north central Pacific region (termed synoptic-scale disturbances), and a decrease in variations in the northwestern Pacific region. These changes in conditions create wind shears that have significant effects on the increases and decreases in tropical cyclone activity.

Li *et al.* discovered that global warming weakens the trade winds in the Pacific, and that the Walker circulation is weakened, causing a weakening of the North Pacific monsoon season. The weakening of heating caused by the monsoon season leads to a reduction of tropical cyclone frequency. In contrast, in the central Pacific, the SST gradient is reduced and there is a higher localized SST, which results in an increase in tropical cyclone frequency. The model tends to overestimate tropical cyclone genesis, so the authors suggest caution when interpreting the results—however, the shift of cyclone activity in the Pacific is significant to the millions of people living in Hawaii and central Pacific islands.

Even with the overestimation, developing a model that can accurately predict tropical cyclone activity and take into account so many variables is particularly important. There are still uncertainties with regards to physics in the models uses and SST warming patterns, but being able to take these into account may have implications for determining the effects of tropical cyclone activity on a global scale, rather than limiting it to the Pacific.

Conclusions

It is demonstrated conclusively that global warming has a significant effect on tropical cyclone frequency and activity. Through influencing the many variables that affect cyclone formation such as sea surface temperature, there is a direct relationship between global warming and tropical storm activity. In addition, global warming affects events such as the El Niño-Southern Oscillation, which also ties into weather patterns that affect tropical storms. As stressed by many scientists, further image models and programs need to be created that can more accurately take into account all of the variables when predicting future cyclone events.

References Cited

Bender, M.A., Knutson, T.R., Tuleya, R.E., Sirutis, J.J., Vecchi, G.A., Garner, S.T., and Held, I.M. Modeled Impact of Anthropogenic Warming on the Frequency of Intense Atlantic Hurricanes. Science 237, 454–460.

Collins, M., An, S., Cai, W., Ganachaud, A. Guilyardi, E., Jin, F., Jochum, M., Lengaigne, M., Power, S., Timmermann, A., Vecchi, G. and Wittenberg,

A. The impact of global warming on the tropical Pacific Ocean and El
Nino. Nature Geoscience 3, 391–397.

Knutson, T.R., McBride, J.L., Chan, J., Emanuel, K., Holland, G., Landsea, C.,
Held, I., Kossin, J.P., Srivastava, A.K., and Sugi, M. 2010. Tropical Cyclones and Climate Change. Nature Geoscience, 3, 157–163.

Kossin, J.P., Camargo, S.J., and Sitkowski, M. Climate Modulation of North Atlantic Hurricane Tracks. Journal of Climate, Vol.23. 3057–3078.

Li, T., Kwon, M., Zhao, M., Kug, J., Luo,J., and Yu, W. 2010. Global warming
shifts Pacific tropical cyclone location. Geophysical Research Letters 37,
1–5.

Li,Y., and Stewart, M.G. 2011. Cyclone damage risks caused by enhanced greenhouse conditions and economic viability of strengthened residential construction. Natural Hazards Review, 9–18.

NOAA-Tropical Cyclone Structure. Accessed 2 April 2011.
http://www.srh.noaa.gov/jetstream/tropics/tc_structure.htm.

Villarini, G., Vecchi, G.A., and Smith, J.A., 2010. Modeling the dependence of
tropical storm counts in the North Atlantic basin on climate indices.
Monthly Weather Review 138, 2681–2705.

Zhou, X., Liu, C., Liu, Y., Xu, H., and Wang, X., 2011. Changes in tropical cyclone number in the Western North Pacific in a warming environment as implied by classical thermodynamics. International Journal of
Geosciences 2, 29–35.

12. Global Food Security: Effect of Climate Change on Agricultural Yields

Whitney Dawson

Today, two of the major problems we face are climate change and food security, intertwined and adversely impacting each other on a global scale. They will require a series of trade-offs. Climate change has been confirmed in numerous scientific reports, and is beginning to become publically accepted. The rise in climate expected to occur will affect the agricultural industry greatly, dramatically impacting it even in the next few decades. Where as some crops may become better off, those already in semi-arid climates will be impacted most from the heat. In northern parts of Europe where the climate is more temperate, climate change may have a positive effect on agriculture with increased productivity and range of species. Unfortunately, the semi-arid regions are typically in developing areas, such as Sub-Saharan Africa, where meeting crop demand is already a struggle. Many of the grain crops are expected to be affected most severely, which would be detrimental to the diets of the region. Corn, for example, is a staple crop for many regions, and is highly sensitive to the warming climate because of its high water requirements. Root crops will be less affected by climate since they are less exposed to it and grow underground. Livestock production is also strongly affected by climate conditions through impacts to animal performance, the supply of feedstuffs, and disease distribution. The environment experiences a significant amount of destruction from agriculture, and the harm contributes to climate change. An example of this is deforestation, a common repercussion from agricultural expansion that increases the intensity of climate change. The economy will see consequences of climate change as well, through price responses to the necessary changes in the agricultural industry. Prices for agricultural commodities are expected to increase, causing a decrease in household incomes.

Solutions for the agricultural industry's negative impacts from climate change have been presented in a variety of research papers. Numerous studies have been completed, discussing the extent of the impact of climate change on crop yields, but also present various prescriptions to the rising problem. Government involvement is crucial for the majority of the solutions to reach food security. Wide scale change is unlikely to occur without significant policy changes, providing incentives for adoption. The European Union has seen success from a change in the agricultural policy to link farmer payment to respect for the environment. The most frequently discussed climate mitigation strategy is Reducing Emissions from Deforestation and Forest Degradation in Developing Countries (REDD). Increased fertilizer use will also increase crop yields substantially, but is expensive and infeasible in many regions without government aid. Another common proposal is the potential of carbon sequestration. This process mitigates climate change by taking carbon out of the atmosphere and storing it in the ground, but also improves soil quality for increased crop productivity. Also discussed is the possibility of land that will eventually become unsuitable for agriculture to be used for the production of biofuels and biomaterials from biomass, reducing our current reliance on fossil fuels.

Poverty and Crop Yield Consequences From Climate Changes by 2030

The latest IPCC report concluded that the climate is expected to be 1 °C warmer by 2030, regardless of any change in greenhouse gases. Agriculture is the most dependant industry on climate and is expected to be the most impacted. Although it only accounts for 2.4% of global GDP, agriculture has a much larger share in poor countries and is of great importance. Past research has not provided decision makers much guidance on who is expected to gain or lose, since it has focused primarily on linking climate impacts on crop yields and agricultural output in given areas; this is somewhat irrelevant on the macro scale due to the interconnectedness from trade. Hertel *et al.* 2010 embed disaggregated data on household economic activity within countries in a global trade model to observe how new levels of agricultural productivity from climate change will affect poverty in poor countries. The models ultimately result in a poor predictor of welfare impacts due to the role that international trade plays in the market, mediating the impacts of climate shocks. Price increases in agricultural commodities due to changes in the climate may reduce some households' income level, but may also have a positive effect on those incomes directly related to the agriculture industry.

Hertel *et al.* 2010 used the Global Trade Analysis Project (GTAP) global trade model, along with its database and poverty modules. The models have been recently validated by their correct predictions of price impacts from shocks in a previous study. Effects on agriculture production and poverty implications from climate shocks can be seen in the macro economy with use of these models. In the study, households were stratified within countries by their primary source of income. Productivity shocks from climate change were based on six commodities: rice, wheat, coarse grains, oilseeds, cotton, and other crops, and low and high productivity outcome estimates were made. The low productivity estimates assume rapid temperature change and high impacts, where the high productivity estimates represent slower warming and low sensitivity.

Coarse grains, such as maize, are expected to see the largest negative outcome, because they are very sensitive to extreme heat. Wheat and rice yields see gains where climate is currently colder. Commodity price changes estimated from GTAP are small, with the exception of an expected 15% increase in coarse grain prices. On a macro level, the most direct impacts of climate change on agricultural losses are on crops in the Sub-Saharan Africa region, and large losses for the US and China are seen as well. The demand for food throughout the world is mostly inelastic, and the decreases in production produce significant price increases in agricultural commodities. Some losses in productivity may be offset through international trading, such as in New Zealand and Brazil. However, the study points out that climate change causes global trade to shrink, therefore resulting in efficiency loss.

While it may be true that rising world prices for staple agricultural commodities could cause a decrease in real income and an increase in poverty, they could also have a more positive effect on changes in earning. Hertel *et al.* 2010 also found that although the prices rise by a significant amount, the actual average impact on the cost of living is much more modest. An increase in earnings is seen for households whose incomes rely on agriculture, where households with incomes completely independent of the agricultural industry have a more negative affected earning level. This same idea transfers to expectations in poverty levels as well, with a similar lack of symmetry in results and a large variation in poverty impacts across different countries.

Estimates of climate change impacts did not include the possibility of any adaptations that could reduce negative outcomes, such as introduction of new crop varieties or expanded irrigation infrastructure in a region. There is also limited knowledge about how global poverty will alter over the next few decades. Ultimately, estimating climate change impacts on global poverty requires knowledge on both agricultural shocks, and trade patterns, production, consumption, and poverty in certain countries. The magnitude of poverty changes could be detrimental to some developing countries, where those countries with many agricultural self-employed may adversely see a decrease in poverty.

Whitney Dawson

The Negative Implications of Climate Change on African Agriculture

Sub-Saharan Africa (SSA) claims the highest proportion of malnourished populations in the world, and with an economy dependant on agriculture production. There have been very limited scientific findings in the past that show the level of harm that crops in SSA will endure from climate change. Schlenker and Lobell use historical crop production and weather data to create a model detailing the crop yield response to the expected change in climate. The study found that climate change is expected to negatively impact crops in SSA, and substantial measures of investment are found to be necessary for sufficient agricultural production.

Schlenker and Lobell have created an assortment of models using panel analysis to demonstrate the extent to which SSA agricultural production responds to climate change. In past studies, availability of reliable data has been a problem, and 'best-guess' estimates have been used with uncertainties. The models that Schlenker and Lobell designed incorporate historical data of both crop production and weather, and are applied to the staple African crops: maize, sorghum, millet, groundnuts and cassava. These are thought to be key sources of protein, fat, and calories in the region. It is advantageous to use a data series of historical weather patterns, rather than averaging conditions, because infrequent extreme weather events are accounted for. A panel data set is preferable because it is an observational study, measuring how various constraints affect farmers' reactions to weather shocks. The disadvantage to the panel model is that responses to weather shocks may differ from responses to a permanent climate shift.

The regression model is able to examine how climate change affects the crop yields while keeping all other variables unchanged. However, farmers tend to use production technologies that are suboptimal due to a lack of resources, and fertilizer is underused in many countries. Zimbabwe and South Africa have higher fertilizer use, and therefore higher yields, but are also more susceptible to damage from temperature increases as a result. Schlenker and Lobell fit separate models for countries that use higher and lower amounts of fertilizer since the responses would be varied. Although lower fertilizer use results in less of an impact from climate change, the countries using higher amounts of fertilizer still produce higher yields, still proving the importance of sufficient fertilizer use.

The predicted changes in climate were evaluated under 16 climate change models and 1000 randomly drawn years. Almost all models had significant improvement with no weather variable and predicted negative impacts of warming, with the exception of the cassava crop, a root crop with a highly variable growing season. The mean estimates of total changes in production for maize, sorghum, millet, groundnut, and cassava are –22, –17, –17, –18 and –8%, respectively.

It was found that temperature changes have a significantly stronger impact on crop yields than precipitation changes. The study omits the possible changes in the distribution of rainfall during growing seasons, which could potentially be important. Increasing the precision of the climate change forecasts would allow a more confident analysis. A more regionalized set of data may also prove to be beneficial, however, the broader scale of data analysis can be useful for decision making on the national level.

Major improvements in agricultural productivity are necessary to combat the substantial poverty problems in SSA. The study suggests that the challenge of increasing productivity will become more difficult with time due to the warming climate. The authors suggest that this should be seen as incentive for significant investments in production renovations that will be sustained in the future. Important investments recommended are crop varieties with greater tolerance to heat and draught, improvement of irrigation systems, disaster relief, and insurance programs to help SSA reach a more sustainable agriculture system.

Possibilities and Alternative for Fighting Climate Change and Food Security in Sub-Saharan Africa

Sub-Saharan Africa faces the potential situation of deforestation and land degradation, intersecting with hunger and poverty. The clearing of forests and woodlands for agricultural use is the primary cause of deforestation. Agriculture practices can be linked to the climate mitigation strategy of Reducing Emissions from Deforestation and Forest Degradation (REDD) in Developing Countries. Palm *et al.* (2010) develop four scenarios for increasing agricultural production by differing supplies of nitrogen, and compare the effects to food production, basic caloric needs, and greenhouse gas emissions. The study found that crop surplus area for reforestation is achieved at low population densities where there is high land availability. Conversely, to realize food security and reduce greenhouse gases in highly populated areas with small farm sizes, mineral fertilizers are necessary to make land available for reforestation. The authors believe that agricultural intensification in sub-Saharan Africa with mineral fertilizers, green manures, or improved tree fallows needs policies addressing costs, and incentives to escalate. The authors suggest carbon financing for small-holder agriculture to reduce emissions due to deforestation.

Palm *et al.* study how the increase of biological nitrogen (N) and fertilizers from mineral sources can reverse the nutrient depletion in farm soils due to decades of crop harvest and erosion. Four scenarios for increasing food production are examined in two SSA sites where food security, poverty, and land degradation are high. The sites differ in rainfall, population density, degree of deforestation, and amount of land used for crops. The four different N sources are extensification by clearing additional land, fertilizers, green manure through legume cover crops, and improved tree fallow. Palm *et al.* used an accounting model for estimating and comparing each scenario to crop productivity, determining if deforestation is needed to meet basic caloric needs or if reforestation is able to occur.

Ideally, a greater N input directs emissions of nitrous oxide from soils, and yields improve simultaneously, reducing the need to clear forest for food security. Where landscapes are already heavily used by agricultural production, tree fallows can be used for biomass production to mitigate GHG emissions while still retaining food security. It is assumed that organic sources of N produce lower emissions than mineral sources, and also lower nitrous oxide emissions.

The study showed that in cases of high population density and small farm sizes, green manure and improved tree fallows do not suffice in achieving necessary crop yields to permit reforestation, and fertilizers are needed to reach food security and reduce greenhouse gas emissions. However, in lower populated areas, there is more abundance of land, and larger areas for crops to grow. In these areas, no additional cropland was needed for food security, and yields proved to be highest with fertilizer use, the only scenario that actually freed cropland for reforestation and carbon sequestration. For each scenario, the N supplied from tree fallow improvement was significantly greater than from green manure. The global warming potential was only positive where the population densities are lower and reforestation from use of fertilizer was possible.

Food security requires more than simply meeting the caloric requirement; proper dietary needs, including sufficient proteins and vitamins must be met. An additional problem for some regions studied in the paper is that agricultural land is utilized for tobacco production rather than food crops. The authors point out that any change is unlikely to be implemented on a wide scale without significant policy changes, providing incentives for adoption. Interventions are suggested by the United Nations that detail initially subsidizing costly mineral fertilizers, replacing them after a few crop seasons with legume cover crops and agroforestry practices as a source of N.

European Agriculture Responses to Climate Change

The productivity of European agriculture is generally higher than the world average. In 2003 the European Union decided to change the agricultural policy to link farmer payment to respect for the environment, animal and plant health, and animal welfare standards. The consequences of climate change are expected to cause increasing water shortages and a varying response in cropping systems. Bindi and Oleson (2010) expect increasing yields and suitable crop areas in northern Europe, but expect disadvantages from water shortage and extreme weather in southern Europe. The authors discuss positive possibilities for different use of the land that will become incapable of crop production due to climate change.

Bindi and Oleson find that the impact of agriculture on Europe's water resources should be reduced to reach higher surface and ground water standards. The authors also discuss the changes in climate that are expected to occur using the IPCC 2007 reports. Europe is projected to warm at a rate between 0.22 and 0.52 Celsius degrees per decade, and precipitation is expected to change with increases in the north of up to 16% and decrease in the south from –4 to –24%. Scenarios studied by the authors showed decreases in European cropland by 2080 from 28% to 47%. Heat waves and droughts are also expected to increase in frequency and intensity, leading to reductions in farm income. The authors find that climate change may have a positive effect in northern areas with increased productivity and range of species, but negative effects in the south. Crops that currently grow in more southern areas of Europe will become more suitable in the north, and at higher altitudes in the south. Earlier infestation will be caused by warmer winters, and plant diseases may lead to a greater demand for pesticide use. Negative effects are seen in livestock as well, with higher mortality risk in livestock systems and an increased disease rate.

Bindi and Oleson suggest that adaptation strategies will be necessary to manage the negative impacts that climate change is expected to cause to agriculture in the south. Agricultural activities are a major contributor to greenhouse gas emissions, and mitigation strategies are needed within the agricultural sector. Soil Organic Carbon stocks in Europe will decrease from the increase in temperatures, speeding up organic matter decomposition. The authors suggest an alternative use for the land that will eventually be unsuitable for crops and relevant to our future needs; land use could change to the production of biofuels and biomaterials from biomass, and reduce our current reliance on fossil fuels. However, future technical development, including new crop varieties and better agriculture practices, could offset climate change effects.

Strategies to deal with climate change are discussed, differentiating planned and autonomous adaptations. Autonomous adaptations may be more feasible, as they are at a smaller scale and occur over a shorter time period. Examples include changes in crop varieties, sowing dates, and fertilizer and pesticide use. Comparatively, planned adaptations involve major structural changes, on a large-scale level. A key planned adaptation available is allocating European agricultural land use differently. The authors also discuss the concept that organic farming may have a higher resilience to climate change because it has more options for change, but higher costs, and subsidies would be necessary.

Whitney Dawson

Climate Change and South American Farmers' Livestock Choices

South American farmers choose livestock species for agriculture use based on the range of climate. They specialize in beef and cattle exports, which are the primary species on around 48% of farms, but climate change will likely have a negative impact on agricultural production, and threaten food security. Seo *et al.* (2010) examine how the livestock choices will respond to climate change, looking at five species in seven countries. The multinominal logit model used in the study proved climate variables are highly significant in determining the species choice. Large changes were seen in Andean countries, but overall the impacts from climate change vary by species and climate.

Seo *et al.* developed a multinominal logit model to measure the effects of climate change on livestock species. Farmers from a broad array of climate conditions in seven different countries were surveyed to collect data for the model. The data set includes information on livestock production and transactions, livestock products, and relevant costs. The five primary livestock species that were examined are commonly raised in South America: beef cattle, dairy cattle, pigs, sheep, and chickens. The model controlled for soils, geography, household characteristics, and country fixed effects. Climate data for a 16-year time period were gathered from satellites operated by the US Department of Defense, and the ground weather measurement from the World Meteorological Organization.

The scientific evidence that livestock production is strongly affected by climate conditions is convincing, and seen in impacts to animal performance, the supply of feedstuffs, and disease distribution. A hot and dry scenario showed a decrease in beef cattle by 3.2%, dairy cattle by 2.3%, pigs by 0.5% and chickens by 0.9% by 2060, and an increase in sheep by 7% to compensate. The increase in sheep occurs mostly in Andes mountain countries, but decreases in the higher mountain areas, where chickens are more frequently chosen. A warmer temperature is likely to cause cattle productivity to fall, and to impact reproduction rates. Chickens are opted for in wetter zones, and dairy cattle choice increases with precipitation, but so does the incidence of livestock diseases.

The study was unique in comparison to past similar studies, in that it controlled detailed household level information data in the model. The data included in the model controlled for multiple variables, and household information was controlled to determine how various farm heads would change their livestock choices. Older farm heads prefer cattle, and more educated farm heads prefer beef cattle or pigs. Female farm heads and long time private landowners tend to avoid chickens. These results demonstrate a female tendency to choose less risky species in comparison to younger male farm heads, in their choosing of beef cattle, a more profitable species.

Where many livestock species choices vary across the countries in South America, the choice of beef cattle will decline across the continent. Beef cattle are an important part of the agriculture industry across the continent, and the authors suggest concern on a policy level due to its vulnerability, and the high dependency on the agricultural economy. Although dairy cattle choice will decline across the continent, increases are seen in Uruguay and Argentina. The likelihood of choosing sheep increases across all countries. Climate changes are going to change livestock patterns on a large scale because the entire ecosystem is likely to change. If the current savannah habitat changes to forest, livestock grazing will become difficult. Seo *et al.* found that farmers are more likely to choose livestock over crops as temperature increases, though the livestock species adopted varies greatly.

The authors did not include price as a variable in their model, and do not know how price will change in the future, nor did they examine potential changes in population, taste, technologies, reliance on regional agriculture economy, and in political structures. These unaccounted for changes could affect agricultural practices greatly, and farmer revenue changes would also have a large impact on livestock species choice.

Weakening Climate Change and Reaching Food Security through Soil Carbon Sequestration

There are one billion food-insecure people in the world, with the gap in cereal requirement extremely high in developing regions, and expected to triple by 2015. Many developing countries are seeking means for reducing this gap, and sustainably increasing grain production. Carbon Sequestration in soils has potential to mitigate climate change on a global level. The process results in improvement of soil quality, and therefore also has positive consequences on food security and agronomic productivity. Farmers that participate in enhancing ecosystem services will receive payments, aiding economic development in developing countries. In his paper, Rattan Lal (2010) found the technical potential of carbon sequestration in soils to reduce atmospheric carbon dioxide by 50 ppm by the end of the 21st century, increasing the soil carbon pool (SOC) at a rate of 1 Mg/ha/year. Food security would then be enhanced with cereal and legume production in developing countries increasing by 32 million Mg/year, and roots and tubers increasing by 9 million Mg/year.

Rattan Lal found that agricultural soils used by small landholders in the tropic and sub-tropic regions are significantly depleted of their soil organic carbon pool, and highly susceptible to erosion, breakdown, decline in biodiversity, and overall reduction in quality. Crop yields are therefore very dependant on rainfall patterns, a monsoon easily resulting in crop failure, as seen in India in 2009, due to erosion and structural breakdown. Though few experiments establishing the relationship of SOC concentration and agronomic yield have been completed, the available data show a strong relationship in areas of diverse soils, and a dramatically stronger relationship for soils of semi-arid regions, such as India. India would see significant improvement in crop yields in a decade if SOC concentration increased by just 0.1%. Lal includes an array of data from various studies that continue to prove the strong relationship between SOC concentration and crop yields over every type of climate across the world, including temperate regions. The gains in agronomic production potentially achieved from increased SOC levels all depend on climate and other factors, but ultimately reduce hunger risks.

Lal also proves SOC sequestration to be highly cost-effective overall, especially if farmers and land managers were to be compensated for their efforts in sequestering carbon in their soils. The incentive for farmers to enhance ecosystem services and reduce carbon dioxide levels would be high, as well as the achieving of global food security. The concept "farming carbon" would be promoted through credits of soil carbon sequestered sold to restore degraded soils, treating these credits as a farm commodity. Lal argues that "farming carbon" could generate income that would incentivize farmers to invest in soil restoration.

There is a variety of practices that farmers are suggested to take on to enhance the SOC pools that largely involve managing a higher level of nutrients in the soil. Lal found the optimum range of SOC concentrations in the root zone of soil to be 2–3%, a level at which agronomic yields of crops and pastures would improve if reached. Farmers in developing countries seeking an alternative to expensive chemical fertilizers can do a number of things to reach these SOC concentration levels such as increasing water capacity, improving nutrient supplies, restoring soil structure, and minimizing soil erosion risks. Lal concludes that these processes should have been discussed at the Copenhagen COP-15 meeting, as many were disappointed from the lack of multiple benefit strategies considered. Restoring the SOC pool in depleted cropland soils around the world would benefit the issues of food security, climate change, and soil/environmental degradation.

Climate Change Mitigation Possibilities through Carbon Sequestration in the U.S.

The United States is an active player in the international effort to combat climate change. Although 84% of US net carbon emissions come from fossil fuel consumption and only 7% from agriculture, the changes made in the agricultural system to fight climate change are still essential until new technologies and strategies become prevalent. Agriculture is both largely affected by climate change, as well as a large contributor itself to the growing problem. The management of agricultural systems to sequester carbon dioxide as soil organic carbon (SOC) and to minimize GHG emissions is a partial solution for climate change mitigation. Morgan *et al.* examine the various agricultural sectors in the United States for their SOC potential, distinguishing the different land characteristics.

Morgan *et al.* (2010) explain that the rate of carbon return to the atmosphere is influenced by the rate of photosynthetic carbon dioxide assimilation, which is dependent on soil fertility, climate, and management. Greenhouse gas mitigation is possible through assimilation of atmospheric carbon dioxide by vegetation choices, and moving carbon from plants and animals into soil. Sequestering carbon within the soil organic matter (SOM) is a prime option for carbon storage but has other benefits as well, such as improved soil quality, soil structure and stability, and water holding capacity.

The authors study each agricultural sector, picking apart possible improvements, and recognize valuable questions to be answered. To increase SOC in croplands, the authors recommend increasing cropping frequency, growing high-residue crops, maximizing plant water use, and applying vegetation to shade the surface soil. Grazing lands take up about 37% of total US land area and contribute about 15% of US soil carbon sequestration potential. The amount of carbon stored in grazing lands can be double that of cropland and can be intensified by adjusting stocking rate, plant species, and fertilizer use. Sequestration rates decline in grazing lands over time without added inputs, therefore attention to these areas is key. Agro forestry is the integration of woody plants into crop and livestock systems for improvement of the quality of their environment, while still allowing sustainable production of food. This system sequesters a large amount of carbon and for a long duration. Horticulture land has received little attention for the potential of carbon sequestration in its vegetable, vineyard, and orchard crops. Specialized management of the crops has discouraged the use of much conservation potential but the authors suggest cover crops for sequestering carbon. Wetlands are less than 1% of cropped areas in the US, but have especially high GHG emission rates due to their waterlogged state, which lacks the oxygen needed to decompose organic matter. Drainage of the organic matter would allow carbon dioxide to be released at a higher rate, but the authors conclude that it is not feasible to consider carbon sequestration in these soils.

Biofuels present an emerging issue for land management. About 18% of harvested grain in the US was used for ethanol production in 2007, and more than half of harvested corn grain was for animal feed. Strong interest exists in developing sustainable energies from biofuels, but a number of concerns for environmental problems have risen from intensification of agriculture and may compromise the overall goal of increasing carbon in the ecosystem. Even as new technologies are developed, it is important for agriculture to continue developing successful soil carbon sequestration practices.

Very few experiments have addressed best management practices for improving soil carbon storage, and little research has assessed how different practices may affect carbon sequestration. Morgan *et al.* suggest the need for low-cost carbon and non-carbon dioxide greenhouse gas information on multiple levels. Measurements of GHG fluxes can be used to evaluate the effects of management opportunities and changes in climate on carbon balance, and could be used to estimate large-scale carbon budgets. Development of a national database is needed to make further assessments. The authors recommend direct sampling of soil carbon as a more feasible technique for gathering data, rather than expensive and complicated GHG measurement technology.

Examining the Impact of Thermal Adaptation of Soil Microorganisms and Crop System on Climate Change's Effects on Organic Matter in Tropical Soil

As populations in tropical regions increase and more food is needed, crop yields are decreasing. Increasing the amount of cleared land for crop production has negative impacts on soil quality and crop production as well as increasing the amount of greenhouse gas emissions. Tropical crops are currently at optimal growth temperatures, and therefore decline in yields are expected with even a small increase in temperature. Sierra *et al.* (2010) hypothesize that climate change in tropics affects soil organic matter (SOM) content and soil fertility through the direct effect on the rate of microbial processes and by the indirect effect on crop growth. The authors predict that temperature and rainfall will substantially increase, and affect maize crops significantly more than bananas. Maize yields were found to decrease by 1% under the adaptation scenario studied, where no difference was found in banana yields. Decreasing rates of SOM and C mineralization were predicted for maize, and again no differences were found for banana crops.

Sierra *et al.* model the thermal adaptation, the shift in the intrinsic response of a biological soil process to temperature due to soil warming, of soil microorganisms in response to climate change. This process is then introduced in a crop system model, already calibrated to incorporate SOM dynamics under tropical conditions. The study aims to see how climate change impacts SOM in agricultural tropical soil, and to evaluate the importance of microbial adaptation in SOM dynamics in crops. The two crop systems compared are maize and banana, both currently of great use in the tropics. Models for climate simulation and crop-soil relationships were borrowed from outside sources, selected for their previous calibration to the crops analyzed in this study, and accounting for irrigation effects. The climate is simulated from 1950 to 2099 for tropical humid conditions.

The model predicts a 3.4 °C increase for air temperature and 1100 mm per year increase for rainfall due to an increase in of 375 ppm for atmospheric carbon dioxide concentration in the 2090–2099 decade in comparison to the 1950–1959 decade. By controlling the change in C input, soil temperature, and soil moisture, the crops affects the response of SOM to climate change. Little variation is seen in SOM until 2020, followed by a faster decrease for maize than banana. Banana had positive effects on growth from an increase in temperature, and relatively stable C inputs. Maize growth and cycle length drastically decreased from increased temperature. The difference in results between crops is due to the higher water consumption of banana than maize, affecting the soil temperature as well. SOM is never stabilized in the period studied since C mineralization is always greater than C input. The authors conclude from the models that microbial thermal adaptation does not fundamentally change the temporal pattern of SOM dynamics, but slightly modifies it.

Debate over climate change impacts occurs as a result of the difficulties is examining the relationship between soil, plant, and weather variables affecting SOM dynamics under the scenario of climate change. In the studied period, the factors controlling SOM decrease varied over time and with the crop system, not with a large amount of consistency. It is suggested that progressive thermal adaptation of soil microorganisms can play an important role in mitigating climate change.

Balancing Food Security and Climate Change Mitigation for Sustainable Land Use in the Tropics

Two of today's major problems are the need to increase food production to achieve food security, and the need to mitigate climate change. However, their potential solutions produce a conflict. DeFries and Rosenzweig (2010) look at the trade-offs that the solutions entail in tropical regions, and note that tropical countries highly value both the agriculture and forest sectors, but the extensive land use in these areas tends to exacerbate climate change. On the other hand, global food production is only slightly increased by deforestation-related agricultural development. Redirection of agricultural expansion to already cleared lands, improvement of soil quality and livestock management, and other policy intervention may allow increased agricultural production without exacerbating climate change. The authors find that there is no easy balance for achieving these objectives in the tropics, but place-specific strategies based on regionally varying factors are a start.

DeFries and Rosenzweig use past studies to examine the linkages between climate change mitigation and food security. They find that the greatest possibility to mitigate climate change is through change in agricultural land use. The only remaining biomes where enough land is available for expansion of agricultural production are in tropical forests and woodlands. However, agricultural expansion is the primary cause of deforestation. Estimates from various data sources strongly conclude that deforestation results in a very small increase of agricultural area, but causes a huge increase in carbon dioxide emissions. The majority of greenhouse gas emissions in tropical countries are due to the use of land for agricultural practices, different from most other countries whose mitigation possibilities are in the energy sector. The predominant agricultural activity that emits GHGs is controlled fires for clearing biomass for deforestation. Tropical regions are increasing GHG emissions at the most rapid rate.

Agricultural intensification, or increasing output per area, is identified as a primary focus for increasing food production in a more sustainable manner. Intensification would allow less deforestation to occur due to a more efficient use of land, and would therefore result in less GHG emissions. A possible exception the authors point out is that higher livestock densities and chemical inputs might result from intensification, which would both add to the level of emissions. Based on multiple analyses, the authors concluded that reducing deforestation will not necessarily lead to increased food production.

DeFries and Rosenzweig suggest the need to view landscapes from a cross-sector perspective to recognize opportunities that minimize trade-offs between food production and climate change mitigation. The authors emphasize the need to examine agricultural practices at a local level, since specific areas have a wide array of variables that also affect crop yields. Strategies to achieve the objectives require analyses of options that consider site-specific characteristics. Trade-offs between food production and climate change mitigation vary between small and large-scale agricultural systems.

The foremost opportunity for tropical countries to mitigate climate change arises in the forest and agricultural sectors. Emissions of GHGs are increasing at a more rapid rate in tropical Asia and Latin America than in the rest of the world. Compared to temperate regions, almost twice as much carbon is lost from a unit of cleared land in the tropics, producing less than half of the crop yield. The opportunities for mitigating climate change and increasing agricultural production will not spontaneously occur, but will require the help of policies. Policy options discussed have been heavily focused on the mitigation potential of REDD (Reducing Emissions from Deforestation and forest Degradation), although this option does not consider food security. A careful balance must be made when considering policies that deal with deforestation because food production could be negatively affected. DeFries and Rosenzweig note that policies should aim at locating new production opportunities on land that has already been cleared, rather than clearing new land. They suggest a policy focus on guidelines for international trade that encourage agricultural commodities produced on already cleared land.

Conclusions

The tradeoff between climate change mitigation and increasing agricultural production to meet global food security will require a careful balance. With all of our available knowledge today, policies should be developed to incentivize agricultural practices that would contribute less to the climate change problem. An example of this may be government compensation for farmers for carbon sequestering in their soil. Another suggestion is that where agricultural expansion is necessary for food demands, it should take place on already cleared lands to avoid further deforestation. The challenge of increasing productivity will become more difficult with time due to the warming climate, and a sense of urgency should be felt. The prospect of trade is not taken into account in the majority of the studies, but has a huge impact on the allocation of food. Trade enables regions to consume products that are able to grow in other areas, in addition to what is locally available. Most authors agree on the importance of additional research of climate change effects, and of possible solutions to balance climate change and food security. Funding will be necessary in order to complete satisfactory studies and a solid database of information.

References Cited

Bindi, M., Oleson, J., 2010. The reponse of agriculture in Europe to climate change. Springer-Verlag published ahead of print November 16, 2010, doi:10.1007/s10113-010-0173-x.

DeFries, R., Rosenzweig, C., 2010. Toward a whole-landscape approach for sustainable land use in the tropics. PNAS published ahead of print November 16, 2010, doi:10.1073/pnas.1011163107

Hertel, T.W., et al., The Poverty Implications of Climate-induced Crop Yield Changes by 2030. Global Environ. Change (2010), doi: 10.1016/j.gloenvcha.2010.07.001

Lal, Rattan, 2010. Beyond Copenhagen: Mitigating Climate Change and Achieving Food Security through Soil Carbon Sequestration. Science+Business Media B.V. & International Society for Plant Pathology March, 169–77.

Morgan, J.A., Follett, R., Hartwell Allen, L., Del Grosso, S., Derner, J., Dijkstra, F., Franzlubbers, A., Fry, R., Paustian, K., Schoeneberger, M., 2010.

Carbon sequestration in agricultural lands of the United States. Journal of Soil and Water Conservation 65, 6A–13A.

Palm, C.A., Smukler, S.A., Sullivan, C.C., Mutuo, P.K., Nyadzi, G.I., Walsh, M.G., 2010. Identifying Potential Synergies and Trade-offs for Meeting Food Security and Climate Change Objectives in Sub-Saharan Africa. PNAS 107:46, 19661-19666.

Schlenker, W., Lobell, D., 2010. Robust negative impacts of climate change on African agriculture. Environmental Research Letters 5, 014010.

Seo N. S., McCarl, B. A., Mendelsohn, R., 2010. From beef cattle to sheep under global warming? An analysis of adaptation by livestock species choice in South America. El Selvier published ahead of print August 20, 2010, doi: 10.1016/j.ecolecon.2010.07.025

Sierra, J., Brisson, N., Ripoche, D., Deque, M., 2010. Modelling the impact of thermal adaptation of soil microorganisms and crop system on the dynamics of organic matter in a tropical soil under a climate change scenario. El Selvier 221, 2850–2858.

13. Small-Scale Agricultural Producers adapting to Climate Change

Asa Smith Kamer

Climate change is already affecting the natural systems with which human beings interact. Of most imminent concern for human adaptability to climate change, are those changes in nature which will substantially affect human livelihood. While much of the planet's economic output is generated by industrial production, our food production is inextricably linked to the natural systems of soil, climate, water etc. Climate change is predicted to have significant effects on the way temperatures change, storms happen, water flows, diseases spread and plants grow. Agriculture is by its very nature especially vulnerable to climate change and its consequences by its very nature. While farmers have been historically skilled at adapting to climatic flux, today's anthropogenic climate change is happening so quickly that farmers are facing especially trying conditions. The difficulty of ever less predictable growing conditions will likely continue well into the future. Research on the effects of climate change on agriculture will be crucial to the successful adaptation of agriculturalists worldwide. Not only does most of the world's food come from domesticated plant and animal sources, but billions of people rely on agriculture for their livelihood.

Strzepek *et al.* found that in addition to the stresses of climatic change many farmers now compete for resources with growing urban populations. In industrializing nations, farmers must share water with increasing manufacturing and industrial sectors. Newly built factories and infrastructure demand water for waste disposal, power generation, and cooling of power plants. Growing urban populations also use more water as it is pumped directly into the home, rather than shared at a more easy to regulate central source. Many people transitioning to urban lifestyles quickly begin using much more water *per capita* both through personal use and consumption of water intensive products, like imported produce and electricity. While growing urban populations expect more hygienic and convenient lifestyles, their increased water demand consequently stresses agriculture in the regions with which they share water.

In such regions, agricultural water supply is already under acute pressure: competing for land and water with growing urban areas. These places are those most vulnerable to the effects of climate change. The additional pressure of a drying climate could threaten agriculture because there is already insufficient water in these areas. Immerzeel *et al.* found that melting of Himalayan glaciers will significantly change the water availability to the five major downstream agricultural basins. In areas like Asia, Africa and Latin America, large portions of the population rely on year-to-year agricultural productivity to survive, the social consequences of decreased agricultural water availability could be too drastic to predict. These regions which face acute water pressure from both climate change and increased urban and industrial demand are considered 'hotspots'.

As a response to the rapidly changing growing conditions faced by many of the worlds farmers, efforts to address agricultural adaptation have been undertaken by governments, academia, non-profit groups, and farmers groups. Much of the current research focuses on predicting the large scale effects of a changing climate. However, some research has also focused on the important farm-level responses to climate change. In many ways, the steps which individual farmers can take to ensure their own resilience to climate change are the most promising.

In Africa, farmers who transition from farms which rely only on water-intensive crops are more likely to succeed when they include livestock in their operations. Niggeol-Seol found that profitability will increase for those farmers that have diversified operations. Weather changes which disadvantage one or the other will not fully destroy their operations because they will not be relying on only crops or livestock.

When rural farmers keep livestock it will be advantageous to keep breeds which are locally adapted. Locally bred breeds are specifically adapted to weather conditions and fodder availability in a home region. However, the global trade in breeds created for one product, such as milk or meat, is increasing. These breeds are created to be economical for large scale production. The success of these breeds however, does not translate to small scale pastoralists in marginalized landscapes. Most peoples who subsist exclusively on small flocks of livestock are especially connected to environmental conditions. Changes in these conditions, like those predicted to occur as a result of climate change, will have substantial effect on pastoral livelihoods. Hoffman found that locally bred genetic diversity of livestock will be substantially more resilient to the systematic shocks presented by climate change and the prioritization of these breed could be an effective measure of support for vulnerable rural peoples.

In addition to livestock genetic diversity, crop genetic diversity also acts to protect farmers from climatic variance. Because each species of crop thrives in specific temperature and precipitation ranges, a larger variety of crops on farm means that in unexpected conditions it is more likely that some crops will be able to grow. Without biodiverse farms, it is more likely that crop disease will thrive when praying on homogenous host populations. While some large agencies have recognized the importance of biodiversity of crops as an enhancement of food security, there has been difficulty developing and utilizing plant breeding programs designed to address the problem. Sthapit *et al.* found that breeding programs which focus on on-farm capacity for genetic conservation have the greatest potential to effect the lives of farmers. Farmer-initiated programs to maintain biodiverse crops bases are the most effective.

Farmer-lead initiatives for environmental sustainability are also measures against climate change. Leland and Smith *et al.* both investigated recent efforts by farmer groups to work with non-profit groups and academic researchers in order to meet both of these goals. In Puerto Rico, farmers who were already trained on principals of sustainable agriculture were more likely to take measure of resilience against climate change, such as seed saving, forest conservation and organic practices. In the northeastern United States, another such collaboration had farmers and university breeders working together to connect the breeding innovations of farmers with small seed companies which have the resources to distribute new, locally adapted varieties. The research found that although there is promising enthusiasm among farmers to encourage local breeding, there exist significant socio-economic factors, such as dominance of the seed market by a few multi-national distributors, which discourage this type of development.

Significant resilience to climate change can be ensured for agriculture by farmers themselves. On-farm decisions related to inputs, water use, breeding and land management all have consequences for the ability of communities to withstand the long-term difficulties presented by climate change.

Climate Change and Agricultural Water Scarcity

The effects of climate change coupled with increased Municipal and Industrial (M&I) demand for water will lead to worldwide changes in the availability of water for use in agriculture. However, the exact effects and intensity of climate change remain to be seen and the way a changing climate effects water availability will vary greatly depending on the region. Also, taking into account the environmental flow requirements (EFR) of a region, the amount of water designated to remain in the ecosystem rather than for human use, Strzepek *et al.* modeled the future ramifications for agricultural water availability. The research pointed to certain hotspots, areas such as Africa, India, China and the western United States. In these places the combined effects of a drier climate and increased human demand for urban lifestyles: industrial production, and energy production, all of which indicate increased usage. In these locations water scarcity is predicted to put acute pressure on agricultural productivity.

Strzepek *et al.* identified potentially stressed agricultural regions by focusing on specific geopolitical regions and estimating likely water demands based on trends of increasing or decreasing industrial water need. The increase of both urban populations as well as the increase of a nation's GDP correlate with dramatically increased water usage per capita. Countries which are developing larger cities and industrial economies are likely to require more water in the future. Subsurface water, the most common source for agricultural irrigation, will be placed under increasingly heavy demand as non-agricultural needs grow. Thus, decreased supply was considered in modeling future availability.

In order to incorporate the effects of a changing climate on already threatened agricultural water sources, the modeling methodology used three distinct climate scenarios to predict future supply; a stable unchanging climate, a generally wetter climate and a generally drier climate. Each scenario identifies different threatened areas. For instance, in Europe under the drier scenario, agriculture water supply is threatened whereas in the wetter scenario it is not. Some areas, like Brazil and the U.K. are not likely to face climate change-based agricultural water shortage under either scenario.

The researchers identified a region's likelihood for water shortage by considering how much water is currently available for agriculture, and then factored the likely increased demands from industry and urban use. Many 'developing' countries face a specifically difficult water management challenge. Industrial development requires increasingly large water inputs, especially as a coolant for power plants. The intensive water use of these processes diverts water away from agricultural availability. Urban residents use significantly more water. In many developing countries, this results from a change from limited central sources such as a town pump, well or water truck to direct household plumbing. This allows for the potential of overuse in a local area as individuals use more than what is sustainable for the region as a whole. This trend also appears on a larger scale, as transnational borders dissect rivers and watersheds. In these situations certain administrative regions can overuse, creating scarcity downstream. Here, the researchers identified a global shortage of appropriate agricultural water management as a cause of consistent local misuse and constructed need.

The other demand for water is Environmental Flow Requirements. These are the calculated need for flowing water in an ecosystem which is institutionally maintained in order to secure ecosystem services. The EFR of a given areas varies greatly depending on the type of ecosystem. For example Oceanian water ways require 54 percent of water, while those in the Nile river basin require 23 percent. These values are calculated to satisfy only minimum ecological requirements.

Climate Change and Asian Water Towers

Most of Asia's population is fed with food grown from Himalayan meltwater. 1.4 billion people, over 20% of the world's population, rely on these mountain water sources. Climate change is predicted to have severe affects on their water and food supply. Until this study, much of the research on climate and precipitation predictions under climate change scenarios has been either local yet anecdotal, or general to the continent without specificity to regional variations. This study aimed to identify the main river runoff areas fed by Himalayan water, and predict the effects of climate change on water availability in those areas, considering regional differences. The main components of river basins which will be altered by climate change are the importance of meltwater on downstream hydrology, the changing ice-covered landscapes (glaciers), and the water supply from upstream basins which dictate food security. The authors focused on the Indus, Ganges, Brahmaputra, Yangtze, and Yellow river basins and food growing areas. The predicted effects of climate change will be quite different on each of these areas, according to the results.

Each region features many different types of glacier which each respond differently to climate changes. Immerzeel *et al.* aimed to use hydrology models which would not be affected by reservoirs or downstream extraction which can calculate the discharge into whole basins, rather than from only one type of glaciers. These models found that reduced meltwater would have the most significant effect on the Brahmaputra and Indus river basins. Of the examined basins, these two rely most heavily on snow and glacier water. The other three, the Yangtzee, Ganges, and Yellow river valleys, each have less flow from meltwater for various reasons: relatively larger catchment areas, smaller glaciers, more of a reliance on water from monsoon precipitation. In the Brahmaputra and Indus river valley 40% of downstream water is meltwater, whereas in the other river valleys the contribution of glacial melt is much less significant.

Each of these regions uses upstream dams and reservoirs in order to regulate water availability for agriculture. Any changes of water flow into these holding systems will have significant effects on the downstream populations that rely on local food sources. The data found that although smaller glaciers will mean less available water in all of the 5 river regions, the decrease of meltwater will be somewhat, though not totally, mitigated by increased upstream rainfall which is predicted in climate change scenarios. In the case of the Yellow river, river flow is actually predicted to increase. The authors also mentioned though, that these cumulative results should be treated with skepticism because the current climatology and precipitation modelling techniques are unrefined and so far unproven. Regardless of these uncertainties the Brahmaputra and Indus river valleys show the most vulnerability with predicted consistent decrease of water availability.

The authors connected the predicted future water amounts with measures of food production potential such as water available for irrigation, crop yields, caloric value of crops, and the amount of energy people require from their diets. With these data they were able to predict how many fewer people would be able to be supported in each region as agricultural water supply decreases. They found that compared to current trends predicted future food production will decrease significantly (most significantly in the Brahmaputra and Indus areas because of high populations and strong reliance on meltwater for irrigation).

The authors found in this study that the Himalayan glaciers, Asia's "Water Towers", are sensitive to climate change, and that their melting will have significant effects on downstream human populations. They also found however, that these changes will vary greatly by region, and may not be as severe as previous research has suggested.

Does Crop-Livestock Integration Mean Resilience to African Farmers?

The decision of African farmers to plant only crops, raise only livestock or operate a mixed system which incorporates both, will be largely affected by a changing climate. However, the specific climate changes i.e. increased or decreased precipitation, as well as intensity and abruptness of climate patterns will determine the severity and necessity of adaptation to new methods for farmers all across the continent. *Niggol Seo (2010)* studied the association between temperature and precipitation, and the preferred methods of farmers concerning specialization or diversification of on-farm practices. Using surveys of around 9000 farms from ten countries, the research indicated that a hotter, drier climate will result in many more integrated farms. The expected profitability of an integrated farm as a method for farm resilience does, however, depend on the climate model applied. The research found that by 2060 integrated farms will be much more common and profitable in Africa.

The data for this study was taken from a 2002–2003 growing year collection produced by the GEF/World Bank project on climate change. Countries were selected so that each region of Africa would be represented and data collection took place clustered in villages in order to make survey taking more affordable. The countries were Niger, Burkina Faso, Senegal and Ghana representing West Africa, Cameroon for Central Africa, Kenya and Ethiopia for East Africa, South Africa and

Zambia for southern Africa, and Egypt for Northern Africa. These data reflected decisions already made by farmers regarding their farm management choices in response to varying environmental factors of the preceding years. The data collectors attempted to understand how African farmers react when forced to continue profitability despite lower yields as temperature and precipitation change threaten previously profitable methods. The data on these previously executed decisions by farmers was then extrapolated to explain what farmers will do under circumstances predicted by climate change models. Of those surveyed, 7% specialized in livestock while 40% specialized in crops, making about half of the respondents specialized, and half integrated. The profitability of integrated farms was higher per hectare than it was for specialized farms. Livestock only farms and mixed farms tended to be in hotter and drier regions, while milder areas with more precipitation featured many more crop only farmers. Farmers in areas which had access to heavy springtime stream flow tended to be crop farmers because of the available water at planting time and the potential to store water for the hotter summer, whereas farmers in regions which get more summer rains tended to have livestock only because local irrigation is less viable for planting. In addition to lands of high water flow, specialized farms tended to be in areas with electricity.

Distinct ecological and agricultural regions are diverse and plentiful in Africa. The farmers surveyed live in landscapes from high mountains to flat plains, and the resulting crop and livestock used can be quite different. Accordingly, the way that farmers adapt to climate change will also show a diversity of strategies. However the research did show that across the board, the switch to integrated farms will be profitable into the future. An increase in temperature of one degree C is expected to raise the number of integrated farms and lessen the number of either kind of specialized farm. An increase in precipitation of any amount correlates with an increase of the number of farms with any crops, be they mixed or specialized.

The research found that any significant and abrupt change in climate would be greatly harmful to African farmers, causing a possible 75% reduction in productivity. However, even under extreme climate changes, diverse farms are estimated to fare better than specialized ones. Given the predicted long term and consistent nature of the changing climate, farmers will likely have to continue adapting their practices to new temperatures and precipitation levels. Farms which remain livestock or crop only will continue to face mounting ecological pressure to integrate as time goes on and the climate continues to change. The paper suggests that aid and government programs attempting to help farmers in the process of climate adaptation should do so with an eye toward the regional differences in ecology and policy. They also suggest that their data on adaptation was created assuming the current practice of communal land for grazing and planting, and that aid projects which alter those land use patterns would also alter the predicted results of this research.

Livestock Biodiversity an Important Measure of Climate Change Adaptation

Research on climate change mitigation within agriculture often highlights methods of GHG reduction which simultaneously act to increase climate change adaptability. Livestock production is a sector in which possibilities for these dual-purpose systematic transformations are robust. Among the 33 types of livestock kept worldwide there are many degrees of reliance on natural resources, dependence on external inputs, use of expensive technological equipment, and types of knowledge systems used to breed livestock. The authors identify two main styles of livestock production which coexist globally: concentrated, livestock rearing facilities which focus on the yield of only one product (milk, eggs, etc.) and rural forage-based systems which require low external input, use animals for many products (in cows for example, meat, milk, fabric, fertilizer, work as well as value to the 'cultural landscape'), and maintain genetic wealth through indigenous knowledge systems. The focus of the paper was to evaluate these two types of livestock management practices in light of the requirement to adapt and possibly mitigate the effects of climate change. Specifically the authors examined the potential of genetic diversity to play a role in the ability of livestock systems to remain resilient despite the substantial and long-term consequences of climate change.

Hoffman researched the 'growing dichotomy' between commercial operations and small-scale pastoralists who live on the land. Since genetic diversity is considered to be an important measure of agricultural systems facing systematic shocks such as climate change, the genetic characteristics of these two types of production were examined. The commercial model is genetically narrow featuring a small number of globally distributed breeds which have been researched and distributed to many developed countries because of one productive trait. Regions which have built industrial livestock systems are the ones which have suffered the greatest loss of breed diversity in the past century. These systems are not able to quickly adjust to sensitivities from new temperature, precipitation, or disease conditions caused by climate change because they generally rely on only one breed which is specifically adapted to the existing set of conditions. The author discusses how livestock physiology and nutrition changes when temperatures rise above the animals' adaptive range, significantly decreasing their ability to produce milk and/or meat. In the context of climate change more research is required to elaborate on this paper's prediction that current concentrated feeding operations may face severe challenges as their animals live in different conditions. On the other hand hot arid climates in many parts of the world provide limited natural resources and only support agricultural systems like low input pastoralism. Thus, many of the world's locally kept and bred livestock breeds already live in the types of climates which could be created or exacerbated by climate change. The people who raise local, small herd, forage livestock are generally economically and ecologically marginalized.

Since livestock bred by local people and methods will be more suited to the local environment than those imported from other countries, local herds will likely support the adaptation to climate change for rural peoples much more effectively than foreign breeds in concentrated operations. According to the author it is more important that countries develop their own genetic livestock pools than simply import them for economic reasons, however, the author suggests that should climate change make certain local livestock populations unsuited for new conditions, exchange of breeds among regions which share similar environments could be necessary. Thus climate change will increase the necessity for genetic exchange of livestock among countries. Since many of the world's local breeds are uncharacteristic, that is not cataloged and registered internationally for their traits, it is difficult for outsiders to gauge the strengths and weaknesses of local breeds, making their potential for exchange with international livestock breeding programs poor. In order to integrate pastoral populations and rare local livestock breeds with global climate change adaptation measures, it is important to characterize local breeds and prioritize agricultural biodiversity as a key measure of climate change adaptation.

On Farm Crop Conservation

Climate change represents a threat to the genetic security of the crop base of many farming regions. Plants which have been bred to exist in certain climatic conditions will face new ranges of temperature, precipitation, and disease prevalence. Farmers face the long term challenge of gradually changing conditions which will consistently threaten production and livelihood if not met with effective adaptation of genetic resources. Greater agricultural biodiversity instills resilience for farmers by giving them a wider set of potentially effective crops. The necessity of plant breeding to this end has been recognized and approached in two manners: ex-situ conservation; breeding centers and storage collections operated by governmental or academic institutions, or in-situ conservation; on-farm efforts to maintain genetic diversity both to satisfy the economic needs of the producer and the ecological need for biodiversity of the community and natural environment. Specifically, farmers saving their own seed, rather than buying it from afar, allows for a locally adapted network of productive genetic resources which are especially resilient to local disturbances. *Sthapit et al.* examined the necessity of in situ conservation systems as a measure to ensure food security, particularly respondent to climate change. The authors also make recommendations as to how to best implement programs which conserve agricultural biodiversity despite the pressure of social and market forces which threaten local seed conservation practices.

The range of plant diseases and pests will change substantially as temperatures change. This poses a direct threat to agricultural areas which do not feature a diverse range of crops. Areas with only one or several strains of the same crop are particularly threatened by pathogens which are not known to farmers. Without biodiversity, diseases which effect one crop can devastate production and livelihoods by damaging large acreages. Areas which have a great agricultural diversity will be much less damaged by any one disease. A large portfolio of genetics is a crucial resource for communities which rely primarily on agriculture for their subsistence. Although many areas which are now adopting the farming practice of monocropping may not find maintenance of genetic diversity to be economically effective, it may become more attractive in changing climate conditions.

Sthapit *et al.* addressed the reasons why in-situ strategies for plant genetic conservation have not yet been able to have a significant effect despite being recognized by large agencies which seek to enhance food security. The authors' research revealed that although there is a significant scientific effort to encourage genetic conservation, there is also a lack of knowledge of how best to implement farmer-initiated conservation measures. Most projects which already exist are ex-situ breeding facilities which do not provide access of findings or success to farmers. These facilities also have difficulty incorporating local informal farmer knowledge, often a region's most significant source of agronomical information. These facilities are often isolated from the farming communities which could benefit the most from professional and well-funded efforts at biodiversity breeding.

The current institutional mindset does not favor farmer projects. It has been a challenge to identify economically sustainable incentives which encourage farmers to practice conservation breeding. It was found by the researchers that farmers who actively conserve biodiversity on site generally do so because it serves an immediate benefit to their livelihood. Considering the general increase in market forces being experienced by farmers of all scales worldwide, it is unlikely that practices which encourage agricultural biodiversity will continue unless they are economically competitive. The authors note that economic incentives from governments or information campaigns by non-governmental organizations could also potentially encourage these practices. Although successful models of this type of intervention do not yet exist, the authors point to them as an important future focus of research and funding.

Climate change is expected to increase extreme events such as floods, draughts and landslides. However, farmers will experience warming patterns most severely as a long term increase of uncertainty. By integrating a diverse range of crops, trees, livestock, and aquatic species farmers can build the capacity to produce a livelihood in a wider range of possible climates. Given the importance of encouraging local on-site biodiversity conservation, the authors give criteria for evaluating a community's current and potential resources to ensure agricultural biodiversity: the specific community processes which purposely or inadvertently produce agricultural diversity, the specific local actors who maintain genetic diversity, and the factors which encourage farmers to continue or abandon traditionally effective methods of seed saving. These features contribute to the relative strengths or weaknesses of a community's food security.

Prospects for Farmers-lead Plant Breeding in the U.S.

Climate change will increase the needs of farmers to have crops which can withstand increasingly variable growing conditions. Conventionally, American farmers have enjoyed a cooperative relationship with breeding programs operated by large universities in agricultural areas. At their outset, these programs were designed to provide farmers with seeds that would be resilient to local conditions and meet market demands for crop quality. The authors of this paper argue that this relationship has become eroded by market forces which encourage the university programs to undertake research for large commercial agriculture firms. The seed supply for the nation's farmers has become increasingly controlled by a smaller number of production and distribution companies, so the university programs are being aimed at an ever smaller set of clients. In this way the bio-diversity of seeds is quickly decreasing, as is the infrastructure which has traditionally connected between seed companies, farmers and university breeders. It is argued by the authors that a strong network of communication and collaboration between these groups will be necessary to strengthen agricultural biodiversity.

The focus of university breeding research on an increasingly small base of crops, bred for a few commercial characteristics, has greatly reduced the availability of breeding programs which focus on the needs of small farmers. Large seed companies and participating university breeders focus on a small number of profitable crops for the ideal climate and soil conditions in which they generally operate. Small growers often have much different needs, growing on smaller plots which do not have standardized conditions. Therefore, the small seed base produced for large, mechanized and chemically treated farm operations does not meet the needs of small growers who are selling directly to consumers and are more vulnerable to crop failure onset by dysfunctional seed.

The trend toward industrial agriculture is rapidly decreasing the biodiversity of crops worldwide. The need for increased agricultural biodiversity has been widely promoted by advocates for sustainable agricultural practices. However, models which successfully integrate a greater range of crops as an alternative to industrial mono-cultures have not become widespread. There are also differences of opinions on how to best design and implement breeding programs which return the benefits of agricultural biodiversity to farmers. Leland presents a case study on one method known as participatory plant breeding (PPB). PPB is a model in which farmers, as well as university breeders, are encouraged to breed locally adapted crops, which can then be distributed to farmers in similar geographic and climatic conditions by seed companies. By using a case study of a prototypical PPB program in one agricultural region of the United States, the author shows its potential utility and current limitations in place because of restrictive socio-economic conditions.

The case study, named the Seed Project is located in the Northeastern United States. It was organized as a collaboration between farmers, university breeders and their staff, other university researchers, industry based breeders, USDA personnel, and farmer's representatives. The project brought together these various actors in the hopes of discovering ways of encouraging connectivity between them. In order to understand the current state of seed production and distribution, the researchers conducted extensive interviews, reviewed documents such as grant applications and material transfer agreements, and conducted participant observation at the project's workshops, meetings, and field days. The project took over a year to begin because it relied on many personal relationships which took time to develop. When it did get off the ground, it quickly developed and distributed new vegetable varieties. The farmers were particularly interested in improved resistance of varieties to local diseases, just as predicted in the literature as a theoretical advantage of the PPB model.

By bringing together these separate groups, the project illuminated important missing trade links which were missing and showed where lack of knowledge was preventing growth of PPB. The researchers found that continued growth of PPB was not restricted merely by breeding behaviors of researchers but by larger forces of genetic homogenization created by monopolistic agricultural companies. Although PPB is believed to be a possible method of reforming these socio-economic obstacles to agricultural biodiversity, this study showed some of the current challenges facing efforts toward that goal. Primarily, securing funding remained difficult for the program organizers exactly because of the program's success. The researchers found that funding organizations which provided short term grants, such as the USDA, were unlikely to renew grants to the project once it showed three years of successful organizing. The authors pointed out that long term grants may be needed in order to more firmly establish regional PPB networks. The brevity of the project, three years, was found to be an obvious roadblock to networking, and represents a potential obstacle for similar projects in other areas.

While the project's official ending was somewhat of a letdown to many participants, the unofficial connections can remain in place as farmers and interested university breeders can collaborate with small seed companies to integrate greater diversity into local food systems.

Costa Rican Farmers Use Sustainable Agriculture to Adapt to Climate Change

Current agricultural land management strategies in tropical regions will likely not be appropriate or stable under the effects of changing temperatures and precipitation levels brought on by climate change. To satisfy economic and socio-ecological demands, landholders will need to change their practices in order to adapt to the conditions of a changing climate. In many cases, systematic-farm level changes which promote long-term farm sustainability, such as local seed banks and integrating trees into farm systems are potentially effective climate change adaptation strategies. A popular sustainable practice examined by the researchers is the integration of forests with agricultural land (agroforestry) to increase yield of fruits and nuts, provide livestock fodder, and clean the water and air. The use of trees on farms accelerates the connectivity between wild and agricultural ecosystems for both economic and ecological gains. Smith and Oelbermann (2010) evaluated the awareness of climate change of a rural Costa Rican agricultural village and analyzed which sustainable agriculture practices already in place could also serve as climate change adaptation measures.

The conversion of forest and grassland into agricultural land is one of the most significant sources of GHG emissions. In Costa Rica this occurs most significantly when native forests are converted into either livestock grazing area or plantation farming of coffee or other cash crops. While small farmers do not have as large an individual impact as larger types of agriculture, they do make decisions which have an effect on GHG output. When trees are felled or conserved, or replanted to be integrated into an agricultural system, there is both a local and regional environmental effect on erosion, soil health, wildlife habitat, and water quality. As land changes from forest into agriculture, not only is there a global externality of GHGs but there is also a degradation of soil quality and marginalization of productivity as agriculture is implemented. Unless sustainable agriculture practices aimed at alleviating these consequences are implemented, there will be a continued decrease in food productivity, a significant social vulnerability, as well as continued environmental damage. Those practices may also be tools to adapting to climate change.

Smith and Oelbermann chose the village of Durika, Costa Rica, to examine the local knowledge of farm level responses to climate change. The village is located on former plantations which badly degraded the soil by removing all trees, overplowing, and overusing agricultural chemicals. Establishing a village on that site necessitated incorporation of sustainable techniques to rejuvenate lost soil productivity, reverse erosion, and improve water quality. The residents have already been exposed to information regarding sustainable practices from scientists and NGO's who have sought to use the success of sustainable practices there as a model for the many other Costa Rican villages suffering the effects of overgrazing, abandoned plantations, and deforestation.

The authors picked a random sampling of residents from the village to questions about their agricultural practices, knowledge of climate change, and opinions of the village's adaptive capacity to climate change. The participants were asked about their observations about the climate change that has already affected their area and how they predicted it will continue, the type of adaptation strategies being implemented and their results, and their beliefs on Durika's ability to continue to adapt. According to the respondents, increased temperatures and decreased precipitation have not yet caused significant damage to productivity. However, the livestock-predator species of snake ferdelance was reported to be increasingly active in farm areas, which was a cause of concern.

Some respondents believed that based on current patterns the increased severity of change will be a threat to their farms. Also, changes in wildlife and plant dispersal patterns were expected by farmers to be a future catalyst of change for their livestock management practices. The respondents displayed a generally good understanding of climate change and are already beginning to instigate adaptation strategies. The respondent's main concern was that adaptive measures to climate change must not hinder current livelihood or food production. The researchers believe that good local knowledge of climate change is an advantage in initiating necessary changes. Also reported was that already existing social networks such a government agriculture extensions and non-governmental organizations were crucial resources in the village's efforts to be aware of coming challenges and meet them with appropriate on-farm techniques. This finding was believed by the authors to be broadly generalizable to rural farmers. Villagers were also encouraged to share their successes with one and other so approaches can be continually improved.

Conclusions

Research on the effects of climate change on agriculture are becoming increasingly common and important. The efforts of agriculturalists to adapt will have significant humanitarian and economic consequences worldwide. The challenge of climate change could have largely destabilizing effects on many agricultural regions, or could be the impetus needed for millions of poor farmers to adapt sustainable practices which will allow them to continue to produce and maintain a successful livelihood for years to come. Non-industrialized farmers across the world are not responsible for the current climate crisis, but how well they are able to react to it will be revealing of humanity's ability to respond to this unprecedented problem.

References Cited

Hoffman, I., 2010. Climate change and the characterization, breeding and conservation of animal genetic resources. Animal Genetics 41, 32–46.

Immerzeel, W., Van Beek, L., Bierkens, M., 2010. Climate Change Will Affect the Asian Water Towers. Science 328, 1382–1385

Leland, G., 2010. Socioeconomic Obstacles to Establishing a Participatory Plant Breeding Program for Organic Growers in the United States. Sustainability 2, 73–91.

Seo, S., 2010. Is an integrated farm more resilient against climate change? A microeconometric analysis of portfolio diversification in African agriculture. Food Policy 35, 32–40.

Smith, C., Oelbermann, M., 2010. Climate Change Perception and Adaptation in a Remote Costa Rican Agricultural Community. The Open Agriculture Journal 4, 72–79.

Sthapit, B., Padulosi, S., Ma, B., 2010. Role of On-farm/In situ Conservation and Underutilized Crops in the Wake of Climate Change. Indian Journal of Plant Genetic Resources 23–34.

Strzepek, K., Boehlert, B., 2010. Competition for Water for the Food System. Philosophical Transactions of the Royal Society Biological Sciences 365, 2927–2940.

14. Agricultural Greenhouse Gas Emissions: How They Can Be Sequestered And How Their Production Can Be Measured

Nitya Chhiber

Climate change is an important issue in today's world, driven primarily by greenhouse gas emissions. Agriculture, which is essential to human survival leads to the release of greenhouse gases. On the other hand, sometimes agricultural conditions are such that greenhouse gases are sequestered or taken up, for example, by soil. There are two types of agriculture: plant-based, in the form of crops and animal based, in the form of livestock. This chapter emphasizes crop-based production of greenhouse gas emissions and how they might be reduced.

In studying these emissions, it is common to consider different scenarios such as changes in fertilization levels or the type of soil conditions. Alongside scenarios, simulation modeling is commonplace.

The papers reviewed in this chapter consider a range of soil ammendments—including manure, biochar and straw—that have the potential to change the nature of soil and may reduce agriculturally-induced climate change. The addition of these was studied in the light of other agricultural practices being carried out at the same time, for example, addition of fertilizers.

Many of the materials that were added to the soil changed its physical properties and, sometimes, the way in which such items were applied was also important. For example, in the first of three scenarios for the process of tillage, tillage was not carried out at all, in the second it was carried out in a conventional manner, and, in the third it was carried out it in a reduced manner. Each of these scenarios interacted with other factors such as rainfall and application fertilizers. Some of the scenarios included the addition of crop residue.

Overall carbon footprint was also a consideration. The idea of carbon footprint is related to carbon sequestration because the lower the carbon footprint of a process, the lower the amount of carbon emissions into the atmosphere, which could be looked at as a form of sequestration. Therefore, in the process of getting a particular crop to the dinner table for consumption, a range of processes is involved, all of which need to be studied in order to calculate carbon footprint.

The greenhouse gas emissions that were studied include methane, carbon dioxide and nitrous oxide. Some gas emissions were more responsive to various treatments than others. The scenarios pertaining to greenhouse gas emissions from agriculture considered many variables, including rainfall's influence alongside N fertilization levels as well as cultural factors that influence whether particular methods to limit climate change are chosen or not.

Increased yield was accompanied by increased nitrous oxide and nitric oxide emissions were an increase in the level of yield. These emissions were also increased by higher soil temperature, which can be explained by the fact that higher soil temperatures allow a greater level of activity by nitrifiers and denitrifiers. Carbon dioxide fluxes increased due to tillage, as this process caused soil loosening, but were not consistently influenced by the addition of biochar. Biochar additions, however, caused increases in methane emissions. Furthermore, methane was sensitive to the interaction between biochar and N fertilization.

In order to set the scene, the application of a range of materials on soil will be considered first. Ideally, the simple application of material that decreased greenhouse gas emissions would be the easiest way to limit climate change. However, not all gases show the same effects across a range of added materials.

Impact of rainfall on Soil Carbon Dioxide Flux should be Considered in Agriculture

Tillage loosens the soil and therefore causes soil carbon dioxide flux. Alvaro-Fuentes *et al.* (2010) studied the impact of different degrees of tillage in terms of soil carbon dioxide flux, keeping in mind that soil conditions are additionaly affected by fertilizer application and precipitation. The authors found that soil carbon dioxide flux increased with rainfall and therefore carbon dioxide emissions depended on how wet or dry the soil was.

Alvaro-Fuentes *et al.* wanted to understand the impact of soil tillage, vis-à-vis the process of soil carbon dioxide fluxes. The climatic conditions during the three year period of this study could be described as being of the Mediterranean type. Different tillage systems were used, namely no-tillage system (NT), conservation tillage system (MT) and finally conventional tillage (CT), and the soil carbon dioxide flux was measured five times each year. Three abiotic factors that affected the soil were also measured: soil temperature, soil water content, and fertilizer application. As water content was to be considered, measurements of the soil were only carried out during fallow periods. Statistical analysis of data was carried out using analysis of variance.

It was found that tillage caused an increase in the soil carbon dioxide fluxes, as there was an increase of the air transport coefficient from soil loosening. Precipitation also influenced the soil carbon dioxide flux, which increased after rainfall. Soil carbon dioxide fluxes also increased when there was increased substrate availability, which in turn occurs when there is soil organic content accumulation, crop residue production, and fertilization. Most importantly, the level of soil carbon dioxide flux levels was determined by the fluctuation of the soil between dry and wet points. Furthermore, the combination of rainfall with either a no-tillage system or conservation tillage system led to increased carbon dioxide fluxes.

The Usage of Organic Waste can Lead to an Increase of Greenhouse Gas Emissions Including Fluxes from Soil

Heller *et al.* (2010) carried out a study of different tilling and soil fertilization practices which mainly consisted of adding different types of organic was to see how different types of organic waste impact soil. The authors found a correlation between ammonia in soil and the emissions of nitrogen oxide and carbon dioxide fluxes into the air. In addition, carbon dioxide fluxes were correlated with soil water content, whereas nitrogen oxide fluxes were correlated with air temperature.

Heller *et al.* exposed soil to a variety of different scenarios, including variations in the intensity of tillage, type of organic residue applied and whether the plot was planted in corn. In control cases of no tillage, no organic residue (NR) soils were included. Emissions of carbon dioxide and nitrogen oxide from the soil were measured and the soil organic content was monitored.

The results show that the most carbon dioxide was released after the addition of pasteurized chicken manure and after irrigation, even under the no-tillage system scenario. Nitrogen dioxide emissions also increased with the addition of pasteurized chicken manure, as well as with tillage. The occurrence of rainfall, which increased soil moisture content, led to peaks of carbon dioxide and nitrogen oxide release. Therefore, concentrations of carbon dioxide emissions from soil are related to the percentage of water content. Nitrogen oxide fluxes were higher only if there was rainfall after the application of inorganic fertilizer. Nitrous oxide emissions were reduced when crops were growing on the plots owing to the competition for ammonium ions from the crops. Furthermore, there is a strong correlation between the content of ammonia in soil and the emissions of carbon dioxide and nitrogen oxide; ammonia in soil forms due to the combination of nitrogen fertilizers and carbon from organic waste.

Usage of Biochar Leads to Higher Yields and Methane Levels but Lower Nitrogen Dioxide Levels

Rice is a staple crop in many Asian countries, including China. However, like many other crops, rice also releases greenhouse gases. In fact, rice paddies are one of the biggest anthropogenic sources of greenhouse gas production and so there is a great need to be concerned about them vis-à-vis climate change. In order to decrease the amount of greenhouse gases released from the soil, the application of biochar, which is a form of charcoal, was tried. Zhang *et al.* (2010) also changed soil conditions by the application of N fertilizer. There was interaction between biochar, N fertilization, and the inherent soil conditions, and methane emissions were sensitive to the interaction in soil between biochar and N fertilization. The authors conclude that there is still some hesitation about the usage of biochar, but found increased yield level and methane emissions with the application of biochar and decreased nitrous oxide emissions.

Zhang *et al.* generated data for this study from a plot of land that was divided into three parts and all treatments were implemented in triplicate. Some subplots received N fertilization and biochar, whilst others were controls. The concentration of nitrous oxide and methane released was measured by gas chromatography throughout one whole rice-growing season in southeast China.

The addition of biochar decreased nitrous dioxide emissions. On the other hand, methane emissions increased. Another difference between nitrous oxide and methane emissions was such that nitrous oxide emission levels decreased regardless of the presence of N fertilization; on the other hand, methane emission levels were sensitive to the interaction of biochar with N fertilization. However, in the case of carbon dioxide, the addition of biochar in soil increased carbon dioxide emissions. There is still some uncertainty with regards to carbon emission, which can be the basis of future studies. Furthermore, in soils containing biochar and no fertilizers, there were higher yields compared to soils containing biochar and N fertilization.

Biochar's Impact on Greenhouse Gas Fluxes: Different Gas Fluxes are Correlated with Different Parameters

The release of greenhouse gases from agricultural soil is important in the light of climate change. However, at the same time, the study of emissions from agriculture needs to take into account many variables, increasing the difficulty of pinpointing exactly what is causing the agricultural flux of greenhouse gases. Kurhu *et al.* (2011) wanted to study the impact of biochar on the release of greenhouse gases from soil in Southern Finland. They found that there were differences between the levels of carbon dioxide and nitrous oxide emissions between soils to which biochar had been added and soils to which it had not. Furthermore, although they found that biochar increased methane uptake, and also became aware of many limitations of studying biochar's impact on the level of greenhouse gases released into the atmosphere.

Karhu *et al.* studied the affect of biochar on agricultural soil that was undergoing a process of five-year crop rotation. Plots were of mainly of two types: those with the addition of biochar and those without the addition of biochar. Fluxes of carbon dioxide, nitrous oxide, and methane were measured, and using linear method, related to soil water holding capacity, soil temperature, air temperature, and grain yield.

Carbon dioxide emissions were positively correlated with temperature, however, the addition of biochar increased methane uptake by a great deal but had no effect on nitrous oxide and carbon dioxide fluxes.

Methane was an interesting case as it responded greatly to rainfall; when it rained and there was higher soil water content, there was a higher methane flux from soil into the atmosphere, especially when the soil was wet and there was no biochar in the soil.

In the literature, no pattern can be found between biochar and the fluxes of carbon dioxide and nitrous oxide across experiments due to the fact that the type of biochar used in each experiment varies. Other reasons that there may be no pattern is that nitrous oxide can be produced under both aerobic and anaerobic conditions, and that higher applications of biochar may be needed in soil to actually see a difference in the fluxes of these two gases.

Impact of Crop Straw and Other Conditions on the Release of Greenhouse Gases from a Wheat-Maize Rotation Site

The economy in China is very much based on agriculture and therefore this was the ideal location to carry out a study on means for reducing greenhouse gas emissions from soil. Lui *et al* (2011) wanted to study the emissions of nitrous oxide and nitric oxide from soil by observing the reaction of organic residue in the form of both wheat and maize straw that were applied to the soil along with the amount of N fertilization applied. They found that nitrous oxide and nitric oxide emissions did decreased along with yield. Furthermore, the level of N fertilization under the improved treatment was better vis-à-vis the greenhouse gas emissions and yield as opposed to the level of N fertilization under the conventional treatment.

The plots of land that were chosen in this study were based in a province in China that had cinnamon soil, and a temperate, continental climate. During this study, the land on which these plots were located was going through a cycle of cultivation from wheat to maize. Half of the plots did not receive any straw whereas the other half did. There were five different scenarios in total: two scenarios were characterized by different levels of N fertlisation, two scenarios were related to straw – the lack or the presence of straw. Finally the last scenario was characterized by no fertilization and the presence of straw. Finally, the emissions of nitric oxides and nitrous oxides were measured using chambers in an automated measuring system. The relationship between conditions in soil such as soil temperature, soil moisture and the emissions of nitrous oxides and nitric oxides was described by using non-linear regression.

The presence of organic residue increased yields of both wheat and maize, and the lack of any fertilizer decreased them. The overall water management and N fertilization application levels under the improved treatment condition were better for the soil and especially for the level of maize yields than under conventional treatment. Furthermore, the level of nitric oxide and nitrous oxide emissions decreased under improved treatment. Both nitric oxide and nitrous oxide emission levels increased in the presence of high soil temperature, which could be explained by the fact that higher soil temperatures allow a greater level of activity by nitrifiers and denitrifiers.

It is not only the addition or the application of materials that can be used in agriculture. The effect of increasing yields should also be studied. Furthermore, one should note that agricultural sequestration is a process but concepts such as that of carbon footprint do exist, which provide a parallel type of application of this same process.

Increasing Yields Decreases Greenhouse Gas Emissions

Interest in agricultural practices peaked around 1961, a time period which was eventually known as the Green Revolution. Currently, we are living during a time when a variety of methods is being sought to limit climate change, and agricultural practices also need to be considered as they also release greenhouse gases, which are the drivers for anthropogenic climate change. Burney *et al.* (2010) have considered three agricultural development scenarios. One (RW) is based on the real world situation, the second (AW1) focused on land expansion, and the third (AW2) is characterized by increased yield. The final recommendation was that if agricultural practices are carried out so that there is emphasis on the quantity of output rather than the quantity of input, there will be lower greenhouse gas emissions, thus making the third scenario the most beneficial for the climate.

Burney *et al.* (2010) wanted to understand the best combination of factors for ensuring the least impact of agricultural practices on climate. As certain parameters were difficult to measure quantitatively, they were converted to other units; for example, yield was measured using monetary values in the form of global spending on yield investment between 1961 and 2005. In this study other parameters that contributed to yield improvement, such as fuel use and transport were not considered. Graphs were drawn depicting emissions of nitrous oxide, methane, carbon dioxide that corresponded to levels of yield improvement.

Focus on outputs produced the least impact on climate. For example, increased yields that resulted from an increase in efficiency of fertilizer usage, was more effective in reducing emissions than increasing yields by agricultural land area. It was also found that the AW2 scenario minimized greenhouse emissions, not because AW2 was marked by yield improvements, but because it maintained 1961 standards of living and thus was characterized by an overall lower pressure on land by the population. Therefore land expansion, also known as extensification, was lessened in this particular scenario.

Carbon Footprint and the Production of Potatoes Requires Taking Note of Uncertainties

A carbon footprint is a concept that is being applied in a variety of contexts, including agriculture. This concept is important because it relates to climate change. The potato was chosen to be studied by Roos *et al.* (2010), because it was a staple national crop. The study showed that it was not an easy task finding out the carbon footprint of potatoes due to the high uncertainty levels involved with parameters. They concluded that the Climate Labelling for Food had the best value in terms of production of carbon dioxide but they also encourage further understanding of carbon footprint as a concept.

Roos *et al.* had the desire to study the uncertainties associated with carbon footprint of the potato in order to apply the results on the real-world implementation of carbon footprint, which was via a labeling system. There were no uncertainties in the methods used; instead there were uncertainties associated with finding out the carbon footprint of the potato as there are so many variables, especially

those categorized under Activity Data (AD) that affect it and that are in turn difficult to measure. As a result, there is a high degree of uncertainty associated with
each variable. In the study, the processes that contributed to the carbon footprint of
the potato were the nitrogen dioxide content and the carbon dioxide content in
soil, fertilizer production, the packaging, seed distribution, fuel tillage, and some
others. In order to ensure that all parameters were considered from the agricultural
aspect of growing the potato to the time the potato reaches the consumer, another
category of parameters was also considered known as Emission Factors (EF), which
consisting emissions from soil, emissions from transport and production of inputs,
and finally emissions from the transport of the final goods.

It was found that two parameters, yield and nitrogen content in soil, affected the carbon footprint. Furthermore, it was recognized that decreasing yield
will reduce carbon footprint. The authors also acknowledged the need to set up a
system that will take into account a variety of conditions that affect soil apart from
nitrogen content. The results show that the amount of carbon released from a regular two-kilogram paper bag is higher than the amount of carbon released from
packaging following the Climate Labeling Food Project guidelines. Such a discrepancy between the values of carbon highlights the drawbacks of using carbon footprint as a concept. Such a drawback needs to be considered when setting up a system identifying the carbon footprint of agricultural crops.

Mitigation Potential of Agricultural Emissions using a Variety of Options in the Tropics

The release of greenhouse gases, primarily methane is an important
issue that needs to be considered in the agricultural sector. However, other gases
are released from the agricultural sector as well, including carbon dioxide and nitrous oxide. Furthermore, in the context of climate change, changes made in agricultural practices as well as changes made in livestock-related practices, can play a role
in reducing greenhouse gas emissions. Thornton and Hererrero (2010) used a method that involved the estimation of four different types of adoption on the production of carbon dioxide and methane. Each adoption could be applied at two levels:
complete adoption and optimistic, but plausible adoption rates. Furthermore, they
used two different types of methods: carbon sequestration of degraded rangelands
and the usage of agroforestry practices. Both these methods were applied in tropical
regions, namely in tropical Central and South America and sub-Saharan Africa.
The authors found that despite the mitigation potential rates having not much impact on the global total from agricultural greenhouse gas emissions, the resulting
carbon payments from offsets in gas emissions could be a source of income for farmers who are not very well off.

Thornton and Herrero used the RUMINANT model to provide estimates of production of methane, milk, and meat. This model is structured around inputs and outputs. The inputs are the fermentable nutrients and the outputs are the products of fermentation, which include methane. The study involved analyzing four different mitigation options under two different types of adoption rates: complete adoption and optimistic but plausible adoption. The four mitigation options mainly had an impact on the production of carbon dioxide and methane gases.

The highest mitigation potential for greenhouse gas emissions was the one associated with the method of restoration of the degraded rangelands in sub-Saharan Africa and Central and South America at observed or plausible adoption rates. The next two methods, which are beneficial in terms of their mitigation potential, are the agroforestry option and improvements in the use of improved pastures and crop residue digestibility. It is interesting to note that despite having one of the highest mitigation potentials of all options, the agroforestry option, which involves the sequestration of carbon due to the replacement of concentrates by leaves of *Leucaena leucocephal* in their diet, there are cultural manifestations. In countries in the developing world, the number of livestock is a form of symbolic capital but this method is related to the reduction in livestock numbers.

Conclusions

Agricultural production of greenhouse gases does occur. However, if certain substances are applied such as biochar, the amount of greenhouse gas emissions can be limited. Furthermore, one must consider their interaction with other natural phenomena such as rainfall. Due to the broad variety of crops and broad variety of habitat conditions that were used in the experiments, it is difficult to make one single, conclusive statement vis-à-vis the best procedure to use to decrease the occurrence of global warming, but it is hoped that by reading this chapter, one has got an understanding of the greenhouse gases that are produced during agriculture and the possible materials that can be used to sequester them.

References Cited

Alvaro-Fuentes, J.,Cantero-Martinez, C., J.,Lampurlanes, Morell, F.J., 2010. Soil carbon dioxide fluxes following tillage and rainfall events in a semiarid Mediterranean agroecosystem: Effects of tillage systems and nitrogen fertilization. Agriculture, Ecosystems and Environment 139, 167–173.

Bergstrom,I.,Karhu, K.,Matila,T.,Regina,K.,2011. Biochar addition to agricultural soil increased CH4 uptake and water holding capacity – Results from a short-term pilot field study. Agriculture, Ecosystems & Environment 140, 309–313.

Burney, J.A.,Davis, S.J.,Lobell,D.B.,2010. Greenhouse gas mitigation by agricultural intensification. PNAS 107, 12052–12057.

Chen, D., Han, S., Liu, C., Meng, S., Yang, Z., Zheng, X., Zhou, Z., 2011. Effects of irrigation, fertilization and crop straw management on nitrous oxide and nitric oxide emissions from a wheat–maize rotation field in northern China.Agriculture, Ecosystems & Environment 140, 226–233. doi:10.1016/j.agee.2010.12.009

Crowley, D., Cui, L., Hussain, Q., Li, L., Pan, G., Zhang, A., Zhang, X. 2010. Effect of biochar amendment on yield and methane and nitrous oxide emissions from a rice paddy from Tai Lake plain, China; Agriculture, Ecosystems and Environment 139, 469–475.

Heller, H. (2010). Effects of Manure and Cultivation on Carbon Dioxide and Nitrous Oxide Emissions from a Corn Field under Mediterranean Conditions. Journal of Environmental Quality 39, 437–448.

Herrero, M. and Thornton, P.K. 2010. Potential for reduced methane and carbon dioxide emissions from livestock and pasture management in the tropics. Proceedings of the National Academy of Sciences 16, 19667 – 19672, doi: 10.1073/pnas.0912890107

Roos, E., Sundberg, C., Hansson, P., 2010. Uncertainties in the carbon footprint of food products: a case study on table potatoes. The International Journal of Life Cycle Assessment 15, 478–488.

Section III—Ecological Impacts of Climate Change

258

15. Impacts of Rising Sea Levels

Michelle Schulte

Sea-level rise due to human-induced climate change has caused concern for coastal areas since the issue emerged more than twenty years ago. The large and growing concentration of people and assets in coastal areas mean that the potential impacts are high. It is estimated that at least 600 million people live within 10 m of sea level today, and these populations are growing more rapidly than global trends (Nicholls *et al.,* 2011). Sea-level rise causes a range of impacts for coastal areas including submergence/increased flooding, increased erosion, ecosystems changes, and increased salinization (Cazenave *et al.,* 2010). Hence, the magnitude of global sea-level rise during the twenty-first century is of great importance.

Since the Intergovernmental Panel on Climate Change (IPCC) Fourth Assessment Report, the possible magnitude of sea-level rise has attracted renewed attention, and a number of authors have suggested that this report underestimates the extent of potential sea-level rise during this upcoming century (Nicholls *et al.,* 2011). Renewed concerns about the stability of the Greenland and west Antarctic ice sheets reinforce these messages (Nicholls *et al.,* 2011). The risk of a rise of over 1 m in sea level cannot be ruled out. A substantial sea-level rise has important and direct consequences for coastal society, and more widespread indirect effects in terms of potential disruption and displacement of people, and economic activities and flows. The purpose of this chapter is to present the current state of research on the global effect of sea-level rise. In order to provide a complete picture of this growing field of study, the following sections summarize eight studies published in science journals from 2010–2011. These studies examine the economic, ecological, and physical impacts of various scenarios of sea-level rise at both a global and an ecosystem scale.

Michelle Schulte

Positional and Morphological Adjustment of Coral Reef Islands Due to Sea Level Rise

Low-lying coral reef islands are considered physically vulnerable to erosion in response to sea- level rise. Webb and Kench (2010) analyzed the physical change in 27 atoll islands located in the central Pacific Ocean over the past 20 to 60 yr, a period over which instrumental records indicate an increase in sea level of the order of 2.0 mm yr^{-1}. They found that 86% of islands remained stable or increased in area over the timeframe of analysis. Only 14% of study islands exhibited a net reduction in island area. Despite small net changes in area, islands exhibited larger gross changes in island surface configuration and location on the reef platform. Over 65% of islands examined have migrated toward the lagoon. These results contradict widespread perceptions that all reef islands are eroding in response to recent sea level rise. The data illustrate that reef islands are geomorphically resilient landforms that thus far have predominantly remained stable or grown in area over the last 20–60 years. Given this positive trend, reef islands may not disappear from atoll rims and other coral reefs in the near future. However, islands will undergo continued geomorphic change. The pace of geomorphic change may increase with future accelerated sea level rise. The style and magnitude of geomorphic change will likely vary between islands. Therefore, island nations must better understand the pace and diversity of island morphological changes and reconsider the implications for adaptation.

This study examines the morphological change of 27 atoll islands located in the central Pacific. The islands are located in three Pacific countries, in four atolls, and span 15° of latitude from Mokil atoll in the north (6°41.04′ N) to Funafuti in the South (8°30.59′S). The atolls examined include Funafuti, Tarawa, Pingelap, and Mokil. The atolls vary significantly in terms of size, structure and number of islands distributed on the atoll rim. The atolls also vary in potential exposure to tropical cyclones. All 27 islands in the study are located on atoll reef rims of Holocene age. A total of 27 islands were examined using comparative analysis of historical aerial photography and remotely sensed images. The timeframe of analysis varied from 19 to 61 years depending on aerial photograph coverage and availability. Using ERDAS Imagine 8.4 software and Quickbird satellite imagery, the images were all rectified and ground control points for each island were established. The analysis involved the overlay of the historical time series for each island. Webb and Kench analyzed the islands for areas of accretion or erosion as well as the configuration and position of the island on reef platforms. Changes in island area were calculated and compared to establish change through time.

Webb and Kench show that all islands have undergone physical change over the respective timeframes of analysis and over the period in which the instrumental records indicate an increase in sea level. The data indicate that islands have undergone contrasting morphological adjustments over the period of analysis. Furthermore, the magnitude and styles of island change show considerable variation both within and between atolls in the study. Only 43% of islands have increased in area by more than 3% while 15% of islands underwent net reduction. The net changes in island area mask larger gross changes in surface configuration and location on the reef platform. Modes of island change include: ocean shoreline displacement toward the lagoon, lagoon shoreline progradation, and, extension of the ends of elongate islands. Over 50% of the examined islands experienced ocean shoreline adjustment via erosion. Additionally, accretion of lagoon shorelines was detected in 70% of the islands. Collectively these adjustments represent net lagoonward migration of islands in 65% of cases. The results show that a significant number of islands exhibit ocean shoreline erosion which may reflect shore readjustment to increased sea levels over the study period and potentially increased wave energy incident at shorelines.

Webb and Kench illustrate that reef islands are morphologically dynamic features that can change their position on reef platforms at a range of timescales. The mechanisms that drive island change can include a combination of sea-level rise, decadal-scale variations in wind and wave climate and anthropogenic impacts. This study contradicts existing paradigms of island response and has significant implications for the consideration of island stability under ongoing sea-level rise in the central Pacific. First, islands are geomorphologically persistent features on atoll reef platforms and can increase in island area despite sea-level change. Second, islands are dynamic landforms that undergo a range of physical adjustments in responses to changing boundary conditions, of which sea level is just one factor. Third, erosion of island shorelines must be reconsidered in the context of physical adjustments of the entire island shoreline as an island may experience both erosion and accretion at opposite points. The authors conclude that the style and magnitude of geomorphic change will likely vary between islands. Therefore, island nations must place a high priority on resolving the precise styles and rates of change that will occur over the next century and reconsider the implications for adaptation.

Economic and Ecological Effects of Sea Level Rise on Coastal Wetlands: A Case Study from Galveston Island, Texas

Coastal salt marsh wetland plants are expected to migrate upslope with the rise in sea level, but human development is expected to limit the potential migration. Feagin *et al.* (2010) explored the ecological and economic effects of projected Intergovernmental Panel on Climate Change (IPCC) 2007 report sea level changes at the plant community scale using the highest horizontal and vertical resolution data available. Their findings demonstrate that salt marshes do not always lose land with increasing rates of sea level rise. The lower bound of the IPCC 2007 potential rise actually increased the total marsh area, resulting in a net gain in ecosystem service values on public property. The upper rise scenario resulted in both public and private economic losses for this same area. Overall, Feagin *et al.* highlight the trade-offs between public and privately held value under the various IPCC 2007 climate change scenarios. As wetlands migrate inland into urbanized regions, their survival is likely to be dependent on the rate of return on property and housing investments.

The authors chose Galveston Island, Texas, USA as the study site for projected sea level rise as the sea level has been well documented in the past. The coastal salt marshes at the study site exhibited the zonation patterns common to other *Spartina alterniflora*-dominated marshes in the U.S.. Five plant community zones have been previously defined as: open water, low marsh, salt flat, high marsh, and upland. The authors then created a map of the plant community zone based on elevation using the highest horizontal (1 m) and vertical (0.01 m) resolution Light Detection And Ranging (LIDAR) data available. Because the resolution of this model is quite fine, spatially and species-wise, Feagin *et al.* illustrate the effect of sea level rise within a discrete 6 x 6 km extent. Three IPCC scenarios were implemented in a time step fashion up to the year 2095 using a low rise (0.18 m increase in sea level), a mid rise (0.39 m), and a high maximum rise (0.59 m).

After running the model, the expected plant habitat loss/gain was calculated for all of the scenarios, both including and excluding potential barriers to plant migration. The authors' goal was to best represent the different plant community zones in this salt marsh relative to one another, in terms of market and non-market based values. The ecosystem services being provided by each plant community at the study site were identified. Monetary values were associated with recreation, hunting and bird watching tourism values, carbon sequestration, storm protection, fisheries support, and market-based property appraisal values. To estimate gains and losses, the authors calculated ecosystem service values considering the different areas covered by each ecosystem, given the modeled climate change.

The zonal migration of the plant community zones primarily depends on the relative sea level rise rate, the accretion rate as specific to zone and location, and the availability of land at a suitable base elevation. Also, the choice of whether to remove human-erected barriers greatly affects the availability of the land on which this migration could occur. There is no significant change, except at the high-marsh-to-upland interface, in the plant community zones for the low-rise scenario between 2005 and 2095. The rate of sea level rise equaled the rate of accretion. The anthropogenic barriers limited plant migration in the upland areas while protecting the developed land. In the mid-rise scenario, there was a net loss of *Spartina alterniflora*-dominated low marsh. There was, however, a net gain of salt flats and high marsh as these two plant communities found more locations at suitable elevations as they migrated upslope. Under the IPCC high scenario, the low marsh and salt flat zones surprisingly fared better than in the mid rise scenario because of the topographic relief. The slope appeared to be the primary factor in determining the plant community distribution in the study area.

In the different SLR scenarios, it was predicted that the economic losses will generally outweigh the gains. The models indicated that there will only be economic gains in *Spartina alterniflora*-dominated low marshes during a low rise event. The uplands, with large property appraisal values, are likely to show large economic losses in all the projected scenarios. In addition, if property investments accumulate at a 3% rate, the net economic value will be greater when the barriers to plant migration are removed. But if this value increases to a rate of 6%, then the optimal solution is to leave the barriers in place. This divergence highlights the trade-offs between public and private value because low marshes and open water are on public property; they are navigable waters and sit below the mean tide line.

This study shows that a salt marsh does not always lose land with increasing rates of sea level rise. The response of each individual plant community zone is more nuanced. Direct human activities and intervention in the migration process are estimated to account for the large majority of the losses that are predicted to occur this century. Rising sea levels and inflating property values will likely interact to reduce the incentive to save wetlands. The results show that the financial incentive to secure private property with barriers will increase by several orders of magnitude, given the IPCC high SLR scenario over the low-rise scenario. In conclusion, as wetlands migrate landward, their survival is also dependent on the rate of return on property and housing investments. Local conditions and human proclivities will radically differentiate the benefit and costs of sea level rise around the world.

First Global Assessment of Terrestrial Biodiversity Consequences of a 1–6 m Sea-Level Rise

Considerable attention has focused on the effects of global climate change on biodiversity, but few analyses and no broad assessments have evaluated effects of sea-level rise on biodiversity. Menon *et al.* calculated the total area lost for all terrestrial ecoregions using new maps of marine intrusion under scenarios of 1 and 6 m sea-level rise. Areal losses for particular ecoregions ranged from nil to complete. Marine intrusion is a global phenomenon, mostly affecting Southeast Asia and nearby islands, eastern North America, northeastern South America, and western Alaska. Assuming that fauna respond to reduced ecoregions in a predictable manner, the authors estimated likely numbers of extinctions caused by sea-level rise. They found that northeastern South America is most susceptible to marine-intrusion-caused extinctions, although anticipated extinctions in smaller numbers will be scattered worldwide. This assessment is the first global analysis of sea-level rise impacts on terrestrial biodiversity, complementing recent estimates of losses owing to changing climatic conditions.

Past studies indicated that the rate of future melting of polar ice sheets and related sea-level rise could be faster than widely thought, resulting in a sea-level rise of 4–6 m by 2100. Menon *et al.* used geographic information systems (GIS) to delineate potential inundation areas resulting from projected sea-level rise of 1 and 6 m. In this analysis, cells below a projected sea-level rise that connect to the ocean and are not presently inland water are designated as inundation cells. The authors used the Terrestrial Ecoregions GIS Database and the Terrestrial Ecoregions Base Global Dataset as a source of geospatial data showing the global extent of ecoregions, as well as providing data on numbers of endemic species in each ecoregion. Menon *et al.* used values for strict endemic species and near-endemic species across all 827 terrestrial ecoregions in this analysis. They then converted the vector-format terrestrial ecoregions coverage into a grid, so as to estimate the area lost from marine intrusion by overlaying it with the 1 and 6 m inundation scenarios grids and performing raster map algebra.

A decrease in the area of an ecoregion can be used to estimate biodiversity losses under certain sets of assumptions. Past studies have employed the relationship between the numbers of species present and area under consideration (species–area relationship, or SAR) to calculate future extinctions. The SAR is a steady-state relationship between number of species (S) and area (A) of the form $S = cA^z$, where c and z are constants estimated empirically. If the present number of species S_{now} is existing in an area A_{now}, which is reduced to A_{future}, and if c and z remain constant, then the number of species will eventually decrease to a new steady state $S_{future} = S_{now} (A_{future}/A_{now})^z$. The authors estimated z in two different ways: as the overall SAR across all ecoregions globally, and SARs for 3 latitudinal bands (polar, temperate, tropical). The authors calculated S_{future} for each ecosystem under the general z and the latitude-specific z, and estimated confidence intervals for each S_{future}.

Globally, 0.7% of global land was inundated and therefore lost under 1 m of sea-level rise, and 1.5% of global land area under 6 m of sea-level rise. Proportional losses in ecoregions ranged from 0 to 100%. The most affected ecoregions were Southeast Asia and associated islands, northeastern South America, eastern North America, and western Alaska. Even under a 1 m sea-level rise scenario, 21 ecoregions are expected to lose >50% of their land area, which include 8 mangrove-dominated ecoregions, lowland forest and scrub on 8 islands, and 5 low-lying continental areas. Thus, sea-level rise manifested as marine intrusions is expected to greatly affect terrestrial ecoregions.

For the global SAR fitting, z was estimated at 0.124 ± 0.015 s.e., although the overall fit was not particularly tight. Out of a total of 18,628 endemic or near-endemic species in single ecoregions, this single SAR yielded a calculated loss of 117 $\pm$ 27 species for the 1 m sea-level rise scenario, and 221 ± 51 species for the 6 m scenario. Splitting SAR regressions into polar, temperate, and tropical subsets, important regional differences were observed. The slope of the SAR (z) was highest in tropical regions, and lowest in polar regions. Also, these SAR differences translated into different rates of estimated species loss under the 1 and 6 m scenarios: 0 of 35 polar species under both scenarios; 10 and 30 out of 3,117 species in temperate regions; and 170 and 307 out of 15,476 species in tropical regions. Overall, with region-specific z estimates, global species losses sum to 181 ± 23 species under the 1 m scenario and 337 ± 44 species under the 6 m scenario, out of 18,628 current species.

Past studies have criticized on a number of grounds the use of the linear relationship of species and area to estimate future extinctions. Menon *et al.*, however, controlled for the possible errors given the data limitations in resolution of area and in the taxon, range, and fragmentation of species. Certainly, both the marine-intrusion and the biodiversity distribution summaries could be improved significantly. For the marine-intrusion scenario, improvements are needed in the horizontal (from 1 km to 10 m resolution) and vertical (<1 m) resolutions. Also, moving from crude ecoregion-based summaries to actual species-specific distributional information would improve the estimates of the biodiversity distribution. Finally, because some species, such as keystone species, may play more critical roles in maintaining communities than others, categorizing the individual species as to their relative 'importance' in community structuring will clarify the magnitude of secondary effects.

Overall, the authors present a valid preliminary assessment of likely biodiversity consequences of sea-level rise and marine intrusion caused by climate change. The most realistic scenario of the two that were explored is a rise of 1 m by 2100, although the 6 m scenario is still very possible given the effects of glacial calving and ice-sheet loss. This analysis does not account for second-order effects on biodiversity caused by humans affected by rising sea levels, such as migrations and land use shifts, which may cause yet more negative effects on natural systems.

Sea Level Rise Expected to Flood Mangrove Forests in Bangladesh, Killing Native Tiger Populations by 2100

The Sundarbans mangrove ecosystem is recognized as a global priority for biodiversity conservation, housing the only tiger (*Panthera tigris*) population in the world adapted for life in mangrove forests. The mean elevation of most of the Sundarbans is less than one meter above sea level. Consequently, sea level rise (SLR) poses the single greatest climate change threat to the viability of the Sundarbans forests. Using scale-appropriate elevation data, Loucks *et al.* (2010) illustrate that the Sundarbans, and its biodiversity, is vulnerable to small increases in sea level. Both tiger habitat and tiger populations will likely reach a critical threshold at SLR between 24 and 28 cm. At a 28 cm rise in sea level, the Sundarbans tiger population is unlikely to remain viable. The authors assert that a 28 cm sea level rise is likely to occur around 2070. If actions to both limit green house gas emissions and to increase resilience of the Sundarbans are not initiated soon, these tigers will become early victims of climate change-induced habitat loss.

Given that only a small portion of the land surface of the Sundarbans is over 1 m above sea level (asl), Loucks *et al.* estimated sea level rise in mm asl. They used 80,584 elevation points to create a continuous digital elevation model (DEM) with sub-meter accuracy. The DEM was based on 1991 elevation data collected by FINNMAP. The authors used 4 mm year $^{-1}$ as a conservative estimate of annual SLR upon which to predict potential impacts to tiger habitat. So as to account for the difference in sea level from 1991 to 2000, the authors factored in a 3.6 cm increase in sea level, equivalent to a SLR of 4 mm yr^{-1} for nine years. Next, for each of the time steps, the authors identified the land area that would fall below the rising elevation of the sea. This land area would be permanently underwater, and thus removed from the potential habitat layer. This analysis was repeated for each time step. Increasing sea level can cause both direct habitat loss as well as increased fragmentation resulting from new or expanded streams and channels. To estimate tiger populations at each time step, the authors utilized a maximum dispersal distance of 5 km across water between potential tiger habitat patches. Second, they defined the minimum potential tiger habitat patch as being 10 km². To assess the potential range of tiger population for each time step, the authors factored in the relative tiger abundance of each patch of land, the average female tiger's home range size, as well as the female:male ratio.

Both tiger habitat and tiger populations will likely reach a critical threshold at SLR at 24– 28 cm. At a 28 cm rise in sea level, the Sundarbans tiger population is unlikely to remain viable as the remaining habitat will have decreased to 3.8%, and the number of breeding individuals will be less than 20. Using a conservative rate of a 4 cm per decade increase, which is consistent with the 4th IPCC report on sea level rise and local tidal gauge records, the authors predict the Sundarbans will realize a 28 cm increase in sea level between 2060 and 2100. Uncertainty persists within the study because the authors only assessed tiger abundance in relation to habitat size. The biodiversity of the ecosystem relies on intricate and complex abiotic and biotic interactions. There is uncertainty regarding prey abundance and possible prey responses to SLR that could then alter tiger abundance.

Furthermore, the study does not incorporate potential effects of geological processes, drainage, withdrawal of water, and sedimentation; factors which may reduce or increase the level of permanent inundation. In addition, there is likely a time lag from inundation to non-use of the area by tigers or their prey that was not accounted for.

Although there is considerable uncertainty regarding the degree of future habitat loss due to SLR, it is still imperative to act now to mitigate the potential habitat loss. Globally, action should include limits on carbon emissions to slow climate change. Locally, management activities that conserve habitat or limit threats include building dykes, developing and planting mangroves that can adapt to the rising seas and changing salinity, and limiting poaching or killing of tigers and their prey.

Sea-Level Rise Expected to Cause Significant Habitat Loss on the Barrier Islands in New York, Thereby Reducing Breeding Habitat of Piping Plover

Habitat loss, a leading threat to wildlife, is expected to escalate under global climate change resulting in the extinction of many species. Climate change is likely to raise sea levels by 0.18 m to 2 m over the next century, threatening many low-lying coastal areas such as the mid-Atlantic shoreline. Seavey *et al.* (2010) assessed the threat of sea-level rise (SLR) on the federally threatened piping plover (*Charadrius melodus*) on the barrier islands of Suffolk County, New York. The authors determined the extent of habitat change over the next 100 years under several SLR predictions. The results illustrate that if plover habitat cannot migrate, SLR is likely to reduce breeding areas. However, if habitat is able to migrate upslope and inland, breeding areas could actually increase. Unfortunately, this potential habitat gain is stymied by human development, which was found to reduce migrating habitat by 5–12%. The migration of potential habitat area was inhibited mostly by the spatial configuration of developed areas rather than the intensity of development. If the relative amount of plover habitat increases, human-plover conflict will likely arise as well. Finally, a large hurricane could flood up to 95% of plover habitat, thereby highlighting the risk from the synergism between SLR and coastal storms. To assure the future of plover habitat on these barrier islands, the authors assert that management needs to promote natural overwash and habitat migration, while minimizing development adjacent to future breeding habitat.

To study the potential change in piping plover breeding habitat with rising sea levels, the authors analyzed the barrier island system of Suffolk County, which spans 93 km of barrier island and peninsula shoreline along the southern coast of Long Island, New York. Multiple inlets break this barrier system into four segments. The islands are approximately 6 km by 0.1 km for the smallest and 50 km by 2.6 km for the largest. These dimensions are not stable, as island profiles are shifting and dynamic. The elevation of these islands is almost entirely below 3.5 m. Human development within the system is highly variable. Seavey *et al.* modeled two possible responses of plover habitat to SLR: static and dynamic. In the static habitat response, it was assumed that SLR would occur at a rate that outpaces the migration of habitat and the islands themselves. In this model, the spatial distribution of habitat was fixed and the rising sea level simply submerged land and existing habitat, resulting in a new spatial configuration of remaining habitat. A static habitat response is expected if the rate of SLR outpaces the ability of flora and fauna to migrate upslope and/or if development blocks movement of the landform. The second response model allowed for a dynamic habitat response wherein habitat could shift upslope and inland, redistributing itself based on the underlying landform. This habitat response was based on a plovar breeding habitat map created previously.

Using a global positioning system, the authors delineated the inland habitat boundary based on the presence of dense vegetation, steeply eroded banks, or human-made structures along the entire barrier island coastline of Suffolk County. The ocean-side habitat boundary was delineated as the high water line. The final format of this habitat map was an ESRI raster grid with 5 m horizontal resolution. This grid served as the base map for the analysis of the static habitat response and the binary response variable in a logistic generalized linear model (GLM) used to predict plover breeding habitat under the dynamic habitat response. Four well-supported SLR scenarios were chosen to model habitat changes. Each scenario represented a 30-year average SLR prediction, centered on 2080. Three of the four SLR scenarios are based on Intergovernmental Panel on Climate Change (IPCC) and New York City Panel on Climate Change estimates. The scenarios are B1 (0.38 m rise). A1B (0.47 m rise), and A2 (0.5 m rise). The fourth SLR scenario was based on recently verified rates of ice sheet loss and it stipulated a SLR of 1.5 m, higher than IPCC predictions. The four SLR scenarios, plus no SLR, were applied to both the static and dynamic habitat response models.

In addition, development data including buildings, roads, jetties and groins were digitized to create a development intensity surface. The authors wanted to compare the influence of development on the dynamic habitat response models by systematically examining each SLR scenario under various levels of development intensity. Next, Seavey *et al.* examined the risk of storm-induced plover habitat flooding under the 1.5 m SLR. Three types of storms were used: 5-year storm surge average (1.65 m), category-two hurricanes (0–2.4 m), and category- three hurricanes (0–3.7 m). The amount of plover habitat flooded by each storm type was calculated by clipping the resulting 1.5 m dynamic SLR with development habitat map by each storm flood extent.

The response of the barrier island plover habitat to SLR (i.e., static versus dynamic response) can make a large difference in predictions of future habitat. Habitat migration allowed for an increase in plover habitat with SLR in Suffolk County, New York. This increase resulted from the specific topography of these particular islands, which has more land area at higher elevations and inland compared to the current position of plover habitat. However, the ability of plover habitat to migrate across this particular landscape is uncertain and complex. Without considering the influence of development, the pattern of habitat change under increasing SLR differed greatly between the static and dynamic habitat response models. Potential piping plover breeding habitat area was reduced by as much as 41% under the static response model. In contrast, in the dynamic model habitat area grew by as much as 15%. This increase in relative amount of habitat reflected the steady loss of the barrier island system in this model. Under the dynamic response, the study area was also lost due to flooding; however, the habitat redistributed itself across the landscape in greater proportion. As the SLR estimate increased, the amount of plover habitat went from 32% to 65% of the total barrier island system. Furthermore, the authors assert that the future of plover habitat with rising sea levels will be dictated, in large part, by how coastal development is zoned and managed.

Regardless of the migration response, SLR in combination with the predicted increase in storminess due to climate change is likely to increase nest failure. Storm surge flooding impacted a large proportion of the projected habitat under the 1.5 m SLR with development scenario. The 5-year storm and category-two hurricane surge flooded about 75% of potential nesting habitat; whereas a category-three hurricane surge flooded over 95% of the area. Among the piping plover nests found in the study area during the 2003–2005 breeding seasons, 74% of nests would have been flooded by a 5-year storm, 73% by a category-two hurricane, and 97% by a category-three hurricane. The large impact from all storm types stemmed from the relatively low elevation of the barrier island system in Suffolk County. While it is uncertain what the loss of one breeding season would mean to the overall plover population, the increased frequency of large storms predicted to accompany global climate change may make nest flooding more frequent and likely to increase population risk.

Their results raise concern over the potential for SLR to increase human-plover conflict. Both habitat response models predict an increase in the proportion of the island areas in potential plover habitat over the next 100 years. If the relative amount of plover habitat increases, conflict is likely to arise especially as the human population in the region grows. Moreover, interspecies competition for nesting space and other resources may increase as plovers, American oystercatchers (*Haema-*

topus palliatus), least terns (*Sternula antillarum*), common terns (*Sterna hirundo*), and other coastal species are crowded together.

Habitat loss resulting from SLR, especially along low-lying, developed coastlines, is likely to increase piping plover extinction risk. To avoid the potential loss of plover habitat, management actions must be based on the assumption that coasts are dynamic, highly variable, and will shift with rising sea levels. Today's plover nesting habitat is unlikely to be suitable, or even exist, in the near future. Management will need to be adaptive and focus on actions that restrict and even reduce development so that ecological processes, such as overwash and habitat migration, are preserved.

The Intertidal Communities on Dissipative Beaches at Risk for Sea Level Rise—The Relationship of Beach Morphodynamics and Species Range.

Sea-level rise is likely to cause significant physical changes to beaches in the higher latitudes, resulting in steeper beaches with larger particle sizes. These physical changes have implications for beach invertebrate communities, which are determined largely by sediment particle size, and hence for ecosystem function. Previous studies have explored the relationships between invertebrate communities and environmental variables such as particle size, beach slope, and exposure to wave action. Yamanaka *et al.* (2010) quantified the abundance of meiofauna and macrofauna across a range of beaches in the UK. The authors confirmed the predominant role of beach physical factors in determining infaunal species composition on the less wave-dominated beaches typically found over much of the European coastline. The more dissipative beaches, or the flat beaches with finer particles and gentler slopes, had a higher density of organisms, but a smaller range of species richness. If predictions that accelerated sea-level rise will move beaches towards a more reflective morphodynamic state are correct, this could lead to potential adverse consequences for ecosystem functioning through the declining abundance of benthic organisms between 0.3 and 1mm in size.

The authors utilized various indices of beach morphodynamic state to quantify the physical characteristics of beaches in three different estuarine locations on the east coast of the UK that experience different tidal ranges, slopes, and range of particle size. The three contrasting field sites in the UK are the Humber estuary, the Ythan estuary, and the Firth of Forth. Five or six sampling sites were selected within each locality, restricted to a short area of the outer estuary or coastal site in order to minimize any potentially confounding effects of salinity. At each station, a cylindrical core was pushed into the sediment to the depth of 10 cm on a randomly chosen surface to sample macrofauna, meiofauna, and sediment. Macrofauna were separated from sediment using a 500 μm mesh, preserved in 70% ethanol, identified to species level, and counted using a microscope. Meiofauna were separated from sediment using a 64 μm mesh, preserved in ethanol, and stained with Rose Bengal, identified to the lowest possible taxon, and counted. Particle size was determined by dry sieving through a tower of mesh sieves. The slope at each sampling station was calculated by measuring the height and distance of the sample site. The exposure at each beach site was calculated using the index derived from wind velocity, direction, duration, and the effective fetch.

Yamanaka *et al.* created new indices to determine the morphodynamic state of the beach and the wave energy. A combination of non-metric Multi Dimensional Scaling (NMDS), and an eigenvector-based approach, DCA, was used, in conjunction with cluster analysis to explore the main trends and patterns in the data in terms of physical and biological variables of the sites. In addition, stepwise multiple linear regression was used to explore the relationships of abundance and number of species with morphodynamic state. One-way analyses of variance (ANOVA) were used to test the importance of each independent variable, and also to test the difference of physical variables between the three areas.

The authors explored the relationships between beach fauna and morphodynamic variables, to test whether more dissipative beaches support a high abundance of macrofauna and meiofauna as well as higher macrofaunal species richness. The authors ask how these relationships may inform our understanding of the impacts of sea-level rise on benthic community structure and function. They compared the differences in the physical characteristics of each of the beaches. Median particle size was not significantly different between estuaries, but beach slope and wave exposure differed significantly. The Humber had a much higher range of exposures and a shallower beach slope than the Ythan and the Forth.

The fauna within these three sites differed in their composition and abundance. There was more overlap in species composition between the Humber and the Ythan, despite an order of magnitude difference in abundance. For each scenario, the more dissipative beaches contained higher abundances of all fauna. So that dissipative beaches with finer particles and shallow slopes generally support a higher abundance of macrofauna.

However, for species richness, Yamanaka *et al.* found that less dissipative beaches generally support higher macrofaunal species richness. Both the Ythan and the Humber had lower species richness compared to the Forth, but differed markedly in the numbers of individuals recorded. The Forth had an intermediate number of macrofauna individuals but the most taxa represented. In addition, the authors found that the length of exposure to the sun and the beach slope affect the abundance of small, benthic organisms. There were no clear relationships between diversity indices and beach physical variables.

Yamanaka *et al.* confirmed the predominant role of beach physical factors in determining infaunal species composition on the less wave-dominated beaches typically found over much of the European coastline. All of the species recorded can be described as deposit feeders, filter feeders, or predators. Past studies illustrate that large polychaetes are disproportionately important for ecosystem processes such as nutrient cycling. Thus, functional diversity and compositional effects rather than species richness, may play an important role in driving ecosystem processes. A greater diversity of large species including polychaete species was found at more sheltered sites on the Ythan and the Forth. If sea-level rise pushes beaches towards steeper slopes and coarser particles, as indicated in the study by Yamanaka *et al.*, then the abundance of these larger species is likely to decline, with consequent reduction in ecosystem functioning.

In summary, the authors illustrate the validity of the trend that more dissipative beaches have a higher abundance of macrofauna and meiofauna compared to reflective beaches when analyzing less wave-dominated beaches. In addition, the authors suggest that sea-level rise could have a significant impact on ecosystem functioning in northern temperate beaches, through the effects of changing particle size and wave exposure on benthic species richness and abundance, especially the larger-bodied polychaetes.

The Optimum Economic Response to Substantial Sea-Level Rise is Widespread Protection of Developed Coastal Areas

Rapid sea-level rise (> 1 m/century) raises concern as it is believed that this would lead to large losses and a widespread forced coastal retreat. Anthoff *et al.* (2010) aimed to estimate economic damages caused by substantial sea-level rise and clarify the extent societies can protect themselves from rising sea levels. While the costs of sea-level rise increase with greater rise due to growing damage and protection costs, the integrated assessment model (*FUND*) suggests that an optimum response in a benefit-cost sense remains widespread protection of developed coastal areas. The benefits of protection increase significantly with time due to the economic growth assumed in the SRES socio-economic scenarios. In terms of the four components of costs considered in FUND, protection dominates, with substantial costs from wetland loss. The regional distribution of costs shows that a few regions experience most of the costs, especially East and South Asia, North America, and Europe. The analysis and computer model contain some limitations so that protection may not be as widespread as suggested in the FUND results. However, the

FUND analysis shows that protection is more likely and rational than is widely assumed, even with a large rise in sea level.

The authors utilize the Coastal Module of *FUND* 2.8n to calculate damages caused by various scenarios of sea-level rise over the next century. The model is driven by five distinct socio-economic scenarios (four well-known SRES scenarios and a control scenario) of population and GDP (gross domestic product) growth on a per country scale. Sea-level rise is treated as a linear interpolation with three distinct scenarios of 0.5 m, 1.0 m, and 2.0 m above 2005 sea levels in 2100. Rising sea levels are assumed to have four damage cost components: the value of dryland cost, the value of wetland cost, the cost of protection (with dykes) against rising sea levels and the costs of displaced people that are forced to leave their original place of settlement due to dryland loss. *FUND* determines the peak amount of protection based on the socio-economic situation, the expected damage of sea-level rise if no protection existed, and the necessary protection costs.

The number of people displaced is a linear function of dryland loss and the average population density in a country. The area of dryland loss is assumed to be a linear function of sea-level rise and protection level up to 2 m of sea-level rise. Wetland value, on the other hand, is assumed to be proportional to per capita income with a correction for wetland scarcity and a cap. Conceptually, the value of wetlands at first rises very rapidly with income, but it increases much more slowly if incomes and wetland values are very high. The average annual protection costs are assumed to be a bilinear function of the rate of sea-level rise as well as the proportion of the coast that is protected. The level of protection is based on a cost-benefit analysis that compares the costs of protection (the actual construction of the protection and the value of the wetland lost due to the protection) with the benefits, i.e. the avoided dryland loss. The authors also continue on to create functions to control for the value of the wetlands lost due to protection and the value of the dryland lost if no protection takes place. Lastly, Anthoff *et al.* used a standard Ramsey discount rate to compute the net present value total damage costs for the period of 2005–2100.

First, the authors analyzed the global damage costs by socio-economic and sea-level rise scenario. Anthoff *et al.* found that while the choice of socio-economic scenario has an influence on the global damage costs from sea-level rise, the damage costs vary more depending on the sea-level rise scenario. The damage costs for a 1 m rise are between 4.8 and 5.2 times as high as the damage costs for the 0.5 m sea-level rise, depending on the scenario. The increase in costs from 1 m to 2 m is only 2.0 times the damage cost of the 1 m sea-level rise scenario. The overall difference between the SRES scenarios is small.

Secondly, the authors broke apart the damage costs by socio-economic and sea-level rise scenarios. At a 0.5 m sea-level rise, protection costs followed by wetland loss are the most important damage cost component for each socio-economic situation. Protection costs are affected by dryland loss and migration costs more so than the socio-economic scenario. When the sea-level rise is then increased to 1.0 m, the wetland costs are the damage components that react roughly linearly. Protection costs increase between 4.2 to 6.6 times compared to the lower sea-level rise while dryland loss and migration costs increase by an order of magnitude. While the step from 0.5 m to 1 m sea-level rise changed the distribution of costs between the four components significantly, the step to the 2 m scenario has no such surprises. All costs roughly double compared to the 1 m scenario. This is not surprising since the model does not have a change in cost assumptions in this step.

Thirdly, sea-level rise damages are not evenly distributed over the world. The regional distribution of the costs shows that a few regions experience most of the costs, especially South Asia, South America, North America, Europe, East Asia, and Central America. Next, under a scenario of no protection, the costs of sea-level rise increase greatly due to the increase in land loss and population displacement; this scenario shows the significant benefits of the protection response in reducing the overall costs of sea-level rise. Furthermore, dikes along the coastline can significantly lower total damages, but only when economic growth enables this sometimes costly investment in protection to occur. Hence protection and economic growth are coupled. In densely populated and rich countries, dike building has a high return in that a small expense prevents substantial damage. If people are dispersed and poor, the pay-off to coastal protection is much smaller. For the 0.5 m sea-level rise, total damages are between 3.4 and 3.7 times higher when no protection is built for that scenario. For 1 m and 2 m sea-level rise the damages in the no-protection scenario are only around 1.4 times as high compared to a protection scenario. This change is due to an increase in magnitude of protection costs as illustrated previously.

Protection may not become as widespread as suggested in this analysis, especially for the 2 m sea-level rise scenario. The aggregated scale of analysis in *FUND* may overestimate the extent of likely protection in certain countries. Also, the SRES socio-economic scenarios are quite optimistic about future economic growth. Lower growth will reduce the capactiy to protect. The benefit-cost approach implies a proactive approach to protection, while historical experience shows that protection is in reaction to actual or near coastal disaster. Lastly, the economics of who pays and who benefits in coastal protection influence society's choices and ability to protect the coast. Despite all of this, the authors assert that the *FUND* analysis shows that protection is more likely and rational than is widely assumed, even with a large rise in sea level.

Protection Against Sea Level Rise and Storm Surge Prevents Severe Economic Losses: A Case Study in Copenhagen

Climate change impacts in coastal cities are expected to represent a major challenge this century, with millions of exposed people and thousands of billions of USD of exposed assets at the global scale. As a low-lying city with a significant number of people and amount of property lying close to the water level, Copenhagen is potentially vulnerable to the effects of sea level rise. In their study, Hallegatte *et al* (2011) illustrate a methodology to estimate economic impacts of climate change at a city scale, taking the example of sea level rise and storm surge risks in Copenhagen. The authors' approach is a simplified catastrophe risk assessment, to calculate the direct costs of storm surges under scenarios of sea level rise, coupled to an economic input–output model. The output is a risk assessment of the direct and indirect economic impacts of storm surge under climate change including production and job losses. For Copenhagen, it is found that in absence of adaptation, sea level rise would significantly increase flood risks. Results call for the introduction of adaptation in long-term urban planning, as one part of a comprehensive strategy to manage the implications of climate change in the city.

Due to local factors such as uplift and changes in ocean circulation, the water level in Copenhagen has risen at a rate of 4 cm a year while globally, the sea level has risen 17 cm over the century. In terms of regional changes, the IPCC found that sea level rise could be greater than the global average around northern Europe, reaching up to 38–79 cm around Denmark. Because of this large uncertainty of sea level rise, several possible amplitudes of SLR are considered, from 0 to 125 cm, and results are presented for all the cases. The authors analyzed the impact of climate change through a series of steps: (1) a statistical analysis of past storm surges in Copenhagen; (2) a geographical-information analysis of the population and asset exposure in the city, for various sea levels and storm surge characteristics; (3) an assessment of direct economic losses in case of storm surge; (4) an assessment of the corresponding indirect losses—in the form of production and job losses, reconstruction duration etc.—using an adaptive regional input–output model (ARIO); and (5) a risk analysis of the effectiveness of coastal flood protections, including risk changes due to climate change and sea level rise.

Hallegatte *et al.* found that in the absence of protection, potential losses would increase over time. The authors analyzed the total, direct losses of public and private (insured) land, defining direct losses as the repair and replacement cost of damaged buildings and equipment due to flooding. With 25 cm of mean sea level rise, total losses caused by a future 100-year event would rise from €3 billion to €4 billion. When this storm was coupled with a 50 cm sea level (or a total SLR of 2 m), the damages increased by 55% to roughly €5 billion, and to €8 billion with

100 cm sea level. Thus, without protection, sea level rise increases the risk of flooding significantly.

Direct losses caused by an event are usually significantly lower than the exposure to this event. There is a complex link between exposure to high sea level and the destruction and losses caused by such episodes. The total cost of flooding in Copenhagen is equal to the sum of direct and indirect costs. The indirect cost is the reduction in production of goods and services across the economy due to the disaster. The authors analyzed the impact of a 2 m increase in sea level above present-day values on 8 sectors of value added (VA). In the early period following a storm surge, the losses and gains in VA are estimated to roughly balance each other due to reconstruction efforts. However, a total of 7,500 jobs are lost in the 3 months after the disaster and 500 jobs are lost 1 year after the shock. The sectors that are most impacted include wholesale and retail trade, finance and business activities, and transportation. However, the authors argue that adaptation measures have to focus on direct loss reduction (using dikes or reinforced buildings) as direct losses are much more vast than indirect losses.

Copenhagen is currently easy to protect against storm surges, but needs additional protection against rising sea levels. While annual mean losses can reach several billions of Euros with protection of less than 1 m, they decrease very rapidly with protection height. Economic losses decrease to less than €100,000 per year for 180 cm of protection, and null for protection higher than 202 cm. Therefore, the authors estimated that construction cost of coastal flood protection of 2 or 3 m to be a few hundred million Euros for the city. Hallegatte *et al.* assert that despite 202 cm of protection, a 25 cm SLR causes €1 million a year in damages while a 100 cm SLR causes €4.2 billion per year. On the other hand, with 300 cm protection, damages only occur if SLR are >1 m. In addition, the timescale of the increases in losses cannot be determined, because of uncertainty in future SLR. In the most optimistic scenarios, sea level rise should not exceed 25 cm by 2100 while the most pessimistic studies show that SLR could exceed 1 m by 2100.

Copenhagen is very well protected against storm surges and coastal flooding due to its high standards of defense. First, in the city center and the harbor, quays are at more than 2 m above current sea level. Considering that the authors estimate the maximum possible storm surge at 2 m, this protection level suggests that this part of the city is not at risk. In locations that are at-risk, protection is present in the form of dikes. In addition, even a large SLR could be managed by the current protection system. Only a few areas could be affected by storm surges with the current sea level and with higher sea levels. In these areas, protection will have to be upgraded to prevent coastal flood risk from increasing rapidly across the ranges of SLR considered in this study.

Conclusions

Although the exact rise of sea level by 2100 has yet to be determined, one cannot dispute that the sea level is rising at a quicker rate since the early 1990s than during the previous decades. Many scientists argue that the rate of SLR is greater than previously thought and that sea levels are likely to rise in excess of one meter in a century. However, the focus of this chapter was not to quantify the possible rate of sea level rise but instead to summarize the possible economic, biological, and physical effects of an increased sea level. The above papers utilized a variety of methods and even a range of sea-level rise scenarios to quantify the impact of the changing sea level on our world.

The first paper by Webb and Kench (2010) analyzed the positional and morphological shift in barrier reef islands, which are considered to be the most vulnerable habitat for sea-level rise. Next, Feagin *et al.* (2010) quantified the economic and ecological impact of sea-level rise at a specific ecosystem level. The next set of papers investigated the impact of a rising sea level on the biodiversity and survival of animal and plant communities at a global and an ecosystem scale. Lastly, two papers examined the possible economic impact of the rising sea level with and without protection at both a local scale in Copenhagen as well as a global scale.

In summary, research shows that barrier reef islands and various beaches will still remain present with a rise in sea level as long as the sea level does not completely inundate them. However, the coasts will undergo morphological and physical changes. Depending on the rate of sea-level rise, plants and animals may not be able to migrate at a quick enough rate to escape the rise in sea level whether they are meiofauna like the polychaetes and copepods in the UK or the top predators such as the tigers in Bangladesh. In addition, human development stymies possible habitat migration as illustrated with the piping plover in New York. Overall, this chapter has demonstrated that sea level rise can cause a significant loss in global biodiversity. In addition, sea-level rise especially when coupled with storm surges can cause significant economic damage at a city and global scale. While the costs of sea-level rise increase with greater rise due to growing damage and protection costs, the integrated assessment model as employed by Anthoff *et al.* (2010) suggests that an optimum response in a benefit-cost sense remains widespread protection of developed coastal areas. Considering the highly negative impact of future sea level rise for society, the multidisciplinary aspects of sea level rise (observations, modeling, coastal impact studies) should remain a major area of future climate research.

Michelle Schulte

References Cited

Anthoff, D., Nicholls, R., Tol, R., 2010. The economic impact of substantial sea-level rise.
Mitigation and Adaptation Strategies for Global Change 15, 321–355.
Cazenave, A., Llovel, W., 2010. Contemporary sea level rise. Annual Review of Marine Science 2, 145–173.
Feagin, R.A., Martinez, M.L. Mendoza-Gonzalez, G, Costanza, R., 2010. Salt marsh zonal migration and ecosystem service change in response to global sea level rise: A case study from an urban region. Ecology and Society 15, 14–32.
Hallegatte, S., Ranger, N., Mestre, O., Dumas, P, Morlot, J.C., Herweijer, C., Wood, R.M. 2011. Assessing climate change impacts, sea level rise and storm surge risk in port cities: A case study on Copenhagen. Climate Change 104, 113–137.
Loucks, C., Barber-Meyer, S., Hossain, M.A.A., Barlow, A., Chowdhury, R.M., 2010. Sea level rise and tigers: Predicted impacts to Bangladesh's Sundarbans mangroves. Climatic Change 98, 291–298.
Menon, S., Soberón, J., Xingong, L., Peterson A.T., 2010. Preliminary global assessment of terrestrial biodiversity consequences of sea-level rise mediated by climate change. Biodiversity Conservation 19, 1599–1609.
Nicholls, R.J., Marinova, N., Lowe, J., Brown, S., Vellinga, P., De Gusmão, D., Hinkel, J., Tol, R.S., 2011. Sea-level rise and its possible impacts given a 'beyond 4 °C world' in the twenty-first century. Philosophical Transactions of the Royal Society A 369, 161–181.
Seavey, J.R., Gilmer, B., McGarigal, K.M., 2010. Effect of sea-level rise on piping plover (*Charadrius melodus*) breeding habitat. Biological Conservation 144, 393–401.
Webb, A., Kench, P.S., 2010. The dynamic response of reef islands to sea-level rise: Evidence from multi-decadal analysis of island change in the Central Pacific. Global and Planetary Change 72, 234–246.
Yamanaka, T., Raffaelli, D., White, P.C.L., 2010. Physical determinants of intertidal communities on dissipative beaches: Implications of sea-level rise. Estuarine, Coastal and Shelf Science 88, 267–278.

16. Ocean Acidification: Impacts Beyond Calcification

Emily Putnam

Increases in CO_2 in the atmosphere are absorbed into the ocean. The dissolved CO_2 disrupts the natural chemical equilibrium of seawater and results in a decrease in pH. This process is widely referred to as ocean acidification. Ocean pH is already 0.1 pH units lower at the surface than it was before the Industrial Revolution (Solomon et al. 2007). Current predictions hold that ocean pH will decrease by another 0.3–0.4 units by the end of the century (Orr et al. 2005). Ocean acidification decreases the amount of available $CaCO_3$ for calcifying organisms. For this reason, the strongest and most negative impacts will likely be felt in coral communities. Several studies have already demonstrated reduced growth rates in marine communities where coral is the dominant structural feature (Cantin et al. 2010, Anlauf et al. 2011). The literature on the effects of ocean acidification on calcification has expanded rapidly in the past few years.

However, there has also been a recent trend to investigate impacts on marine communities beyond reduced calcification. Studies over the past year have covered a breadth of potential impacts. Studies on coral have expanded beyond calcification rates to include potential impacts on recruitment (Albright et al. 2010) and productivity (Crawley et al. 2010); both of these processes are vital to successful expansion and resiliency. Physiological impacts on invertebrate species have also been investigated (Wood et al. 2010, Small et al. 2010). Vertebrate fish species have not been excluded from the scope of ocean acidification; early life stage growth (Munday et al. 2011) and the behavioral response to predators (Dixson et al. 2010) are just two of the investigated impacts. Although most of the literature from the past year has focused on ecological and physiological impacts, one study even attempted to draw comparisons between current ocean acidification with historical occurrences in an attempt to better understand the current phenomenon (Kiessling and Simpson 2011). Increasing amounts of literature demonstrate that ocean acidification will negatively affect many marine species.

Ocean Acidification Reduces Recruitment of the Reef-Building Coral *Acropora palmata*

Coral reefs are one of the most diverse ecosystems on the planet. As CO_2 emissions grow, the oceans absorb a greater amount of CO_2 in a process known as ocean acidification. Recent studies have focused on the impact of ocean acidification on corals' ability to grow a calcified skeleton. However, very little experimentation has been done to examine the impact of acidification on the early life stages of coral. A recent study has shown that an increase in dissolved CO_2 has reduced the recruitment abilities of *Acropora palmata* juveniles (Albright *et al.* 2010). Albright *et al.* found that increased acidity resulted in decreased fertilization, settlement, and early growth. Reductions in recruitment can severely impact the size of coral reefs and limit the ability of reefs to recover from large-scale disasters. Thus, ocean acidification places further stress on an already threatened ecosystem.

Albright and colleagues at University of Miami and the National Oceanic and Atmospheric Administration performed assays to determine the effect of increased ocean acidity on the three components of recruitment—the successful development of larvae, the ability of larvae to settle and the growth of larvae after settling. A fertilization assay, a settlement assay, and a growth assay were executed. Each test was performed at dissolved CO_2 levels either consistent with today's values, at the lowest value estimated for the year 2100, or at the highest estimate for the year 2100. The fertilization assay determined the number of successful fertilizations for a range of optimal sperm concentrations as a function of dissolved CO_2. The settlement assay determined the number of larvae settled onto tiles. The growth assay measured the upward growth of the larvae once they were settled. Taken together, these assays measure the recruitment success of *Acropora palmata* juveniles.

Albright *et al.* found a significant decrease in the recruitment success of *Acropora palmata* juveniles. Ocean acidification reduced fertilization success by an average of 12–13%. The number of settled larvae was reduced by 45% at the low estimate and by 69% at the high estimate for dissolved CO_2 levels in the year 2100. Growth was limited by 39% at the low end of the range and by 50% at the high end. The authors conclude that there was a net reduction of 52–73% in larval recruitment. Further studies are necessary to determine whether the mechanisms involved in reducing recruitment success are direct or indirect.

Reduced growth in larval settlement stages further supports the observation of reduced coral skeleton growth in adults under acidified conditions. The authors have found that ocean acidification will negatively impact larval stages in addition to the widely recognized impacts on adult stages. The magnitude of this problem is further revealed when you consider that approximately 75% of coral species reproduce in the same way as *Acropora palmata*. Thus, coral communities throughout the globe may be at risk for reductions in recruitment.

Catastrophic events further degrade and damage coral reefs. Global climate change has contributed to an increase in frequency of catastrophic storms and to an increase in global seawater temperatures. These events have severely weakened the resiliency and health of coral reef systems throughout the world. The success of recruitment is vital to recovery following destructive events. An increase in acidity over the next century will further limit recovery and reduce coral population sizes.

Ocean Acidification Negatively Impacts the Productivity of Photosynthetic Coral Symbionts

Many corals have a symbiotic relationship with symbiotic dinoflagellates. These photosynthetic symbionts are vital to the survival and health of their coral hosts. Ocean acidification has been shown to inhibit the calcification of coral structures, but few studies have focused on the impact on the symbiotic dinoflagellates. Crawley *et al.* (2010) tested the impact of ocean acidification on several key aspects of dinoflagellates of the genus *Symbiodinium* associated with the coral *Acropora formosa*. The authors found that a decrease in ocean pH resulted in an increase of the pigment chlorophyll a per cell, an increase in xanthophyll de-epoxidation, and a decrease in photosynthetic capacity per chlorophyll. Phosphoglycolate phosphatase (PGPase), an enzyme that enables carbon fixation by the symbionts, was also impacted by an increase in ocean acidity. These findings suggest symbiont productivity might increase under conservative increases in ocean acidity, but will likely decrease according to the current trajectory.

Crawley and colleagues at the University of Queensland performed a variety of tests to assess both physiological changes due to increased CO_2 and the genetic expression of the enzyme PGPase. The physical tests executed were respirometry assays, cell counting, and pigment analysis. Respirometry assays are designed to examine photosynthesis as a product of controlled amounts of light. This test determines the amount of respiration produced without light, as well as the photosynthetic efficiency and capacity of the symbionts. The symbiont cells were counted for each trial to see whether acidification impacted the number of dinoflagellates found on a coral specimen. The pigments produced by the symbionts were separated by chromatographic techniques. The authors specifically looked for the pigment xanthophyll and evidence of xanthophyll de-epoxidation. Xanthophyll de-epoxidation is an important indicator for this study because the process of de-epoxidation quenches extra energy from light and protects the symbiont from damage.

Genetics testing centered on expression of PGPase. The sequence for PGPase was obtained from a database and then compared with similar sequences from other photosynthetic organisms, including diatoms and terrestrial plants. RNA was extracted from *A. formosa* specimens. Quantitative real time reverse transcription polymerase chain reaction was performed to measure the expression of PGPase in the symbionts. A test was done using coral RNA with no symbionts to ensure that the primers used to isolate the sequence coding for PGPase did not amplify the coral's RNA as well.

The chlorophyll a concentrations per cell increased along with increases in acidity. The density of cells was not affected by acidification. Xanthophyll deepoxidation also increased as a result of acidification. PGPase expression was reduced by 50% in the severely acidified conditions. Crawley *et al.* claim that a coincidental decrease in photosynthetic productivity suggests a link between PGPase expression and photosynthetic output, but will require further testing to confirm this hypothesis. Productivity increases under conservative increases in acidity, but did not for the current trajectory of ocean acidification. The authors posit that sharp increases in acidity may overwhelm the symbionts capacity for dissipating energy and that the loss of these systems may be involved in the loss of productivity.

Temperature Rise and Ocean Acidification Impacts Physiological Processes of the Brittlestar *Ophiocten sericeum*

The Arctic is considered one of the most threatened areas on the planet. Climate change has already greatly impacted the oceanic landscape of this region. Further increases in temperature and acidity are believed to affect the Arctic more strongly than any other region on Earth. Ocean acidification has been shown to negatively affect the calcification and growth of many marine organisms. Temperature increases have placed organisms under great thermal stress and narrowed the habitat range of species, especially in the Arctic. Wood *et al.* (2011) examined the physiological effects of temperature and acidity increases on the Arctic brittlestar *Ophiocten sericeum*. The authors found that high temperature had no effect on metabolic rate, but resulted in a decrease in muscle density. The results also suggest that a lower pH increased metabolism. Taken together, the authors found that increased temperature and acidity due to climate change could result in decreased survival over the long term.

Wood and colleagues at the Plymouth Marine Laboratory tested the effects of increased temperature and increased acidity on the physiology of *O. seri-*

ceum. Six experimental setups were used—three with ambient temperature seawater and three at a higher temperature. The setups at each temperature were further broken down by pH—current ocean pH, the mid-level pH predicted for the year 2100, and the extreme pH level predicted for the year 2100. Some of the brittlestars were chosen for amputation and either 25% or 70% of an arm was removed. All brittlestars were then randomly placed into one of the experimental setups, where they remained for twenty days. After this time, brittlestars that had been left complete were placed into a metabolic chamber for 2 hours. The amount of oxygen respired was measured. These brittlestars then had one complete arm amputated for examination under microscope of the size and density of muscle cells, changes in calcium content, and the thickness of the outer layer of tissue. Previously amputated brittlestars were measured for the amount of arm regenerated following exposure to acidified and/or heated water. Regeneration was measured by comparing the length of the arm after twenty days to the length just after amputation.

Metabolic oxygen uptake increased under conditions of increased acidity, but not increased temperature. Higher temperatures resulted in a decrease in muscle density and lower calcium contents. Regeneration was affected by both increased acidity and temperature, though pH had a greater effect. Functional regeneration was greater at the more basic pH and greater in all of the high temperature setups.

The increase in metabolic rate at lower pH indicates a highly stressful environment for this species. The brittlestars compensate for the low pH with an increased energy demand. Temperature was expected to have an effect on metabolic rate, but no increase was detected. The authors posit that the temperature used in this study was not sufficiently high to find a significant effect on metabolism. The decrease in muscle at high temperatures suggest that pre-existing muscle may have provided an additional energy source for the brittlestars. Wood *et al.* concluded that increased acidification resulted in an increase in energy demand. This energy demand created additional stresses for the brittlestars, forcing them to use reserve energy. This idea was further supported by the faster regeneration in acidified and hotter waters. The brittlestars use energy faster and require more energy than can be adequately taken in from their surroundings. The authors conclude that *O. sericeum* may be able to survive short-term increases in temperature and acidity, but long-term survival may not be possible under the current predictions.

Velvet Swimming Crab *Necora puber* able to Compensate for Medium-Term Exposure to Ocean Acidification

Tolerance to ocean acidification has not been very well studied, and even fewer studies have examined the physiological basis for this tolerance. The velvet swimming crab *Necora puber* has been shown to be tolerant to acidification on a short-term basis. A recent study examined the physiological implications of a medium-term exposure to acidified conditions (Small *et al.* 2010). The authors examined a variety of parameters to attempt to get a complete look at how this species tolerates decreases in pH. They found that most physiological processes, including thermal tolerance and immune response, were unaffected by lowered pH levels and that the crabs were able to compensate for these harsh conditions. A decrease in oxygen uptake suggests that decreased energy consumption is associated with internal pH regulation, even though more of the remaining energy consumption is presumably diverted to active excretion of hydrogen ions from the gills. This will likely make the crabs less active predators.

Small and his colleagues at the University of Plymouth studied the effects of acidification on a variety of physiological characteristics of a medium–term exposure length of 30 days. Male *N. puber* individuals were collected and held in three acidification conditions—the current pH, the projected pH for the year 2100, and a lower value to mimic conditions of extra CO_2 inputs in addition to acidification. After 30 days, crabs were placed in a chamber for 50 minutes and the amount of oxygen taken up by the crabs was measured as an indicator of metabolic rate. The upper thermal tolerance was determined by finding the temperature at which the crabs began to spasm and the temperature at which they were unable to right themselves from an upturned position. Haemolymph, or circulatory fluid, was extracted by needle and tested for total CO_2 levels and pH. From these values, pCO_2 and carbonate ion concentrations were determined by calculation. The immune response to acidification was determined by examining lipid peroxide concentrations in haemolymph samples. Calcium and magnesium haemolymph concentrations were found by atomic absorption spectrometry. Levels of shell mineralization were found by dissolving a portion of the shell, or chelae, in acid and measuring calcium and magnesium ion concentrations.

The oxygen uptake decreased under acidified conditions, and total CO_2 levels in haemolymph decreased as a function of decreasing pH. Haemolymph calcium and magnesium concentrations also decreased in acidified conditions, but magnesium concentration in the shell increased slightly at lower pH. Thermal tolerance, lipid peroxidation, and calcium ion concentration in the shell were unaffected by acidification.

Small *et al.* concluded that *N. puber* is able to compensate for a medium-term exposure to ocean acidification. This compensation comes without affecting thermal tolerance, or immune response. Decreases in metabolic activity corresponded to increases in calcium in the haemolymph and magnesium in the chelae. Since no impact upon mineralization was observed, the authors concluded that shell dissolution is not the most important process in buffering the body against acidified conditions in the medium term. The ability to buffer pH is likely energetically expensive, which could incur extra costs on physiological processes not examined here. The authors conclude that the decrease in oxygen consumption observed corroborates other papers as a proposed mechanism for conservation of energy and regulation of internal pH in harsh external conditions. As a key predator in its ecosystem, tolerance for ocean acidification will likely give this species an ecological advantage over other predators. However, since oxygen uptake limitations were observed, there could be additional restrictions on the ability of these predators to maintain existing population dynamics in the face of ocean acidification.

Early Growth and Development of the Tropical Fish *Acanthochromis polyacanthus* unaffected by Ocean Acidification

Effects on the calcification and growth due to ocean acidification have been established for several marine invertebrate species. However, little research has been done to examine the effects of ocean acidification on fish. Of the available research, most papers have focused on the acid-base regulatory mechanisms of adult fish, but very few have considered the effects of acidification on juveniles. Munday *et al.* (2011) studied whether ocean acidification affected the early life cycle of the tropical reef fish, *Acanthochromis polyacanthus*. The authors believed that an increase in acidity should affect skeletal growth by reducing calcification. They found that increases in dissolved CO_2 did not significantly affect the growth and development of these reef fishes. The results suggest that marine fish species may be more tolerant to changes in seawater pH than invertebrates in the same locations.

Munday and his colleagues at James Cook University studied the effects of acidification on the growth of *A. polyacanthus* individuals for the first three weeks of their lives. Freshly hatched *A. polyacanthus* juveniles were reared in four acidification conditions—the current pH, the projected pH for the year 2100, and two intermediate acidities. At the end of three weeks, the fish were killed and preserved for study. The standard length and weight of each fish was measured to ascertain overall growth. Otoliths, or small ear bones, were removed and examined by photographic analysis to determine the level of asymmetry. Each fish was then stained and measurements were taken for 29 skeletal reference points. Statistical analyses compared the effects due to parentage versus that of acidified conditions.

Munday *et al.* found that standard length and weight was not significantly different among the treatments. The otoliths were expected to be more strongly impacted by acidified environments because they are composed of aragonite—a compound that is harder to form as pH decreases. However, the authors found that there was no effect of acidification on any aspect of the otoliths. Skeletal measurements agreed with otolith and standard growth measurements—26 of 29 skeletal references were not different amongst the treatments. Statistical analysis showed that these three reference points were not enough to conclude that acidified conditions affected the development of the juvenile. All growth measurements were more strongly connected to genetic variation than to environmental constraints.

Even though early life stages are considered to be more susceptible to environmental conditions, Munday *et al.* found no negative effects on the early life of *A. polyacanthus*. They concluded that marine fishes may be more tolerant to ocean acidification than their invertebrate counterparts. One possible explanation for the observed results is that *A. polyacanthus* juveniles spend all of their early lives on the reef, where large fluctuations in dissolved CO_2 levels are common. Thus, this species may be especially tolerant to changes in ocean pH. The authors also posit that 3 weeks may be sufficient for the juveniles to develop to a life stage where they can actively regulate internal acid-base chemistry to overcome the effects of acidification. Taken together, the authors conclude that more expansive studies of species and juvenile-based growth be undertaken to fully consider the effects of ocean acidification of early life development.

Fish Prefer the Smell of Predators in Acidified Conditions

Ocean acidification as a result of increased CO_2 emissions by human activity has been shown to have a variety of secondary effects on marine organisms. Dixson *et al.* (2010) studied the ability of orange clownfish, *Amphiprion percula*, to detect the presence of predators by smell under acidic conditions. Newly hatched and settlement stage larvae prefer waters that contain no trace of other fish—either predatory or non-predatory. The authors simulated the more acidic conditions predicted for the year 2100 to determine whether fish raised in more acidic conditions would be able to detect predators. Although newly hatched larvae in acidic conditions navigated away from predator signals, settlement stage larvae preferred water containing the chemical signature of predators over waters without any chemical signal and waters containing the chemical signature of non-predators. The results suggest that clownfish may exhibit risky settlement choices as oceans continue to acidify.

Dixson and colleagues at James Cook University compared the ability of settlement-stage larvae and newly hatched *Amphiprion percula* to detect predators. Two species of predators were chosen, *Cephalopholis cyanostigma* and *Pseudochromis fuscus*. Two species of non-predators, *Acanthurus pyroferus* and *Siganus corallinus*, were chosen as further controls on the ability of the clownfish to detect predator signals. The clownfish were raised in water either at pH levels consistent with today's oceans or at pH levels predicted for the year 2100. The fish were then placed individually into chambers with two streams of water. These tests focused on six combinations: normal water vs. normal water, predator 1 vs. normal water, predator 2 versus normal water, non-predator 1 vs. normal water, non-predator 2 vs. normal water, predator 1 vs. non-predator 1, predator 2 vs. non-predator 2. The clownfish were monitored for stream choice every five seconds for two minutes. To account for side preferences unrelated to chemical signals, the fish were allowed to rest for one minute while the streams were switched, then monitoring was repeated.

Although newly hatched and settlement-ready clownfish raised in today's waters preferred normal water and water with non-predatory chemical cues over those of predators, *Amphiprion percula* larvae raised in acidified conditions preferred water containing the chemical signatures of predatory fish and could not make a distinction between the chemical signatures of predatory vs. non-predatory fish. Newly hatched clownfish from acidified conditions followed the preferences of fish from today's waters. The difference between newly hatched and settlement-age fish reflects the vulnerability of these two ages. Newly hatched fish by today's standards would avoid the chemical signals of all fish and swim to the open ocean, whereas settlement-ready fish need to settle on reefs where they are more likely to be near other fish species. This could account for the discrepancy in sensing abilities between newly hatched and settlement-age orange clownfish individuals.

The larvae's ability to detect predators can be directly related to the chance of survival. Fish that are unable to detect chemical cues will be more likely to settle near predators and will increase their chance of becoming food. This risky behavior could contribute to a large decrease in population size and could even lead to extinction. One important thing to note is that the fish in the acidification samples were treated using acidity levels predicted for 2100. It is possible that a gradual increase of ocean acidity could instigate the adaptation of senses to be able to distinguish predators even under acidified conditions. However, the ability to adapt and the exact pH levels at which these fish are affected has yet to be determined. Dixson *et al.* have shown that increases in ocean acidity can affect the ability of fish to determine the presence of a predator and to distinguish between predators and non-predators.

Ocean Acidification Favors the Dominance of Turf Algae over Kelp Forests

Research into habitat effects of ocean acidification are primarily concerned with calcifying coral reefs. While reefs are critical ecosystem builders in tropical areas, these are not the only habitats that could potentially be harmed by acidification. A recent study has examined the effects of increased temperature and ocean acidification associated with global warming on temperate habitats dominated by kelp forests (Connell and Russell 2010). The early stage of temperate algal communities is dominated by algae that form a turf over large rocky surfaces. Following a period of relative stability, kelp (also a type of alga) overtakes the turf algae and creates a forest habitat. Connell and Russell hypothesized that removal of turf algae would result in a greater recruitment of kelp and that turf algae would increase in abundance in high temperature and pH conditions. They found that these hypotheses were true, further solidifying the perception that ocean acidification will have far-reaching effects even in communities not dominated by calcifying organisms.

Connell and Russell from the Southern Seas Ecology Laboratories at the University of Adelaide first tested the ability of turf algae to inhibit kelp recruitment. The authors removed turf algae from square meter plots that were found less than 5 meters from existing kelp canopies. These sites were chosen for their location along a metropolitan coastline. After one year, the number of kelp recruits was recorded and compared to control plots where no turf algae were removed. Mesocosm experiments were set up in large 40-liter tanks where turf algae specimens were exposed to one of four combinations of current summer maximal ocean temperature and pH and predicted temperature and pH for the year 2050. After 14 weeks, visual estimations of algal growth on previously uninhabited substrate were made. The algae from this substrate was then scraped from the substrate, dried for two days and weighed. Chlorophyll fluorescence was measured to determine the photosynthetic, or quantum, yield of the algae. Quantum yield is calculated comparing the relative fluorescence following exposure of the algae to a weak beam of red light and then to a strong beam of light.

Kelp recruitment was greater for all sites where turf algae had been removed. Increased temperature led to an increase in turf algae cover, but increased CO_2 had no effect. Increased temperature and CO_2 combined led to an even greater increase in turf coverage than increased temperature alone. Quantum yield increased slightly with CO_2 increases but decreased with temperature increases. The synergistic effects of increased temperature and acidity on turf coverage suggests that the dual threat of acidification and global warming would further favor the dominance of turf algae at sites that were once home to large kelp forests. While action can be taken to reduce nutrient levels as a means of reducing turf algae on a local scale, any mitigation will eventually be overcome by these global stresses. The gradual dominance of turf algae will also likely result in a further weakening of existing kelp forests due to reduced resilience. While the results from this study apply directly to coastlines with local human populations, even remote habitats will probably be affected by changes in seawater chemistry and temperature. As habitats shift and change, local herbivorous species distributions will adjust accordingly. Thus, temperate marine communities face as much risk as tropical communities in the face of global warming and ocean acidification.

Ocean Acidification is a Possible Contributor to Ancient Reef Crises

Ocean acidification in recent years has been linked to decreases in calcification rates in reef-building corals. Little work has been done to analyze past coral reef crises and ocean acidification events. Coral reefs have one of the most complete fossil records due to their calcium carbonate skeletons. Thus, the coral reef fossil record has been widely studied and documented. Ocean acidification in prehistoric times has been connected with several possible mechanisms resulting in large releases of CO_2 into the marine environment. Like the fossil record, geologic evidence of these events has been collected in a database. Kiessling and Simpson (2011) investigated a possible relationship between past extinction events, reef crises, and ocean acidification trends by examining data from the paleological databases. The authors found that four out of five past reef crises could be partially attributed to ocean acidification and global warming. Out of these five major events, only two had geological proof of a concurrent ocean acidification event.

Kiessling and Simpson from the Leibniz Institute for Research on Evolution and Biodiversity first determined major reef crises by calculating changes in reef volume per time interval and defining crises as significant outliers below the normal. Extinction intensities were found by calculating the rate of extinction from the PaleoBiology Database. The selectivity of these extinctions was determined in two ways—by comparing calcified organisms with all others, and by comparing physiologically pH sensitive organisms with all others. The authors also took into consideration the possibility that ocean acidification could have impacted the preservation of the fossil record by measuring the completeness of the record for groups at each time interval.

Kiessling and Simpson found that reef volume changes vary widely over time and only the most severe decreases in volume can be identified as crises. A total of five reef crises were found from the existing records—Late Devonian, Early Triassic, earliest Triassic, Early Jurassic and early Eocene. Four out of five of these crises followed elevated extinction rates of calcifying organisms, with three of these showing a preferential extinction of these organisms. Five marine biodiversity crises were found—the end-Ordivician, Late Devonian, end-Permian, end-Triassic, and end-Cretaceous. Degradation of the fossil record agreed with fossil preservation hypotheses for acidified conditions.

Analysis of the geologic evidence for possible ocean acidification events revealed that four out of five reef crises could have been at least partially due to ocean acidification. Ocean acidification was not connected to mass extinctions. Thus, ocean acidification in today's world may play a role in reef stress, but may not lead to mass extinctions. Despite the attempt to connect the past with the present, the authors could not offer more information relating the magnitude of the crises with CO_2 levels to determine the potential impact of the current ocean acidification event on coral reefs. Global warming was considered to be an equally likely cause of reef degradation and crisis as ocean acidification. Kiessling and Simpson therefore concluded that the greatest danger to coral reefs comes from the double threat of global warming and ocean acidification.

Conclusions

Ocean acidification has many well-established effects on calcifying organisms. Because ocean acidification is a global phenomenon, the effects of ocean acidification will be felt in almost all marine communities. Recent literature has further confirmed negative impacts on recruitment, productivity and predator detection. Temperate communities are not exempt from the effects of ocean acidification either. However, other studies have established the possibility of physiological tolerance to decreases in pH. Ocean acidification is expected to have many far-reaching effects. Additional impacts on various processes will inevitably be documented in the near future as part of the natural human tendency to investigate the impacts of our activities on our surroundings.

References Cited

Albright, R., Mason, B., Miller, M., Langdon, C., 2010. Ocean acidification compromises recruitment success of the threatened Caribbean coral *Acropora palmata*. Proceedings of the National Academy of Sciences 107, 20400–20404.

Anlauf, H., D'Croz, L., O'Dea, A., 2011. A corrosive concoction: The combined effects of ocean warming and acidification on the early growth of a stony coral are multiplicative. Journal of Experimental Marine Biology and Ecology 397, 13–20.

Connell, S.D., Russell, B.D., 2010. The direct effects of increasing CO2 and temperature on non-calcifying organisms: increasing the potential for phase shifts in kelp forests. Proceedings of the Royal Society B: Biological Sciences 277, 1409–1415.

Cantin, N.E., Cohen, A.L., Karnauskas, K.B., Tarrant, A.M., McCorkle, D.C., 2010. Ocean Warming Slows Coral Growth in the Central Red Sea. Science 329, 322–325.

Crawley, A., Kline, D.I., Dunn, S., Anthony, K., Dove, S., 2010. The effect of ocean acidification on symbiont photorespiration and productivity in *Acropora formosa*. Global Change Biology 16, 851–863.

Dixson, D.L., Munday, P.L., Jones, G.P., 2010. Ocean acidification disrupts the innate ability of fish to detect predator olfactory cues. Ecology Letters 13, 68–75.

Kiessling, W., Simpson, C., 2011. On the potential for ocean acidification to be a general cause of ancient reef crises. Global Change Biology 17, 56–67.

Munday, P.L., Gagliano, M., Donelson, J.M., Dixson, D.L., Thorrold, S.R., 2011. Ocean acidification does not affect the early life history development of a tropical marine fish. Marine Ecology Progress Series 423, 211–221.

Orr, J.C., Fabry, V.J., Aumont, O., Bopp, L., Doney, S.C., Feely, R.A., et al., 2005. Anthropogenic ocean acidification over the twenty-first century and its impact on calcifying organisms. Nature, 437, 681–686.

Small, D., Calosi, P., White, D., Spicer, J.I., Widdicombe, S., 2010. Impact of medium-term exposure to CO2 enriched seawater on the physiological functions of the velvet swimming crab *Necora puber*. Aquatic Biology 10, 11–21.

Solomon S, Qin D, Manning M, Chen Z, Marquis M, et al., 2007. Climate Change 2007: The Physical Science Basis: Contribution of Working Group I to the Fourth Assessment Report of the Intergovernmental Panel on Climate Change. Cambridge University Press, New York.

Wood, H., Spicer, J., Kendall, M., Lowe, D., Widdicombe, S., 2011. Ocean warming and acidification; implications for the Arctic brittlestar *Ophiocten sericeum*. Polar Biology 34, 1–12.

292

17. Impacts of Climate Change on Fisheries and Aquaculture

Lauren Lambert

It is clear that changes in the earth's climate will continue to increase the temperature and have an effect on all ecosystems. Carbon dioxide and other greenhouse gases are building up in the atmosphere, changing the Earth's climate, oceans and coasts, and freshwater ecosystems. Environmental conditions that are affected by climate change include increases in air and sea surface temperatures, rainfall, wind patterns, and intensity of cyclones and hurricanes. Many wet areas will become wetter, while dry areas will become drier, increasing flood and drought tendencies. The increased extremity of weather will create variation in water supplies that drive agricultural systems and have an effect on food availability. Rising water temperatures may reduce upwelling in the ocean, which decreases the amount of nutrition and food sources that are available to marine organisms. This will also lead to acidification of the water, causing many issues for the organisms as well as their food sources. Changes in water temperature, precipitation, wind velocity, wave action, and sea level rise can negatively affect marine ecosystems and those communities that rely on them. Fisheries production is heavily impacted by climate change. Global aquaculture production has been increasing in response to depletion of wild fish supplies.

Fisheries and aquaculture provide food supply, food security, and income generation to the global population. A majority of jobs in developing countries come from this sector. Aquatic foods have a high nutritional value and contribute significantly to global protein intake. Fish products provide approximately 20% of protein to the world's population with an average export value of 86 billion dollars in 2006 (Badjeck *et al.* 2010). As global population continues to rise, the demand for aquatic food supply will increase dramatically. While the output of capture fisheries has remained relatively stable over the last decade, growth in aquaculture has significantly contributed to the global output of fish. Capture fisheries and aquaculture are particularly vulnerable to climate change. The changes have affected productivity of marine and freshwater species through biological processes and alteration of food webs. Future production levels and food security is uncertain. In response to the stresses of climate change on marine ecosystems includes demographic, economic, and policy changes on the local and national level (Perry *et al.* 2010). Many communities that depend on fisheries tend to live in poverty with a lack of services and infrastructure and it will be these that suffer the most.

National economies are vulnerable to the impacts of climate change because of the depletion of global food security. Countries that depend on fish as the main source of protein do not have the capacity to adapt to the change fast enough. Annual losses in the billions are unevenly distributed, with developing countries suffering a two to three times larger loss than others (Barrange *et al.* 2010). Countries located around the tropics will be threatened the most. As global temperatures rise, current surface water temperatures in existing fisheries will become too extreme for marine organisms to survive. Fisheries capture will decline in these areas and increase in higher latitudinal regions to an ideal temperature. Fish species distribution has already been shifted as a result of increased sea surface temperatures (Badjeck *et al.* 2010). In response to this redistribution, advances in aquaculture have been able to increase the amount of fish products available in the food industry. Coastal sites farm fish for a more sustainable approach to food security. However, controversy surrounds this method because of the use of hormones, quality of fish feed, disease outbreak, and damaging effects to the surrounding ecosystem as a result of waste and exposure to the open water. Aside from the direct effects of waste materials that create dead zones beneath fish farm facilities, the current transports this toxic material further into the ocean. Disease is also carried out to wild populations, further threatening their existence.

Data used to determine past effects of climate change does not serve as an accurate model to predict future changes in aquaculture. Future planning for the uncertainty of fish availability and productivity needs to be implemented immediately. Models for future climate change predictions are important for agricultural and mariculture activities that are largely affected by climate change. These models implement scenarios in which effects of climate change can be investigated. Through these scenarios, possible solutions to this issue can be proposed and hopefully implemented in the future.

How Fisheries Respond to the Effects of Climate Change

The productivity of fisheries is significant factor in human society because of influences on food supply, employment, and income. The effect of climate change on marine communities is of particular importance because of the strong influences that these communities have on marine food web function and fisheries yield. Climate can effect the function, distribution, and structure of fish communities. The distributions of fish species is expected to shift towards the poles as a result of climate change. Many studies have focused on how climate has affected abundance levels as well as the consequences of this decline. The changes in productivity of specific and whole populations will determine how these fisheries are responding to climate change. Jennings and Brander 2010 proposed that it is possible to make predictions about the community level responses to climate that are independent from knowledge about identity and dynamic of component populations. Community level approaches could be used to determine total fishery productivity, however population specific productivity will need to be based on each individual population. The fluctuation of a species population size can have negative effects in all countries.

Jennings and Brander 2010 addresses several methods in which population and community based abundance levels change as a result of climate change. Abundance is related to total production size, so lower intercepts of size spectra in areas with low primary production means that production is reduced by a constant fraction throughout the food web. Primary production is correlated with fish production at large scales. Slopes of size spectra depend on the relative body sizes of predators and prey and efficiency of energy transfer from prey to predators. The former is measured as the mean predatory-prey mass ratio (PPMR), while the latter is mean trophic transfer efficiency (TE). Because slopes of size-spectra are constrained by these factors, the mean trophic level of the community is also constrained. Based on evidence for a relatively constant slope at a range of temperatures, it can be concluded that temperature will influence rates but will not change relative abundance at size. Jennings and Brander 2010 noted that species with faster life histories responded more rapidly to climate change. Studies also showed that smaller prey species moved while their predators did not. This could potentially disrupt the food chain if other species do not replace their absence. The effects of climate change on primary production will be the main factor driving changes in abundance and production.

Due evidence from previous publications, Jennings and Brander 2010 presented information regarding six different climate model simulations to show the response of primary production in ocean ecosystems in relation to climate change from the beginning of the industrial revolution to 2050. This provides insight to a rule-based categorization of global marine system into biogeographic production zones, estimates of change in primary production within these zones, and an overview of the limitations of making projections of ocean production. It has been suggested that global primary production may increase by 10% by 2050, however there is not much confidence in the accuracy of this estimate. Large scale plankton sampling shows actual observations of declining phytoplankton and chlorophyll levels over the past 20–50 years. This evidence is consistent with the expected consequences of reduced nutrient supply.

Over the next 4–5 decades, global marine primary production is not expected to significantly change, but there is a stronger basis for predicting changes at a regional scale particularly in the North Pacific and North Atlantic. These changes largely rely on regime scale and event scale factors such as El Niño effects. In the Arctic Ocean, a rising climate will lead to reduction in ice cover, resulting in a greater amount of phytoplankton production in these areas because of the increased availability of sunlight. While the productive area will rise, the existing food web will be disrupted. For example observations show that there has been a switch from krill to salps as the major nektonic species in some areas of the Antarctic. Increase in vertical stratification will also be a result of increased freshwater input from rivers. This is likely to result in negative consequences for fisheries and cause shifts in relative productivity of benthic and pelagic species in this size spectrum.

To assess the effects of climate change on fish communities, two methods have been proposed. Scaling up from predictions of climate on the individual species within the community could be used, or identification of aggregate properties of communities and the expected responses. Both of these approaches done simultaneously will provide the best understanding of ecological as well as community effects of climate change. Productivity of communities is likely to be predictable but species composition is not. The expected capacity to develop shipping vessel designs that allow for switching between different species will change the market in that they will need to accept and sell a more diverse range of fish and fish product. For the future, the main challenges in predicting the effects of climate change are to refine the current models for primary production at global scales as well as developing individual population based models that are consistent with community based models. Flexible ways of incorporating species dynamics in size-based models also needs to be developed.

A Warming Climate Leads to Redistribution of Fisheries around the World

Most fisheries throughout the world are over–exploited and are pushed past their biological limit. With an expected rise in greenhouse gas emissions, fisheries yield could suffer a dramatic decrease. Countries that strongly rely on food and revenue outcomes of fisheries will be negatively impacted both in terms of food supply and socioeconomic factors. Theoretical and experimental studies have shown that physiology, life history, productivity, and distribution of marine organisms are dependent on conditions of the ocean such as temperature, currents, and coastal upwelling which are all factors affected by climate change. Through various climate change scenarios, Cheung *et al.* 2010 aims to project future changes in the maximum catch potential of marine fish and invertebrates in global oceans from 2005 to 2055. It is expected that climate change will have an effect on the ocean, which will result in an effect on goods and services provided by marine ecosystems. Alteration of current ocean conditions can have an effect on primary productivity, species distribution, community, and food web structure. It has been observed that marine fish and invertebrates shift distribution according to climate change. They generally move towards a higher latitude and deeper water where temperatures are less extreme. While production could increase in higher latitudinal areas, those with lower latitudes will suffer. This will have a direct effect on human society around the world.

Cheung *et al.* 2010 used several models to make their predictions about maximum catch potential by the year 2055. The empirical model can be applied to evaluate how fisheries productivity could be affected by climate change based on primary production and distribution range of 1066 species of exploited fish and invertebrates. Future distributions of these species are represented using dynamic bioclimate envelope models. These models identified species preferences with environmental conditions such as water temperature, salinity, distance from sea ice, and habitat types. A large range of taxonomic groups was used, including krill, shrimp, anchovy, cod, tuna, and sharks. The distribution of each species was determined from an algorithm that estimated the relative abundance of species. Habitat type was also taken into consideration. These included coral reef, seamounts, estuaries, inshore, offshore, continental shelf, continental slope, and abyssal habitats. The models assume that species distributions are dependent on latitude, bathymetric, and habitat gradients. Two climate change scenarios were included in the study with both high and low greenhouse gas emissions. To predict primary production from the world ocean, published empirical models and algorithms were used. Primary production was predicted by looking at surface chlorophyll content and distribution, light supply, vertical attenuation, and temperature of surface. The annual maximum catch potential was calculated based on total primary production for the two climate change scenarios.

Cheung *et al.* 2010 found that climate change may have a significant effect on distribution of catch potential between tropical and high latitude regions.

Results from the higher greenhouse gas emission scenarios show that impacts in Indo-Pacific regions are the most intense, with up to 50% decrease in catch potential by 2055. Semi–enclosed areas and many coastal regions also show a decline. Catch potential showed a more than 50% increase in higher latitudinal regions. In contrast to the results of this model, the pattern of changes under the low greenhouse gas emission scenario is less clear. Changes in catch potential by 2055 for all regions under the high range scenario were 1.6 times higher than the changes under low range scenario. This suggests that climate change may have a large impact on distribution of maximum catch potential, which is extremely important in predicting the potential impact that climate change could have on fisheries productivity.

Species distribution will undergo a shift in range as the ocean temperature increases, resulting in a decrease in catch potential in these areas. High latitude regions will open up new habitat for lower latitude species, causing catch potential to increase. These projected changes could have implications for global security. Climate change may have a negative impact on food security in tropical communities that are dependent on fisheries production as a food source and revenue. With rising agricultural problems as a result of climate change, this additional stress will have an extremely negative effect on the food security dilemma. The distribution change from coastal regions to offshore could also have an effect on the cost of fishing because boats will be forced to travel further away from land and be at sea for a longer period of time. The conclusion is that greenhouse gas emission could result in a worldwide redistribution of maximum catch potential.

Are Fish Farms the Answer in Supplying Our Growing Population?

There is a great controversy surrounding production through fish farms as opposed to a reliance on wild fish sources. Wild fisheries populations are declining, however aquaculture could become the most sustainable source for protein for humans. Currently there is a reliance on meat from livestock, and food consumption is increasing worldwide. The population is estimated to increase from an already high 6.9 billion to 9.3 billion people by 2050. With this in mind, the question arises about where global meat will come from. Raising livestock uses up a vast amount of land, freshwater, fossil fuels, and results in organic waste and fertilizer run-off that has a negative impact on rivers and oceans. These same issues apply to fish farming and other aquaculture, which results in fish sewage, depletion of mangrove forest for shrimp growth, and densely packed salmon farms that cause disease and parasites, which kill off their populations and infect native species as well. Larger offshore pens are much cleaner and could serve as a place for expansion of aquaculture and could even become more sustainable than wild fish or raised beef.

Simpson (2011) addresses the benefits of aquaculture and fish farming as a solution to the global food security issue. Coastal fish farms pollute the ocean with fish excrement and food scraps, particularly in the shallow waters. Offshore sites such as Kona Blue Water Farms have eliminated the pollution issue by submerging paddocks that are anchored in the presence of rapid currents that quickly dilute and sweep away the harmful waste before it can become a problem for marine ecosystems nearby. These paddocks are cone shape and made from solid material that is strong enough to keep sharks from getting into the fish supply. They contain massive amounts of domesticated yellowtail, which serve as an alternative to wild tuna. These fish are fed pellets of fishmeal and oil made from smaller fish. The yellowtail could survive on a purely vegetarian diet, but their meat would not contain the fatty acids and amino acids that produce a healthy, good tasting fish. Other farms raise seaweed and filter feeding animals such as mollusks near the fish pens to use up the waste. Cutting edge designs for fish pens are submerged, steered by large propellers, and ride on ocean currents to stimulate fish maturation. The pens would then return months later to the starting point or designated destination for delivery of fresh fish to market.

The fishmeal used to feed the fish farms is of concern because of the rapid decline of smaller fish species such as anchovy. Anchovy concentration in feed pellets were reduced from containing 80% in 2005 to 30% in 2008 by adding a higher concentration of soybean meal and chicken oil. However as the demand for fish farms increases, sardine and anchovy populations are in jeopardy of a decline in population size. Aquaculture is the fastest growing food production sector in the world, expanding at a rate of 7.5% per year since 1994. At this rate, fish and all of its products could be exhausted by 2040 and therefore, the main goal is to eliminate the use of wild fish from feed products altogether. One possible solution is to use docosahexaenoic acid (DHA) from microscopic algae because of the need to eliminate all agricultural resources from feed, and push towards a reliance on easily grown seaweed and zooplankton.

The world health organization predicts a 25% increase in meat consumption by 2050. Simpson leans towards aquaculture for the global protein supply. Cattle eat a large amount of heavily fertilized crops, and pig and chicken farms are extremely polluting to the environment. Raising Angus beef requires 4,400 times more high quality pastureland than seafloor needed for the equivalent weight of farmed Atlantic salmon. However fish farms also have their flaws. Areas below coastal fish farms have huge dead zones, similar to the results of fertilizer run-off from the Mississippi River into the Gulf of Mexico, or harmful algal blooms from pig farms in the Chesapeake Bay. Although fish farms are relatively detrimental to ecosystems, marine ecosystems have the ability to recover in less than a decade, whereas a cattle farm would take centuries to overcome the damage.

Fish farming reduces the size of marine fishing fleets, so that although fuel consumption and emissions are higher on an offshore farm, they are not as high as would result from fleets catching equivalent amounts of wild fish. Aside from these advantages, inefficient and harmful fishing methods such as trawling and dredging kill millions of animals as bycatch, that are regarded as worthless and tossed aside. Fish farming is also more efficient in that the raised fish do not have to waste energy searching for food, avoiding predators, and reproducing. Most of their diet goes into growth, so they mature at a faster rate.

Fish farming already accounts for 47% of global seafood consumption, and could potentially rise to 62% of total protein supply by 2050. Although there are many benefits to this method of food production, society is not yet ready to switch to these measures. But Americans do not yet accept this transition to an increased reliance on aquaculture; the public accepts domestication on land, but has a perception of the ocean as a wild frontier. Perhaps at some point this will change.

Effects of Fish-Farms on Marine Biodiversity Along the Mediterranean Coast

The expansion and growth of offshore mariculture is a growing business. The environmental effects of this industry are of particular concern because of the impacts they have on marine habitats and biodiversity. Mirto *et al.* (2010) investigated the effects that fish farms have on the metazoan meiofaunal communities existing in areas exposed to fish farms along the coast of the Mediterranean Sea. The potential effects of fish farm effluents on the abundance and community composition of meiofauna were analyzed by comparing two different habitats in four different regions with different background trophic conditions. It was found that there are conflicts between aquaculture and the conservation of marine habitats and benthic primary producers. The organic enrichment of sediments falls beneath the sea cages used by fish farms. This sedimentation of particulate waste products from the fish farm has a direct effect on the local habitat. The continuous deposition of feces and food pellets from fish cages can alter the quantity as well as biochemical composition of sediment organic matter. The extent to which these areas are affected differs in different regions/habitats. Investigating meiofaunal assemblages in different regions of the Mediterranean Sea identifies the changes that are caused by aquaculture on benthic ecosystems and can provide insight to what is going on in these marine communities.

Mirto *et al.* (2010) hypothesized that fish farms influence the meiofaunal assemblages of existing habitats. This includes abundance, community structure, and diversity. Four regions along the Mediterranean Coastal zones were selected in order to provide a variety of different environmental conditions. Two different habitats were selected, meadows of seagrass vs. soft non-vegetated bottoms. Control sites were also chosen to match conditions and environmental features found at the bottom of fish farm cages. These sites were located at a distance of at least 1000m upstream from the fish farms to be certain that this habitat would not be affected. The sediment protein, carbohydrate, and lipid contentents were determined. The amount of meiofauna was determined by sieving through 1000 mm sieve for macrobenthos and macroalgae, and 32 mm sieve to retain smaller meiofauna. The differences between control and impact sediments were calculated using three-way-analysis-of-variance (ANOVA). When significant differences were observed between the two groups, a post-hoc Student-Newman-Kuels test (SNK) was also used to assess this information.

The observations of the study showed differences between impacted and control sites as well as in the four geographical areas. SNK tests revealed a consistent increase in biopolymeric C concentrations in farm-impacted vegetated sediments in Cyprus, both habitats in Greece, and in non-vegetated sediments in Italy. Protein to carbohydrate ratio increased in both habitats in Italy and non-vegetated sediments in Spain. A decrease in impact sediments was observed in both habitats of Greece. The SNK test indicated a significant increase of meiofaunal abundance in impacted sites with vegetated sediments in Cyprus, in non-vegetated sediments in Italy, but no difference between control groups in other regions. In summary, Mirto *et al.* found that the differences between control and sites impacted by fish farms varied depending on the region.

Differences between impact and control sites in the meiofaunal community composition were only significant in non-vegetated sediments in Cyprus or Greece. Nematodes and Copepods were the most dominant taxa followed by polychaetes, ostracods, turbellarians, oligochaetes, gastrotrichs, and all other taxa. The richness of meiofaunal taxa decreased significantly in impacted sites in non-vegetated sediments but no significant differences between impact and control sites were observed in sea grass sediments. The taxa that disappeared beneath the cages varied throughout the sites, but always compromised the rare taxa which make up <1% of total meiofaunal abundance.

Fish farms typically have an effect on the attributes of the benthic environment beneath cages and show a significant amount of modifications in the abundance, biomass, species composition, and evenness of meio and macrofauna. However these observed changes associated with the presence of fish farm effluents are often not consistent because meiofaunal abundance may increase or decrease beneath the cage depending on characteristics of the site or farm. The abundance of meiofauna was generally higher in fish farm sediments, which could be a result of limited organic enrichment in the sediments beneath the cages. There is a clear and consistent meiofaunal response to the fish farm deposition in sea grass sediments. *Posidonia oceanica* is the sea grass existing on the sites that plays a key ecological role for many of the organisms and assemblages by preserving biodiversity. It is difficult to detect effects of fish farm biodeposition on sea grass meadows because the grass masks the changes in organic composition. The presence of a large number of filter feeders and detritus feeders within sea grass beds can also act as a buffer for the organic enrichment because of the amount of biodeposits that they consume.

Lauren Lambert

Actual changes are difficult to know because of these supplemental factors. However in the long term, the increased sedimentation and waste particles that result from these farms does lead to the deterioration of the sea grass system and will eventually result in disruption of the ecosystem in place. Fish farm biodeposition in the Mediterranean Sea can provoke changes in meiofaunal abundance, community structure, and biodiversity. Because of the amount of variation between the sites, it is important to use indicators of fish farm impact in vegetated and non-vegetated systems in the future.

Implications for Disease Control in Aquaculture

With over-exploitation of coastal fisheries and rising disease rates of ocean populations, fish abundance levels have been dramatically decreasing. The outbreak, persistence, and eradication of infectious diseases are often dependent on the density of the host population. The growth of aquaculture has produced a large density of fish in fish farms, making them more susceptible to disease. They are often open to the surrounding ecosystem and therefore are exposed to wild fish populations as well. Krkošek (2010) explores the connection between outbreaks of parasites in wild salmon and density threshold in aquaculture growth. High densities lead to higher transmission rates of infectious diseases because of increased contact with infected individuals. Wild-farmed populations can exceed host density threshold from an influx of migrating individuals, increases in aquaculture production, or environmental changes such as global warming. In contrast, populations with lower densities show a much lower rate of susceptibility and slower rate of disease spread. Fisheries reduce abundance levels of wild populations, which should lead to a decrease in disease and parasite abundance as well. However when a predatory population declines, the prey population increases and therefore increases susceptibility of disease.

Krokšek proposed a series of models to test density threshold levels in relation to disease susceptibility and transmission. Industrial aquaculture and number of fish farms are growing. They often have larger domesticated abundance than wild populations. These domesticated populations are concentrated by pens, nets, cages, rafts, or ropes that are open to the surrounding areas. Therefore any disease or parasites that arise in these populations will be open to the surrounding ecosystem and can be transmitted to wild populations. This is a major challenge for the aquaculture industry because of the concern for conservation of the wild marine ecosystem. The most common measure of disease persistence is known as R0, or the net reproductive value. If R0 >1, the parasite population can invade host population. If R0 <1, infections do not replace themselves and parasite populations will eventually die out. This is the process of disease eradication. Populations are susceptible to microparasites such as viruses, bacteria, and protists. Dynamics of microparasite diseases can be modeled by dividing host populations into categories determining status of infection (susceptible, infected, recovered). Individuals become infected by being exposed to others that are infected. Even if an individual recovers, over time it becomes more susceptible to disease and could become infected again. The number of infected individuals generated by a single individual can be determined by multiplying the average duration of infection period by the rate at which hosts become infected.

Macroparasites include helminths and arthropods such as intestinal worms and ectoparasitic copepods. Unlike microparasites, these must leave the initial host in order to complete their life cycle. They also produce sexually in or on a host. For example, sea lice reproduce on the surface tissue of fish. Models describing macroparasites must track free-living stages as well as number of parasites per host, per population. Birth and death rates, rate of infection of hosts, and host/parasite mortality rates are also determined.

Theory predicts that host density thresholds are important for host-parasite dynamics. For example, increases in sea lice in salmon were associated with small incremental changes. This is consistent with the theory in which a small increase in host density that crosses threshold triggers a sudden outbreak of disease. Threshold capacity could have been decreased by environmental conditions such as temperature, leading to an acceleration of an epidemic. Vaccination has contributed to the eradication of diseases in fish farms despite the large increase in fish production. Most developments of vaccines can only treat bacterial and viral diseases, and not parasitic ones.

Spatial scale of thresholds is dependent on physical characteristics that influence dispersion and survival of free-living parasites and infectious agents. Pathogens existing in marine environments are long lived and widely dispersed compared to those on land because they are able to be transported over long distances in a more stable condition of temperature and moisture. This is especially true in the case of wild marine populations that have hosts that are highly mobile or migratory which leads to spread of infection at a much more rapid rate. Outbreaks have been shown to follow the direction of currents, predicted using hydrodynamic modeling. With these migratory fish spreading disease to other populations, epidemics in fish farms can be spread over very large scales. However the infection is likely to decline with increased distance from the source population.

Parasitic life cycles are influenced by a variation of environmental factors such as temperature, moisture, and salinity. Global climate change can have a profound influence on these parameters. Developmental rates of parasites are highly dependent on the consistency of temperature. Knowledge of disease outbreaks and its possible influences has important implications for coastal fish farm planning.

Lauren Lambert

Minimizing transmission of pathogens among farm fish to wild hosts could increase
the size of wild populations. This can be done by placing farms further away from
wild fish migration routes and in locations that have low ocean tides and currents,
to minimize rates of disease spreading. Selective breeding of fish that are resistant to
disease can also provide the future populations with a higher survival rate. Increased
vaccinations of fish, increased circulation of facilities, and maintaining lower density levels in these fish farms provides advances in disease control.

Global Fish Meal and Aquaculture Production in Response to Climate Change

Climate variability and change has the potential to alter the balance of
marine systems. Global aquaculture systems rely on small pelagic fish populations,
fisheries productivity, fishmeal supply, and fish oil production. Aquaculture is dependent on fishmeal as food to serve as a primary source of protein, lipids, minerals, and vitamins. Fishmeal is produced using small pelagic fish such as sardines,
anchovies, and mackerels. These species are short lived and fast growing, so their
production is highly susceptible to environmental changes. Fisheries production has
stabilized over the last decade, however aquaculture has continued to increase, particularly through production of low-value freshwater fish. Prediction of changes in
fisheries yield that result from climate change are important to estimate. Merino *et
al.* (2010) used bioeconomic models at two temporal scales with the objective of
investigating environmental and human induced changes to aquaculture systems.
Short-term economic hypotheses were that (i) there is no relationship between aquaculture production and fishmeal consumption, given that technological advances
will reduce the dependency on fishmeal production; and (ii) fishmeal demand is
linearly related to aquaculture expansion. Long-term models were based on two
socioeconomic scenarios until the year 2080. The World Markets scenario was estimated using prices based on recent average and highest price records while The
Global Commons scenario predicted limited expansion of aquaculture and population growth.

Merino *et al.* expect that climate change will have a negative effect on marine resources through reduced levels of primary production. Global aquaculture
production relies on both carnivorous and herbivorous species. The majority of
carnivorous species include salmonoids from Chile and Norway, and shrimp from
Thailand and China. Herbivorous species, mainly from China, make up 55% of
global aquaculture production. Carnivorous species are dependent on fishmeal,
however the amount of fishmeal used for herbivorous species is rising because of the
improved growth rates and profits. The models combine the uncertainties of future
climate and market effects on global fishmeal production and consumption.

The first model used short-term impacts over a 10-year simulation to find the annual variable production rate of individual small pelagic fish stocks aquaculture. The second was long-term (2080) and estimated environmental impacts on the same stocks by using primary production predictions as proxies for carrying capacities of fish stocks. The short-term simulation investigated the consequences of short-term climate change on fish and fishmeal systems. Biological, economic, and activity/investment components were observed through this simulation. The biological component computed expected yields and was modulated by expected primary production. The economic component estimated net profits for regional production systems by combining their costs with revenue from the global market. This was driven by outputs from the biological component, activity component, fishmeal price function, transformation, and shipping costs. The parameters of the global market are price records from 15 international fish markets. Activity and investment components express exploitation patterns in terms of catchability and fishing activity of specific stocks. The results of this simulation were presented in the form of bioeconomic indicators such as global exploitation index, estimate of global small pelagic fish caught, and a measure of traded fishmeal to global markets as well as average prices.

The fish stocks show fluctuation according to random variability in fish production. In years that fish stocks decline, the costs of obtaining fish at the same yield show a slight increase, and the small pelagic and fishmeal supply remains relatively constant. As fishmeal markets expand, fish production fluctuates as a result of climate change. Through this simulation, Merino *et al.* found that in years with negative environmental conditions the price of fishmeal would need to be increased while production levels stay the same. At the end of the 10-year simulation, the fish stocks global indicator was 23% of optimal levels. Under these same conditions, the combination of random negative environmental impacts and increases in demand will continue to reduce the size of the fish stocks.

Long-term simulations investigated the impacts of changes in primary production under two different management scenarios. These are short and long term models that use actual data from 1997–2004 for 3 regional production systems. The import and export data from the International Fishmeal and Fish Oil Organization (IFFO) was used to estimate the size of these fish stocks, fleets, and transforming industries. The global market only works under the condition that fish stocks are currently exploited at their maximum sustainability capacity and that the differences in fishmeal production are reflective sof the difference in available fish stocks, fleets, and technology. This allows for investigation of impact of climate variability on production systems that trade products in the global commodity markets. The Global Commons management scenario showed that resulting fish biomass, exploitation levels, fish yield, and market trade are similar to present conditions. The World Market scenario shows a decline in all parameters that were tested. The model showed that production appears to be sustainable over the 10-year period, but fishmeal prices will rise.

The results of the long-term scenarios show changes in biomass of small pelagic fish, index of global exploitation level, total production of small pelagic fish, and quantity of fishmeal in the markets. Sustainability of small pelagic resources is more dependent on how society responds to climate change than to the magnitude of the alterations. There is a link between global climate change and aquaculture dynamics in relation to the demand for natural resources and limits of ecosystem services. Ecosystems are expected to respond to global warming through variations in primary production and species capacity parameters.

Advances in Discovering Solutions to Sustainable Fishing and Aquaculture through Satellite Remote Sensing

The global capture fisheries production has remained relatively stable over the past decade, while aquaculture production continues to rise. Capture fisheries face issues such as overfishing, depletion of key species habitats, and unstable global fuel prices. Aquaculture faces challenges such as competition for space, feed, labor, and disease outbreaks. Both methods face the impacts of climate change in the future. A solution to this problem is to apply satellite remotely sensed (SRS) information to fisheries. Saitoh *et al.* (2011) provide an overview of selected SRS systems along with two case studies investigating capture fisheries and aquaculture. The first case study discusses the application of SRS environmental data and vessel monitoring in a skipjack tuna fishery in the western North Pacific. The second focuses on the impact of climate change on scallop aquaculture in Funka Bay, Hokkaido Japan. These studies aim to provide perspective on the future of fisheries information systems.

Saitoh *et al.* briefly describe operational fisheries oceanography in pelagic fisheries to gain a better perspective on how these information systems work. Operational oceanography provides high quality observational and modeled data for practical application. *Inter alia* provides services that allow for minimal search time by directing fishing fleets and vessels to areas with optimum catch availability. SRS systems measure sea surface temperature (SST), ocean color, sea surface height anomaly (SSHA), currents, and winds. These are the most important sets of data that shape operational oceanography. One application of SRS includes the ability to identify potential fishing zones (PFZ). SRS allows for a clear demonstration of relationships between target species and environmental factors. It also contributes to minimizing bycatch of endangered species. For example, SRS was used to keep loggerhead turtles from being caught while fishing for swordfish and tuna in the

North Pacific. A tool used to decrease the amount of southern Bluefin from being caught in the eastern quota was also developed. The ability to study behavior and habitat utilization is important in fisheries oceanography.

Commercial fishing applications are mostly aimed to minimize search time and save fuel. TOREDAS is a fishery information system service that facilitates near-real-time data transfer through satellite connection during fisheries operations, predict PFZ's based on scientific findings, and provide high value-added fisheries oceanographic information for global oceans. Skipjack tuna were studied using high-resolution spatial VMS data obtained via TOREDAS from pole and line fishing vessels from 2007 to 2009. Data consisted of latitude and longitude positions logged by the vessel's GPS system. Vessel speed was calculated using distance travelled between polling points relative to travel time (~1 minute). A histogram of estimated vessel speeds was used to categorize vessel activity. Only data that was transmitted during hours of skipjack tuna fishing were used. Scallop aquaculture used SRS to explore potential impacts of climate change on aquaculture. The model consisted of two steps. First the suitability of sites for scallop aquaculture was determined using integrated remote sensing as well as a model based on geographic information system (GIS). The second modeled the effect of SST warming on the previous model using temperature increases of 1, 2, or 4°C. This will provide framework for evaluating the impacts on climate change on aquaculture.

Searching for tuna schools is the most time consuming part of fishing. This results in increased fuel and labor costs that takes away from net profits. Satellite based VMS data are used to provide high-resolution temporal and spatial information on fishing activity to minimize search time. VMS data are more accurate than fishing logbooks because data can be accumulated much faster and are more accurate and complete. These data provide improvements to operational fishery forecasting models and management measure such as designing protected marine areas or effort control measures. Daily vessel trajectories are conducted from June 19-23, 2008. During pole fishing the vessel does not move, so fishing activity is therefore characterized by points associated with slow speeds. The vessel travels slower during fishing, gear deployment and retrieval, so this allows for simple data separation. However there are other factors that are not taken into account for why the vessels are slowed or stopped. For example, identification of fishing activity can be initiated when a school of fish swims by but does not respond to the bait and therefore provides false information. The vessel stops and data are collected, but no fish are caught.

The Japanese scallop is the most successful marine shellfish in japan with greater than 40% of Japanese scallop production coming from aquaculture farming. Changes in water temperature will affect the timing and levels of productivity across all coastal and pelagic marine systems. It threatens optimum grow out temperatures through changes in weather and ocean temperatures. After application of IPCC scenarios in the models for scallop aquaculture production, the sites had changed dramatically relative to original models. A STT increase of 1°C resulted in relatively no change, but 2 and 4°C changes decreased the most suitable area for production by 52 and 100%. These results suggest that climate change will have an influence on the development of scallop aquaculture through changes in suitability of sites. One solution to this problem is to implement a shellfish breeding program to increase temperature tolerance of these species.

Future research includes use of oceanographic datasets from satellites. The increasing miniaturization of communication devices and low cost of transmitting information make these systems more practical for delivering future oceanographic information. Programs such as Google Earth could be vital in advancing this process. Products would provide useful information for fisheries and aquaculture such as fishing ground updates, site suitability for aquaculture facilities, and safety information. SRS data is important in providing information from satellites that is vital for research, monitoring, and management of marine fisheries and sustainability of aquaculture systems.

Conclusions

Many models have shown that climate change may alter species diversity and the structure of marine ecosystems. Climate change is just one of the many stresses on marine ecosystems. Human activities such as over-fishing, pollution, and habitat destruction contribute to this problem, exerting a great amount of pressure on fish production. From social to economic issues, global economies will suffer as a result of these changes. Long-term strategies must be developed in response to climate change. Global food security is an important issue that requires immediate attention. Fisheries are over exploited and average capture will continue to decline as a result of increasing demand. As the climate warms fisheries production will undergo a regional shift, altering the local availability of species. The communities that rely on the availability of preferred species will suffer with the declining fish population. Projecting future effects of global climate on fisheries and aquaculture will help to maintain economies as well as fish populations. Over-exploitation of capture fisheries has negative effects to marine ecosystems that rely on the existence of key species. The growth of aquaculture is an adequate solution to the current issue. Although fish farm production is under controversy because of the potential harmful effects on the environment, reliance on fish farm products allows for wild fish populations to recover from exploitation. These fish can also be selectively bred to withstand an increase in water temperature, while wild populations will need to retreat to cooler waters in higher latitude areas.

Implementing climate change scenarios is an effective way to predict global temperatures and impact on marine ecosystems. This is useful because it provides a practical model in which species production and distribution can be determined for future purposes. However predictions about marine systems are uncertain due to lack of adequate oceanographic and ecosystem models and satellite data. Impacts of climate change cannot be accurately predicted without taking into account simultaneous changes at all levels including air and water temperature, reactions of individual species, primary production levels, etc. This is particularly hard to do because of the uncertainty of global economy and future community reliance on these systems. Models used to describe future effects must also provide information for an array of species to pinpoint effective strategies. Although there have been many advances in science of climate change and aquaculture, the response of marine ecosystems must be further researched to provide a better understanding. This ability will contribute significantly to global nations' future responses to climate change.

References

Badjeck M, Allison E, Halls A, Dulvy N. 2010. Im pacts of climate variability and change on fishery-based livelihoods. Marine Policy 34, 3, pp. 375–383.

Barrange M, Cheung W, Merino G, Perry R.I. 2010. Modelling the potential impacts of climate change and human activities on the sustainability of marine resources. Current Opinion in Evnironmental Sustainability. 2, 5–6, pp. 326–333.

Cheung, William W. L., Lam, Vicky W. Y., Sarmiento, Jorge L., Kearney, Kelly, Watson, Reg, Zeller, Dirk and Pauly, Daniel. 2010. Large-scale redistribution of maximum fisheries catch potential in the global ocean under climate change. Global Change Biology, 16: 24–35.

Jennings, Simon, and Keith Brander. 2010. "Predicting the Effects of Climate Change on Marine Communities and the Consequences for Fisheries." Journal of Marine Systems 79.3-4 418-26.

Krkošek, M., 2010. Host density thresholds and disease control for fisheries and aquaculture. Aquaculture Environmental Interactions 1: 21–32.

Merino G., Manuel B., Christian M., 2010. Climate variability and change scenarios for a marine commodity: Modelling small pelagic fish, fisheries and fishmeal in a globalized market. Journal of Marine Systems 81, 196–205.

Mirto, S., Silvia B., Cristina G., Maja K., Antonio P., Mariaspina S., Marianne H., and Roberto D., 2010. Fish-Farm Impact on Metazoan Meiofauna in the Mediterranean Sea: Analysis of Regional Vs. Habitat Effects. Marine environmental research 69,1 38–47

Lauren Lambert

Perry R.I., Ommer RE., Barange M., Werner F. 2010. The challenge of adapting marine social-ecological systems to the additional stress of climate change. Current Opinion in Environmental Sustainability 2, 356–363.

Roberto D., 2010. Fish-Farm Impact on Metazoan Meiofauna in the Mediterranean Sea: Analysis of Regional Vs. Habitat Effects. Marine environmental research 69,1 38–47.

Saitoh S-I., Mugo R., Radiarta I N., Asaga S., Takahashi F., Hirawake T., Ishikawa Y., Awaji T., In T., and Shima S. 2011. Some operational uses of satellite remote sensing and marine GIS for sustainable fisheries and aquaculture. ICES Journal of Marine Science, 68: 687–695.

Simpson, S., 2010. The Blue Food Revolution. Scientific American 304, 54–61

18. Assorted Responses of Fungi to Climate Change

Daniella Barraza

The repercussions of anthropogenic climate change have an immense effect on the environment. It is impossible to find any place on Earth to be unaffected because all biotic and abiotic factors are intertwined in complex processes that sustain life. The published literature of these effects is numerous, but only a small portion concerns the impact on fungi whose presence in the environment is vital. In the kingdom of fungi, the fungi undertake many roles that can be detrimental or beneficial to other organisms. The parts they play involve predatory, parasitic, or pathogenic behaviors, formation of incredible symbiotic relationships, and decomposition of elements that even bacteria cannot break down. Therefore, studies attempting to link climate change and fungi are a needed addition to the growing knowledge on global warming.

Oftentimes, the link is subtle with repercussions that seem like side effects rather than anything of serious consequence; for example, the ability to store high amounts of silver. The fungi residents of the rhizosphere recycle many elements as part of the biogeochemical cycle, and they can store them for a long period. Their efficiency at absorbing elements is equally noticeable. As results show for the absorption of silver, the concentration found in the soil is lower than that found in the mycelia Borovička et al. (2010). Some fungi are even categorized as hyperaccumulators for their efficacy at absorption. The case in question, though, refers to the reason behind the large amount of silver in the soil. Most soils have low levels of silver, but levels increase when activities such as mining and lead smeltering are occurring nearby. There seems to be no detrimental effect on the fungi themselves as they as they are able to store silver safely, but there are still many unknowns regarding consumption of fungi with a large stored amount of silver or other metals; especially as radioactive or toxic metals are not excluded from the absorption process. There are also possibilities for useful applications of this bioaccumulation capacity. One suggestion is the bioremediation of metal pollution.

Already, the bioremediation process by fungi is being considered for the treatment of wastewater. A very common source of pollution is the industrial discharge of effluents. Though usually treated, the current depuration process can be improved through bioremediation. Degradation by fungi can be a more sustainable and economic method than other filter systems (Panagiotis *et al.* 2011).

Fungi, however, can have negative effects on society which are exacerbated by climate change. For example, certain fungi which are associated with agricultural change produce toxic secondary metabolites known as mycotoxins. Mycotoxins are harmful and some are carcinogenic. They are not easily eradicated and can spread quickly, especially in warm temperatures which are favorable to the output of mycotoxins. Crops in temperate climates are most at risk as temperatures increase due to global warming (Lewis *et al.* 2005).

Spores of certain fungi are allergenic and are grouped with other airborne allergens responsible for worsening symptoms of asthma and allergies. The increase in carbon dioxide levels in the atmosphere has increased the production of allergenic spores (Wolf *et al.* 2010), so more people are predicted to be diagnosed with these conditions due to climate change and urbanization (Schmier & Ebi 2009). This study focused on *Alternaria alternata*, a fungus that is both saprobic and pathogenic towards its host plant. This relationship is beneficial to only one organism, but symbiotic relationships do commonly take place.

Fungi form symbiotic relationships with plants by colonizing the roots. With dark septate endophytic fungi, the benefits towards both involve an exchange of the host plant's net primary productivity for greater resistance to droughts and infections. Another mutualistic result is nutrient exchange. Ericoid mycorrhizal fungi can decompose organic compounds like protein, cellulose, and chitin supplied by the host plant. Then, this decomposition releases amino acids and amino sugars which are taken up the plant (Olsrud *et al.* 2010). However, urban settings can compromise this partnership. Twenty-six species of trees growing in an urban area had lower colonization by mycorrhizal fungi compared to trees in their native habitat. The reasons can be attributed to the composition of the urban soil called technosol which lowers the infectivity of the soil. These soils have a different pH than non-urban soil, lack sufficient aeration, and contain pollutants. Also, in urban areas, the density of possible hosts is greatly decreased making it more difficult for the fungi to spread. Negative effects caused by lower fungal colonization have not been pinpointed since there have been enough fungi present in the rhizosphere to form a structure. Nevertheless, one possibility is decrease in size and longevity of the tree; inoculation has been proposed as a remedy although further research needs to be done (Bainard and Klironomos 2010).

Finally, the effects global warming will have on the physiology and behavior of the fungi is studied. Temperature increases have caused fungi that fruit in the spring to fruit earlier. Temperature and precipitation levels of the previous year have had the most effect on the timing of fruiting. The season for fruiting has advanced, but the end of the fruiting season has remained the same (Kauserud *et al.* 2010). The influence this might have outside of the fungi's activity is not known, but there is a possibility of having a significant effect on the carbon cycle. Fungi play an important role in the carbon cycle, so their longer fruiting season would release more carbon dioxide in the atmosphere. Increase in temperatures will also have a different effect on fungi living in woodland streams in colder regions. Aquatic hyphomycetes are the main decomposers of organic matter falling into the stream, and the increase in water temperature augments their decomposing activity. What will result from a more rapid decomposition rate is not known, but the link between climate change and fungi is demonstrated by the results (Ferreira and Chauvet 2010).

Determination of Silver Accumulation in Ectomycorrhizal and Saprobic Macrofungi

Silver (Ag) has an average concentration below 1 mg kg^{-1} in soil and presence in the rhizosphere makes it susceptible to uptake by plants, bacteria, and other soil organisms. However, little is known about its biogeochemical cycle. (Borovička *et al.* 2010) consider macrofungi because they are vital in the biogeochemical cycles of many elements and have the ability to accumulate Ag. Silver in its non-charged state is not considered a toxin, but there are locations that have acquired an excess of silver where it might be. It is known that Ag-polluted areas have a positive correlation with Ag concentration in ectomycorrhizal and saprobic macrofungi. The research presented here combines a review of related published literature with a summary of the data on accumulation and distribution of Ag, and original research on Ag concentration in fungi in pristine and Ag-polluted areas.

Borovička *et al.* collected samples of soil and fungi from various regions throughout the Czech Republic. For Ag-polluted areas, macrofungal samples were gathered from a forest in Lhota. The macrofungi were a mixture of ectomycorrhizal and saprobic fungi and consisted of 30 different species encompassing 22 genera. Lhota is polluted by a nearby lead smelter and mining activities. The topsoils in this area were reported to have values of up to 78 mg kg^{-1}. The soil samples for verification were also collected from this area near a Norway spruce. The sample was a soil profile with five organic soil horizons: O1 (needles), Of (decomposing matter), Oh (well-decomposed matter), and mineral soil horizons, Ah and Bw. A representative part of each soil horizon was used for analysis. For the case study, a fungus *Agaricus bernardii* was chosen and was collected from the center of Prague. The soil profile from Prague was a technosol which is soil whose composition is altered by urban and industrial activity. To detect Ag concentration in the fungi, the fruit-bodies of a specific species were cleaned, cut, and dried to a constant weight. These samples were then ground and analyzed by instrumental neutron activation analysis (INAA). This method involves exposing the sample to a neutron flux so it will produce characteristic gamma rays. Silver concentration in soil was determined with the same method. For *A. bernardii,* Ag concentration in the caps and stipes of 19 fruit-bodies was also measured using the same technique. The authors also did a meta-analysis of related literature. They included only papers stating Ag concentration values for ectomycorrhizal and saprobic fungi from pristine places. The data were separated into eight classes based on concentration ranges and compared to the original data the authors had collected from pristine places in another, unpublished, study.

In pristine areas, the median Ag concentration was 0.79 and 2.94 mg kg^{-1} in ectomycorrhizal and saprobic fungi, respectively. The macrofungi have higher Ag concentrations than soil suggesting that they are very potent in absorbing Ag from the soil. The effectiveness of absorption can sometimes be intense and leads to the term hyperaccumulation. A hyperaccumulator is a species with 100 times higher concentration than the surroundings. A few fungi from the *Amanita* genus, an ectomycorrhizal fungi hyperaccumulators. In Ag-polluted areas with Ag concentration in the soil around 26.9 mg kg^{-1}, the median concentration for both types of macrofungi was 24.7 mg kg^{-1} unlike the differences between the two types of macrofungi in pristine areas. The highest Ag concentrations were found in the ectomycorrhizal fungi. The hyperaccumulators had concentration values of 287–692 mg kg^{-1} and *Boletus edulis* had a Ag concentration of 206 and 242 mg kg^{-1}. In saprobic fungi, the highest Ag concentrations were found in *Lepista nuda* with a value of 84–123 mg kg^{-1}. This is the opposite case in pristine areas where ectomycorhizzal fungi, of the genus *Amanita,* have the highest Ag concentrations . The reason saprobic fungi have lower values is because they absorb other metals besides Ag. The best competitors for silver for uptake by saprobic fungi are probably cadmium and mercury. In soils containing these two metals, an increase in Ag concentration does not result in an Ag concentration increase in the fungi. Ecotmycorrhizal fungi, however, do differentiate between metals. As another study showed, these fungi near a gold deposit absorbed the Ag but not the gold. The results of the case study show that caps accumulate twice as much Ag as the stipes. The caps had a range between 81–544 mg kg^{-1} and the stipes has values between 31–303 mg kg^{-1}. For both parts, there was positive correlation between Ag concentration and biomass.

Other results show that there is no current risk of metal poisoning associated with consuming fungi. The most common fungi on the market are *Agaricus bisporus* and their Ag concentration does not surpass 1 mg kg^{-1}. There is even less risk of bioaccumulation in humans since mushrooms comprise a small part of the consumer's diet.

There are many unknowns still remaining about macrofungi. A few unknowns are which tissues favor Ag accumulation, how age of the fungi plays a role in the Ag accumulation, or the purpose of hyperaccumulation. It appears that the reason why fungi are able to accumulate high concentrations of Ag is because they can store excess metal safely so that it does not interfere with cellular processes.

The Possibility of using Fungi as a Treatment for Wastewater

If effluents are released without treatment, the industrial chemicals in the surroundings will lead to environmental pollution. To prevent this, wastewater treatment has become common practice and numerous systems have arisen. Specifically, in the fruit packaging industry the chemicals found in wastewater are typically from fungicides and pesticides. To combat the high concentration of a certain fungicide, a depuration system based on pesticide adsorption was patented and the result was a reduction of that fungicide by 7000 times. However, the costs for implementing this system on a large scale basis are too great to be efficient. Similarly, a filter system to treat this wastewater removed more than 98% of certain fungicides; however, its implementation was also impractical in terms of cost and volume capacity. Panagiotis *et al.* (2011) recognize the need for a viable option; therefore, they suggest the bioremediation of these chemicals by fungi. Irreversible chemical degradation by microbes has already been studied. It is known that white rot fungi (WRF) can degrade various organic pollutants. *Aspergilus niger* has also been shown to degrade several pesticides. This study focuses on the bioremediation by these two types of fungi on fungicides and pesticides in the wastewater of the fruit packaging industry. Another aim is to increase the understanding of the enzyme's role in this degradation process.

Panagiotis *et al.* used *A. niger* and three different types of WRF: *Phanerochaete chyrsosporium, Trametes versicolor*, and *Pleurotus ostreatus*. From the WRF, the enzymes lignin peroxidase (LiP), Mn dependent peroxidas (Mn), and laccase (Lac) can be studied since WRF has an extracellular enzymatic system called lignin mineralizing enzyme (LME) system that produces these three enzymes. The pesticides used were CHL, TBZ, OPP, IMZ, DPA, and TM. The evaporated residues of these pesticides were place in two different media selected to mimic the natural environment of the fungi. The first is a soil extract medium (SEM) and the second is straw extract medium (StEM). The soil in SEM is sandy loam with a pH of 6.5. StEM is composed of the supernatant of chopped and sterilized wheat straw and has a pH of 5.5. For the experiment, flasks were divided into two categories: non-inoculated and inoculated. The non-inoculated flasks contained either medium and evaporated residues of one pesticide. The inoculated flasks allowed a strain of fungi to grow before adding pesticides on the third day. After this addition, samples were taken in set intervals until 30 days had passed. Another part to this experiment was to investigate the ability of *T. versicolor* to degrade really high concentrations of the fungicides TBZ, OPP, IMZ, and DPA; and its ability to degrade mixtures of these pesticides as would be expected from the fruit packaging industry such as the post-harvest treatment of citrus fruits which would contain TBZ, OPP, and IMZ. For the enzymatic portion of the experiment, pesticide-free flasks were made for comparison to determine if pesticides have an effect on the enzymes.

In StEM, WRF degraded most of the pesticides. *T. versicolor* and *P. ostreatus* almost completely degraded DPA and TM within the first two days. *P. chyrsosporium* had a slower rate of degradation for the same pesticides and was not able to degrade OPP. In non-inoculated flasks, the rate of degradation for all of the pesticides was much slower around 50% and 80% slower for DPA and TM, respectively. In SEM, the results were slightly different. Within the first two hours, *T. versicolor* and *P. ostreatus* were able to completely degrade DPA, TM, and OPP. However, WRF did not degrade IMZ in SEM whereas it had completely degraded it in StEM. The reason is because WRF are adapted to ligninocellulosic material like straw and not soil. *P. chrysosporium* and *A. niger* rapidly degraded DPA. *A. niger*, however, despite being in a medium similar to its natural environment had the slowest degradation rate for OPP comparable to the degradation rate in the controlled flask. In both SEM and StEM, activity for the enzyme LiP was not detected. Activity for the enzymes MnP and Lac were detected in flasks containing *T. versicolor* and *P. ostreatus*. There was a positive trend between the rapid degradation of DPA and OPP by *T. versicolor* and *P. ostreatus* and the activity of MnP and Lac which suggests that the enzymes play a strong role in degradation. A reason for this is because MnP and Lac are known to oxidize phenol rings of lignin and these two pesticides contain phenol rings in their molecules. This result further suggests that other enzymes are responsible for the rapid degradation of other pesticides. Finally, *T. versicolor* was able to degrade high concentrations of pesticides and mixtures of pesticides except with a few discrepancies the reasons which remain unknown. WRF, especially *T. versicolor* and *P. ostreatus*, had the best records for degradation of pesticides and can serve as depuration systems for the fruit packaging industrial wastewater.

Mycotoxin Production and Growth Changes due to Predicted Climate Change

A constant concern in agriculture is the productivity and health of the crops. Diseases, droughts, and a growing human population are contributors to this concern. Magan *et al.* (2010) focus on the damage mycotoxins can cause to crops, both pre- and post-harvest, in light of climate change Mycotoxins are the toxic secondary metabolites of certain fungi, with varying harmful effects. This paper concentrates especially on three mycotoxins: aflatoxin B, ochratoxin A, and deoxynivalenol (DON). Aflatoxin B is produced by *Aspergilius flavus*; ochratoxin A is produced by *Aspergilius carbonarius*; and DON is produced by *Fusarium graminearum*. Besides crops, mycotoxins can also be harmful to consumers. They are often carcinogenic and highly heat-tolerant which allows them to survive the processing after harvest. The European Union has the strictest laws setting limits on how much mycotoxins crops and their products can contain. In African countries, export crops are regulated; therefore, for residents, the risk to health is high. In Kenya, in 2004, there was an outbreak of aflatoxicosis with 125 deaths (Lewis *et al.* 2005). Climate change is predicted to affect the relationship between mycotoxins and crops by stimulating growth of the mycotoxigenic fungi and changing the physiology of plants so that they are more susceptible to pests and pathogens. Due to climate change, CO_2 concentrations are prognosticated to rise 1.5 μmol per year, global temperature is expected to increase 0.03 °C per year, and water activity (a_w) will decrease significantly in certain areas. Water activity is similar to water availability, however, aw has more to do with the chemical interaction between water and other solutes. The more solutes interact with water molecules, the less water there is available for hydration leading to values lower than 1.0 (pure water).

Magan *et al.* reviewed the scientific literature to examine influence of climate change on pre-harvest and post-harvest mycotoxin contamination, the relationship between increased CO_2, increased temperature, and decreased a_w, and whether models based on molecular and ecological data can be used to reliably predict mycotoxin levels of risk. Under each topic, they include studies utilizing different models and systems for analysis.

For pre-harvest contamination, an historical occurrence the impact climate change might have. In the years 2003 and 2004, northern Italy experienced very hot and dry spells. *A. flavus* and *Fusarium verticilloides* are two competing fungi pathogens in maize grown in this area, but because of the arid conditions, the more xerotolerant *A. flavus* was able to gain an advantage. Maize contamination was high and, as a result, cow's milk became heavily infected with aflatoxins since maize was used as animal feed. This contamination resulted in great economic losses. Other crops that are easily contaminated by aflatoxins because of dry conditions are peanuts and cottonseed. One way to determinate which crops will be at high risk of contamination because of dry conditions is through geostatistics. A three year study used goetstatistics to find the relationship between meteorological data and contamination, indicating that contamination was highest just before harvest. This method can be useful for understanding the spatial (latitude and longitude) and temporal variations in mycotoxin contamination and can be useful in determining the timing of fungicide application and pest control. An agricultural production systems simulator which relates seasonal temperature and soil moisture can also be useful in determining the aflatoxin risk index (ARI). For the mycotxin DON, the DONCAST takes into account weather conditions including number of rain days before anthesis and after ripening, and temperature variations. A systems approach can also be taken for DON prediction which takes a look at the life cycle of *F. graminearum*. However, these models are very simple and don't demonstrate complex interactions. They have yet to include many important factors such as levels of CO_2 and ongoing changes to the physiology of host species and mycotoxigenic fungi.

Post-harvest storage of crops and processing that occurs to turn them into marketable products can also incur risk of mycotoxin contamination. Crops stored at high temperatures and in damp conditions are at risk and any infection with aflatoxins or ochratoxin A can result in the loss of the entire crop. Fungistatic preservatives are used, but they are likely not completely effective, even applied at the most appropriate concentration. Higher temperatures and damp conditions increase the volatility of these fungistatic preservatives thus cutting their job short.

Atmospheric CO_2 concentrations of 800–1000 ppm, triple the current levels, may not have a much effect on fungi. Although they can withstand extremely high levels, atmospheric CO_2 will not be the only variable to change. In combination with temperature and a_w, CO_2 does have an effect. With higher a_w, aflatoxin growth is restricted under atmospheres containing 25% and 50% CO_2. Atmospheres with 75% CO_2 resulted in greater growth restrictions despite changes in a_w levels. Elevated CO_2 mixed with N_2 have a different effect on aflatoxin B. A 70% CO_2 concentration with 0.80 a_w prevented spoilage of bakery products. Focusing only on temperature and a_w, contour maps have been used to predict mycotoxin production at +3 °C and +5 °C with varying a_w. One discovery was that exactly 0.90 a_w and temperature +5 °C will cause no mycotoxin production.

To relate the genetics of mycotoxins and ecological data, a microarray was developed. A key marker gene under study is *aflD* which produces aflatoxin B. The microarray established that there are two peaks for mycotoxic production. The first is the exact intersection between temperature and a_w which is most conducive to production, and the second peak is when the mycotoxic fungi is under stress and overreaching the demonstrated extremes. Changes in CO_2, temperature, and a_w can be modeled based on understood gene expressions.

There are still many questions left to answer especially since models need improvement and more studies need to be made. Future questions that need to be addressed should be more specifically determining the impact of climate change on the physiology of host species, on the life cycle of mycotoxigenic fungi, and how to improve storage for post-harvest crops.

Carbon Dioxide Levels have a Significant Effect on Allergenic Fungal Spores

Airborne allergens commonly include pollen and fungal spores. These allergens aggravate allergy and asthma symptoms. In light of global warming, pollen has increased because CO_2 levels have increased. However, the effect of CO_2 concentrations on fungal spore production has not been significantly investigated. Wolf *et al.* (2010) investigate whether there is a clear relationship between CO_2 levels and fungal spore production. The fungi under study are *Alternaria alternata* and *Cladosporum phlei*. *A. alternata* spores are sensitized by 11.9% of the asthmatic global population. On a more local scale, they are sensitized by 28.2% of asthmatic people residing in Portland, Oregon. People diagnosed with severe asthma are more likely to be sensitized to *A. alternata*. *C. pheli* does not produce allergenic spores. However, other *Cladosporum* species do produce them. These fungi, of course, do not grow alone. They grow on plants, either on live or dead tissue. The plant for this experiment was the perennial C3 monocot timothy grass (*Phleum pratense*).

Wolf *et al.* grew the fungi and timothy grass separately. The authors' main focus was to study the indirect effect CO_2 has on production of fungal spores through the host species, timothy grass. Timothy grass was grown in two chambers at different CO_2 concentrations: 300, 400, 500, and 600 µmol/mol. These concentrations correspond to preindustrial levels at the beginning of the 19th century, current ambient levels, and projected levels in 2025 and 2040, respectively. Each chamber maintained two different CO_2 concentration levels at different times. These levels were replicated four times. Each chamber contained ten pots with a single timothy plant. The controlled variables in the chamber were temperature and photosynthetically active radiation (PAR) supplied by high-pressure sodium and metal halide lamps. Temperature was changed gradually from the lowest at night, 20 °C, to the highest in the afternoon, 30 °C. PAR was also changed gradually in conjunction with temperature and lasted 14 hours. After 60 days, the timothy grass was stripped of the leaves. Ten leaves from each plant were analyzed for total area, mass, and nitrogen and carbon concentrations. The rest were then inoculated by recently prepared fungal inocula and then placed in a sterilized media bottle. After one week, the spores were dislodged from the leaves and counted. For *A. alternata* spores, the antigen protein was extracted.

The ratio of C to N in the ten leaves was significantly higher in timothy grass grown at the highest CO_2 concentrations, 500 and 600 µmol/mol. Leaf mass was significantly higher at 600 µmol/mol. There was no significant change in area. *A. alternata* spores produced per gram of leaf showed a positive and significant relationship with C to N ratio. However, the antigen produced per spore was negatively correlated with C to N ratio. In other words, in the two highest CO_2 concentrations, the number of spores produced tripled, and as a result, the antigen produced was doubled. This doubling occurred because there more spores were produced rather than an increase of production of antigen per spore. The decrease in antigens can be attributed to the decreasing nitrogen in the timothy grass. There was no relationship between the size of the spores and the C to N ratio. For *C. phlei*, the production of spores also increased with the C to N ratio, but the *C. phlei* spore production did not reach the quantity that *A. alternata* produced.

There are still lots of unknowns but the relationship between global warming and allergenic fungal spores such as the effects of increasing temperatures and the more significant role that nitrogen has in spore production. This study showed that increased levels of CO_2 will increase allergenic fungal spores through their relationship with a host plant. This will decidedly have an effect on allergy and asthma symptoms.

Effect of Global Warming on the Aymbiotic Relationship between Fungi and Plants

The ecosystems of mycorrhizal fungi take place below ground in symbiosis with plants. These ecosystems are not well researched despite their significant contribution to their surroundings. The fungi under study are ericoid mycorrhizal (ErM) fungi, fine endophytic (FE) fungi, and dark septate endophytic (DSE) fungi. ErM fungi can decompose a broad range of organic compounds such as protein, chitin, cellulose, hemicellulose, and starch. This decomposition releases amino acids and amino sugars which are then received by the symbiotic plant. FE fungi can improve host nutrient uptake. DSE fungi are ascomycetous but perform as mycorrhizal fungi in harsh environments. Plants in symbiosis with DSE fungi can resist droughts and infections better. In return, fungal symbionts receive approximately 20% of their plants' net primary production. Olsrud *et al.* (2010) present research of the effect on these symbiotic relationships due to global warming factors, elevated atmospheric CO_2, and temperature. The area under study is a subarctic birch forest understory in Sweden at latitude 68°21'N. Compared to regions of low latitude, global warming will have an appreciable effect on regions of high latitude.

Olsrud *et al.* conducted a six-year long study (2000–2006) on the responses of the three fungi to global warming. How plant cover and C, N, and P concentrations in leaves responded to global warming was also examined. Six 0.45 m by 0.75 m experimental plots were established and surrounded by an open-top chamber (OTC). Each plot was divided into fifteen 0.15 by 0.15 m subplots. Four out of the six chambers were randomly selected for treatment. One of the chambers was heated so that soil and air temperatures were 5 °C above ambient temperatures. Another chamber was CO_2 enriched to double the ambient concentrations. The third chamber was both heated and CO_2 enriched. Finally, the last chamber was a control so there was no change in CO_2 or temperature from the ambient. For the heated chambers, resistance cables were run through the upper layer of the soil to warm the soil. These were controlled by a data logger which was programmed to switch on and off every two minutes to maintain the temperature difference. To heat the air, infrared lamps were suspended above the soil surface. For the CO_2 enriched chambers, CO_2 concentration was increased to 730 ± 25 ppm. Two tanks were placed on opposite sides of the chamber to blow CO_2 enriched air into the chamber. Their position was to maintain an even concentration of CO_2, to maintain an even blowing effect, and to reduce convective heating.

In each of the four experimental plots, one subplot was randomly chosen for analysis. The presence of symbiotic plants was recorded using point-frequency analysis. This involved recorded the species present at 5 cm intervals using a sheet of Plexiglass with 97 holes of 5 mm diameters. The plant cover, roots and leaves, was then harvested to calculate for biomass. Plant cover and biomass increased throughout the study. The three dominant plants found were *Vaccinium myrtillus, Vaccinium vitis-idaea,* and *Deschampisa flexuosa.* The leaves and roots of these plants were then analyzed for C, N, and P concentrations.

To examine the fungi, soil samples were taken. Three soil samples of 2.1 cm in diameter and 7 cm in depth were obtained from the center of each of the randomly selected subplots. The soil samples were placed on ice and transported to a cooling room at 2 °C in the laboratory. There, the soil samples were sorted for hair roots and grass roots. Hair roots belong to *V. myrtillus* and *V. vitis-idaea* whose symbiotic fungi is ErM. Further analysis of ErM Fungi involved a staining method and a visual examination. Grass roots belong to *D. flexuosa* whose main symbiotic fungi are FE and DSE fungi. Colonization of these fungi also involved visual examination. Visual examination refers to the process where 81 cm roots are examined under X400 magnification and 0.5 cm intervals.

Warming, CO_2, and fungi root colonization were analyzed using two-way ANOVA. There was a significant increase in plant cover under elevated temperatures, but not under elevated CO_2. Under elevated CO_2, *V. myrtillus* and *V. vitis-idaea* had a lower N concentration in leaves, and the C to N ratio was higher. Nitrogen deficiency prevents plants from growing, but not root density. ErM colonization in these plants increased under elevated CO_2 since plants will transfer more carbon to the fungi to obtain more N. Future global warming will allow ErM fungi to dominate the ecosystem. In *D. flexuosa,* FE fungi colonization was lower in CO_2 treated and in higher temperature plots. DSE fungi colonization increased in warmer temperature plots, but there was no significant change in CO_2 enriched plots. A reason FE fungi are affected by temperature is because they are not adapted to dry conditions. Higher temperatures can lead to dryer conditions. The response of

FE fungi to CO_2 can be explained by their slow growth compared to the fast growth of the roots. For DSE fungi, the main explanation for their response is competition with FE fungi. Under lower FE fungi density, they were able to flourish. However, further investigation needs to be done on their functional capabilities. There were no significant changes in P concentration for none of the plants.

Comparison of Mycorrhizal Colonization between Urban and Rural Environments

Human populations continue to grow and with it the urbanization of natural environments. There are numerous implications associated with this transformation, the greatest being the destruction of the ecosystem. It affects the air, the land, and all the organisms residing in the area. Characteristics of urban areas are buildings, square miles of concrete, and artificial mixes of vegetation. Usually, the introduction of exotic species takes over the remaining patches of habitat for native species. The exposed soil also undergoes drastic changes including lack of aeration, higher pH, and appearance of pollutants. Bainard and Klironomos (2010) focus on one of the effects urbanization produces on the mycorrhizal colonization of 26 tree species It compares the colonization of the tree species between urban and rural forests in Ontario, Canada; and it seeks to expand the literature on the effect of urbanization on mycorrhizal fungi.

Bainard & Klironomos identified 26 tree species, found in both urban and rural environments, as their focus for mycorrhizal colonization. The rural area consisted of forests in southern Ontario and the urban area consisted of parks, streetscapes, and residential areas in southern Ontario. The species belonged to the genera *Acer, Aesculus, Betula, Cercis, Fraxinus, Gleditsia, Juglans, Juniperus, Populus, Prunus, Quercus, Robinia,* and *Thuja*. In urban and rural environments, five different locations were chosen for each of the tree species. The locations were chosen at 5 km intervals. Besides their location, another difference between tree species is that most trees found in the urban environment were grown in nurseries before being transplanted into their current location. At each location, three trees were chosen to represent their species, and all the chosen trees were mature at 20–25 years of age. For analysis, a soil core was obtained from beneath the trees. The soil cores were collected between May 26 and June 21 to keep seasonal changes at a minimum. From the soil cores, tree roots were examined for ectomycorrhizal (EM) and arbuscular mycorrhizal (AM) fungi colonization. To determine EM fungi colonization, root tips with mycorrhizal structures and a hartig net were counted and percent EM colonization was calculated. A hartig net is the hyphal network for nutrient exchange and its presence is to ensure that the symbiotic relationship between tree and fungi is active. To determine AM fungi colonization, roots were observed under a microscope since they are smaller than EM fungi. Percent AM fungi colonization was also calculated. Statistical analyses were computed to find out the insignificant and significant difference between colonization in urban and rural areas.

In both areas, all of the tree species were colonized by AM fungi and only seven were colonized by EM fungi. These seven species were also colonized by AM fungi and this relationship is called the tripartite association. Across the board, the species showed lower AM and tripartite association colonization in urban areas. For AM fungi, the range for percent colonization was broad from 2.4 % to 53.5 %. For EM fungi, the range for percent colonization was from 14.4 % to 50.8 %. In tripartite associations, the colonization of AM fungi was the lowest. This result accords with the trees' stages of growth and fungal colonization. During the early stages of growth, the tree is colonized by AM fungi, but as it matures, the EM fungi become more prominent. As mentioned, the studied trees were all mature trees.

However, there is one exception to lower fungal colonization in urban areas. *Populus deltoides* with a tripartite association had a significantly higher AM fungi colonization in urban areas. When the data collected from each tree were averaged, AM colonization was significantly lower in urban areas; in tripartite association, AM colonization was not significantly different in urban areas.

The reasons for lower colonization could be discovered in the composition of urban soils, they're pH, presence of pollutants and nutrients, and lack of aeration. Another reason can be attributed to the density of tree species in urban areas. There are fewer hosts for fungi to colonize since the trees are relegated to certain areas in the city. Finally, in disturbed soils, such as urban soils, fungi have more competition from other plant species, thereby reducing the fungal infectivity of the soil. However, not all disturbed soils result in lower fungal infectivity; some disturbances like clear-cutting have no effect on fungi colonization.

It is not known what the causes are for lower fungal colonization in urban areas, and it is not known what negative effects can occur. A suggestion for possible negative effects is inoculating the trees with mycorrhizal fungi. Although definitely more research needs to be done since trees in urban areas seem to be doing fine, and there is enough mycorrhizal fungi colonization to form structures for symbiosis.

Climate Change Causes Earlier Fruiting in Fungi in Norway and the UK

Current climate change has been linked to changes in the phenology of many organisms. There have been many attempts to understand organismal response to certain climatic factors, however, few have been in-depth investigations of fungi. Kauserud *et al.* (2010) examine which climatic factors are directly related to earlier fruiting, including weather from the preceding year, differences between

Norway and UK fruiting, and effects of climate change on the thermal time of the fungi. The results indicate that the differences between the two countries arise from the effects of longitude/latitude and species-specific distinctions. Higher winter temperatures as well as warm and wet summers have a direct relationship with earlier fruiting. There was no clear link found between earlier fruiting and changes in thermal time suggesting that there is no fixed thermal time for fungi.

Kauserud *et al.* obtained data for the fungi from the Norwegian Mycology Database and the Fungus Record Database. Climate data were obtained from the Norwegian Meteorological Institute and the Biotechnology and Biological Sciences Research Council (BBSRC). The period set was between the years 1960 through 2007. Statistical analyses were divided into two parts: analysis of spatial and temporal trends and analysis of effects on climate on fruiting day and thermal time. The first analysis was to determine if differences existed between earlier fruiting in Norway and in the UK. Temporal trends were evaluated and compared to longitude and latitude. Species-specific changes were evaluated and compared to average fruiting. Longitude and latitude results reveal a 10.2 % contribution to the variation in early fruiting in Norway and 5.0 % in the UK. The greater percentage in Norway can be attributed to possessing a more heterogeneous climate than the UK. Species-specific effects contribute 11.6 % in Norway and 19.3 % in the UK which can be attributed to a longer spring-fruiting season in the UK. There is a 79.9 and 77.6 % leftover variation that can include climatic factors in Norway and the UK, respectively.

The second analysis examined which climatic factors were causing earlier fruiting and how thermal timing was affected. The results showed that higher winter temperatures led to earlier fruiting. In Norway, an increase of 1°C in January causes earlier fruiting of one day. In the UK, an increase of 1°C in January and February causes earlier fruiting of three days. Summer (July and August) temperature and precipitation play a significant role in the timing of initial fruiting. A warmer and wetter summer causes earlier fruiting. Warm winters will also cause earlier fruiting. However, warm temperatures in October delay initial fruiting.

This analysis also examined changes of thermal time which indicated that spring-fruiting fungi do not have a fixed thermal time. Thermal time is a unit of heat or the sum of the temperatures to determine the stage an organism is during its lifetime. It is a more reliable method to predict an organism's current situation than a specific date or season. Throughout the period under observation, the thermal time for the fungi was not the same during fruiting. Therefore, there is no relationship between initial fruiting and length of fruiting.

One important question for future research concerning climate change and fungi is the effect earlier fruiting might have on the carbon cycle. The lengthier fruiting of fungi leads to more respiration in the ecosystem than in the past.

Effects of Increasing Water Temperature and Nutrient Concentration on Fungi Activity and Subsequent Litter Decomposition

Woodland streams are characterized as small forest streams located in moderate to high latitude and altitude magnitudes. The ecosystem of these streams is dependent on the decomposition of organic matter which is primarily decomposed by aquatic hyphomycetes. The streams do not obtain energy through photosynthesis because riparian vegetation, aside from supplying organic matter, provides a lot of shade to the streams. This shade, in addition to the streams' location, causes the streams to have low water temperatures, and be, therefore, more susceptible to temperature increases from global warming. Two factors associated with global warming and which are expected to have a great impact on litter decomposition in streams are water temperature and nutrient concentrations (Ferreira & Chauvet 2010). These two factors are expected to increase and to affect litter decomposition, specifically alder leaves; aquatic hyphomycetes will also be affected as they are the primary decomposers. The hypothesis states that increases in water temperature and nutrient concentration will increase hyphomycete activity and decomposition rates.

Ferreira and Chauvet simulated stream-like conditions at the lab by creating fungal microcosms. A microcosm consisted of a glass chamber with an opening at the bottom for air to enter and create turbulence for the leaf discs. The leaf discs represent the organic matter to be decomposed. Inside the discs are samples of *Alnus glutinosa* (alder) leaves. Also, at the bottom, was a valve to allow the glass chamber to drain and to obtain the conidial suspension for analysis. A conidium is an asexual spore of the hyphomycete. The strains were acquired from a conidium found in three streams of different biomes. A total of six species were collected to form an assemblage for experimentation to represent the fungal diversity of a decomposing leaf in a stream. This number was indicated as adequate by another study. *Articulospora tetracladia* was gotten from a lowland stream in Portugal. *Clavariopsis aquatica, Flagellospora curvula*, and *Tetracladium marchalianum* were gotten from a Mediterranean stream in the French Pyrenees. *Heliscus lugdunensis* and *Tumularia aquatica* were gotten from a temperate mountain stream in the southwest of France. These strains were grown in petri dishes until they produced conidia. These conidia were then placed in a solution to be used in the microcosm. There were six microcosms and they were replicated twelve times. The treatment each microcosm received was a variation of the pair of factors being studied: water temperature and nutrient concentration. Water temperature was three levels: 5°C, 10°C, and 15°C. Nutrient concentration (NP) was two levels: low and high. The information procured from the microcosms was rate of oxygen consumption of the leaf discs, biomass of hyphomycetes by converting from the mass loss of the leaves, and fungal carbon budget which is the percentage of carbon dioxide the hyphomycetes produced. The data was statistically analyzed through three-way ANOVA and Tukey HSD.

The results were consistent across the whole spectrum and fell in line with the stated hypothesis. High NP levels and high water temperatures (10 °C and 15 °C) resulted in higher hyphomycete activity and higher decomposition rates. This means that if global warming does not occur and temperatures stay low, despite high NP levels, hyphomycete activity will remain low. Placing these results into the scenarios of eutrophic waters versus oligotrophic waters yields different interpretations of the results. In eutrophic waters, carbon mineralization might occur due to stimulation of decomposition rates and oxygen consumption rates but this might not occur in oligotrophic waters. It might not occur in oligotrophic waters because the maximum predicted global temperature increase is 6.4 °C for this century. Oligotrophic waters need at least a 10 °C increase in temperature to stimulate decomposition and oxygen consumption rates before carbon mineralization can take place. Carbon mineralization is the process by which fungi (and other organisms) obtain carbon from the decomposing litter which they then respire and release into the atmosphere as carbon dioxide. Therefore, litter decomposition rates in oligotrophic waters will remain relatively the same in spite of the global warming.

Conclusions

Studies into the climate change and fungi link have been few, but revealing. The established knowledge has demonstrated that a variety of different fungi are affected by the changes induced by the burning of fossil fuels. This question has been only partly answered, however, as it is impossible to experiment with every known fungus and the many roles they execute. What is certain is that as the studies progress many more fungal responses to global warming and climate change will be discovered.

References Cited

Bainard, L., Klironomos, J., 2010. The mycorrhizal status and colonization of 26 tree species growing in urban and rural environments. Mycorrhiza 21, 91–96.

Borovička, J., Kotrba, P., Gryndler, M., Mihaljevič, M., Řanda, Z., Rohovec, J., Cajthaml, T., Stijve, T., Dunn, C., 2010. Bioaccumulation of silver in ectomycorrhizal and saprobic macrofungi from pristine and polluted areas. Science of the Total Environment 408, 2733–2744.

Ferreira, V., Chauvet, E., 2010. Synergistic effects of water temperature and dissolved nutrients on litter decomposition and associated fungi. Global Change Biology 17, 551–564.

Kauserud, Havard, E., Heegaard, M. A., Semenov, L., Boddy, R., Halvorsen, L. C., Stige, T. H., Sparks, A. C., Gange, N. C., Stenseth, 2010. Climate change and spring fruiting-fungi. Proceedings of the Royal Society B 277, 1169–1177.

Lewis, L., Onsongo, M., Njapau, H., Schurz-Rogers, H., Luber, G., et al., 2005. Aflatoxin Contamination of Commercial Maize Products during an Outbreak of Acute Aflatoxicosis in Eastern and Central Kenya. Environmental Health Perspective 113, 1763–1767.

Magan, N., Medina, A., Aldred, D., 2011. Possible climate-change effects on mycotoxin contamination of food crops pre- and post-harvest. Plant Pathology 60, 150–163.

Olsrud, M., Carlsson, B., Svensson, B., Michelsen, A., Melillo, J., 2010. Responses of fungal root colonization, plant cover and leaf nutrients to long-term exposure to elevated atmospheric CO_2 and warming in a subartic birch forest understory. Global Change Biology 16, 1820–1829.

Panagiotis, K., Perruchan, C., Exarhou, K., Ehaliotis, C., Karpouzas, D., 2011. Potential for bioremediation of agro-industrial effluents with high loads of pesticides by selected fungi. Biodegradation 22, 215–228.

Schmier, J., Ebi, K., 2009. The impact of climate change and aeroallergens on children'shealth. Allergy and Asthma Proceedings 30, 229–237.

Wolf, J., O'Neill, N., Rogers, C., Muilenberg, M., Lewis, Z., Halvorsen, 2010. Elevated Atmospheric Carbon Dioxide Concentrations Amplify Alternaria alternata Sporulation and Total Antigen Production. Environmental Health Perspectives 118, 1223–1228.

19. Plant Diseases and Climate Change

Daniela Hernandez

Increases in plant diseases and their implications are important potential aspects of global warming. Even though some plants are expected to react positively to the effects of global warming, others are expected to face problems. Research on the subject varies depending on the type of plant as well as on the climate change factor being considered. Temperature increase, elevate carbon dioxide levels, and changes in precipitation are the factors expected to have the most significant effect on plant disease and severity in the future.

Two of the ways researchers have analyzed the effects of global warming on plant disease are through disease severity and disease incidence. Disease severity is measured as the magnitude of the lesion area from affected leaves. Disease incidence, however, is measured as the proportion of the plant infected by the disease. McElrone *et al.* (2010) measures this as the percentage of leaves infected from the random sampling taken. To analyze the effects of atmospheric change on plant disease incidence and severity, researchers employ the use of Free-Air CO_2 Enrichment, or FACE, facilities. These facilities allow scientists to grow plants under elevated CO_2 levels, while giving the opportunity for other factors, like temperature and precipitation, to fluctuate naturally. Plants are grown within plots in the FACE facilities and are exposed to certain amounts of carbon dioxide. Researchers, such as Eastburn *et al.* (2010) have further used this technique to investigate the impact of elevated O_3 levels, as well as in combination with elevated carbon dioxide levels.

Temperature increase was found to perpetuate the disease incidence in some plants. Roos *et al.* (2010) found that an elevation in temperature would elongate the vegetation period in some crops, which would then cause disease pathogens to be more resilient. This trend is true for some rust diseases in wheat and barley grown in Sweden. Madgwick *et al.* (2010), however, found that the increase in temperature would actually cause a shortening in the flowering period, or anthesis, in other crops. Their study suggests that the shortening of the anthesis date will increase fussarium ear blight incidence in some winter wheat crops cultivated in the

United Kingdom. Research conducted by Evans *et al.* (2010) also indicates damaging effects. They found that hotter temperatures will result in ideal conditions for phoma stem canker disease and thus lead to an increase of its occurrence in oilseed rape crops.

Other data support the idea that temperature increase will cause a decrease in disease incidence in other plants. Evans *et al.* found that light leaf spot disease affecting oilseed rape will cause less yield loss under future projections of elevated temperature because this disease thrives in cooler and wetter climates. Another study conducted by Luck *et al.* (2011) suggests that elevated temperature will negatively affect the life cycle of the pathogen Pst, and thus decrease wheat yield loss associated with this rust inducing pathogen.

Global warming is caused by an increase in carbon dioxide levels in the atmosphere. Some research suggests that elevated CO_2 will cause a decrease in the severity of certain diseases. Eastburn *et al.* found that an increase in CO_2 will cause a decrease in downy mildew severity in soybean, although this is not conclusive. These same researchers found that an increase in CO_2 will increase brown spot severity in soybean. The same results are expected with a combined increase of CO_2 and O_3 levels. Ghini *et al.* (2011) found that elevated CO_2 levels would cause a decrease in the latent period of coffee leaf rust, thus posing a serious threat to the crop. Even so, an increase in CO_2 can have no significant effect on plant disease. This is true in both brown spot disease and sudden death syndrome incidence in soybean crops (Eastburn *et al.* 2010).

Some research suggests that an increase in precipitation during the winter could lead to substantial damage in certain crops. Changes in the freezing process can damage the roots of plants and thus make the plant vulnerable to pathogenic invasion (Roos *et al.* 2010). Eastburn *et al.* also found that higher levels of annual rainfall will have negative effects. According to their data, there will be an increase in downy mildew severity in soybean caused by the increase in precipitation. Data gathered by Luck *et al.* further supports this claim. According to the researchers, an increase in precipitation coupled with an increase in temperature will make some potato crops more susceptible to certain bacteria.

The effects of global warming can also have secondary implications. Because insects tend to thrive under warmer conditions, their numbers are expected to increase with rising temperatures. This has the potential to escalate the kinds of pathogens available to infect plants (Roos *et al.* 2011). The increase in frequency of storms caused by global warming can also contribute to the dispersal of plant pathogens (Luck *et al.* 2011). Of additional concern is that the increase in natural disasters can cause an influx of diseases such as leaf scald in sugarcane (Ghini *et al.* 2011).

Certain crops are economically crucial for manufacturing goods while others are significant as food sources. Therefore, it is crucial to consider the effects that varying global warming parameters will have on plant pathogens and diseases. Some researchers suggest the need for further research in genetically modified crops to offset the yield loss associated with plants in which disease incidence and severity are expected to increase (Roos *et al.* 2010). Other researchers advocate for the use of models to predict the impact that global warming will have on plant disease infection (Madgwick *et al.* 2010). Alternative opinions lie on the need of plant disease management strategies and further research in this area. Juroszek *et al.* (2011) promotes the idea that disease management strategies should cater to the specific type of plant, location, and pest of the disease in question.

Climatic Changes in Sweden Cause an Increase in Crop Diseases

Roos *et al.* (2010) surveyed the effects of climatic changes on plant diseases and pests of various crops in Sweden. The crops investigated include: *Brassica* crops, cereals, potatoes, sugar beets, and tomatoes. Traditionally, the climatic conditions in this region have protected crops from several diseases; the cold winter temperatures have usually prevented the survival of various pathogens. With the increase in average temperatures, however, crops have become increasingly susceptible to pathogenic invasion. The prolongation in the vegetation period caused by these climatic changes was shown to be a root cause of the observable increase in disease resilience. Changes in precipitation have also demonstrated negative effects on crops. The authors observed the increasing damage in crop health caused by global warming, projecting an increase in severity in the future. Furthermore, Roos *et al.* promote further investigation in preventative strategies, citing options such as genetically modified crops to alleviate the ramifications of increasing temperatures.

Sweden is currently facing climatic changes that have the potential of dramatically altering the integrity of food crops. Studies have shown that the region is expected to experience a higher temperature change than the global mean change. Roos *et al.*, at the Swedish University of Agricultural Sciences, project that these changes will ultimately alter vegetation periods. A temperature increase of 4 °C is predicted to cause an increase of one to two months in the longevity of the vegetation period; it is also predicted that in the southern regions the change could be up to three months. The projection for the southern regions is of special interest since the bulk of crops grown in Sweden are in the southern temperate zone. The climatic changes are also expected to lead to an overall increase in rainfall during the winter, which could ultimately affect crop health. Due to the recurring freezing and thawing processes these environmental changes would result in, plant roots are expected to undergo severe damage. The damages to the roots could make the crop susceptible to pathogenic invasion. Furthermore, the authors conclude that although a certain crop might be better adapted to withstand winter conditions, the crop might not be able to survive the added stresses caused by the climatic change.

The increase in longevity of the growing season, coupled with the changes in precipitation, suggests that Swedish crops will increasingly become more vulnerable to disease and pests. For example, wheat and barley are expected to face an increase in attack by some rust diseases, such as brown and yellow rust, caused by the prolongation of the vegetation period. Additionally of great concern, is the potato disease, late blight, which is caused by the oomycete, *Phtophthora infestans*. Trends of higher temperatures and increased humidity are expected to create favorable conditions for late blight to thrive in. The authors also suggest that an increase in mean temperature will result in an increase in the number of insects, which will result in an influx of different kinds of pathogens.

Roos *et al.* recommend an overall increase in measurements for protecting crops against the ramifications of global warming. To mediate the damaging effects of diseases on crops caused by climatic changes in Sweden, the authors suggest further development in genetically modified crops that can withstand pathogenic aggression. Additional research is warranted to decrease the dependency on pesticides in order to protect crops against disease, and thus also decrease the risk of potential damages to human health.

Effect of Climate Change in the Anthesis of Winter Wheat in the United Kingdom and the Resulting Impact on Fussarium Ear Blight Incidence

Fussarium ear blight is one of several diseases that affect the winter wheat crop cultivated in the United Kingdom. Madgwick *et al.* (2010) investigated the impact of climatic changes on the flowering period, or the anthesis, of the winter wheat and the effect this anthesis change has on fussarium ear blight incidence. The authors researched this question by constructing two models: the Sirius Model that projects anthesis dates and another that projects fussarium ear blight. To develop the Sirius model, Madgwick *et al.* gathered weather parameters as well as sowing dates for the wheat. In order to create the fussarium ear blight model, they used weather data in addition to the observed anthesis dates. The research showed that climatic changes will progressively shorten the anthesis date for the wheat and this in effect will increase the incidence of fussarium ear blight. The increase in infection can ultimately have a significant impact on this crop's availability; therefore, Madgwick *et al.* suggest further research.

The specific weather data gathered to develop the models were temperature, rainfall, and solar radiation, measured in °C, mm, and MJ d^{-1} respectively. The researchers gathered the weather data from several weather stations to complete the gaps in existing information. Sowing dates for the winter wheat were also collected. The predicted anthesis dates based on the model were then plotted against observable anthesis dates to find the correlation, if any. The observable anthesis dates were based on information from the time period of 2003 to 2008 for two regions: southern and northern England. The plotted data showed that there was a general correlation between the predicted anthesis dates based on the Sirius model and the actual observed anthesis dates, thus validating the purposefulness of the model.

The authors also created a model for fussarium ear blight in winter wheat grown in the United Kingdom. The weather data investigated were: minimum and maximum daily temperatures (°C) and total rainfall (mm). Additionally, the observed anthesis dates for crops in northern and southern England were gathered. Using these sets of data, and an equation derived by the researchers, a model was created for the prediction of winter wheat crops infected by fussarium ear blight. The authors then compared these predictions with the actual observed cases of the crop disease during the time period 2004–2008. The comparisons did not show an immediate relationship; however, the authors attribute this to the fact that there were some inconsistencies in the weather data that this model could not overcome. However, the researchers note that this model can still be useful in showing some general trends for projections of the impact of climate change on fussarium ear blight.

Both the Sirius model and the fussarium ear blight model were used to extrapolate into the future. The authors found that the dates of anthesis will come increasingly earlier throughout the United Kingdom; their model projects 11–15 day earlier anthesis dates. Of significant interest is the fact that the impact of climatic change will ultimately be larger in the southern regions of the United Kingdom than the northern regions. The fussarium ear blight model predicts an increase in crop disease infection caused by the shortening of the anthesis date. It also predicts that by the year 2050, the severity of fussarium ear blight will be greatest in the southern regions of England.

With their projections of faster anthesis dates of winter wheat based on climatic changes, and the resulting increase in percentage of crop infection by fussarium ear blight, the authors suggest further research in this topic. In light of issues related to food security, they ultimately validate the importance of the construction of models that demonstrate the relationship between weather parameters and disease infection on crops.

Daniela Hernandez

The Effect of Climate Change on Winter Oilseed Rape Diseases

Both phoma stem canker and light leaf spot are diseases that currently affect the production of oilseed rape crops cultivated in the United Kingdom. Evans *et al.* (2010) researched the effect of climate change on future projections of these diseases and the yields of this crop. The researchers found that the canker thrives in hotter temperatures. They also noted that the light leaf spot disease generally prefers a cooler and wetter climate. Climate change, therefore, is expected to affect the yield of fungicide-treated oilseed rape crops differently based on the two diseases. The authors predict that there will be an increase of phoma stem canker severity on yields and a decrease in yield loss as a result of the light leaf spot disease. The authors validate these predictions and suggest further research to fully understand the effect of climate change on phoma stem canker and light spot disease that affect the oilseed rape crop.

For their research, the authors created five different climate scenarios: baseline, 2020s low CO_2 emissions, 2020s high emissions, 2050s low emissions, and 2050s high emissions. The scenarios were based on projections they gathered from sources such as the UKCIPO2, the HadCM3, and the IPCC. Using these scenarios, Evans *et al.* produced the following weather data for fourteen different areas in the United Kingdom and projected it for thirty years: daily minimum temperature, daily maximum temperature, daily rainfall, and daily solar radiation. The researchers then used these data as the parameters for three already established models; the first model projected the yield of oilseed rape treated with fungicide, the second looked at the severity of phoma stem canker on oilseed rape, and the third predicted the occurrence of light leaf spot on oilseed rape. The models were adjusted to reflect United Kingdom particularities and were then employed to investigate the effect of climate change on the two oilseed rape diseases.

The authors measured the damaging effects of the phoma canker disease on the oilseed rape crop by quantifying the yield loss. To find out how much was lost, they compared the total fungicide-treated crop yield to the untreated crop yield when infected by the disease. Evans *et al.* also investigated the impact of climate change on light leaf spot incidence. They used these projections to estimate yield loss caused by the disease. The results projected that there will be a significant increase in the severity of phoma stem canker disease infection throughout the UK. Conversely, it was shown that there will be a decrease in infection of the oilseed rape by light leaf spot. Overall, however, the researchers found that there will be a notable yield loss caused by the combination of the diseases on the yield of the crop. To fully understand the total scope of the yield loss, both diseases were taken into consideration, showing that the positive correlation between the decrease in light leaf spot occurrence and climate change will not offset the negative results of phoma stem canker without the use of fungicides.

However, the authors found that climate change will increase oilseed rape yield in fungicide crops; this trend is expected for all the climate scenarios. The greatest increase in crop yield is projected to result from the high CO_2 scenario, and is thought to be especially true in eastern Scotland and northeastern England. Furthermore, Evans *et al.* also investigated the predicted economic costs involved, *ceteris paribus*, with the change in treated oilseed rape yield predicted as a result of climate change. The predicted decrease in yield caused by the phoma stem canker and light leaf spot diseases is expected to counter the predicted increase in the treated oilseed rape yield caused by the climate changes. Therefore, the UK is expected to face a low economic cost for the treated crop. Further research is warranted to have a more complete understanding of the costs involved and the effects these diseases will have on crop yields.

The Effect of CO_2 and O_3 Levels on Soybean Diseases

This experiment analyzed the effects that a change in the atmospheric composition will have on the diseases that infect soybean crops. Specifically, Eastburn *et al.* (2010) researched the implications associated with an increase in CO_2 and O_3 levels, comparing these results to ambient conditions. The three soybean diseases observed were brown spot, downy mildew, and sudden death syndrome (SDS). The results showed that, throughout the span of the study, both an increase in CO_2 and a combined increase in CO_2 and O_3 are expected to cause a decrease in downy mildew severity but an increase in brown spot severity. However, the different atmospheric conditions did not have a significant effect on either the brown spot or the sudden death syndrome incidence. The data also showed that higher levels of precipitation lead to greater downy mildew severity. Generally speaking, warmer conditions exacerbated both brown spot and downy mildew severity, but chemical analysis showed no change in the structural and chemical composition of the soybean.

Eastburn *et al.* conducted the present study throughout a three-year time span from 2005 to 2007. The researchers did not want to discount the effects that certain climatic parameters might have on the soybean diseases. Instead of growing soybeans under controlled conditions, they, therefore, used the soybean free air concentration enrichment facility, SoyFACE, located on the University of Illinois campus, in which conditions such as temperature and precipitation could occur naturally. The four atmospheric composition conditions tested in the present study were: ambient conditions, elevated CO_2, elevated O_3, and a combination of elevated CO_2 and O_3 levels. Conditions were measured regularly to calculate the adequate level of CO_2 and O_3 that the plants needed to be exposed to.

The authors conducted random samplings of the soybean plants in the varying plots. They tested leaves of those plants showing signs of infection to see whether the diseases (brown spot, downy mildew, and sudden death syndrome) were the actual cause of the symptoms. Brown spot disease affects plants by causing brown spots bounded by chlorotic tissue on the leaves. The symptoms of downy mildew show up as spots on the top surface of leaves and lesions on the bottom surface. Although sudden death syndrome is actually a root disease, the leaves also show spots when infected.

To quantify the effect of atmospheric changes on the soybean diseases, both disease incidence and severity were measured through visual inspection and a digital image analysis (ASSESS: *Image analysis software for plant disease quantification*), respectively. Disease incidence was measured as the positive or negative infection of the plant and number of lesions, calculated as a percentage. Severity, however, was quantified by measuring the proportion of the leaf area that was infected as well as the individual lesion size, again calculated as a percentage. Because they are a way of understanding plant defense, cuticle wax as well as carbon and nitrogen content were measured from the leaf tissue using a chemical analysis. These values offered a further insight as to the impact the diseases had on the soybean.

Soybean is an economically and practically significant crop; its use ranges from food products to the production of biodiesel. Therefore, it is crucial that research be done to expand on current knowledge of the effect of climatic and atmospheric change on the crop and to implement future management strategies.

A Review on the Impact of Climate Change Factors on Wheat, Rice, Soybean, and Potato Diseases

Luck *et al.* (2011) conducted a review of the impact of climate change on diseases that affect wheat, rice, soybeans, and potatoes. Because these crops are a key source of food and oil, understanding the factors that affect their availability is crucial. The authors found that the relationships between climate change, pathogens, and host crops vary among crop type and the location in which they are cultivated. Additionally, the data show varying crop responses to differing climate change factors such as precipitation, temperature, storm frequency, and atmospheric CO_2 levels. The authors conclude that further research is warranted to gain a deeper understanding of the complex relationship between climate change and plant disease incidence.

The authors suggest that an increase in temperature will negatively affect the wheat stripe rust-causing pathogen, *Puccinia striiformis* (Pst). Data gathered from China between the years 1950 and 1995 showed that an increase in temperature caused a decrease in Pst infection. Moreover, this correlation shows that an increase in temperature is projected to cause a general decrease in wheat yield loss caused by this pathogen. Additionally, changes in precipitation are expected to affect wheat diseases. Wet cool summers, for instance, are expected to create more favorable conditions for aphids that will ultimately intensify the spread of yellow dwarf viruses.

The data gathered on rice diseases show how different climate factors affect epidemics in different ways. In general, rice blast, a disease caused by the pathogen *Magnaporthe grisea*, is expected to increase under most scenarios, with temperature change being the most influential factor. In cool subtropics, increasing temperature was shown to cause an increase in the rice blast severity; however, an increase in temperature also showed a decrease in rice blast epidemics in warm/cool humid subtropics. The effect of CO_2 changes on rice crop diseases was also observed. The data show that rice grown under higher levels of CO_2 has more severe leaf blast epidemics; conversely, panicle blast incidence remains unchanged under the same conditions.

The literature on the subject also points out that an increase in the frequency of storms, caused by climate change, will result in an increase in the dispersal of plant pathogens. Luck *et al.* researched this correlation through data focused on soybean crop diseases. Hurricane Ivan, for example, introduced *Phakopsora pachyrhizi* to Louisiana and succeeded in spreading it throughout eight different states. This pathogen affected the soybean crops by causing Asian soybean rust on the plant. Another severe storm, hurricane Wilma, was linked to the dispersal of the pathogen, *Xanthomonas citri*. This pathogen attacked citrus orchards and spread throughout the state of Florida. Thus the researchers found that climate change factors will not only affect pathogens biologically, but will also affect their dispersal.

Luck *et al.* indicate that climate change is expected to cause a general decrease in potato yield by 18–32%, but the effect on the potato diseases will vary among the climate factors. An increase in CO_2 levels, for example, is predicted not to cause a significant change in early blight incidence caused by the pathogen, *Alternaria solani*. Furthermore, data also show that an increase in temperature coupled with changes in precipitation will increase the potato crops' susceptibility to bacteria such as *Pectobacterium carotovorum* and *Pectobacterium chrysanthemi*.

The present research conducted by Luck *et al.* briefly reviewed changes in some of the most pressing diseases that affect wheat, rice, soybeans, and potatoes; the effects of climate change on these diseases were also reviewed. Since there are several climate variables that can affect pathogens, the authors suggest more experiments be conducted measuring the severity and dispersal of crop diseases under a combination of these factors. Moreover, they also recommend data be collected to take into account the effect of disease management practices on pathogens.

A Review on the Impact of Climate Change on Diseases Affecting Tropical and Plantation Crops

Ghini *et al.* (2011) reviewed and researched the effect of climate change on disease epidemics of coffee, sugarcane, eucalyptus, cassava, citrus, banana, pineapple, cashew, coconut, and papaya. The authors explain the importance of analyzing crop diseases specifically in the tropics because of this ecosystem's unique conditions. Projections show that although the tropics are expected to experience only a slight increase in temperature, the impact will be of greater magnitude than in other ecosystems. Insect species living in these tropical areas, for example, tend to live under optimal temperatures so that a small increase in temperature would, therefore, have a significant impact on the viruses and disease that are generally transmitted by these insects. The authors found that the impact of diseases on these crops depends on host-pathogen interactions and it therefore varies significantly from one disease to another. The authors promote further research in the subject as well as further research in disease management strategies.

Using historical data and projections from models, the authors of a previous study found that under the A2 and B2 IPCC scenarios the number of monthly coffee nematode and leaf miner generations is expected to increase in Brazil. The increase in generations will thus cause an increase in the pathogen and insect infestation of coffee crops. An experiment cited by the authors also shows that increasing CO_2 levels will generally cause a decrease in the latent period of coffee leaf rust. This disease is caused by the fungus *Hemileia vasatatrix* and is a serious threat to coffee crops in the tropics; the shortening of latent period for this disease is therefore also of great concern.

Some studies predict that the spread of several sugarcane diseases, such as smut and leaf scald disease, are expected to remain unaffected by climate change because of the systemic nature of these diseases. Other studies, however, project that increases in natural disasters caused by climate change will result in an increase in diseases like leaf scald. Conversely, an increase in temperature is expected to cause a decrease in the severity of other diseases such as pineapple disease since it thrives best in cooler soil temperatures.

Ghini *et al.* also found that certain diseases affecting eucalyptus are expected to increase in severity. Diseases spread by *Ralstonia solanacearun, Xanthomonas* sp., and *Quambalaria eucalypti*, for example, thrive under higher temperatures; global warming, therefore, would augment the spread of these diseases. The incidence of secondary pathogen infection to eucalyptus is also expected to increase due to changes in both temperature and precipitation.

When researching the cassava crop, the authors found some general trends linking temperature and bacterial blight epidemics. The data show that in areas whose temperatures are above the optimum range for the bacteria, which is about 22–26 ºC, increasing temperatures will either have no effect or cause a decrease in blight incidence. Conversely, in areas where the temperatures are below the optimum, an increase in temperature will likely cause an increase in blight incidence.

In citrus crops, the data suggest that black spot and floral rot would increase in severity as a result of increasing temperatures.

For bananas, studies show that under both the A2 and B2 scenarios, the severity of black Sigatoka, one of the diseases that greatly affects banana yield, will decrease in Brazil. Predictions of a decrease in humidity will likely cause a decrease in the area in which the disease can thrive. Conversely, the incidence of Panama disease is expected to increase. An increase in temperature and a decrease in precipitation are expected to magnify the aggressiveness of the pathogen that causes Panama disease, *Fusarium oxysporum* f. sp. *cubense.*

As for pineapple, Ghini *et al.* note that disease occurrence and severity will also vary with climate change. An increase in temperature and decrease in precipitation is expected to lessen the severity of pineapple fusariosis, which is spread by *Fusarium subglutinans.* Pineapple mealybug wilt, however, is expected to be increased in severity by warmer temperatures.

Literature on the subject also shows that climate change will create favorable conditions for powdery mildew to infect cashew crops in Africa and Brazil. Conversely, projections demonstrate an increase in anthracnose infections, which is the most significant disease that affects cashew cultivated in Brazil.

For coconuts in Brazil, projections suggest that climate change will cause a decrease in severity of black leaf spot, phytomonas wilt, and heart rot epidemics; leaf blight, however is expected to increase in impact.

For papayas, an increase in temperature will lead to a decrease in yield caused by papaya ringspot virus.

The effect of climate change on diseases in topical and plantation crops is not fully understood yet because there are few empirical data on the subject. Moreover, it is difficult to project the disease management strategies that would be necessary to mitigate crop infections. Additionally, little information is known about the impact that climate change will have on biological control of pests. In order to minimize loss in yield of tropical and plantation crops and to understand climate change impacts, Ghini *et al.* propose future research be conducted.

Daniela Hernandez

Impact of Higher Atmospheric CO_2 Concentrations on Tree Diseases

McElrone *et al.* (2010) studied the ways in which higher atmospheric CO_2 concentrations, as well as variance in precipitation and temperature, are expected to affect plant diseases. The authors specifically analyzed *Cercospora* leaf spot diseases affecting two deciduous trees: sweetgum (*Liquidambar styraciflua*) and redbud (*Cercis canadensis*) trees. Their experiment was conducted at the Duke Forest Free-Air CO_2 Enrichment (FACE) facility located in Duke Forest, North Carolina. *Cercospora liquidambaris* and *Cercospora cercidicola* were found to be the leading pathogens infecting the redbud tree and the sweetgum tree respectively; these spot diseases affect the trees by causing lesions on the plants' leaves. Moreover, the authors determined disease incidence and severity by analyzing a sample of random leaves. A chlorophyll fluorescence imaging analysis and leaf chemical analysis were also conducted to determine the affect of CO_2 concentration on these disease parameters. The results varied with the differing climatic factors. Because these diseases affect several crops that are economically significant, the results of the present study can be instrumental in implementing management strategies.

The researchers randomly sampled about 174 to 336 leaves per year from the different experimental plots. McElrone *et al.*'s experiment was conducted over the years 2000–2001 and the year 2005. The incidence of the diseases was found by analyzing the percentage of leaves infected. The severity of the diseases, however, was found by analyzing the percentage of leaf area affected and by calculating the lesion area. Observable lesions on the sample leaves accounted for disease incidence. Disease severity was analyzed by measuring the areas of the lesions using ASSESS: Image analysis software for plant disease quantification.

The Duke Forest FACE facility used in this experiment operates by surrounding experimental plants with rings of CO_2 emitters, which allow concentrations of CO_2 within the rings to be controlled. The trees analyzed in the present study were planted in 1998 and placed into sub-plots of the FACE rings. For the purposes of this experiment, the trees were grown under both elevated CO_2 and ambient conditions in the FACE facility. The natural precipitation and temperature in the site were left unaltered. The effect of CO_2 levels on the plant diseases was determined through a chlorophyll fluorescence analysis and through a chemical analysis, using leaves from the plants to test this effect.

McElrone *et al.* found that lower than average temperatures cause a greater disease incidence in sweetgum. Additionally, the results showed that there was a greater *Cerspora* leaf spot disease incidence during wetter years particularly evident in the sweetgum tree. Conversely, the years that faced lower than average precipitation, demonstrated lower disease severity in the rosebud and a lessening of leaf lesions in both tree species. Taking into account the instances in which the plants were significantly affected, the authors found that both disease incidence and severity were favored under the higher CO_2 conditions.

However, the authors found that there was no significant change in the leaf chemistry among the plants grown under the differing CO_2 concentrations. Through the chlorophyll fluorescence imaging analysis, McElrone *et al.* also concluded that although the plants might experience an increase in *Cercospora* leaf spot disease under higher CO_2 levels, the net effect is offset by the increase in photosynthetic activity by the uninfected leaf area. The authors suggest further research be conducted to analyze the effect that both the atmospheric CO_2 concentration and the resulting climate changes have on these diseases.

Plant Disease Management Strategies Under Climatic and Atmospheric Change

Research shows that increasing population growth will cause an intensification of food scarcity. Therefore, plant disease management practices must be improved to mitigate the damaging effects of already induced yield loss. Because pests and diseases have varying effects on plants, however, control practices must be catered to the specific location, crop, and type of pest. With climatic and atmospheric changes, plant disease management strategies have to adjust in accordance with these new conditions. Some ways in which temperature change and atmospheric change may affect the relationship between plants and pathogens are by altering the host plant's susceptibility and by reducing the pathogenic resistance, as well as other changes. Juroszek *et al.* (2011) conducted a review on disease management practices and researched the ways in which these tactics will have to be altered in accordance with climate change. The authors specifically looked at fungal plant pathogens in agriculture and horticulture.

The authors researched some possible agronomic practices that can mitigate the impact of plant diseases. Generally speaking, planting a diverse set of crops may significantly decrease the threat of plant disease associated with monocultures. The authors additionally point at the importance of crop rotation as a disease management strategy, especially under climate change. Other strategies include changing the harvest date, to avoid pathogen infection, as well as planting cultivar mixtures and intercropping. The benefit of the latter two strategies is that they have the potential of slowing down the rate of epidemics. At the same time, however, the intercrop implemented can outcompete the crop being managed, thus reducing yield. The authors suggest more research be conducted to investigate the extent of these effects.

Juroszek *et al.* also researched the implementation of resistant crops as a disease management strategy under the climate change criteria. According to the authors, some of the factors that need to be taken into consideration when looking at disease resistance and the implementation of possible resistant crops are temperature, "...leaf wetness, nutrient status (e.g. nitrogen fixation), soil type and availability of water (105)." Research suggests that increased CO_2 levels can lead to acceleration in the pathogen evolution for increased aggressiveness. Juroszek *et al.*, however, resist making any ultimate correlation, as much more research is needed.

The researchers additionally looked at fungicides as possible disease management strategies under climate change. Studies show that increasing CO_2 will require an additional amount of fungicides to those plants negatively affected by this change in atmospheric condition. Other studies, however, show how increasing temperatures reduce the efficiency of certain fungicides against pathogens. An increase in CO_2 and temperature can also lead to morphological changes to the plant, which can ultimately reduce the effectiveness of the plant protection products (PPPs). The authors suggest that optimizing the time at which the PPPs are used can help increase this effectiveness. The ideal fungicide application will be dependent on the specific disease and crop, since climate and atmospheric change might alter the favorability of the disease in a positive or negative way.

Another type of disease management practice the authors analyzed was the application of biological control agents (BCAs). The adoption of this technique is also dependent on the specific antagonistic organism's reaction to temperature and atmospheric change. Some studies imply that pathogens may be favored under these changes, while other studies suggest the antagonistic organism might be favored.

Adopting integrated pest management (IPM) as a management practice was also researched in this review. IPM is a preventative strategy whose main goal is long-term effectiveness of preventing plant disease. It uses a combination of other strategies such as "...biological control, use of resistant cultivars, habitat management and cultural practices (108)." Juroszek *et al.* recommend models be used to predict the long-term consequences in order to adopt the ideal IPM.

The authors ultimately suggest that the ideal disease management strategy must be implemented given the specific plant, pathogen, and environmental factors. They find that disease-forecasting models will be key in analyzing this based on the effect of climate and atmospheric change on plant disease instance and severity.

Conclusions

As most of these summaries suggest, there is much more research that needs to be done in order to fully understand the effects of global warming on plant diseases. Not only is it important to analyze the impacts of climate change, but also to further investigate the impacts of precipitation variability as well as changes in atmospheric conditions, among other factors. As the research presented in this chapter demonstrates, not all plants react the same way to these changes related to global warming. Therefore, it is crucial that future research focus on a variety of plant types that are also geographically diverse.

References Cited

Eastburn, D., Degennaro, M., Delucia, E., Dermody, O., McElrone, A., 2010. Elevated atmospheric carbon dioxide and ozone alter soybean diseases at SoyFACE. Global Change Biology 16, 320–330.

Evans, N., Butterworth, M., Baierl, A., Semenov, M., West J., Barnes, A. Moran, D., Fitt, B., 2010. The impact of climate change on disease constraints on production of oilseed rape. Food Security 2, 143–156.

Ghini, R., Bettiol, W., Hamada, E., 2011. Diseases in tropical and plantation crops as affected by climate changes: current knowledge and perspectives. Plant Pathology 60, 122–132.

Juroszek, P., von Tiedemann, A., 2011. Potential Strategies and future requirements for plant disease management under a changing climate. Plant Pathology 60, 100–112.

Luck, J., Spackman, M., Freeman, A., Trebicki, P., Griffiths, W., Finlay, K., Chakraborty, S., 2011. Climate change and diseases of food crops. Plant Pathology 60, 113–121.

Madgwick, J., West, J., White, R., Semenov, M., Townsend, J., Turner, J., Fitt, B., 2010. Impacts of climate change on wheat anthesis and fussarium ear blight in the UK. European Journal of Plant Pathology published ahead of print January 04, 2011,doi:10.1007/s10658-010-9739-1

McElrone, A., Hamilton, J., Krafnick, A., Aldea, M., Knepp, R., DeLucia, E., 2010. Combined effects of elevated CO_2 and natural climatic variation on leaf spot diseases of redbud and sweetgum trees. Environmental Pollution 158, 108–114.

Roos, J., Hopkins, R., Kvarnheden, A., Dixelius, C., 2010. The impact of global warming on plant diseases and insect vectors in Sweden. European Journal of Plant Pathology 129, 9–19.

20. Effects of Climate Change on Animal Ecology

Emily Cole

Having a diverse biological population is generally acknowledged to be a desirable trait (Garroway *et al.* 2010). The positive effects of biodiversity range from the stabilizing of local ecosystems, to the well being of humans (Sala *et al.* 2000). Important as it is, however, climate change is altering biodiversity at rates never seen before (Sala *et al.* 2000). While these changes are a representation of all biological life, it is undeniable that the fluctuation of animal species plays a key role. This is just one reason that the effects of climate change on animal behavior is such an important topic.

Within the field of climate change and its effects, studies about animals are often geared toward the question of whether or not the species is likely to become extinct, with the goal of preventing such a fate. While phenotypic changes in species are a common focus of studies, the analysis of the potential impact of climate change on any one population is far more complex than a simple analysis of phenotype permits. The effects of climate change are often countered by behavioral adaptations. These adaptations sometimes come at a cost and are therefore often mediated by outside factors such as predation, or sexual competition In addition, the direct effects of climate change, such as increased temperature or rainfall, will often lead to indirect effects such as a change in plant growth (Møller 2010), or an increase in parasites (Chapman *et al.* 2010), which can also be harmful to animal populations. In order to properly predict a species' potential for survival in the oncoming years, one has to consider a complex web of factors. In this chapter, with its overview of current articles pertaining to the effects of climate change on animal behavior, I hope to demonstrate this.

Articles examining the effects of climate change on animal behavior often revolve around two important questions. The first is how the climate is changing. Not all studies experiment with the same aspect of climate change. Some only examine rising temperatures, some changing rainfall patterns, and some incorporate both. In addition, some studies bring to light aspects of climate change less frequently considered, such as rising temperature variation.

The second important question found in many articles is how climate change is affecting particular species. This often takes the form of an examination of coping mechanisms of the species. In most cases, the article either examines a species' ability or inability to adapt to a certain aspect of climate change, or it examines the species' ability or inability to move to a new habitat, and the possible consequences of that move. Because analysis of climate change and species welfare is so complex, not all articles cleanly answer these two questions.

As climate change is such a broad topic, its specific meaning varies from paper to paper. One study, which examined resting time as an ecological constraint—Korstjens *et al.* 2010—focused on the temperature aspects of climate change, mainly variations and increase in temperature. The researchers for this project examined the constraints thermoregulation places on an animal. They found that although an animal may be capable of thermoregulation at a certain temperature, if it has to spend too much time doing so it loses its ability to do other things, such as forage, effectively impeding its survival.

However, not all papers on climate change focus on temperature. Chapman *et al.* (2010) developed an experiment in which they examined the effects of increased rainfall, and thus a wetter habitat on colobus monkeys. The researchers found that the monkeys living in wetter habitats suffered higher instances of parasites. This led them to the conclusion that a wetter climate could lead to more parasites, an instance of climate change indirectly causing harm to the species.

While articles may vary in the aspects of climate change they examine, they also differ in the behavioral mechanism they are addressing. Some articles examine a species' ability to cope with climate change through avoidance, that is, by changing habitats. These articles may examine an unforeseen behavior that prevents that species from moving into more climate-appropriate territory. Jankowski *et al.* (2010) for example, demonstrated that interspecific competition and dominance is likely to prevent some species of tropical birds from expanding into cooler territory.

Conversely, other articles may examine a species which was successful in moving and is now exhibiting an indirect effect of climate change due to its new location. Garroway *et al.* (2010) document such an effect in two species of flying squirrels, which, due to a shift in habitat bringing the populations together, have begun to hybridize.

On the other hand, some articles study a species' ability to adapt to climate change without changing habitats. In the case of articles pertaining to animal behavior, these adaptations are often unforeseen behavioral patterns that may either aid or harm the animal in its success. Hassall *et al.* (2010) present an example of a helpful behavior in their study of the aggregation of isopods. The isopods were able to clump together, simultaneously reducing their exposed surface area and producing a moister microclimate in their immediate vicinity. Although, much like the resting time, this behavior can only increase so much, this is still an important factor when considering the species ability to survive.

In another example of climate adaptation, Møller (2010) considered song post height employed by songbirds. He found that the birds raised their perches higher off the ground to compensate for changes in the vegetation brought on by climate change. This behavior is also a good example of an adaptable behavior that was modified by other factors. The birds could raise their perches only so high, due to predation by the sparrow hawk.

Brashares *et al.* (2010) demonstrated yet another factor to keep in mind: the Allee effect. The Allee effect is a phenomenon characterized by a sharp decline in a population, once it falls below a certain threshold. The Allee effect is independent of the aspect of climate change being examined, as well as the coping mechanism the species employs—it simply relates to whether or not the species suffers a decline. It is an excellent example of the complicated web of factors that must be taken into account when predicting a species' response to climate change.

Resting Time as an Ecological Constraint on Primate Biogeography

The act of resting is not often treated as an aspect of animal behavior that directly impacts survival, and is more frequently perceived as time that could be used for other activities. While this is true of some resting time, animals do need a certain amount, known as enforced resting time, to perform necessary biological processes such as regulating body temperature (thermoregulation) and digesting food. In turn, the amount of resting time an animal requires can affect where it is able to live. In order to demonstrate this, Korstjens *et al.* (2010) performed an analysis of climate and common animal behavioral data. The team of scientists chose to focus on primates for this analysis because they are frequently studied, and have a wide range of dietary specializations and geographic distributions. The scientists compared observation data on primate resting times with dietary needs as well as social groupings and climate data. They found that while the percent of the day a primate spent resting was significantly affected by social group size, annual temperature variation, and the percentage of leaves in the primates diet, only temperature variation and percentage of leaves significantly affected enforced resting time. In addition, the researchers found that the minimum amount of enforced resting time a primate required affected it's geographical location. These discoveries bring new insight to models that predict how a species will fair with the oncoming climate change.

Korstjens and her partners chose data sets for this analysis based on several parameters. The data had to include observations on resting time, diet, and group size, and had to have been carried out over 8 months or for multiple seasons. If a data set failed to meet these requirements it was not used. The scientists then compared these data to several climatic variables, including average annual rainfall, average annual temperature, variation from month to month of rainfall, and monthly variation of temperature. These data were either gathered by the same scientist who made the primate observations, a colleague or, in the absence of these, through the Willmott and Matsuuras climate model.

The scientists found three parameters that significantly affected resting time. Dietary needs, specifically the amount of leaves consumed, were one. Primates who's diet was made up of more than 33% leaves (folivores) needed far more resting time than those who consumed fewer leaves, presumably to aid in digestion. The monthly variation of temperature was also found to have a significant effect, especially on folivores, with higher variation leading toward more resting time probably because more thermoregulation was required. It was also hypothesized that temperature could affect the quality of the foliage consumed by the primates, thus heightening it's impact. The size of the social group the primates participated in also significantly affected resting time, however the researchers argued on theoretical grounds that this only affected uncommitted resting time and not the enforced resting time of interest.

From the data, the researchers were able to extrapolate an equation that predicted the minimum amount of enforced resting time a generic primate would require based on monthly temperature variation, the constraints placed on this by mean annual temperature, and the amount of leaves in the primates diet. Using their equation, the researchers found that the predicted resting time was significantly higher for areas in which primates were absent, than for areas in which they were present. This implies that resting time does influence geographic distribution. This is most likely because places that require too much enforced resting time draw time away from other vital activities, such as foraging. The researchers found that almost any area that required more than 33% of the day for rest was uninhabited and inferred this to represent the maximum enforced resting time, above which it would difficult for a species to sustain itself.

Using their new-found equation, the researchers went on to predict the enforced resting times for primates that would be needed in scenarios of climate change where the mean temperature would rise by 2 °C or 4 °C. They found that nonfolivore distributions would remain relatively unaffected in the 2 °C scenario, while African folivore distributions would be largely affected in either case. South

American folivore distributions, however, would remain largely unaffected in the 2 °C scenario as well. The scientists hypothesized that this was due to the fact that South American primates are largely arboreal, while their African counter-parts are often at least semi-terrestrial.

The findings imply that enforced resting time plays a key component in both the survival and distribution of a species. As such, this paper presents yet more important aspects to consider when predicting the effect climate change will have on animal behavior and, ultimately, biodiversity.

Colobus Monkey Parasite Infections in Wet and Dry Habitats: Implications for Climate Change

The effect of climate change on animal behavior is an often-studied phenomenon, however the effect of climate change on animal relationships is a less frequently examined sub-topic. In this experiment, Chapman *et al.* (2010) studied the host parasite relationship and the likely changes it will encounter, should climate change grow more severe. Using the colobus monkeys of Kibale National Park in Uganda as a model, the researchers created a comparison between the monkeys frequenting wet habitats, and those that preferred drier ones. The researchers took fecal samples from the monkeys and analyzed them for gastrointestinal parasites. Two forest sites were chosen for this experiment, Kanyawara and Mainaro. The monkeys were studied in three groups, those who frequented the wet lowlands and dry highlands of Kanyawara, and those who frequented the highlands of Mainaro only. The researchers found that in all cases, the moneys in the wetter areas did show increased instance of intestinal parasites. The effects of parasites such as these on the colobus population have yet to be determined, however some theories suggest that they could be extreme. As climate change is expected to make some drier areas wetter, these findings have implications for the future of colobus monkeys and many other animal populations as well.

The researchers chose two study sites for their difference in rainfall per year, but also for their similarities in forestation. While Kanyawara is 30 km north of Mainaro and receives 361 more mm of rain, both sites have comparable biodiversity of the tree community with similarly sized trees, although the species content of the two forests does differ. Primate densities at each site were generally alike, with the exception that *Cercopithicus mitis* was not present in Mainaro.

Fecal samples were collected from groups of moneys that frequented the highlands and the lowlands of Kanyawara, and also those who frequented the highlands of Mainaro. As colobus monkeys have a small home range, it is unlikely that one group visited both areas. Samples were only collected in May and June of 2005 and 2006 to avoid a seasonal skew of the results. Prior to processing, the samples were stored in a solution of 10% formalin. They were then processed using sodium nitrate and evaluated visually for intestinal parasites.

The researchers found that the monkeys living in wetter areas showed higher amounts of gastrointestinal parasites. The prevalence of specific parasitic species such as Trichuris sp. was found to be higher, the wetter the area. In addition, the species richness of the parasite community was found to be higher in the lowlands of Kanyawara than in the drier highlands, while both of these areas exhibited higher species richness than the drier Mainaro site.

While it is not proven that gastrointestinal parasites have severe effects on the populations of their hosts, some studies have suggested they do, especially when their hosts are pressed for food. Chapman *et al.* also offer up the postulate that since climate change has been shown to alter growth patterns in plants, sometimes inducing food scarcity, it could exacerbate parasitic effects. In any case, the effects of climate change on the host parasite relationship is certainly relevant to the future of many animal populations.

Squeezed at the Top: Interspecific Aggression may Constrain Elevational Ranges in Tropical Birds

The effect that climate change will have on many endangered species is currently a hot topic in the field of environmental analysis. While many sophisticated predictions are being made in terms of the abiotic impact climate change will have, rarely do researchers take biotic effects into account. Jankowski *et al.* (2010) performed an experiment that explored one possible biotic aspect that will influence species survival in the event of a temperature change, namely, niche habitats and the species interactions that maintain them. The researches studied tropical birds in the Cloud Forests of Costa Rica, who are known for their strict elevational distribution. By playing pre-recorded bird songs to target birds, the researchers tested the hypothesis that the birds use interspecific competitive interactions to enforce their spatial boundaries. The results the researchers obtained indicated that the bird's ranges were enforced as a result of interspecies competition, and that when combined with the effects of climate change, this dynamic could lead some species to extinction far sooner than anticipated through abiotic considerations alone.

While the mechanism the birds use to maintain their range is still in debate, this is the first study to provide experimental evidence supporting the theory that the birds use interspecific competition to maintain their elevational boundaries rather than phenotypic specialization or some other attribute. Jankowski *et al.* experimented with five species of bird, two of which were known to inhabit lower forest elevations: the White-breasted Wood-Wren and the Orange-billed Nightingale-Thrush, two of which inhabited higher forest elevations: the Gray-breasted Wood-

Wren and the Slaty-backed Nightingale-Thrush, and one, the Black-headed Nightingale-Thrush, which inhabited a narrow strip between the other two Thrushes. Each of these birds has been known to maintain strict elevational boundaries and is highly subject to species replacement.

In order to discern whether these birds were maintaining their elevational distribution through species interactions, the researchers played pre-recorded birdcalls, both from birds of the same species and from birds of a different species but the same genus, to the target birds. The target bird's behavior was observed and recorded before the recordings, after the first recording, and after the second recording. The researchers established the extent of each species' territory by listening to birdsong and watching individual birds' movements. They played the recordings to birds at varying distances from the edge of their territory, to see if they exhibited a distance-based change in behavior. A recording of either the Golden-crowned Warbler or the Lesser Greenlet, which are both known to cohabitate at many elevations, was also used as a control. No differences were found between the target bird's behavior before this recording and after it however, so these behavioral observations were added to the general pool of uninfluenced target bird behavior.

The researchers found that the birds of each genus responded aggressively to the songs of birds from the other genus, indicating that there was interspecies competition. In addition, in almost all the species, aggressive reactions grew stronger closer to the edge of the territory where the chances of meeting an outside bird increased, indicating that the aggressive behavior was learned, and therefore flexible, allowing for responses to change based on population density, etc. Finally, it was detected that certain species showed more aggression in their reactions toward the birdsong of other species than vice versa. This demonstrates a certain interspecific dominance, which could have large repercussions should the climate change. If, for example, the higher elevation species was subordinate and warming were to allow lower dominant species to expand into higher elevations, the subordinate upper elevation species would then be forced into an even smaller amount of land, possibly too small to sustain it's population. In an alternate scenario a dominant upper elevation species could prevent the expansion of a lower elevation subordinate species, squeezing it between the dominant species' territory and the increasing temperature. In this case at least, biotic factors play a key role in anticipating the effects of global warming on endangered species.

Climate Change-Induced Hybridization in Flying Squirrels

While there are many studies examining the effects of human activity on biodiversity, fewer examine the anthropogenic effects on the evolutionary mechanisms that govern biodiversity. This study, conducted by the research team Garroway *et al.* (2010) takes a closer look at one such mechanism: hybridization. For this experiment, the researchers examined the DNA of two separate species of flying squirrel, *Glaucomys volans* and *Glaucomys sabrinus*. Though the two species classically reside in habitats that are close but not overlapping, a recent series of warm winters, brought on by global climate change, led *G. volans* to expand it's territory 200 km north, and into that of *G. sabrinus*. The researchers hypothesized that this would create instances of hybridization between the two species. They found that not only were there examples of genetic hybrids between the two species but that there was also evidence of backcrossing without extensive introgression, implying that the hybridization was recent and therefore an indirect result of the recent climate change. This is likely the first report of contemporary climate change acting as a catalyst in the creation of new hybrid zones.

The researchers collected specimens through live trapping in two separate locations. The first was Ontario, Canada where they designated 26 different sites ranging from the north shore of Lake Erie to the southern edge of the boreal forest, which encompassed the original upper bound of *G. volans's* habitat prior to its 200 km northward expansion. They collected specimens here from 2002–2004. They also conducted live trapping at 19 sites in Pennsylvania, USA . The results from this study site showed that all remaining *G. sabrinus* populations in the state were coexisting with *G. volans*, indicating a widespread shift in habitat.

Once the squirrels were trapped, the researchers obtained their DNA through removing 20–30 hairs and suspending them in a solution at 37 °C for 12 hours. After processing the DNA the squirrel's genotypes were analyzed and scored. Each animal was assigned a Q value, which represented the amount of that individuals genome devoted to a certain species. An individual was defined as highly assigned to a species if it's Q value was greater than 0.95 for that species. Hybrids were defined as individuals with Q values greater than 0.20 but less than 0.80.

Using these criteria, the researchers discovered a total of 11 hybrid squirrels, which constituted 4% of the population sampled. They also found squirrels with Q values high enough to be assigned to one species but which also contained genetic markers for the other species. These were assumed to be the offspring of hybrids who had crossed back again with the parental species, or possibly, but less likely, with another hybrid. They were taken as evidence of hybrid fertility. As there were instances of extensive introgression the researchers concluded that the hybridization was recent and most likely an effect of the new habitat boundaries. While the researchers conceded that hybridization can be a positive result if it aids in adaptation, they also stated that it is generally considered a negative process as it results in a net loss of biodiversity. This article exemplifies some of the effects that can be expected when a species copes with climate change through migration rather than adaptation.

Predicting the Effect of Climate Change on Aggregation Behaviour in Four Species of Terrestrial Isopods

On the subject of biological organisms and climate change some topics are studied more than others. Changes in territory, migration, morphology, and breeding patterns are all frequently examined, however less often studied are animal behaviors that attempt to cope with extreme climate through modifying it. Hassall *et al.* (2010) performed one such study in which they investigated the ability of woodlice to alter their microclimate by aggregating, or gathering together in tight groups. This behavior allows the woodlice to reduce their individual water-loss, both by decreasing the area of their bodies exposed to the air, as well as by creating a moister microclimate around the group. The researchers studied the tendency of the lice to aggregate in environments of altered temperature, humidity, and vapor pressure deficit (VPD), the difference between the current level of moisture in the air and the amount it holds at saturation. The scientists found that those species of woodlice more physically disposed toward water loss gathered together more frequently at higher temperatures and lower humidities, indicating an ability to adapt to climate change, through the technique of altering microclimate.

Hassall *et al.* studied four different species of woodlice: *Armadillidium vulgare*, *Philoscia muscorum*, *Oniscus asellus*, and *Porcellio scaber*. *A. vulgare*, which is native to drier habitats than the other species, was the best equipped for preventing water-loss. *O. asellus* and *P. muscorum* were the least protected and *P. scaber* possessed an intermediate level of fitness. The woodlice were collected from two different areas. *O. asellus* was collected from Norwich, UK in January of 2006 while the remaining species were collected from Corsham, Wiltshire, UK in August of 2006. Throughout collection the woodlice were kept at a constant temperature of 17 °C.

In order to test the tendency of the woodlice toward aggregation, the researchers placed ten individuals into a petri dish which was divided into eight equal segments with a marker. The largest and smallest 5% of the population were not used, and age and gender were allowed to fluctuate randomly. The lid of the petri dish had a hole cut into the top, which allowed air to circulate, and the dishes were placed into an environmental chamber, highly controlled for humidity and temperature, for 20 minutes. At the end of the experiment the dishes were carefully removed and the number of woodlice in each segment was counted. In the event that a woodlouse lay in two segments, it was counted as being in the one that over half its body was in. If the louse was exactly between segments it was counted as being in the segment in which it's head lay. When woodlice were found sharing a segment it was interpreted as aggregation. The researchers performed two different sets of tests, testing *P. scaber* with *O. asellus* as well as with *P. muscorum* and *A. vulgare*. The two separate groups were tested at different temperatures and humidities.

Hassall *et al.* hypothesized that aggregation would increase with decreasing humidity and also with increasing temperature, even at a constant VPD. They also predicted that the species which possessed more physical adaptations to prevent water-loss would aggregate less frequently. Their findings were supportive of their hypotheses. They found that, with the exception of the woodlouse most adept at water conservation, *A. vulgare*, all of the species aggregated significantly more at lower humidity and at higher temperatures. *P. scaber*, the species, which after *A. vulgare* was most water-loss resistant, aggregated less frequently than *O. asellus* and *P. muscorum*. The researchers saw no significant difference in aggregation resulting from fluctuating VPD, which suggests that the behavior is closely related to temperature. This in turn indicates that woodlice will respond to climate change by aggregating more frequently. As different species aggregated more frequently than others, these responses will most likely be species specific. The extra time spent aggregating may come at a cost to foraging or reproduction, and the fact that this behavior necessitates several individuals to be viable, could spark an Allee effect, should the population slip beneath a certain density. Further study is needed to better predict the effects increased aggregation would have on the terrestrial isopod population.

When Climate Change Affects Where Birds Sing

While the effect of climate change on animal behavior is a known and visited topic, rarely do researchers delve into the effects of climate change on subcategories of animal behavior, such as communication. In this experiment Møller (2010) studied the effects of climate change on sound through documenting changes in the height of song posts selected by songbirds. This was the first experiment to study the effects of climate change on vocalizations. Møller hypothesized that an increase in air temperature could alter sound absorption and through this, affect birdcalls. He also predicted that vocal communication could be affected by a change in plant phenology brought on by temperature change and an increase in rainfall. Møller believed that these effects would manifest themselves in an overall change in song post height. He also believed, however, that these changes would be complicated by several variables, namely, sexual competition, susceptibility to predation, height of surrounding vegetation, and migration. To test these hypotheses Møller collected two sets of data on songbird post height, 20 years apart.

Møller chose the village of Kraghede, Denmark to serve as the study sight. He collected data during the months of April, May, June, and July from 1986–1989 and then again in 2010. The area was 25km² and consisted of farms, houses, open fields, hedgerows, woodlots, shrubs, and trees. The exact same area was studied during both periods of the experiment. To gather data Møller walked through the area recording no more than a single individual at each site. This was to avoid recording one bird as two. Birds don't travel much during their breeding season so this was most likely an effective method. Møller recorded both the position of the bird on the vegetation and the maximum height of the vegetation using his own height as a comparison. He recorded all height values in multiples of his own height. In order to verify this method he used a hypsometer, an instrument that measures height, in addition to his visual judgment for 300 observations. The results of the two separate methods were extremely close. Møller collected mean temperature and rainfall data from April through August 1971–2010 for his study from the Danish Meterological Institute.

Møller expected that song post height would depend on many variables, the first of which being song post habitat. He felt that species living in habitats with higher vegetation would necessitate higher song posts. To compensate for this he rated habitats on a three-point scale using 0 to represent grassland, 1 to represent brush and scrub, and 2 to represent forested areas. If a species fell into both categories he assigned it the higher number.

In addition Møller predicted that the results would be affected by sparrowhawk predation, with more susceptible species showing lower song post heights. Thus he employed another numerical scale where 0 implied a species of bird was consumed as much as would be expected from it's abundance, +1 implied that it was being consumed 10 times more frequently than would be expected from it's abundance, and -1 implied that it was being consumed 10 times less frequently than would be expected. A higher number implied that a species was more susceptible to predation and would most likely have a lower song post height.

Møller also hypothesized that song post height would be influenced by sexual competition within a species. He thought that species with higher levels of sexual competition would exhibit higher song post heights. He anticipated two situations in which a species would experience higher levels of sexual competition: species with growing population trends, and species in which the male and female were different colors.

Finally Møller anticipated that the results would be influenced by whether a species of birds migrated or not. He believed that migrating species were less likely to quickly adapt their phenology to a changing environment than their residential counter-parts, and thus more likely to experience impaired environmental conditions. To account for this he recorded an estimate of each species migratory distance by averaging the northern most and southern most latitude for both the breeding and wintering locations and then subtracting the wintering mean from the breeding one.

Møller found that many climatic aspects for April–August did indeed shift from 1971–2009. The mean temperature increased by 2 °C or almost 20% and annual precipitation increased from about 250mm to about 300mm or by about 30%. Møller concluded that such a change in temperature and rainfall would only produce negligible changes in sound absorption, if any, and thus discarded his hypothesis that this would affect song post height. However, song post height did increase on average 1.2 m, with species deemed more susceptible to sparrowhawk predation showing a smaller increase than those less preyed upon. While Møller did not find any significant changes in relation to migration, species anticipated to have higher levels of sexual competition showed a larger increase than others, as did those singing in higher vegetation. Møller stressed that this was not simply a case of birds singing in higher vegetation having higher options for song posts than those in lower areas, such as grassland, because such areas often contained barns and other high posts. He found his results to be consistent with the idea that changes in plant phenology led to this increase in height. This article is an excellent example of the broadness of variables that need to be examined when anticipating the effects of climate change.

Social 'Meltdown' in the Demise of an Island Endemic: Allee Effects and the Vancouver Island Marmot

The Allee effect is a biological phenomenon originally proposed by Warder Clyde Allee. This phenomenon is characterized by a sharper decline in an already diminishing population once it is reduced past a certain threshold. The effect is driven by a shift to an inverse density-dependant relationship; the population becomes so small that, rather than increasing, it shrinks as population density decreases. Although the Allee effect has been observed in some controlled experiments, it is rarely documented in nature and attempts to stimulate it outside of a highly controlled environment are often impractical and unsuccessful. Despite this, Brashares et al. (2010) have conducted a study in which they not only observe the Allee effect take place naturally in the population of the Vancouver Island marmot, but also document the causes which induce it. This makes theirs one of few papers to present empirical evidence of the mechanisms of the Allee effect in a wild population. Their results indicate that some of the actual causes of population decline as density decreases are: larger home ranges and increased difficulty in finding mates, diminished ability to detect and evade predators, and a decrease in foraging, either to make more time for vigilance or because a more bountiful environment was compromised for a safer one. Further knowledge of the mechanisms of the Allee effect, and the thresholds at which populations reach it, may be very important for population forecasts and conservation in the face of oncoming climate change.

Brashares and his colleagues conducted their study, in part, through the use of the behavioral observations of the Vancouver Island marmot (VIM) gathered by D. C. Heard in 1973, 1974, and 1975. At that time the population of the VIM was stable at about 350 individuals. Using these observations, and a contemporary set that the researchers collected themselves, Brashares *et al.* were able to make a comparison between the behaviors of the VIM of a stable population, and those of an inverse density-dependant population. They also drew from observations of contemporary congeners of the VIM at stable populations. In order to reduce bias and error, the researchers used the same methods as Heard when collecting and analyzing data whenever possible. Heard collected his samples in the Nanaimo Lakes area of Vancouver Island. Brashares and his fellow researchers also made observations at the Nanimo Lakes area, as well as an additional site, Mt Washington, from 2002 to 2005. Over this period they observed a total of 38 individuals, which at that time comprised 70% of the population. The researchers made their observations by means of binoculars and spotting scopes, and were always 40–300 m away from the animals. They also gathered data from radio transmitters implanted into the marmot's ears, which allowed for effective tracking. A. A. Bryant describes the implantation of these transmitters in his 1999 report, *Metapopulation ecology of Vancouver Island marmots*. Many of the marmots were already embedded with the transmitters, however the researchers did implant a small number each year to compensate for deaths.

The researchers found drastic differences in the behaviors of the populations of the 1970s and the 2000s. The contemporary marmots exhibited much larger home ranges, those of males up to 45 times larger and females 30 times larger than those of the past. Social behavior was widely varied as well, with the marmots of the 2000s interacting with each other at less than one twentieth the rate of their ancestors. In addition, when they did interact, they demonstrated significantly fewer greetings, and significantly more aggressive behaviors such as fighting and chasing. Finally, modern marmots were far more active during midday than historic, and far less active during morning and evening. They devoted more time to belowground activities and when aboveground, more time to vigilance. In total, modern marmots spent less than 15% of the time foraging that their 1970s counterparts did.

The researchers believe that these behavioral changes are, for the most part, related to the modern decrease in population and population density of the VIM. They argue that the increased home ranges are a result of the increased distance between colonies, which forces the marmots to travel farther in search of both mates and safety. In addition, their social behaviors are perceived as a possible result of natural selection for personality types more fitted to a less populated environment. Finally, the marmot's shift in time management is also viewed as a development of their more unaccompanied lifestyle. A separate historic study, Schwartz and Armitage (1997), demonstrated that solitary marmots spent up to twice the time on vigilance that their more social counterparts did.

While it is rare to see the Allee effect manifest in a wild population, the Vancouver Island marmots appear to be a clear case. In addition their behaviors suggest the mechanisms by which low population density depletes small populations. As the Allee effect represents a sharp positive feedback cycle, it is easy to see how more research on its mechanisms and the population thresholds at which they come into effect could benefit species conservation. Especially in the anticipated environmental changes ahead.

Conclusions

It is clear that an animal species' ability to cope with climate change relies on far more than its phenotypic attributes. Animals are able to respond to climate change in a variety different ways, including behavioral adaptations and relocation. However the net effects of such responses are not simple. Though a particular species may have the tools to deal with climate change, there may be outside factors, such as predation, preventing it from using them. In addition, animals that choose to relocate may face unique challenges of their own. Some may encounter unforeseen boundaries like the territory of a dominant species. Others may face consequences from their move, like hybridization. Even if a species surmounts the direct effects of climate change there are still such indirect effects as higher parasite population or altered vegetation to consider. In order to accurately predict the survival of a species, one must take into account an enormous amount of variables.

References Cited

Brashares, J., Werner, J. R., Sinclair, A. R. E., 2010. Social 'meltdown' in the demise of an island endemic: Allee effects and the Vancouver Island marmot. Journal of Animal Ecology 79, 965–973.

Bryant, A. A., 1999. Metapopulation ecology of Vancouver Island marmots. PhD thesis, Univ. of Victoria, Victoria, Canada.

Chapman, C., Speirs, M., Hodder, S., Rothman, J., 2010. Colobus parasite infections in wet and dry habitats: Implications for climate change. African Journal of Ecology (In Press).

Garroway, C. J., Bowman, J., Cascaden, T. J., Holloways, G. L., Mahan, C. G., Malcolm, J. R., Steele, M. A., Turner, G., Wilson, P. J., 2010. Climate change induced hybridization in flying squirrels. Global Change Biology 16, 113–121.

Hassall, M., Edwards, D. P., Carmenta, R., Derhé, M. A., Moss, A., 2010. Predicting the effect of climate change on aggregation behaviour in four species of terrestrial isopods. Behaviour 147, 151–164.

Jankowski, J., Robinson, S., Levey, D., 2010. Squeezed at the top: interspecific aggression may constrain elevational ranges in tropical birds. Ecology 91, 1877–1884.

Korstjens, A., Lehmann, J., Dunbar, R., 2010. Resting time as an ecological constraint on primate biogeography. Animal Behaviour 79, 361–374.

Møller, A. P., 2010. When climate change affects where birds sing. Behavioral Ecology (Advance Access Publication).

Sala, O., Chapin, F., Armesto, J., Berlow, E., Bloomfield, J., Dirzo, R., Huber-Sanwald, E., Huenneke, L., Jackson, R., Kinzig, A., Leemans, R., Lodge, D., Mooney, H., Oesterheld, M., Poff, N. L., Sykes, M., Walker, B., Walker, M., Wall, D., 2000. Global Biodiversity Scenarios for the Year 2100. Science 287, 1770–1774.

About the Authors

The authors of this book are students at all five of the Claremont Colleges. The book is a work product of Biology 159: Natural Resources Management taught by Emil Morhardt in the Joint Science Department of Claremont McKenna, Pitzer, and Scripps Colleges. Each student picked a topic, did a full literature search, and selected ten papers written within the past year that exemplified the state of the science.

Their task was to write journalistic summaries capturing the essence of the papers but eschewing technical terms to the extent possible—to become, in effect, science writers. The summaries were due weekly and were returned with editorial comments shortly thereafter. The chapters are compilations of the individual summaries with additional introductory and conclusionary material.

The editor is Roberts Professor of Environmental Biology at Claremont McKenna, Pitzer, and Scripps colleges, and Director of The Roberts Environmental Center at Claremont McKenna College. He remembers how difficult it is to learn to write and appreciates the professionalism shown by these students.

Index

heat pump, 47
Heliscus lugdunensis, 325
Hemileia vasatatrix, 338
Himalayas, 178
Holocene, 260
hurricane, 203, 205, 206, 207, 210, 267, 268, 269, 293, 337
hybrid, 47, 86, 139, 140, 141, 142, 143, 144, 149, 153, 154, 155, 157, 309, 352
hybrid vehicle, 139, 140, 142, 157, 309
hydraulic fracturing, 40, 41
hydrokinetic energy extraction (HEE), 38
hydropower, 31, 38, 39, 48, 72, 177
ice sheet, 10, 175, 176, 177, 178, 179, 180, 181, 182, 183, 184, 185, 259, 264, 268
Iceland, 179, 184
India, 76, 123, 189, 223, 234
Indus river, 235, 236
Intergovernmental Panel on Climate Change (IPCC), 16, 17, 29, 33, 40, 45, 50, 164, 176, 181, 182, 210, 216, 221, 259, 261, 262, 263, 266, 268, 275, 291, 308, 334, 338
International Atomic Energy Agency (IAEA), 199
intertropical convergence zone, ITCZ, 211, 212
IPCC A2 scenario, 45, 268, 338, 339
IPCC B1 scenario, 268
IPCC B2 scenario, 338, 339
iron, 35, 90, 115, 121, 145, 165, 166, 171
iron fertilization, 165, 166
isotope, 20, 83, 84, 86
ITCZ, 211, 212
keystone species, 265
Lepista nuda, 314
Leucaena leucocephal, 255
life cycle assessment (LCA), 31, 35, 36, 38, 43, 44, 49, 50, 78, 79
lignin, 315, 316
Liquidambar styraciflua, 340
Long Island Rift Basins, 162
Magnaporthe grisea, 337
maize, 93, 217, 218, 226, 227, 252, 256, 317
manure, 37, 220, 247, 249
methane (CH4), 17, 31, 40, 41, 42, 43, 50, 89, 93, 248, 250, 251, 253, 254, 255, 256
Microcystis aeruginosa, 107
Mongolia, 124
monsoon, 178, 213, 223, 235
mycotoxin, 312, 317, 318, 327
Nannochloropsis, 105
Nannochloropsis sp, 105
Necora puber, 283, 284, 291
net primary production (NPP), 320

New York, 10, 52, 86, 144, 267, 268, 269, 277, 291
New Zealand, 23, 182, 217
Newark Rift Basin, 161
Niger, 236
Nile, 200, 201, 235
nitrogen, 6, 20, 28, 86, 90, 91, 93, 96, 97, 98, 109, 114, 125, 130, 132, 133, 134, 157, 167, 171, 184, 190, 219, 220, 230, 248, 249, 250, 252, 254, 255, 260, 278, 284, 290, 309, 310, 319, 320, 321, 327, 336, 342, 343, 359
nitrogen fixation, 342
nitrogen, N, 6, 86, 109, 125, 157, 171, 184, 190, 219, 220, 230, 248, 250, 252, 260, 278, 284, 290, 309, 310, 319, 320, 321, 327, 343, 359
nitrous oxide (N2O), 93, 168, 220, 248, 250, 251, 252, 253, 254, 256
Northwest National Marine Renewable Energy Center (NNMREC), 52
no-till (NT) agriculture, 249
nuclear proliferation, 78
ocean acidification, 10, 279, 280, 281, 282, 283, 284, 285, 286, 287, 289, 290, 291
Ocean Nourishment Corporation (ONC), 167
Oniscus asellus, 353
Ophiocten sericeum, 282, 291
Oryza sativa (rice), 217, 250, 256, 336, 337
overfishing, 306
ozone, O3, 33, 37, 38, 39, 79, 329, 330, 335, 343
Pacific Northwest (PNW), 43, 45
parasite, 302, 303, 349, 350, 358
parasites, 298, 302, 303, 345, 346, 349, 350
Pectobacterium carotovorum, 337
Pectobacterium chrysanthemi, 337
Pennsylvania, 144, 146, 352
pesticide, 91, 93, 221, 315, 316
Phakopsora pachyrhizi, 337
Phanerochaete chyrsosporium, 315
phenology, 323, 354, 355, 356
Philoscia muscorum, 353
Phleum pratense, 319
photosynthesis, 88, 281, 325
Phragmites communis, 107
Phtophthora infestans, 332
phytoplankton, 165, 167, 168, 295, 296
Pleurotus ostreatus, 315
plutonium-239, 82
pollen, 319
Populus deltoides, 323
Porcellio scaber, 353
Portugal, 52, 325

www.ingramcontent.com/pod-product-compliance
Lightning Source LLC
Chambersburg PA
CBHW062155270326
41930CB00009B/1539